BEHIND THE MASK

Behind the Mask

Regulating health and safety in Britain's offshore oil and gas industry

JOHN PATERSON
University of Westminster, London

Routledge
Taylor & Francis Group
LONDON AND NEW YORK

First published 2000 by Dartmouth Publishing Company Limited and Ashgate Publishing

Reissued 2018 by Routledge
2 Park Square, Milton Park, Abingdon, Oxon, OX14 4RN
711 Third Avenue, New York, NY 10017, USA

Routledge is an imprint of the Taylor & Francis Group, an informa business

A Library of Congress record exists under LC control number: 00132805

ISBN 13: 978-1-138-73621-4 (hbk)
ISBN 13: 978-1-138-73618-4 (pbk)
ISBN 13: 978-1-315-18606-1 (ebk)

Contents

List of Figures

Acknowledgements

Many people, too many to mention, from all aspects of the industry have helped me by giving me their time and advice during the writing of this book. I am extremely grateful for that help.

I want particularly to thank: Gunther Teubner, now of the University of Frankfurt and the London School of Economics, who was my supervisor whilst I was a researcher at the European University Institute, Florence, Italy; Jacques Lenoble, Director of the Centre de Philosophie du Droit, Louvain-la-Neuve, Belgium, where I was able to progress this work (recherches réalisées dans le cadre du programme 'Pôles d'attraction inter-universitaires' financé par l'Etat belge – Théorie de la norme et régulation démocratique); Susan Nash, Chair of the Department of Postgraduate Legal Studies, School of Law, University of Westminster, London, where I was able to complete the book; and my wife, Debora, for her love, support and patience throughout this project.

This book is for my parents, for their love and support through all the years.

John Paterson

London
December 1999

List of Abbreviations

AcoP	Approved Code of Practice
ALARP	As Low as Reasonably Practicable
API	American Petroleum Institute
APRT	Advance Petroleum Revenue Tax
AUOSG	Aberdeen University Offshore Study Group
BNOC	British National Oil Corporation
CIMAH	Control of Industrial Major Accident Hazards
CRINE	Cost Reduction Initiative in the New Era
CT	Corporation Tax
DEn	Department of Energy
FA	Finance Act
FAI	Fatal Accident Inquiry
FSA	Formal Safety Assessment
FY	Fiscal Year
HSC	Health and Safety Commission
HSE	Health and Safety Executive
HSWA	Health and Safety at Work etc. Act
ILGRA	Interdepartmental Liaison Group on Risk Assessment
IP	Institute of Petroleum
IPE	International Petroleum Exchange
FPSO	Floating Production Storage and Offloading vessel
LRFD	Load Resistance Factored Design
MG	Metallgesellschaft
MODU	Mobile Offshore Drilling Unit
MWA	Mineral Workings (Offshore Installations) Act
NPD	Norwegian Petroleum Directorate
NPV	Net Present Value
NYMEX	New York Mercantile Exchange
OILC	Offshore Industry Liaison Committee
OIM	Offshore Installation Manager
OPEC	Organisation of Petroleum Exporting Countries

OTC	(in text) Over The Counter (in bibliography) Offshore Technology Conference
PE	Petroleum Economist
PED	Petroleum Engineering Division
PPS	Petroleum Press Service
PR	Petroleum Review
PRT	Petroleum Revenue Tax
PTW	Permit to Work
QRA	Quantitative Risk Assessment
QUASCO	Quality Appraisal Service Company
RIDDOR	Reporting of Injuries, Diseases and Dangerous Occurrences
SMS	Safety Management System
SPD	Supplementary Petroleum Duty
TLP	Tension Leg Platform
TUC	Trades Union Congress
VSC	Voluntary Safety Case
UKCS	United Kingdom Continental Shelf
UKOOA	United Kingdom Offshore Operators Association
WSD	Working Stress Design

1 Regulating and Evaluating

Lawyers...like Underworkmen...are expert enough at making a single Wheel in a Clock, but are utterly ignorant how to adjust the several Parts, or to regulate the Movement. *Jonathan Swift*

1 The Development of the Law Relating to Health and Safety at Work Offshore

1.1 Introduction

The collection of photographs recently published under the title *Century* and representing 'one hundred years of human progress, regression, suffering and hope' includes an image of the burning remains of Piper Alpha, the North Sea oil platform destroyed by a series of explosions on the night of 6 July 1988 with the loss of 167 lives. In many respects, that image encapsulates the progress, regression, suffering and hope that characterise the thirty-five year history of the oil and gas industry on the United Kingdom Continental Shelf.[1] The vast scale of the platforms that were floated out from mainland fabrication yards captured the public imagination and appeared to symbolise another step in the triumph of technology over hostile nature as the industry moved into the most demanding environment it had yet encountered. Piper Alpha was part of the vanguard of the huge first generation platforms. The progress, however, was not achieved without setbacks. Already by the time Piper Alpha began production in 1976, there had been significant accidents, lost rigs, deaths and injuries. Nor was there any let up in what seemed to be a steady stream of such incidents, prompting one commentator to state that '[t]hroughout the years which have elapsed since exploration for gas and oil first began...a relentless...price in death and injury has...been exacted in the race to get Britain's offshore wealth ashore' (Carson 1981, 5). Almost twenty years after that comment was made, it is striking to find that the caption which accompanies the photograph of the burning Piper Alpha in *Century* reads 'this is sometimes the price of oil' (Bernard 1999, 936). That caption seems to express a fatalism about such industrial accidents, a belief that when technology is pushed so far out to the limits then problems are somehow inevitable. And yet the Piper Alpha disaster was supposed to represent a turning point in the way in which occupational safety was viewed by all concerned in the industry. Out of the tragedy, the hope was widely expressed that the offshore industry had now overcome its dubious and dangerous past - a past that had on occasion seen it accused of having the worst accident record of any industry.[2]

By the time of the Piper Alpha disaster, safety in the UK offshore industry had already been the subject of two inquiries and the legal approach had shifted from a licensing system to a detailed code of prescriptive regulations. The disaster prompted a further inquiry and a further radical change in the way the law was deployed to ensure occupational safety - this time involving a shift from detailed prescription to goal-setting and a greater emphasis on self-regulation. And yet despite this unprecedented history of external scrutiny and ongoing legal innovation, there have been indications in the years since Piper Alpha that the offshore industry is continuing to resist the best efforts of law to achieve improved occupational safety. Those years have seen continuing angry exchanges on the question of safety between representatives of the oil companies on the one hand and trade unions[3] and academic commentators[4] on the other. The same period has seen a number of successful prosecutions in relation to offshore safety[5] and, most embarrassingly for the industry, a series of explosions and apparently unresolved safety problems aboard the offshore platform which replaced the Piper Alpha and which had been put forward as the state of the art regarding safety.[6] Further, an international conference on safety was told during that period that nearly half of all offshore workers in the UK sector of the North Sea were worried that the platform they worked on could suffer explosion or collision damage.[7] That those fears might still be justified is evident to some observers in the evacuation of Shell's North Cormorant platform as recently as June 1999 following a gas leak.[8] While a generous interpretation would highlight the success of emergency response procedures, a less sympathetic reading would point to the shift that was supposed to be achieved post-Piper Alpha from a reactive stance towards safety to a proactive and preventive one which emphasises the need to ensure operational safety on an ongoing basis. Worryingly, leaked confidential reports appear to support the latter view.[9] While it is therefore disturbing that a trade union boss should have cause to express fears that another Piper Alpha-scale disaster is possible fully eleven years after the event,[10] it could be tempting to suspect that he has an axe to grind and is deliberately exaggerating to gain maximum publicity. Such a view, however, may be complacent. Only a month earlier, a Health and Safety Executive Inspector agreed with a proposition in Aberdeen Sheriff Court that a failure by two companies which led to conviction and fine for breach of health and safety regulations could in the appropriate circumstances have a produced a disaster on a par with the events of 6 July 1988.[11] Regarding the regulation of health and safety in this area we might, as a result, be tempted to agree with the somewhat pessimistic sentiments expressed in the opening quote from Swift: on the face of it, and within its own terms, the law may seem comprehensive and coherent but when it comes into contact with the object of its concerns it experiences continuing difficulties in achieving its goals. Perhaps the fatalism of the caption accompanying the picture of the stricken Piper Alpha in the collection of some of the century's most dramatic images is justified after all.

As a problem of reaching desired ends, then, the regulation of occupational safety offshore appears to be a particularly intractable one for law. This may not be surprising given that there is no denying that the field occupied by the oil industry is large (indeed global), complex and with multiple connections. That said, there has been no shortage of explanations for this state of affairs of the sort which not uncommonly attach to the operation of big business - especially when it is involved with something as politically and economically important as oil. For all the complexity of the field, it is neither difficult to imagine, nor indeed to take seriously, the reading of the situation which sees the workforce as just another expendable resource in a high-stakes game played out between a profit-driven industry and a revenue-hungry government. Admittedly this is a gross simplification of the argument, but it is the basic theme running through much of what has been written on the subject, whether from a political, sociological or economic point of view. Equally, there has been a general rejection by the same writers of any explanation which relies on the technological complexity of the industry or on the hazardous environment it finds itself in - a rejection which has particular significance given that these were the reasons most often cited for the separate arrangements for the regulation of safety offshore which, as will be seen, have subsisted throughout its history.[12]

It is legitimate to ask then whether, in the light of such a broad consensus on the part of those who have written about offshore safety, anything more remains to be said. To a great extent, it may transpire that not much more on a purely descriptive level does remain. The precise *orientation* of any description is, however, of the utmost importance given that it has profound implications for any prescription which follows and it is in this regard that it would seem that something more does remain to be said. When existing assessments of the situation, whether by academics or by government-sponsored inquiries, are considered it can be seen that, as time goes on, the prescriptions which have been progressively made are ultimately characterised as part of the problem rather than as anything approaching a substantial solution. And when the most recent legal reforms come to be criticised in terms of the approach which had previously been regarded as inadequate, the danger of a vicious circle is clear. There is a need, then, for a reconsideration not only of what the law is doing when it enters such a sphere of society in an attempt to regulate it, but equally of what legal sociological research involves when an attempt is made to describe and account for the experience of regulatory success or failure.

It can be objected immediately that the benefit of hindsight is indeed a significant luxury - especially after thirty-five years of offshore history and with an ever-growing amount of data and information with which to work - but something more profound is at stake here. Law, especially in the form of regulation, in contemporary society has been instrumentalised by politics, has become an interventionist tool in attempts to deal with uncertainties, to provide guarantees, and increasingly it seems to respond to a public demand that risks be removed from every aspect of daily life. Equally, law in these circumstances is frequently perceived to have failed. Thus, if both the law and evaluations of the law are not to continue to be found wanting by ongoing experience and to result in continual changes in legal regimes, it would seem that both must adopt an orientation which is radically different from what has traditionally counted as a model of law. It is contended in this book, therefore, that an alternative model of law may help to break this cycle of dissatisfaction. By altering the understanding of the process of regulation, the limits and the opportunities, it reveals the masking effects of the assumptions underlying previous legal sociological assessments and forces a change in the orientation of the empirical description. In this way, the possibility arises of new perspectives and new prescriptions which can transcend what risks becoming a futile debate.

In the remainder of this first section the history of the offshore industry will be traced in fairly broad outline with particular attention to the regulation of health and safety at work. While this will serve to orient the reader, additionally an integral component of this description will be the findings of the three government-sponsored inquiries which have considered the topic.[13]

1.2 The Background to the Prescriptive Regulatory Regime in the UK

Investigations into the possibility that there might be significant oil and gas resources under the North Sea began in the early 1960s following the discovery that the Groningen onshore gas field in the Netherlands extended offshore. Despite a degree of uncertainty and continuing scepticism that there would be any oil, the North Sea was geologically attractive to oil companies. Equally important, however, were the economic, political and legal factors. The economic and political attractions were clear: the North Sea was surrounded by some of the world's most prosperous and politically stable nations. The legal factor, however, was not something which the oil companies could take for granted. Although initial exploration could proceed without much in the way of intervention from the law, the massive investments involved in the production of the resources which were eventually discovered meant that those financing operations, whether internal or external to the oil companies, wanted the security offered by a more definite legal framework. The UK responded with the rapid passing of the Continental Shelf Act 1964,[14] which was based on the United Nations Convention on the Continental Shelf of 1958 that had conferred 'sovereign rights' in the continental shelf on coastal states.[15] The particular legal regime which the UK imposed on the exploitation of offshore mineral resources, however, was a more or less straight lift of the onshore regime which dated back to the Petroleum (Production) Act 1934. In particular, this meant that all mineral resources were vested in the Crown and those who wished to exploit them had to obtain a licence. Regulations governing the grant of licences had been promulgated in 1935 under the authority of the 1934 Act, with Model Licence Clauses annexed,[16] and these were now substantially repeated for offshore licences.[17] The most relevant clause in the light of present concerns stated:

> The Licensee shall comply with any instructions from time to time given by the Minister in writing for securing the health, safety and welfare of persons employed in or about the licensed area.[18]

In practice, the Minister wrote to each licensee instructing them in this regard to follow the Institute of Petroleum Model Code of Safe Practice in the Petroleum Industry (IP Code) which had been issued in October 1964.[19] The haste with which the 1964 Act was passed and the minimal attention that was paid to important matters such as safety in operations have been seen as being a result of the government's economic concerns at the time, in particular its preoccupation with the balance of payments deficit, to which oil imports made a significant contribution (e.g. Carson 1981, 141ff; see also L. Turner 1983; Levy 1984). There are certainly indications from those who were then present within the Treasury that this preoccupation became at times an obsession (Cairncross 1992).

While a licensing approach is generally regarded as one of the most interventionist forms of regulation (e.g. Ogus 1994, 214ff), it should be noted that the question of health and safety was not in fact subject to any detailed scrutiny whatsoever as part of this process. Thus, the legal arrangements at this time can be characterised as largely *formal* inasmuch as there was no direct substantive intervention by the government in the question of health and safety at work and the law could rather be seen as playing only a facilitative role.[20] The net effect of the centrality of the licence (itself a contract) was that much was left to contracts between different parties in the industry, including contracts for the development of equipment and technology, for the supply of services and of employment.

That these arrangements for safety were not adequate became apparent very soon after with the sinking of the Sea Gem jack-up rig in December 1965 when 13 men died. This event had a particularly high profile as the Sea Gem had been the rig which had discovered the first commercial gas field for BP in April 1965.[21] It was not simply the loss of the rig which pointed up the shortcomings of the law but also the fact that the Minister of Power was unable to set up an inquiry into the incident that could compel the appearance of witnesses because the rig did not fall into any category which was recognised by the law (see Ministry of Power 1967, 1). An inquiry was nevertheless set up and its eventual success depended upon the voluntary compliance of witnesses. Chaired by a lawyer, the recommendations of this Inquiry ultimately led to the establishment of a comprehensive prescriptive regulatory regime.

There is no doubt that many shortcomings of the licence approach can be identified. It has been criticised, for example, on the ground that enforcement was difficult in that the IP Code was neither legally authoritative nor prescriptive, and on the ground that the contractual nature of the licence made it difficult to regulate the behaviour of third parties (see generally Bentham 1984; 1991). While the Inquiry's eventual recommendation of a regulatory approach met these criticisms, its rationale was significantly different. The Inquiry focused on the difficulties that *the law* faced in dealing with a Code of Practice which had been drafted by *the industry*. There are references, for example, to part of the IP Code being 'a prescription for unlimited litigation' and to the fact that a 'court of law might have considerable difficulty in determining what' a particular technical operation meant (Ministry of Power 1967, para 8.8). These concerns, then, led the Inquiry to recommend 'a code of statutory authority with credible sanctions' (para 10.2(i)). This is not a surprising recommendation in its own terms but is nevertheless rather startling when read in conjunction with the immediately foregoing finding of the Inquiry that the area in question was 'so large and the evidential material so complex' that 'generalisations could well be both inapt and dangerous' (para 10.1). Ironically, there was also an implicit recognition of the difficulties faced in trying to produce a comprehensive code for complex technologies in circumstances which could not be foreseen: where the IP Code had been unequivocal, the strict adherence to its terms had led to most of the deaths on the Sea Gem.[22] Nevertheless (and evidently encouraged by the comparison that was drawn by the Inquiry between an offshore installation and a ship to which the Merchant Shipping Acts applied),[23] there was a fundamental belief, firstly, that responsibility for ensuring safety lay with the government and, secondly, in the ability of law to come to terms with the problems so as to provide a comprehensive regulatory code which, if enforced, could ensure safety in the industry.

1.3 The Prescriptive Regulatory Regime

This, then, was the background to the Mineral Workings (Offshore Installations) Act 1971 which was the statute eventually enacted to enable the formulation of the detailed safety regulations called for by the Sea Gem Inquiry. It might be suggested that this amounted to the beginnings of the 'juridification' of the relationship between employers and employees in the industry where:

> [a]n interventionist policy...entails increasingly dense materialization of the law...Social conflicts are no longer hidden behind purely formal regulation, but are openly addressed through clearly substantive provisions. (Simitis 1987, 124-5)

Indeed, Simitis himself mentions occupational safety provisions in general as an instructive example of juridification:

> [t]he original rudimentary rules have been gradually replaced by a long list of mandatory standards and control mechanisms that guarantee both the transparency and permanent monitoring of employers' activities. (1987, 121)

This is not a point which can be pushed too far in the context of the North Sea, however, as there were continuing differences between the rights and protections applying respectively to onshore and offshore employment, and the net effect was that certain relationships (perhaps even affecting the majority of offshore workers) remained invisible to the law.[24] Nevertheless, the orientation of the law with regard to health and safety at work offshore had now changed from one based on a formal rationality to one founded on a *substantive* or *material* rationality in that government now sought to intervene directly with a view to ensuring health and safety at work offshore.[25]

The 1971 Act first required that every installation be registered and then certified as fit for purpose by a Certifying Authority. Thereafter, the concerns of the Sea Gem Inquiry as to the size and complexity of the field were recognised by the government in the form of the 1971 Act as a framework statute with provision for the making in due course of more detailed regulations. It was believed that such subordinate regulations could be more easily modified and updated to take account of changing technology.[26] The regime relating to health and safety at work offshore which was in place immediately prior to the Piper Alpha disaster in July 1988 consisted of some eleven pieces of subordinate legislation in the form of Statutory Instruments progressively introduced between 1972 and 1980 under the 1971 Act - although until 1976 they dealt with largely administrative aspects of safety rather than substantive issues. They covered everything from construction and survey of installations and well control, through fire-fighting and life-saving equipment, right down to the contents of first aid kits.[27] Although the responsibility for safety in the offshore industry had passed between several different government departments since the early 1970s, a point emphasised by many commentators is that the department responsible for health and safety was always the same department as was responsible for licensing and ensuring the maximisation of oil production (e.g. Carson 1981, 163; Bentham 1991, 267; K. Miller 1991, 178-9). For the majority of the period from 1971 to the Piper Alpha disaster the responsibility for safety lay with the Petroleum Engineering Division (PED) of the Department of Energy (DEn).[28]

The special status accorded to the offshore industry as compared with other industries is evident from the fact that while the 1971 Act was passing through Parliament, a committee set up by the government, the Robens Committee, was considering the question of the regulation of health and safety at work in general and ultimately reported in 1972 (Robens 1972).[29] In contrast to the regime which had just been set up for the offshore industry, this Committee came down firmly against a prescriptive regulatory approach, citing the following principal objections: (1) there existed too much law relating to health and safety at work and the detailed prescription of every aspect of work had the effect of persuading people that health and safety was purely a matter of government regulation and not of individual responsibility; (2) too much of the existing law was irrelevant to real problems; and (3) there was a major disadvantage in attempting to address the problem of health and safety with the wide array of administrative agencies then engaged in the field (Robens 1972, paras. 28, 30 and 41). Its main conclusion was as follows:

> There are severe practical limits on the extent to which progressively better standards of safety and health at work can be brought about through negative regulation by external agencies. We need a more effectively self-regulating system. This calls for the acceptance and exercise of appropriate responsibilities at all levels within industry and commerce. It calls for better systems of safety organisation, for more management initiatives, and for more involvement of work people themselves. The objectives of future policy must therefore include not only increasing the effectiveness of the state's contribution to health and safety at work but also, and more importantly, creating conditions for more effective self-regulation. (Robens 1972, para 41)

There was a clear tension here with the fundamental beliefs behind the Sea Gem Inquiry's recommendations of five years previously and, indeed, the outcomes of the two reports were quite different. The result of the Robens Report was the Health and Safety at Work etc. Act 1974 (HSWA 1974) which provided for a tripartite approach to health and safety for onshore industries with negotiations taking place between government, industry and unions. In contrast to the offshore approach, onshore '[t]he state intervened to support and promote autonomous regulation' (Clark and Wedderburn 1987, 179). Further, the government's function was centralised in the Health and Safety Commission and the Health and Safety Executive (HSC/E) instead of the broad array of industry-specific agencies which had existed previously.[30] It would be going too far to say that this approach has been generally accepted as a total success (see e.g. Kinnersley 1973, 228-230; Baldwin 1987; Dawson *et al.* 1988; James 1992; Ogus 1994, 188), but a measure of the perceived differences in the value of this approach as opposed to detailed regulation enforced by the offshore industry's 'sponsoring' department may be gained from the numerous calls there were prior to the Piper Alpha disaster for responsibility for offshore safety to be transferred to the HSC/E, for example at the Burgoyne Committee in 1980.[31]

It should be noted that the regulations created under the 1971 Act were not the totality of the regime affecting offshore health and safety. While the regulations under the 1971 Act were centred around the installation itself, there were also regulations created under the Petroleum and Submarine Pipelines Act 1975 in relation to offshore pipe-laying operations.[32] Equally, the general principles contained in the HSWA 1974 were expressly extended offshore,[33] including the duty to provide a safe system of work and a safe workplace, although, significantly for many commentators, the provisions relating to workforce involvement such as safety committees and safety representatives were not similarly extended. Daintith and Willoughby (1984, 1-857) make the general point that the two different regimes (that under the 1971 and 1975 Acts and that under the 1974 Act) operated on the basis of different enforcement procedures. The former relied on criminal penalties and, in the ultimate, the power to suspend operations, while the latter relied on a more flexible system of improvement notices, prohibition notices and lastly criminal penalties. Equally, they point out that the two regimes each envisaged different inspectorates and that the industry was concerned that the HSE would not understand the special problems faced in the offshore situation, including the extreme cost of delays. This issue was ultimately dealt with by the PED carrying out the HSE's inspection function under an agency agreement between the HSC and the DEn.[34] Fundamentally, questions arose as to how the spirit of the 1974 Act could survive *without* the workforce involvement envisaged by that Act and precisely *with* the sort of inspectorate that the Robens Committee had criticised.

That there was concern about the new regime was clear when, in response to the heightened profile of offshore safety in the wake of the blowout on the Ekofisk Bravo platform in the Norwegian sector in April 1977, a further inquiry was established.[35] While this committee agreed with the Sea Gem Inquiry's fundamental belief in the ultimate responsibility of the government for ensuring safety in the offshore industry (Burgoyne 1980, para 6.5) and shared its faith in enforcement and monitoring as the means of achieving this end (para 6.2), there was a significant shift in emphasis as regards the appropriate role of the law. Whereas the Sea Gem Inquiry called for 'a code of statutory authority with credible sanctions', and whereas the government in passing the 1971 Act had expressed its faith in the ability of the framework statute approach to allow regulations to keep pace with technology,[36] the Burgoyne Committee appeared to withdraw from any notion that the law could achieve a comprehensive coverage in its regulations. Rather it suggested that the role of government was 'to *set objectives* designed to achieve a uniformly high standard of safety throughout the Industry' (para 6.2; emphasis added) and later made this clearer when it stated that '[t]he Government shall discharge its responsibility for offshore safety via a single Government agency whose task it is to *set standards* and to ensure their achievement' (para 6.5; emphasis added). And it departed even further from the ideas of both the Sea Gem Inquiry and the government at the time of the passing of the 1971 Act when it recommended that '[m]ethods of implementation should be advised as fully and flexibly as possible in guidance notes, which should be recognised as being non-mandatory' (para 6.15).

An indication as to the reason for this shift can be found at one level in the evidence of what might be called ongoing problems of definition. These were of course most obvious at the time of the Sea Gem collapse when it was discovered that the category of an offshore installation did not exist in law. Similar problems were highlighted by the Burgoyne Committee as regards the 'legal status of floating installations moored alongside and attached by walkway to a fixed platform' (para 6.14), a description which covers such structures as 'flotels' or floating installations used for accommodation of workers. It seems that the definition of an installation contained in s1(3)(b) of the 1971 Act (as modified by s44 of the 1975 Act) had not always been interpreted by the PED as covering such a structure (para 5.3).[37] Further, the conflict set up by the existence of separate regimes under, on the one hand, the 1971 and 1975 Acts and under, on the other hand, the 1974 Act was especially evident in the contradictory conferral of responsibility on the Offshore Installation Manager and the Employer respectively (para 6.19). Lastly, there was the problematical position of workers involved in the construction of installations in the North Sea. This work could be taking place on a structure to which the 1971 Act regulations could not readily be applied and to which no Certificate of Fitness had been granted. But these problems, serious as they undoubtedly were and difficult to resolve in practice as they may in certain cases have been, are of a different order to a more profound tension between the law and the regulated area which was evident in the Sea Gem Inquiry and which made another appearance in the Burgoyne Committee's report. It is perhaps this problem that more adequately explains the apparent withdrawal on the part of the Burgoyne Committee from any notion of a comprehensive role for law in regulating the safety aspects of the offshore industry.

Whereas in the Sea Gem Inquiry emphasis was laid on the inability of the law to understand a Code of Practice which had been drafted within the industry, the Burgoyne Committee was confronted by evidence that the converse problem had now arisen and difficulties were being encountered *by the industry* in dealing with regulations drafted in accordance with the needs *of the legal system*. The PED described the problems as follows:

> It is...difficult to draft regulations which can be readily understood by a person without legal training. We accept, however, that legal conventions must be respected and that, in the ultimate, regulations must be able to stand up in a court of law. We think that the regulations under the 1971 Act are now understood by the offshore oil industry, largely through explanation and interpretation from the Inspectorates to educate the industry through guidance notes.[38]

The Burgoyne Committee seems to have shared the PED's faith that it could make the regulations understood by the industry provided that it restricted itself to setting objectives as, despite strong opposition from the Trades Union Congress members on the Committee, it decided in favour of retaining the role of the PED rather than handing it over to the Health and Safety Executive (Burgoyne 1980, para 6.6). That said, the Committee clearly also recognised that the PED could not carry out its role with regard to occupational safety without help from the HSE and it therefore recommended a strengthening of contacts between the two (para 4.24). Further, it also recognised the way in which the offshore industry had fallen behind in comparison with the onshore as regards worker participation. To this end, it made a series of recommendations which reflected to some extent the terms of the Safety Representatives and Safety Committees Regulations 1977.[39] Significantly, however, and despite explicit mention of the onshore regime (para 5.94), the Committee did not call for its extension offshore nor did it 'consider it essential to embody these principles in mandatory regulations' (para 5.97). This, along with the failure to hand responsibility over to the HSE, was one of the main points of dispute with the TUC members of the Committee which led them to issue a Note of Dissent. They totally rejected the approach of the Committee with regard to the safety representative and safety committee position and pointed out that the tripartite Offshore Industry Advisory Committee had recently reached agreement in principle regarding the extension of the onshore regulations.[40] Whereas the Burgoyne Committee might have taken a tougher stance in recommending the mandatory implementation of its own proposals in this regard, its failure to recommend extension of the onshore regulations may have included a recognition that these operated so as to allow employers who did not recognise trade unions to avoid the mandatory involvement of safety representatives (see Kloss 1998, 137). This is a significant point in the context of the offshore industry, which had historically manifested a very low level of unionisation (see Andersen 1987; Woolfson *et al.* 1996, 44ff).[41] Nevertheless, the controversy surrounding the Burgoyne Committee was largely restricted to the issues of safety representatives and committees and the continued role of the PED. With regard to this latter issue, the Note of Dissent mentioned fears of the 'possibility of shared values and membership of closed groups'[42] as between industry and regulator, an assessment which provides an interesting contrast to the difficulties in communication perceived by the PED mentioned above.

1.4 Beyond the Prescriptive Regulatory Regime

The offshore industry and its regulators then largely disappeared from the public eye as far as the safety aspect was concerned until it burst upon the scene once more with considerable drama on 6 July 1988. On that night a series of explosions ripped through the Piper Alpha production platform, largely destroying it and claiming the lives of 167 men. Not only was this by far the worst accident in the history of the UK sector of the North Sea, it was also the worst disaster the industry had ever experienced anywhere in the world. The scale of the disaster meant that the only response the government could make was to announce the setting-up of a Public Inquiry.[43] This was established under the chairmanship of a senior Scottish judge, Lord Cullen, and was principally to answer two questions: 'What were the causes and circumstances of the disaster...? and What should be recommended with a view to the preservation of life and the avoidance of similar accidents in the future?' (Cullen 1990, para 1.1).

There can be no denying that the Report of the Public Inquiry into the Piper Alpha Disaster (Cullen 1990), which was the product of one of the lengthiest and most thorough inquiries ever seen in Britain, is a damning indictment of the state of safety in the UK sector of the North Sea and very few aspects emerge unscathed. The principal cause of the disaster was found to be a breakdown in the permit to work (PTW) system which served as a means of communication between the day and the night shift on the platform. This failure led to plant being used which was in fact undergoing maintenance and a gas escape and explosion resulted (Cullen 1990, Chapter 11).[44] Thereafter, the scale of the disaster was exacerbated by a number of factors: firstly, the Claymore platform, to which the Piper Alpha was connected, continued to pump oil to the Piper, hence feeding the fires which resulted from the explosion (paras. 7.37-40); secondly, the Offshore Installation Manager 'took no initiative in an attempt to save life' (para 8.35); thirdly, emergency systems, especially the fire-water system, failed as a result of the intensity of the explosion; fourthly, the platform's Stand-by Vessel, the *Silver Pit*, proved ineffective in the circumstances (para 9.42) as did the *Tharos* fire-fighting vessel, which was actually on hand at the time of the disaster (paras. 9.49-57). The platform's owners, Occidental Petroleum, were severely criticised by Lord Cullen for this state of affairs. They were said to be unprepared for this sort of emergency and to have adopted a superficial attitude to such risks. Adequate safety arrangements were frequently not in place and where they were they were often ignored: this was the case vitally with the PTW system (Chapter 14). Beyond the criticism of Occidental, the PED also came under fire from Lord Cullen. The inspections carried out by the PED were 'superficial to the point of being of little use as a test of safety on the platform' (para 15.48) and not really an effective means of assessing the management of safety (para 15.50).

In light of such thoroughgoing criticism, it is not surprising that the Report concluded with no fewer than 106 recommendations which constituted a radical reorientation of the approach to the regulation of safety in the offshore industry. There was a resonance with some of the principles which were evident in the Burgoyne Committee's report but in the Cullen Report they were worked into a comprehensive system. From an organisational point of view, and in line with the demands of the dissenting voices on the Burgoyne Committee (although not for the same reasons), Cullen recommended that the functions of the PED should be transferred to the HSE. At the level of the form of the regulatory approach, the fundamental recommendation was that the operator should be required to submit to the regulator a Safety Case (literally, making the case that the installation is safe) in respect of each of its installations. This Safety Case should demonstrate that certain objectives have been met, including the following: that the Safety Management System (SMS) of the company and that of the installation are adequate to ensure that the design and the operation of the installation and its equipment are safe; that the potential major hazards to the installation have been identified and appropriate controls provided; and that adequate provision is made for ensuring, in the event of a major emergency affecting the installation, a temporary safe refuge for personnel and their safe and full evacuation, escape and rescue (para 23.2). Whereas there may seem here to have been a call similar to that of the Sea Gem Inquiry for a comprehensive approach, there were in fact very significant differences.

Cullen largely abandoned any faith in the ability of the law, even in the form of more adaptable secondary legislation, to cover all the options. Instead he placed much of the responsibility on the operator both to identify risks and to demonstrate, by means of Quantified Risk Assessment (QRA) where appropriate, that they have been minimised and how this has been or is to be put into practice. He departed from the views on the location of responsibility expressed by both the Sea Gem Inquiry and the Burgoyne Committee, stating that 'a regulator cannot be expected to assume direct responsibility for the on-going management of safety...this is and remains in the hands of the operator' (para 21.4). He went so far as to suggest that an operator may want to depart from procedures outlined either in regulations or in official guidance and if so this would be permissible so long as the approach was justified in the Safety Case. Equally, he called for regulations to be reviewed and their prescriptive orientation replaced with a goal-setting orientation, albeit that some prescription would continue to be required.[45] Significantly, Cullen argued that prescriptive regulation could be part of the problem rather than a solution as this approach encouraged a compliance mentality rather than a wider consideration of safety (para 21.51) and was unable to cope with the overall interaction of components (para 21.42).[46] Such a shift in orientation for the regulations meant a different notion of compliance and equally implied a change in the role of the regulator. The operator under the new regime must satisfy itself by means of audits that the Safety Management System is being adhered to and the regulator is to review the operator's audit and to ensure that the output from the SMS is satisfactory (para 21.60). A further change was evident in the degree of freedom which was to be given to the operators to specify themselves which standards will be used to comply with the goal-setting regulations (para 21.70). This fits in, however, with Cullen's view that the primary function of the Safety Case is to ensure that every company produces a Formal Safety Assessment (FSA) to assure itself that its operations are safe and to derive the benefits therefrom. Only secondarily is it a matter of demonstrating this to the regulators, although this meets the legitimate expectations of the workforce and the public and provides a sound basis for regulation (para 17.35). This is a further example of the extent of Cullen's departure from a traditional view of the process and function of regulation.

The recommendations regarding the use of FSA, QRA and other such procedures are another interesting feature of Cullen's approach. He was explicitly impressed by the HSE's use of such methods and it was one of the factors which helped him decide which agency should be given responsibility for regulating offshore safety (paras. 22.28 and 22.34). Interestingly, in contrast to the fears of shared values expressed by the dissenting voices of the Burgoyne Committee as regards the PED and the industry, Cullen found no evidence to suggest a lack of independence on the part of the PED or that its actions had been influenced by considerations related to the exploitation of the hydrocarbon resources (para 22.38). Equally, he seems to have shared the concerns which were expressed by the PED at that time as regards the difficulty in achieving communication between law and the regulated area. Whereas the Burgoyne Committee went some way towards addressing this problem in its recommendations of non-mandatory guidance and flexibility, Cullen met the problem head-on and recommended an approach which meant that the regulators would be speaking to the industry in a language which it could understand. In evidence to the Inquiry, the HSE explained that it used QRA as a means of founding legal or political judgements as much as possible on a rigorous scrutiny of the facts because the technologically based industries or scientifically numerate organisations it dealt with expected a structured and logical approach (para 17.53).

One major point remains to be discussed with regard to the Cullen Report, namely the involvement of the workforce in health and safety. While the Inquiry was ongoing, the DEn brought in a set of regulations which provided for workforce involvement.[47] This was not an extension of the corresponding onshore regulations but rather reflected the approach recommended by the Burgoyne Committee. As a result, in the course of the Piper Alpha Inquiry, there were calls for these to be amended to incorporate trade union involvement.[48] While Cullen was sympathetic to the view that the appointment of representatives by trade unions could be beneficial with regard to credibility and the ability to resist pressure, he concluded that the particular circumstances of the offshore workforce in terms of its low level of unionisation and its fragmentation meant that such a change would have the effect of removing representation from a large number of workers (para 21.85).

With the changes recommended by Cullen now well into the implementation stage under the Offshore Safety Act 1992, it could be said simply that the broad philosophy of the Robens Report has belatedly been brought to the North Sea. It is possible to go further, however, and suggest that many of the features of the new regime indicate a significant transcendence of both the former substantive rationality and the onshore regime set up after Robens by the HSWA 1974. Regulations requiring the submission of Safety Cases for each of the installations operating in the UK sector of the North Sea (a figure somewhat in excess of 200) were introduced in 1992[49] and the HSE announced in November 1995 that it had achieved the successful assessment and acceptance of all Safety Cases for existing installations before the statutory deadline. At this time, the HSE signalled the extent of the break with the view of responsibility held by the Sea Gem Inquiry and the Burgoyne Committee when it stated that acceptance of a Safety Case 'cannot guarantee' that safety management systems are working effectively but rather allows inspectors to 'target their continuing intervention'.[50] Further, the process of introducing the new goal-setting regulations is also well-advanced.[51] When the degree of responsibility handed back to the operators in this regard is considered together with the new auditing role of the regulators, it is not difficult to draw parallels with notions such as responsive law or reflexive law which have gained increasing currency in recent years (Nonet and Selznick 1978; Teubner 1983; 1985; 1993a). One might even be tempted to suggest a cultural change in the industry, in that it now concedes the existence of difficulties in the past in claiming that these have now been transcended (e.g. Taylor *et al.* 1991). There are limits, however, to the survey so far undertaken and in the next section it will be seen that a too ready acceptance of the conventional wisdom both on the past and the current situation might be dangerous.

2 External Evaluations of the Law

As mentioned at the beginning of this chapter and as demonstrated in the foregoing outline of the history of the regulation of health and safety at work offshore, there has been a tendency for the solutions put forward in the aftermath of a disaster or as the result of an Inquiry to come to be seen in due course as a part of the problem. In brief, the formal approach of the early days was seen eventually as hopelessly inadequate, while the dreams of a prescriptive solution were already in question by the time of the Burgoyne Committee and were abandoned by Cullen. While it might be thought that the approximation to, and even transcendence of, the Robens philosophy achieved by Cullen constitutes a triumphant homecoming for the law in this field after years in the ideological wilderness, the continuing occurrence of dangerous incidents and the ongoing tension between workforce and employers mentioned at the beginning of this chapter would appear to imply that caution is required.[52] The story told so far, however, relates very much to the internal transformations of the law - the public inquiries were very much a part of the legal process - and so perhaps it should not be a surprise if the degree of change effected at each stage was not as radical as was really called for by the circumstances. It might be speculated that a certain inherent conservatism in the law leads to a reluctance fully to grasp the nettle and abandon all of that which has been implicated in the definition of the problem. It is a question, therefore, of looking also at what 'outsiders' have said about the situation - the way in which the period under discussion has been described by academic commentators. In the following sections four academic approaches which cover the different periods of development discussed above will be considered to see how they compare with the 'internal' assessments of the law.

2.1 Carson - The Other Price of Britain's Oil

This book (Carson 1981) has been until very recently the most authoritative discussion of the health and safety at work situation in the UK sector of the North Sea, continuing to be quoted with approval many years after its publication (see e.g. K. Miller 1991; Cotterrell 1992). Carson emphasises the impact of larger political and economic pressures in the oil industry and beyond on the regulators and on the workforce. Equally, one of his principal concerns is to dispel the 'myth' that accidents in the offshore oil industry were the result of the use of leading edge technologies in a hostile environment. The economics and politics of oil throughout the 1970s and the early years of the 1980s and their perceived impact on the law relating to safety can hardly be adequately described in a few paragraphs, but a summary of Carson's thesis can be given as follows.

The situation of the British economy in the 1960s sets the scene for all that is to follow in Carson's analysis. A political inability to come to terms with the UK's new and diminished world status led to a delay in the devaluation of sterling. This contributed to a chronic balance of payments deficit which was significantly affected by oil imports. Despite a relative fall in the price of oil on the world market at this time with the arrival of cheap supplies from the likes of Libya, any potential impact on the balance of payments was offset by an increasing use of oil in the UK. The discovery of commercial quantities of first natural gas and then oil in the

North Sea was, therefore, regarded by the government as something akin to manna from heaven, and a policy of rapid exploitation which would yield the earliest possible impact on the ailing current account was almost beyond question. This situation is perceived to have largely persisted throughout the period of Carson's survey and to have survived changes in the political complexion of the government. The pressure for production was only added to by the oil shocks of 1973 and 1979 when OPEC flexed its muscles and sent the price of oil rocketing. Such events merely confirmed the importance of the strategic political question of security of supply in addition to the simple question of economics. Equally, from the point of view of the industry, a rising price made an area such as the North Sea with its high capital and operating costs (relative to, for example, onshore Middle Eastern oil fields) much more attractive. Carson concludes his survey of the national economic and political situation by noting that as the 1970s progressed, the first revenues from the North Sea reached the Treasury and the effects on the visible trade deficit were seen on the current account. Gradually, the preoccupation with the balance of payments and currency valuation disappeared but as Carson was writing, the Conservatives were in the early years of their marathon term in power and even at this stage he was able to discern the government's pressing need for revenue to finance its election promises, which significantly included tax-cutting measures. It would not be difficult to gain acceptance of a continuation of Carson's thesis throughout the years of the Conservative term in office - a term marked by drastic cost-cutting and a central and powerful position for the Treasury in the administration.[53]

This desire to get oil ashore quickly and also to ensure that companies did not move their operations elsewhere led to the industry being handled with kid gloves in terms of regulation, Carson believes. In addition to this factor, the government was for a long time (and to a lesser extent even at the time Carson was writing) at the mercy of the industry in terms of information both about the size of the reserves and the technical aspects of their operations. These factors are seen as having contributed to the industry being given a free rein technologically. To compound what Carson sees as an already shaky position for safety in this equation, the fact that the safety inspectors were part of the same department promoting the maximisation of production provided at least the potential for an unacceptable conflict of interests. The inspectors, from the inception of the Petroleum Engineering Division of the Department of Energy in 1977, are seen as having worked with the industry in concentrating on disaster prevention to the exclusion of occupational safety so that security of production was guaranteed. To this end the inspectorate rejected the option of prosecution for breach of regulations in favour of a more 'softly softly' approach. As Carson puts it: the 'detailed application of legal rules had a tendency to become technologically negotiable' (1981, 179). The differences between the onshore and offshore health and safety regimes after the passing of the HSWA 1974, which were discussed above, are seen as especially significant. The industry is perceived as having put the emphasis on rapid production to maximise profit, leading to undue pressures on the workforce, and to have weighed the costs of compliance against the costs of breach of regulations in purely monetary terms. Equally it is seen as having victimised and blacklisted workers who questioned safety procedures, and actively discouraged unionisation. In the end, the view of accidents as the inevitable consequence of the combination of new technology in a hostile environment is rejected (cf. Kitchen 1977, 126ff).[54]

2.2 Wright - *'Routine Deaths: fatal accidents in the oil industry'*

This much more restricted survey (Wright 1986) is based on the evidence presented at a number of Fatal Accident Inquiries[55] following work-related deaths offshore. Like Carson, Wright has been struck by the accepted view both within and of the industry of the inevitable risks associated with new technology in a hostile environment. Whereas he is not concerned with the broader economic and political picture but rather with the organisational level, he confirms Carson's findings as to the relatively mundane and unexceptional nature of many accidents in the industry. He concludes that accidents nearly always resulted from what appeared to be a breach of normal working procedures and thus could be attributed to a common-sense understanding of what is involved in an accident, namely that 'they occur in abnormal, unpredictable, unexpected or novel situations and are brought about by individuals' consequent idiosyncratic behaviour' (1986, 276). Thus, the circumstances of accidents can be accepted as indicating the present limits of bureaucratic control.

Contrary to this common-sense view, however, Wright argues that in each of the cases he examines what was characterised as abnormal was in fact part of the normal work routine and was thus 'abnormal' only insofar as it had not been anticipated in the rules for work (1986, 279). The fact that these events were actually normal thus calls in question the adequacy of bureaucratic rationality which attempts to provide solutions for all eventualities in advance within formal rules. He also finds examples of unusual circumstances being dealt with by a process of normalisation, that is by fitting them into the ambit of formal rules when no procedure exists. Like Carson, Wright sees one of the principal factors in all of the accidents as speed: the pressure to get work done as quickly as possible because of the high costs of delays whether in construction, operation or maintenance. The second principal factor identified by Wright is poor communication whether between managers and workers on the installation or at other levels of the industry, for example between the designers, manufacturers and operators of equipment. According to Wright, a prime reason for the existence of such poor communications in an otherwise technologically advanced industry is the widespread use of subcontracting, which means that the workforce onboard an installation will normally be composed of the employees of several different companies with perhaps only a few men being employed by the installation's owner or operator. The result of such a situation is 'uncertainty over the location of legitimate authority and decision-making, ignorance about work conditions and the responsibilities of personnel and confusion over safety procedures' (1986, 284). Significantly, however, '[t]his confusion is caused not by the lack of communications and authority structures in the industry but by the existence of too many of them' (1986, 285). Despite the confusion, Wright finds that the system is economically rational for operators as it avoids the need to retain expensive specialists for particular tasks and allows market forces to push contractors to maximise output in the shortest time. Nevertheless, the result is also organisational inefficiency and ultimately injuries and death.

2.3 Tombs - 'Piper Alpha - A Case Study in Distorted Communication'

This study (Tombs 1990) is specifically restricted to the case of the Piper Alpha disaster but its findings are possibly generalisable given that many of the issues raised are common in the North Sea. Tombs's analysis proceeds from the work of Barry Turner (1978) who claims that disasters and accidents are often the result of 'complex and systemic, human and organisational factors, rather than inherent technological weaknesses'. He follows Turner in arguing that a 'socio-technical perspective' needs to be developed. Fundamentally, both writers are concerned with information and its availability to the appropriate people at the appropriate time. Recalling what was said about the Piper Alpha disaster by Lord Cullen (in particular the failure of the permit to work system and the basic organisational shortcomings in Occidental of which this was but one symptom), there is clearly much cogency in this point of view.

In greater detail, Tombs basically follows Turner's division of relevant information into four categories:

> (i) that which is completely unknown;
> (ii) that which is known but not fully appreciated;
> (iii) that which is known by someone, but is not brought together with other information at an appropriate time when its significance can be realised;
> (iv) that which was available to be known, but which could not be appreciated because there was no place for it in existing/prevailing modes of understanding. (Tombs 1990, 100)

He believes that this analysis can 'largely be subsumed under Habermas's more general concept of "distorted communication"' (Tombs 1990, 100). This allows him, after he has discovered informational problems in the Piper Alpha disaster, to make progress towards their solution. He follows Habermas's (1970) notions of intersubjectivity and the ideal speech situation and in particular he quotes the following: '"[i]n normal communication an intersubjectivity...develops and is maintained in the relation between individuals, who acknowledge one another"' (Tombs 1990, 100). With regard to 'acknowledgement' of one another, Tombs stresses that the participants in a dialogue '*must recognise each other as legitimate potential participants in any dialogue that may occur, and thus be prepared to act upon this recognition*' (1990, 100; emphasis in original). For him, '...a precondition of approaching ideal speech is a recognition of the socially constructed obstacles to that ideal speech situation. The degree of distortion in communication is related to the degree of repression within a given social system' (1990, 101). Tombs maintains that, in the case of Piper Alpha, vital information was not acted on because managers did not take workers or their organisations seriously, but rather regarded them as 'outside groups'. As a result, communication was systematically distorted; there was no approximation to the ideal speech situation as there was no 'intersubjectivity'; the parties to the communication did not 'acknowledge' one another in the sense meant by Habermas. Tombs identifies this state of affairs as being related to the following points:

> (i) the sources from which such information derived;
> (ii) a general technocratic hubris;

(iii) a general set of power relationships characteristic of, but not unique to, the offshore oil industry (1990, 105).

His conclusion is that a precondition of improved safety management is for workers to become subjects in, rather than objects of, health and safety efforts (1990, 106). There is thus a strong resonance with Carson, the dissenting voices of the Burgoyne Committee and with Cullen in his endorsement of the Offshore Installation (Safety Representatives and Safety Committees) Regulations 1989. In a further work (Tombs 1991), Tombs suggests that the way to achieve a situation where the workers become subjects in, rather than objects of, health and safety efforts is to grant them 'formal legal rights' to communicate information they possess which could help to avert accidents. At the very least such information should be recorded so that in the event of an accident it can be used to determine whether management had done all that was reasonably practicable. Further, he calls for the right to refuse to do dangerous work (1991, 34). Beyond these reactive measures, he wants to see a proactive role for the workforce in the development of working practices because they will often be the ones with a better knowledge of the 'practical realities' of operating the plant (1991, 34-5). In order to deal with what he sees as an imbalance of power between employers and workers, he calls for a stronger role for unions as opposed to simply giving rights to workers (1991, 36). With these views in mind, Tombs concludes pessimistically that '[t]he Inquiry and Report of Lord Cullen recommended nothing which would result in a shift in the nature and extent of distorted communication in the offshore oil industry' (1991, 39).

2.4 Woolfson, Foster and Beck - Paying for the Piper: Capital and Labour in Britain's Offshore Oil Industry

This more recent and very comprehensive work (Woolfson *et al.* 1996) effectively brings the story told by Carson up to date - indeed it has been wholeheartedly endorsed by the latter in an afterword to the book. While concentrating on the relationships between capital and labour in the offshore industry and in particular on the question of union organisation, the authors have significant things to say about the regulation of health and safety. In common with Tombs, theirs is a very negative assessment of the regime instituted after the Cullen Report.

This book is all the more striking because it conflicts seriously with the general perception of the new regime which has prevailed in recent years. In the immediate aftermath of the Cullen Report's publication, the mood was uniformly upbeat (see e.g. K. Miller 1991) and since then the feeling has been that the corner has been turned and that a cultural change has occurred in the industry's approach to safety. Woolfson, Foster and Beck, however, suggest that this perception is due more to the industry's strenuous efforts to project a new image and bears little relationship to a reality of continuing problems (1996, 360-1). The authors contend that while the industry has abandoned the policy of capture employed with regard to the PED, it has nevertheless adopted an equally effective 'strategy of containment' with regard to the HSE. This has been manifest in resistance to regulatory reconstruction and has produced a gradual erosion of regulatory reform (1996, 328). Equally, it has been made easier because of certain features of the new regime.

In contrast to the hopes expressed for the new regime, the authors are concerned that it is, in fact, fatally flawed. They make three principal points in this regard: 1) Safety Cases place the major burden of responsibility on line management in a highly technocratic way which few understand - especially because they have often been produced by external consultants; 2) the handling of compliance is also technocratic because the HSE now audits processes rather than checking to see if its regulations are being observed - the authors believe that goal-setting regulations can only be effective if anchored in genuine workforce involvement and this is affected by their third point; 3) there is a lack of trade union support for the safety representatives who form the cornerstone of workforce involvement (1996, 346).

The goal-setting approach of the new regime has allowed the industry to emphasise self-regulation and thus to argue against all forms of regulatory intervention (whether emanating from the national or European level) which can be characterised as introducing any element of rigidity or prescription (1996, 362). The regulations which Cullen foresaw as 'underpinning' the Safety Cases have therefore come to be attacked rather as 'diluting' them. Bad as this response would be on its own, according to the authors, matters are made far worse by the fact that the HSE is perceived to have acquiesced in this approach - not least perhaps because of the general deregulation drive of the previous Conservative government.[56]

While Cullen himself called for the abandonment of prescriptive regulations, the industry has sought to take matters much further. The HSE's use of Approved Codes of Practice in conjunction with goal-setting regulations has also been resisted. Breach of an ACoP is not in itself regarded as criminal, but failure to observe such a code is regarded by the courts as *prima facie* evidence of guilt (see Kloss 1998, 125). Even if industry concern with ACoPs might, therefore, be somewhat understandable - albeit that they do not really seem to conflict with the Safety Case approach - its opposition also to non-mandatory guidance produced by the HSE demonstrates just how much freedom the industry wants. In place of ACoPs and guidance produced by the regulator, the industry wants to substitute its own guidance. Similarly, it has pressed for the abandonment of the external audit provided by Certifying Authorities, which the authors see as having been largely achieved in the Design and Construction Regulations,[57] which replaces certification with a verification scheme for safety critical elements. The independence requirements for those carrying out the verification do not appear to impress the authors (Woolfson *et al.* 1996, 348-54).

Nor is it the case that the industry is simply concerned to ensure the purity of the Safety Case approach according to the authors. Instead, its response must be seen in the context of the current cost reduction initiative in the industry (CRINE 1994) and the HSE is perceived to be operating also within the terms of the CRINE agenda (Woolfson *et al.* 1996, 338), not least in regard to its opposition to European health and safety legislation.

Woolfson, Foster and Beck appear to disagree fundamentally, therefore, with Cullen's attitude to the former prescriptive regime. Indeed, they employ implementation theory to test the adequacy of the new approach and find it wanting in all regards. Not least among their objections is the lack of a 'sound theory which identifies the principal factors and causal linkages affecting policy objectives' in the enabling legislation (1996, 362). The contrast with Cullen could not be more stark. The result, they say, is a 'gradual erosion scenario' in which 'a legislative agenda, which clearly mandates a behaviour change, gradually deteriorates as it faces a host of "veto points" which emerge when concrete regulations are negotiated' (1996, 363-4). Beyond this, the historical lack of prosecutions for health and safety breaches in the offshore industry is seen as problematical (1996, 375-7). Despite a definite increase in the last few years, and the imposition of a handful of large fines, they complain that the average fine remains low and offers no economic deterrent (1996, 382-3). The authors themselves argue strongly for economic deterrence (1996, 409-12) and the introduction of the crime of corporate manslaughter, and draw a comparison with the success of the prescriptive approach to offshore health and safety regulation in the US, which indicates that their faith lies precisely with the form of regulation which Cullen had found wanting (1996, 430).

3 Evaluating the Evaluations

There is a danger in taking too broad a view of these academic writers in comparison with the internal assessments of the law as carried out by the three public inquiries considered previously, but one general difference does stand out. Whereas the Burgoyne Committee and the Cullen Inquiry have been willing to reorient law away from more direct forms of intervention, there is something of a consensus among the academic commentators in their reluctance to accept the degree of freedom this gives to the industry. Despite differing approaches, there is a tendency to hold faith with the Sea Gem Inquiry's proposals for a strict and comprehensive regulatory regime. In the sections which follow, the ways in which this reluctance to grant a greater degree of freedom to the industry may actually be at odds with the findings of these commentators will be outlined. Further, the aim will be to demonstrate that this failure to draw the conclusions indicated by the findings arises from a particular conception of what the law is and what it can reasonably achieve. Such a conception, it will be suggested, significantly colours the sociological process, hiding much of the picture to be drawn of the area under investigation as well as closing off many prescriptive options from the outset.

3.1 The Economic Analysis of Law

Perhaps the aspect of the oil industry which has the greatest impact on the observer is the sheer scale of its economic power.[58] This leads commentators rightly or wrongly into straightforward economic analyses of its activities with regard to health and safety and produces prescriptions designed to lock into its supposed economic rationality. Such an approach is evident especially in the work of Carson and more recently of Woolfson, Foster and Beck. In both cases, the approaches are more sophisticated but economic analysis firmly underpins their work. Both make reference to the inadequacy of the fines available to the courts for breaches of health and safety at work regulations, fines which in the context of multinational organisations would make not the slightest impact. Carson contends that companies simply apply or ignore the regulations on the basis of cost-benefit calculations (1981, 77-9). Woolfson, Foster and Beck point out that even the then record £250,000 fine handed down following the conviction of ARCO in the Ocean Odyssey case represented a tiny fraction of one per cent of the parent company's annual profits (1996, 414). The implication is, then, that if the fines were only large enough, presumably running into several millions of pounds, companies would comply with what was demanded of them by the law. And this is the basic assumption of the economic analysis of law approach in general with regard to health and safety at work. Without regulation, it is assumed that industry will internalise the costs of injury and death only to the extent that they affect productivity since to go any further would be contrary to profit-maximisation. Regulation, therefore, is seen as forcing the internalisation of the externalities involved in the social cost of industrial accidents; and in order for this process to work, the costs of ignoring the regulations must be sufficiently high to make an impact on profit (see Posner 1986, 311). Now, within its own terms, this is undoubtedly true and one only has to consider the efforts of such companies to ensure that compensation claims are pursued in jurisdictions other than the United States to see the force of this analysis.[59] At bottom, the economic analysis approach aims at an optimal level of safety with intervention seeking to achieve the minimisation of both accident costs and accident prevention costs. The standard problem identified with such an approach within economics is its assumption of a perfect labour market (see e.g. Oi 1974; Kaufman 1994, 390ff; Ogus 1994, 181). Proponents of economic analysis acknowledge that such a perfect market does not exist but insist on the importance of cost-benefit analysis for rational choice. While this is undoubtedly reasonable, further difficulties exist. At the most basic level is the assumption that added safety must equal added cost (e.g. Chelius 1974) - a result of the close link between economic analysis and a detailed regulatory approach to occupational health and safety and consequently an assumption which is increasingly questioned as this approach to regulation is superseded. Beyond this, however, there are more fundamental problems.

A contradiction arises at this point, for example, in the approach of writers who are broadly critical of 'big business'. On the one hand, they use economic analysis to demonstrate that regulation and enforcement strategies which take no account of cost-benefit calculations are unlikely to influence corporate actors. This suggests that regulators must equally engage in cost-benefit calculations if they are to produce desired effects. On the other hand, they are critical of the inability of cost-benefit analysis adequately to reflect social cost. Posner's analysis, for example, suggests that regulation may lead to standards being raised to a point where both employer and employee are 'harmed', the extra cost of safety being passed on to the employee in the form of lower wages. Employees may, therefore, not 'desire' such a high level of safety (Posner 1986, 311). This view would presumably not be acceptable to Carson or to Woolfson, Foster and Beck, for example. Further, the critics are fearful of those who use economic analysis to demonstrate the harmful effects of regulation and 'big government' on business (e.g. Wallis 1977; AGDG 1995). It has also been argued that economic analysis can suggest that so long as there is a pool of unemployed people to replace those killed or injured in industrial accidents, there is no economic incentive to take extra care unless the costs of training and compensation threaten profit, and this may in fact result in a net gain to society as the unemployed also represent a cost (Priest 1988, 133-4). The attempt to pitch sanctions at a level which influences profit is, then, itself a market-based process and depends on regulators as well as industry placing an exact money value on life and limb, whether implicitly or explicitly. It involves the translation of social costs into economic costs and it does not ask where the costs predominantly lie (Ashford 1976). Priest rhetorically suggests testing this approach by asking workers how much they would accept to die (1988, 118). Of course, it is easy to be critical of economic analysis by using examples such as these, and they represent problems which have for long been recognised by economists. Nevertheless, even more complex approaches such as the cost-effective deterrence model (Veljanovski 1984) or yet more modern approaches which accept, for example, that optimality must be allowed to drop out of the picture (e.g. Harris and Veljanovski 1986, 119) still assume that social objectives can be unproblematically subjected to economic criteria. While these difficulties do not unduly trouble writers such as Posner who accept economic analysis as part of a wider faith in the market and in private or common law, they represent fundamental problems for those such as Carson and Woolfson, Foster and Beck who recognise the need to take account of economic analysis but whose concerns are with public policy (see Rose-Ackerman 1992, chapter 2).

Of more concern, however, in the context of a situation as complex as that represented by the offshore oil and gas industry is the considerable simplification which economic analysis can achieve without raising the question of whether such an action is not in fact a potentially dangerous *over*-simplification. There is criticism from within economics of a 'common attachment to a singular conception of how one does economic analysis - the starting point is always with the individual and individual-optimizing behavior' (Darity 1993, 2) - an attachment that goes all the way back to Adam Smith. Greater specification of this problem can be found in the work of Herbert Simon (e.g. 1976; 1978), and his comprehensive account of the difficulties faced by economics in this regard can be summed up in the following quote:

> ...economics has largely been preoccupied with the *results* of rational choice rather than the *process* of choice....we must give an account not only of *substantive rationality* - the extent to which appropriate courses of action are chosen - but also *procedural rationality* - the effectiveness, in light of human cognitive powers and limitations, of the *procedures* used to choose actions. (1978, 2; 8-9; emphasis in original)

Simon is concerned, then, about the way in which economic analysis *assumes* an economic rationale and in this way inevitably produces the kind of prescriptions we have seen from Carson (1981) and Woolfson *et al.* (1996). Now it may be that the dominant presence of an economic rationality in multinational oil companies is not in dispute but it is something nevertheless which remains to be demonstrated. Furthermore, the precise *form* of any economic rationality must be demonstrated rather than assuming a basic programme of profit-maximisation. Equally, with regard to the important technological aspects of the industry at which much of the regulation is aimed, the importance of a scientific rationality cannot be ignored. As Roger Cotterrell has pointed out, 'legal relations are not...solely economic relations nor relations whose content and significance are necessarily explicable in exclusively economic terms' (1992, 5).

Of even greater significance, however, is the fact that an economic approach to law has to make one very important assumption - although one that is not usually considered - namely that the *content* of the law is uncontroversial. In the context of a complex industry which has continually produced new technology to meet new challenges as it has moved into deeper water and attempted to open up smaller and geologically more difficult fields, this is precisely the sort of assumption that cannot be lightly made. Of course, there has also been a consensus among academic commentators that many accidents in the offshore oil industry have not been the result of complex technology but are of a much more mundane nature. While many have indeed been mundane in their immediate causes and results, their relationship to the complex technology involved is perhaps for this very reason too easily dismissed. The fact that the industry in both its management and engineering aspects has continued to lay stress on the importance of the complexity issue is perhaps something which should be addressed rather than being dismissed as a typical piece of obfuscation by big business. The very certainty which the economic analysis of law assumes may simply not be present, in which case its prescriptions may be ineffective or produce unintended detrimental side-effects. The traditional substantive strategies of economic analysis have reached their limits 'when we are seeking to explain the decision maker's behavior in complex, dynamic circumstances that involve a great deal of uncertainty, and that make severe demands upon his attention' (Simon 1978, 14). There is some evidence of an appreciation of this issue in the work of Wright when he discusses the limits of bureaucratic rationality (1986, 286-7) but his prescription for solving the problem - a reduction in the amount of subcontracting - may be somewhat naive. Given that as much as 85% of the offshore workforce is employed by subcontractors (Spiller 1994, 3), it is clear that a major restructuring of the industry would be required to effect any significant change. There is a failure here to consider whether subcontracting is purely economically rational or whether the farming-out of specialist tasks is itself a response to complexity. If this is the case then Wright's prescription becomes part of the problem rather than a solution.

The economic power of the industry, however, also produces an irresistible attraction for commentators towards capture theory explanations of the regulatory situation.

3.2 Regulatory Capture, Containment and Accommodation

This approach is most evident in the work of Carson in his discussion of the PED and a variation of it appears also in the work of Woolfson, Foster and Beck, who term it 'regulatory containment'. In this respect, these authors are part of a larger area of legal sociological research which has discovered many instances of what might be termed an unhealthy closeness between regulatory agencies and the corporations they are supposed to be regulating. This closeness can take a variety of forms and be present in differing degrees. The regulation of offshore health and safety is by no means the only area which has come in for this sort of analysis and other studies have found regulators taking account of the pressures which businesses experience when making decisions about the enforcement of the law.[60] Such situations can be seen, however, in different ways and as well as looking at them from the point of view of the regulator taking account of the needs of the regulated there is the alternative view which sees economically powerful corporations as having greater opportunities to manipulate the regulatory process in their own interests. Many commentators see big business as having in many instances successfully limited either the scope of regulatory control or its enforcement (e.g. Carson 1970).[61]

Fundamentally, studies which allege regulatory capture or accommodation can often be related to the economic analysis of law approach discussed in the above section as there is an underlying assumption that the corporations concerned are seeking to minimise the costs which will be incurred as a result of the demands imposed by regulation. However, other reasons for such relationships between regulator and regulated have also been recognised. Carson, for example, points to the differences in expertise and information between the PED and the industry (Carson 1981, 116ff). On the basis of such findings, commentators see regulators as negotiating with the regulated in order to achieve such measure of implementation as they can.[62] This information imbalance certainly exists but an emphasis on this point relies on a particular conception of the role of government and of law and their ability to have or to find all the answers to the regulation of diverse areas of social life. There must come a point, especially in an area occupied by complex technology, where this particular conception of law and government hits serious, if not indeed insurmountable, difficulties. In a situation where myriad government agencies are competing for scarce resources - which may indeed be diminishing as the regulatory demands increase - and where the actors being regulated will always be in a position (as part of their ongoing operations as economic entities) to deploy significantly more resources, such a conception of the role of law and government risks entering the realm of fantasy, and to continue to operate on such an assumption is to make demands which can simply never be met. And yet, even the most recent assessment of the offshore safety situation suggests clearly that matters could be improved by greater prescription and by inspection based upon such regulations (Woolfson *et al.* 1996, 346; 430).

Another reason exists for accommodatory policies and indeed for attempts by business to moderate the impact of regulation. This is a reason which also explains situations where regulatory agencies are given high degrees of discretion in the implementation and even in the making of regulations. It is a reason, however, which, as we have noted earlier, has been rejected by Carson, Wright and Woolfson *et al.*: the complexity of the area to be regulated. While the government at the passing of the Mineral Workings (Offshore Installations) Act 1971 explicitly mentioned the inevitability of changing technology and indeed the potential for the rapidity of such change in an industry like the oil industry as the reason for the framework form of the legislation, even this approach was found by both the Burgoyne Committee and the Cullen Inquiry to be inadequate for the task in hand in terms of its ability to keep up with the pace of change. These findings sit unhappily with the critics' insistence on the irrelevance of complexity and their apparent faith in the role for law that these inquiries have called into question. Equally, these commentators' findings of regulatory capture or containment and their criticisms of accommodatory strategies by the regulators can take on a potentially very different complexion and the regulators' approach (especially that of the PED) might just as easily be seen as an attempt to come to terms with the shortcomings of the legal form which was eventually swept away by the Cullen Report. Cotterrell, for one, recognises that often in such circumstances 'issues of causation, of allocation of responsibility, and of culpability' present considerable difficulties (1992, 269) which can only problematically be accommodated within a traditional concept of law. The related finding by Carson that prosecution was not an option very frequently chosen by the PED when faced with regulatory breaches can appear much less surprising in such circumstances (see also Richardson *et al.* 1982, 124ff).

With this in mind, the application of implementation theory concepts by Woolfson, Foster and Beck to the new regime - especially the requirement for a 'sound theory which identifies the principal factors and causal linkages affecting policy objectives' in the enabling legislation (1996, 362) - begins to appear rather suspect. Given that the new regime explicitly rejected the style of regulation implied by implementation theory, for it to be found wanting in that theory's terms is less than surprising. That said, the authors are able to point to the apparent success of the prescriptive regime in the US offshore industry in order to support their belief in its superiority (1996, 430). But citing figures such as 99% of key components required by regulations found to be satisfactory during US inspections entirely misses Cullen's criticisms of the 'compliance mentality' and of the inability to cope with the overall interaction of components, and offers no information about the differences between the technological and environmental conditions subsisting in the two jurisdictions. This last omission is particularly surprising given the evident care with which these authors have considered and compared the varying interpretations of the UK offshore accident statistics. As will be seen in Chapter 3, the differences between the two jurisdictions are significant and the failure to recognise them had a considerable impact in the UK. Furthermore, as offshore activity in the US begins to enter areas with more severe environmental conditions and requiring more complex technology, it is interesting to note that a regulatory approach very similar to the UK Safety Case and distinct from the pre-existing prescriptive approach is being adopted - the Deepwater Operations Plan (see Regg *et al.* 1996).[63] In short, insisting on an understanding of law which ignores the complexity of the regulatory area is bound to find more innovative regulatory forms wanting. Equally, it risks masking problems which may ultimately prove fatal. It is perhaps not surprising, then, to find that other writers characterise similar regulatory situations in less condemnatory terms, such as 'partial accommodation', and stress the ways in which such an approach can bring out the common interests of regulator and regulated in, for example, safety or the quality of products.[64]

Accordingly, there is a possible resonance between the question of regulating health and safety at work offshore and a line of legal sociological writing from Eugen Ehrlich through Roscoe Pound and which finds its most recent formulations in the work of Niklas Luhmann (e.g. 1985), Gunther Teubner (e.g. 1987) and Karl-Heinz Ladeur (e.g. 1989). Ehrlich and later Pound stressed the importance of the 'living law' of the areas of social life where state law progressively intervenes (e.g. Ehrlich 1936, 369; Pound 1953, 67ff). To the living law, the law of the state can appear inappropriate and as causing disruption rather than providing solutions. Pound, for example, demonstrated how the rigid categories of the law could be ill-adapted to new developments and discoveries, even when they were merely used as analogies (e.g. 1960, 63-4).[65] Teubner (1987) has continued this line of reasoning, pointing out that law's effect can often be to create uncertainty, hostility, chaos and mistrust and he seeks instead an appropriate relationship between law and other social subsystems in order to prevent this (see also Nisbet 1975, 73; Allott 1980, 121ff; Evan 1990, 127ff). To the commentators on the oil industry we have considered above, of course, if large corporations are disrupted so as to improve safety standards then so much the better. The point is, however, that such disruption only produces such desirable effects where the content of the law is appropriate and uncontroversial. In situations of complexity, of course, this is precisely the matter frequently at issue. The blanket exclusion of complexity as a significant feature in the regulation of health and safety at work offshore risks shutting off the most important questions and excluding from the outset many possible prescriptions. Such an exclusion may, of course, turn out to be justified but it remains to be proved rather than assumed or at best accepted on the basis of relatively superficial findings. The fact that in attempting to regulate the behaviour of the offshore oil industry the law is confronting actors of considerable economic and technological sophistication raises questions of the possible mismatch between the living law and state regulation which are too large to be easily dismissed. Interestingly, all of the commentators discussed above provide evidence of the importance of different rationalities in the regulation of health and safety at work offshore. Wright discusses the limits of bureaucratic rationality and the seemingly economically rational choice of what he sees as the dangerous practice of subcontracting. Tombs concentrates on the differing views of management and workforce and on the need to improve communication between them. Woolfson, Foster and Beck similarly stress the importance of engaging the expertise of the workforce in producing regulation. Finally, a large part of Carson's thesis and that of Woolfson *et al.* is the impact of the broader political and economic importance of oil on the question of health and safety. Nevertheless, despite such recognition, there is a reluctance on the part of all the commentators to abandon a model of law which appears to be at odds with the regulated area on the basis that it is for the regulated area to step into line and not the other way round.

4 Moving Beyond Existing Evaluations

4.1 At the Limits of Modernity

At root, there is in much in the evaluations of the operation of the law relating to health and safety at work in the offshore oil and gas industry which demonstrates an underlying commitment to command-and-control regulation: what Ziegert (1983) calls the 'light-switch' model of law and what Kidder (1983) describes as the 'vaccine' model of law.[66] In other words, there is an assumption that once a particular problem has been discovered, the passing and implementation of certain regulations will bring about an amelioration if not a complete resolution of the problem.[67] Where, once regulations have been passed, there is no sign of what might be regarded as a sufficient improvement in the situation then it is assumed that there must be some problem of enforcement. As certain other writers discussing offshore safety have written: 'law is only effective if it is enforced' (Barrett *et al.* 1987, 80; see also Baram 1985). Beyond this there may at times be an admission that the content of the law is problematic, although this has not been a significant feature of the writers discussed. More often there is a belief rather that more law is required, as is the case with Woolfson, Foster and Beck (see also Kinnersley 1973; O'Riordan 1985). Whatever the particular emphasis and whether there is a predominantly economic analysis approach or a regulatory capture or accommodation approach, the significant point is the priority position which is assigned to law and an unquestioning faith in its ability to deal with the problem in hand. In each case, however, potentially the most interesting and fruitful questions are being avoided.

There is also in such a perception of the situation very much a one-way view of the relationship between law and society, a belief that law changes society but that law is (or ought to be) somehow immune to any influence from society that can be characterised as in any way watering down the rigour of the law. Thus, where resistance is encountered by the law, such an approach constrains us to prescriptions along the lines of more law, better enforcement, more information and so forth. But this then leads to a point where the existence of over-ambition on the part of law or of a situation in the regulated area which law might more reasonably have to live with rather than attempting to change is effectively masked from view (see Allott 1980, 68).

We can see in this situation what has been characterised by some writers as the condition of law in transition from modernity to post-modernity (see e.g. Bauman 1992). Historically, as law freed itself from the constraints of other aspects of culture, it came to be the instrument of government in its attempts to regulate ever more areas of society, being seen as autonomous, comprehensive, principled and systematic and thus superior to other normative systems (see Cotterrell 1992). But gradually in more recent years it has been perceived as showing signs of having reached and even gone beyond the limits of its 'intellectual' capacity (Willke 1990, 237). Equally, there is the suggestion that the law produces only one (legal) record of events which fails to accommodate the plurality, interrelatedness and conflict inherent in modern life: the priority assigned to law is therefore in question (see Goodrich 1986, 219-223; Nelken 1990). Of course, the same sort of story could be told about, for example, economics and science, both of which have been assigned a similar priority by their own proponents.

Recalling what was said about Herbert Simon's critique of substantive economic reasoning, there is a growing number of those who are beginning to question the explanatory power which has been attributed to the discipline. McKenzie (1983), for example, has discussed the limits of economic analysis while Hausman has stated that it is

> ironic that various economists and other social scientists have been making grandiose claims for the universal validity of the economic approach at just that time when so many economists have had qualms about their own discipline. (1984, 2-3)

McCloskey has produced one of the most sustained criticisms of economics, attacking in particular the 'poverty of economic modernism' and pointing out the ways in which economics clings to a rationality long abandoned by other disciplines (1985, 3ff). Gudeman takes these points to their conclusion in what could be described as a post-modern assessment of economics in arguing that 'economies and economic theories are social constructions' (1986, vii), while Dodd puts the point even more clearly when he says that 'information does not have the integrity supposed by economic reasoning. The notion that information is simply "transmitted" and "received", as if its meaning remains constant, is unsustainable' (1995, 1).[68]

Meanwhile in science, a paradox is perceived in that while science produces knowledge at an exponential rate, this very activity produces relative ignorance even more rapidly (Ravetz 1990; Luhmann 1993, 28). Furthermore, the ultimate application of the principles of science to science itself has brought about a crisis of confidence in the great Enlightenment hope that the scientific method would provide the ultimate and irrefutable measure of truth (e.g. Ravetz 1990; Beck 1992). Some in science attempt to deal with such problems by holding a stronger disinterested position for the discipline that would take it further from the firing line (e.g. Harré 1986) but the impossibility of such a 'solution' is clear in a world where economic, political and legal demands for scientific answers increase daily - the famous 'trans-science' of Weinberg (1972).[69] The implications for science in these circumstances are rather depressingly (from the scientist's viewpoint) summed-up by Majone (1989) who stresses the need for scientists involved in the policy process to hone their advocacy skills in the face of the inability of science to provide a final answer - a point echoed by Collingridge and Reeve (1986) in what they see as a new 'ironic' role for science as opposed to its Enlightenment 'heroism', by Jasanoff (1990) who discusses the difficulties for those on the receiving end of scientific advice in this new context, and by Ulrich Beck who talks of the sciences as 'self-service shops for financially well-endowed customers in need of arguments' (1992, 173).[70]

While these problems are at best disappointing for economists and scientists, they present a challenge to law of considerable magnitude and one which would certainly appear to be present in a particularly potent combination in the regulation of such a technologically complex and economically important industry as offshore oil and gas. Some idea of what is involved here can be gained from the recognition that what counts as truth for a traditional model of law is something different from what counts as truth for science. Perhaps the most influential modern account of the nature of science is that of Popper (1972) who holds that science makes only provisional findings of truth which are themselves immediately subject to falsification and hence replacement with another, provisional, truth.[71] It has been pointed out that whereas science can go on making provisional findings of truth, law ultimately requires a definite answer and indeed 'misunderstands' scientific evidence in this way.[72] But the difficulties do not end there. An indication of the feedback effect (or scientific reconstruction) of this legal 'misunderstanding' appears in the scientific 'retreat into ever-narrower specializations' and a weakening of its 'critical function' as the system comes to terms with the possibility of litigation and other adverse reactions and ultimately seeks to avoid controversy (see Wildavsky 1995). And when we see that the same holds true between economics and science with economics similarly constructing scientific answers as absolute and imposing deadlines on what is an essentially open-ended process (see e.g. Collingridge and Reeve 1986), and between law and economics with Heyne asking provocatively whether 'the blind can lead the blind' (1988; see also Balekjian 1979, 377; Summers 1979), then there is clearly the potential for the existence of some very uneasy relationships in an industry such as offshore oil and gas which a traditional implementation approach to law is in danger of exacerbating through its failure properly to recognise them.

4.2 Behind the Mask

It would be going too far, however, to say that the commentators we have considered are not aware of this situation. Carson, of course, stresses the importance of the broader political and economic situation and admits of constraints which transcend the direct exercise of power (1981, 233). There would seem, therefore, to be a question of the process of communication between legal rationality and other rationalities in the broader society. Wright (1986) demonstrates the importance of the limiting construction of reality in bureaucratic rationalities, a point developed much further by Tombs (1990; 1991). There appears, therefore, also to be a question of the process of communication between the different organisations and individuals involved in all stages of the regulatory process and the regulated area. But in each case, despite such tantalising indications of a recognition of such questions, the authors revert to a model of law in their prescriptions which is at odds with that very recognition. This reversion is evident even in the most recent work by Woolfson, Foster and Beck (1996) where there is a scathing attack on the developments introduced after the Cullen Inquiry which seem *prima facie* to address these very issues by a significant reorientation of roles for the regulator and the regulated. In the foregoing discussion, it has been contended that this situation arises out of a model of the legal process which effectively masks the greater complexity of the area under study. In the light of this consideration, the rejection at the outset by Tombs of the categories of information he defined as 'that which is completely unknown' and 'that which was available to be known, but which could not be appreciated because there was no place for it in existing/prevailing modes of understanding' (Tombs 1990,100) seems particularly unfortunate. The degree of uncertainty would seem to be *precisely* what needs to be added back into considerations of the appropriate method of regulation of complex technology. And the influence of prevailing modes of understanding would seem to be *precisely* what needs to be given urgent consideration. As Cotterrell says towards the end of his detailed survey of the sociology of law:

> [s]ociology of law must aim to interpret complexity, rather than replicate it or hide within it; it must seek to reveal the broadest significance of the social details it studies, to build bridges between the legal experience of individuals and of different social groups, to construct perspectives that connect disparate specialised or localised knowledges. (1992, 311)

If the overview of the regulation of health and safety at work in the offshore oil and gas industry and of its evaluation by government-sponsored Inquiries and by academics appears to reveal a situation of complexity unsuited both to traditional regulatory approaches and to evaluation on the basis of such approaches, then there would seem to be a need for a legal sociological approach which can address these issues - one which is sensitive to complexity and which is able to evaluate and accommodate regulatory innovations rather than dismissing them purely on the ground that they differ from traditional models. In other words, there is a need for an approach which can look behind the mask imposed by traditional regulatory and legal sociological approaches to discover the complexity which lies there. If complexity is left behind this mask, then the risks to health and safety offshore may be left there also.

Notes

1 First indications that gas was present in commercial quantities came in September 1965 with first gas ashore 18 months later in early 1967. First oil was struck in the latter half of 1966 with the first sizeable quantities being confirmed in late 1970. First oil flowed from the Hamilton field in June 1975. See *Petroleum Press Service* 1965, 404; 1966, 426; 1967, 144; 1970, 380; *Petroleum Economist* 1975, 253.

2 See Carson (1981, 19-26) Wright (1986, 266) and Woolfson *et al.* (1996, 383ff) for a negative view of the statistical record, see SREA (1989, 19). Historically, however, there have been difficulties in comparing onshore and offshore statistics (see Carson 1981, 17ff; Woolfson *et al.* 1996, 367-72). While Taylor (1993) and Hughes (1994) offer a more favourable reading of the situation in more recent years, their figures have been profoundly questioned by Woolfson *et al.* (1996, 385). Interestingly, calls for uniformity in accident reporting have come from the industry, which feels that it has been disadvantaged by the different standards applied offshore and onshore (Hughes 1994, 4). The Reporting of Injuries, Diseases and Dangerous Occurrences Regulations (RIDDOR) 1995 (SI 1995/3163) raised hopes that within a few years meaningful comparisons between onshore and offshore figures would finally be possible. That this situation may still be some way off, however, appeared from the fact that the Health and Safety Executive felt compelled to launch an initiative aimed at raising awareness of RIDDOR reporting requirements offshore in May 1999. This followed concern that offshore work patterns were contributing to the non-reporting of injuries (see HSE Press Release E092:99, 7 May 1999).

3 See, for example, *The Press and Journal* 7 October and 22 October 1994 for the exchange between Harold Hughes of the United Kingdom Offshore Operators Association (UKOOA) and Ronnie McDonald of the Offshore Industry Liaison Committee (OILC).

4 At the end of 1995, a fairly acrimonious dispute erupted between Charles Woolfson of Glasgow University and Matthias Beck of St. Andrew's University on the one hand and UKOOA on the other as to the interpretation of offshore accident statistics. The two sides presented diametrically opposed interpretations of the same raw data from the Health and Safety Executive (HSE). See *The Press and Journal* 25 October and 1 December 1995. The same researchers together with John Foster produced a book (1996) critical of the industry, which prompted a pre-emptive dismissive

response and led to one bookshop refusing to host the launch - apparently for fear of upsetting industry clients. See *The Daily Mail* 10 December 1996.

5 See www.open.gov.uk/hse/ops_unit/proscomp.htm for the latest prosecution statsistics.

6 See *Petroleum Economist* March 1993, 47 and *The Press and Journal* 28 March 1997.

7 This was the finding of the ongoing risk perception project conducted by the Robert Gordon University Offshore Management Centre and was reported in the paper given by Rachel Gordon to the 13th Leith International Safety Conference at Edinburgh. See *The Press and Journal* 27 October 1994.

8 See BBC Online Network 8 June 1999.

9 See BBC Online Network 8 September 1999.

10 Jake Molloy, General Secretary of the OILC. See BBC Online Network 8 and 9 September 1999.

11 See BBC Online Network 9 August 1999.

12 This technological and environmental uniqueness is a quality which the industry itself has been at pains to reinforce, even in its advertising. See, for example, BP's advertising campaign 'The Gods of Oil must have a Fine Sense of Humour' *The Economist* April 17-23 1993. This would appear to be a recurring theme given that the same point was also noted by Wright (1986, 269 fn5). Greater sensitivity to public concerns about the environmental impact of oil production, especially post-Brent Spar, may account for the fact that the industry has recently been more coy about showing dramatic pictures of production platforms in the midst of seething seas or of pipelines stretching across virgin snowfields.

13 For a fuller account with emphasis on the legal position more generally see especially Daintith and Willoughby (1984).

14 See now the Oil and Gas (Enterprise) Act 1982 and the Petroleum Act 1998. Dr. T. F. Gaskell of the British Petroleum Company told the March 1965 meeting of the Institute of Petroleum in London that the North Sea (among other new provinces under consideration at the time) was only picked out for exploration when the economic, legal and geological conditions became sufficiently promising. See *Petroleum Press Service* April 1965, 127.

15 Art. 2(1). Note that s3 of the 1964 Act purported to extend the onshore law in general to the offshore situation. However, because of the accepted canon of statutory interpretation which holds that statutes are assumed to extend only to Great Britain unless otherwise stated, this section could not have the effect of extending, for example, existing factory legislation. See Bennion (1984, 506-8) for the position on statutory interpretation; also Daintith and Willoughby (1984, paras. 1-507-8; 1-851).

16 Petroleum (Production) Regulations 1935 (SRandO 1935/426).

17 Petroleum (Production) (Continental Shelf and Territorial Sea) Regulations 1964 (SI 1964/708).

18 *ibid.* Schedule 2 Clause 18.

19 For details of this letter of instruction and the IP Code see Ministry of Power (1967, 17-18 and 18-22).

20 The term *formal* is thus used here in the same sense as Teubner (e.g. 1983; 1987) (following Max Weber) to refer to a situation where law provides structures and methodological rules within which actors can order their affairs. Law does not in this orientation intervene substantively to define detailed objectives or to prescribe the ways in which they must be accomplished but rather confines itself 'to the delimitation of abstract spheres for private-autonomous action' (Teubner 1987, 15).

21 See 'Triumph and Tragedy in the North Sea' *Petroleum Press Service* 1966, 5.

22 See Ministry of Power (1967, para 9.2) for details of the requirement to muster on the helicopter deck in the event of an emergency. This instruction had relevance only in the event of a fire and when helicopter evacuation had been arranged, but not in the circumstances of a structural collapse when escape to the sea via life-boats was the appropriate response.

23 In their other recommendations the Inquiry called for an accepted discipline and chain of command similar to the merchant navy (Ministry of Power 1967, paras. 10.2(ii), (iii)); loudspeakers so that orders could be communicated (para 10.2(iv)); the keeping of records of e.g. increases and decreases of loading on the rig, and other matters affecting the rig as a structure (para 10.2(v)); and a daily round equivalent to the ship master's daily round designed to keep 'everybody up to scratch' (para 10.2(vi)).

24 'The Act was structured around the physical entity of the installation, rather than the offshore employment relationship; it is thus addressed only to installation owners and managers, and to the concession owners for whom the installation is working, and can produce, at best, only indirect effects on the situation of other offshore employers and their workers' (Daintith and Willoughby 1984, I-851).

25 Again, *substantive* and *material* are used here in the same sense as Teubner (e.g. 1983; 1987). Substantive or material law is the instrumentalisation of law 'for the purposes of the political system which now takes on responsibility for social processes - and this means the definition of goals, the choice of normative means, the ordering of concrete behavioral programs and the implementation of norms' (Teubner 1987, 14).

26 Hansard HC (Debs) 28 April 1971 col. 648, Under-Secretary of State for Trade and Industry.

27 Offshore Installations (Registration) Regulations 1972 (SI 1972/702); Offshore Installations (Managers) Regulations 1972 (SI 1972/703); Offshore Installations (Logbooks and Registration of Death) Regulations

1972 (SI 1972/1542); Offshore Installations (Inspectors and Casualties) Regulations 1973 (SI 1973/1842); Offshore Installations (Construction and Survey) Regulations 1974 (SI 1974/289); Offshore Installations (Public Inquiries) Regulations 1974 (SI 1974/338); Offshore Installations (Operational Safety, Health and Welfare) Regulations 1976 (SI 1976/1019); Offshore Installations (Emergency Procedures) Regulations 1976 (SI 1976/1542); Offshore Installations (Life-saving Appliances) Regulations 1977 (SI 1977/486); Offshore Installations (Fire-Fighting Equipment) Regulations 1978 (SI 1978/611); Offshore Installations (Well Control) Regulations 1980 (SI 1980/1759).

28 The administrative history of the regulators responsible for offshore health and safety is somewhat complicated. Initially, responsibility lay with the Petroleum Division of the Ministry of Power. In 1969, responsibility was transferred to the Ministry of Technology and a Petroleum Production Inspectorate was set up as a subdivision of the Petroleum Division. Only a year later, however, the function was moved to the Department of Trade and Industry where the responsible division became the Petroleum Production Division. In 1974, the Department of Energy was founded and the Petroleum Production Division became a part of that Department. It was this move in particular which concerned critics who saw safety subordinated in a Department 'for which energy production was the primary concern' (Carson 1981, 163). In 1977, the Petroleum Engineering Division was established and most safety functions became its responsibility. See Carson (1981, 161-163); Burgoyne (1980, Appendix 7).

29 The Robens Committee did not explicitly consider offshore safety. The 1971 Act was noted as one of a category of statutes which, though not considered in detail, the Committee thought capable of, on the face of it, being brought within the proposed unified system perhaps after the main arrangements had been made (Robens 1972, para. 109).

30 It is interesting to note that at more or less the same time a very similar debate was taking place in the United States about the exact orientation of the Occupational Safety and Health Act 1970. Some commentators stressed the detailed regulation requirements of the Act (e.g. Morey 1974) while others pointed to the difficulties with such an approach and conversely stressed the general duty clause (e.g. R. S. Miller 1974; R. S. Smith 1974). Equally, there was a dispute about the location of responsibility with some stressing the Act's aim at wide participation and the Federal government's role as catalyst (e.g. Stender 1974) and others criticising the lack of government leadership and the dangers of an 'arbiter' role between employer and employee (e.g. Page and Munsing 1974).

31 For example, by the dissenting members of the Burgoyne Committee - see Note of Dissent, para 13 (Burgoyne 1980, 60) - and by the Trades Union Congress - see Submission 62, para II (b) (Burgoyne 1980, 292) - cf. the

opposition of the industry put forward by UKOOA - see Submission 43 (Burgoyne 1980, 241, 247-9).

32 Submarine Pipe-lines (Diving Operations) Regulations 1976 (SI 1976/923); Submarine Pipe-lines (Inspectors, etc.) Regulations 1977 (SI 1977/835).

33 Health and Safety at Work, etc. Act 1974 (Application Outside Great Britain) Order 1977 (SI 1977/1232).

34 For the agency agreement see Burgoyne (1980, Appendix 11).

35 The Burgoyne Committee whose terms of reference were as follows: 'To consider so far as they are concerned with safety, the nature, coverage and effectiveness of the Department of Energy's regulations governing the exploration, development and production of oil and gas offshore and their administration and enforcement. To consider and assess the role of the Certifying Authorities. To present its report, conclusions and any recommendations as soon as possible' (see Burgoyne 1980, para 1.1).

36 See note 26 above.

37 The approach which considered such structures as *not* coming within the terms of the legislation followed advice to the PED from the DEn's legal advisers: see the Submission of the Department of Energy - Petroleum Engineering Directorate to the Burgoyne Committee; Submission 37, para 9 (Burgoyne 1980, 228). Contrary to the impression given within the body of the Committee's report, it is not at all clear from the PED's evidence that they were by this time treating such structures as coming within the terms of the legislation.

38 Submission by the Department of Energy - Petroleum Engineering Directorate to the Burgoyne Committee. See Submission 37, para 8 (Burgoyne 1980, 228).

39 SI 1977/500 made under the HSWA 1974.

40 See the Note of Dissent by Mr. Lyons and Mr. Miller, para 25 (Burgoyne 1980, 63).

41 It is also worth noting that the original intention was to allow safety representatives to be appointed by either the workforce or trade unions. This provision in the HSWA 1974 was, however, repealed by the Employment Protection Act 1975 as part of the Social Contract between the then Labour government and the TUC (see James 1992, 90).

42 *Ibid.* note 40 above para 8 (Burgoyne 1980, 59).

43 Set up by the Secretary of State for Energy under the Offshore Installations (Public Inquiries) Regulations 1974 (SI 1974/338).

44 It should be noted that this crucial finding of the Inquiry was disputed by the BBC *Frontline Scotland* programme broadcast on 17 November 1998. The new evidence brought to light in the programme led to a call from the Scottish National Party for the Inquiry to be re-opened, a call ultimately rejected by the government (see BBC Online Network 26 January 1999). While it is unlikely that the new evidence would result in any

recommendations substantially different to those produced by the Inquiry, it may well affect the question of liability. The question of which insurance company should foot the compensation bill for the disaster was decided by Lord Caplan in the Court of Session in 1997 (see *The Scotsman* 3 September 1997) but an appeal is still pending at the time of writing.

45 The recommendation was that the Construction and Survey Regulations, the Fire Fighting Regulations, the Life-Saving Appliances Regulations and the Emergency Procedures Regulations should be revoked and replaced by: (i) Construction Regulations, covering *inter alia* the structure and layout of the installation and its accommodation; (ii) Plant and Equipment Regulations, covering *inter alia* plant and equipment on the installation and in particular those handling hydrocarbons; (iii) Fire and Explosion Protection Regulations, covering *inter alia* both active and passive fire protection and explosion protection; and (iv) Evacuation, Escape and Rescue Regulations, covering *inter alia* emergency procedures, life-saving appliances, evacuation, escape and rescue. Each of these sets of regulations should include goal-setting regulations as their main or primary provisions and should be supported by guidance notes giving advice which is non-mandatory (Cullen 1990, para 21.69).

46 He went so far as to associate himself with the remarks of one witness (Mr. R. E. McKee, the Chairman and Managing Director of Conoco (UK) Ltd.) who claimed that safety could not be legislated (Cullen 1990, para 21.4).

47 Offshore Installation (Safety Representatives and Safety Committees) Regulations 1989 (SI 1989/971).

48 Details of trades union evidence to the Cullen Inquiry can be found in Cullen (1990, para 21.78-80). I have also had sight of the Trade Union Legal Group submission to Part 2 of the Inquiry which has not been published.

49 Offshore Installations (Safety Case) Regulations 1992 (SI 1992/2885).

50 See HSE press release E180:95, 22 November 1995.

51 Offshore Installations (Management and Administration) Regulations (SI 1995/738). Offshore Installations (Prevention of Fire and Explosion, and Emergency Response) Regulations (SI 1995/ 743); Offshore Installations and Wells (Design and Construction, etc.) Regulations 1996 (SI 1996/913). See also the Pipelines Safety Regulations 1996 (SI 1996/825) which also follow the same goal-setting rationale and which revoke the Offshore Installations (Emergency Pipe-line Valve) Regulations 1989 (SI 1989/680), the regulations requiring the installation of emergency valves in the immediate aftermath of the Piper Alpha disaster.

52 A further problem which recalls the earlier fears about the complexity and multiple connections of the regulated area became apparent in 1992. The Sheriff at the Fatal Accident Inquiry (see footnote 55 below) into the helicopter crash at the Cormorant Alpha Platform on 14 March 1992 which

killed eleven, stated that '[a] review of helicopter safety in the North Sea is now overdue and this accident has, I hope, provided lessons from which a totally integrated safety policy for flying can be introduced'. The Sheriff stated that the issue had not been considered in the Cullen Inquiry. Pilot error was blamed in this case. *The Scotsman* 7 April 1993.

53 For Carson's detailed argument as regards the economic and political situation at a national level and its impact on the development of the oil and gas resources of the North Sea, see (1981, Chapter 4).

54 For Carson's detailed view of the operation of the regulations see especially (1981, Chapters 5 and 7).

55 Very broadly the Scottish equivalent of the English Coroner's Court, conducted before a Sheriff in the Sheriff Court with evidence led by the public prosecutor, the Procurator Fiscal, and with legal representation of parties concerned. The function of the FAI is fact-finding and at the end there is no formal attribution of guilt although the Sheriff's findings may point very clearly in a particular direction. While the findings may not be referred to in any subsequent proceedings, they may influence a decision as to whether any further proceedings are appropriate.

56 For an indication of the previous government's policy in this direction see *Lifting the Burden* (Cmnd. 9571: 1985); *Building Business...Not Barriers* (Cmnd. 9794: 1986) and *Releasing Enterprise* (Cm. 512: 1988). That this was not restricted to the Thatcher years is evident from the initiative of Michael Heseltine under the Major administration in setting up the Deregulation Unit and Task Force. The Task Force issued its first report in 1995 in which it explicitly identified health and safety at work as an area where there is a need to ensure that business is not overburdened with regulation. See *The First Annual Report of the Deregulation Task Force* (DTI/Cabinet Office 1995). The Labour government which came to power in 1997 did not dismantle these bodies but replaced 'Deregulation' with 'Better Regulation' in their titles. See *Principles of Good Regulation* (Better Regulation Task Force 1998). Nor is that the end of the story – more recently the Better Regulation Unit has been renamed the Regulatory Impact Unit with an extended role. See *Modernising Government* (Cm 4310: 1999).

57 SI 1996/913.

58 Tony Benn, Secretary of State for Energy in the late 1970s, states in an explanatory note in his diary: 'Some oil companies are comparable in strength and wealth to national governments...As Secretary of State, I learned that relations between governments and oil companies were much like treaty negotiations' (1990, 3).

59 The 'trans-Atlantic' settlement of the Piper Alpha claims at a level substantially higher than would have been awarded by a Scottish or English Court – Occidental ultimately paid out around £150million in compensation – may have an effect on future claims and will no doubt have given some

operators in the North Sea pause for thought (K. Miller 1991). The extraordinary efforts by Shell to avoid US jurisdiction in the claims arising out of the Cormorant Alpha helicopter crash are documented by Woolfson *et al.* (1996, 421ff).

60 For the position regarding the regulation of pollution control in the UK see Hawkins (1983) and for that regarding environmental health see B. M. Hutter (1988).

61 A good definition of this approach which summarises these points is provided by Rottleuthner: '[t]he focus of interest is...the way in which the law, especially administrative law, is applied by state agencies. Within this process of application law and the aims of the legislator are transformed according to the autonomous interests of the agencies themselves and according to the relationships between the agencies and their clients or addressees. Bartering relationships are established between the administrative staff and companies with large investment power. Exceptions to mandatory provisions are made administratively in order to avoid migration of capital. In general, a specific field of implementation evolves with relative autonomy as compared to the legislative objectives' (Rottleuthner 1989, 279-80).

62 Rhodes finds that '[p]revention rather than detection, persuasion rather than coercion, friendly advice rather than the heavy hand of the law - these are the characteristic ways in which enforcement inspectors behave' (1981, 176). See also Hawkins (1983, 129ff).

63 The UK approach has also been influential in the US in regard to Tension Leg Platforms (Curole 1997) and Floating Production, Storage and Offloading vessels (Regg 1999; Nesje *et al.* 1999). Even where US commentators have questioned the blanket adoption of the UK approach, they have acknowledged its usefulness in the UK setting and in comparable circumstances in US waters (Arnold and McCafferty 1997).

64 See, for example, Cranston (1979, 29) discussing the regulation of food manufacturers. The recently announced policy of charging for work done on safety case regimes including that offshore will, however, focus renewed attention on the relationship between HSE and industry. See HSE Press Release C040:99, 16 September 1999.

65 Coincidentally, the example which Pound referred to was the use initially by the American courts of inappropriate analogies for the ownership of oil and gas reserves.

66 For a detailed critique of this approach to law see Stewart (1981, 1263-77).

67 'When all is said about the many difficulties with standards, legal and otherwise, they plainly are the only way to proceed with the enormous task of providing occupational health and safety' (Morey 1974, 611).

68 Similar themes are also evident in Pearce (1976), Bell and Kristol (1981) and Ellickson (1987). There are equally indications that economists are

beginning to respond to this sort of criticism and are attempting to reflect better the complexity of social situations in their economic models. See, for example, Henning and Mann (1981), who problematise the causal assumptions of economics, and Huang and Wu (1994). And see more generally Lawson (1997).

69 This situation is well typified by the ongoing crisis surrounding BSE or mad cow disease and CJD, its human equivalent. Scientists are seen as both the creators of the problem and the source to whom all parties (politicians, regulators, farmers and consumers) turn for solutions. Scientists in turn produce conflicting accounts of the existence of a problem, the degree of any risk and the appropriate response. The more recent debate surrounding genetically-modified food manifests these difficulties even more clearly.

70 More controversially, scientists with an interest in complexity are even beginning to suggest that the future of science lies in non-linearity rather than linearity - something which their critics dismiss as 'fact-free' science (see Horgan 1995).

71 Popper's position is well summed-up in the following passage: 'The empirical basis of objective science has nothing "absolute" about it. Science does not rest upon solid bedrock. The bold structure of its theories rises, as it were, above a swamp. It is like a building erected on piles. The piles are driven down from above into the swamp, but not down to any natural or "given" base; and if we stop driving the piles deeper, it is not because we have reached firm ground. We simply stop when we are satisfied that the piles are firm enough to carry the structure, at least for the time being' (1972, 111).

72 See Lévy-Bruhl (1964) quoted in Cotterrell (1992, 51). See also Yellin (1983, 1312) where he notes the 'important functional distinctions between scientific and legal evidence. Scientific evidence principally serves to define the limits of knowledge and help set directions for further work'.

2 Mapping a New Approach

1 Looking for a New Approach

1.1 Coming to Terms with Complexity

The previous chapter examined the development of health and safety regulation in the offshore oil and gas industry and also the evaluations which have been made of that development. It was seen that despite the emergence of a regulatory form which seeks to accommodate the complexity of the field, there is a continuing yearning on the part of some commentators for more traditional prescriptive regulation. This desire is all the more confusing when the findings of the Cullen Inquiry about the shortcomings of the prescriptive regime are borne in mind. Nor is it the law alone which confronts the challenge of coping with complexity. Evidence was considered from the realms of science and economics also which demonstrated that the previous assumptions of these disciplines are under considerable pressure and are seen to mask as much as they reveal about the world they seek to order.

The issue that lies at the heart of these difficulties currently confronting disciplines such as law, science and economics has been clarified in the analysis of Karl-Heinz Ladeur (e.g. 1989). Traditionally, these disciplines have sought to identify causal connections in the world - the relationships of cause and effect - in order that the means to be deployed if desired ends are to be achieved can be developed. In each case, stable models have been produced which can both describe the nature of the world (physical and social) and prescribe action within it. In recent times, however, it has become increasingly evident that the greater the complexity of the problem under consideration, the less able are these models to describe it or to prescribe action aimed at desired effects. In short, the stable models upon which these rationalising disciplines have been built are now understood to be much more provisional than was previously assumed. As was mentioned in the last chapter, this presents fewer problems for pure science but significant difficulties for law, politics or economics, which to a great extent depend for their survival upon their claimed abilities to provide certainty.

While the desire for more prescriptive regulation may paradoxically, therefore, be a response to the very uncertainty which a challenge to law's assumptions may create, to give into this desire is to risk further (and perhaps greater) problems in the future as the shortcomings of the 'stable' models underlying law's prescriptions become manifest. That said, however, the desire for a return to prescription is understandable in a situation where the regulatory form which has succeeded it is inadequately conceived and implemented or is perhaps simply not well understood. That Woolfson, Foster and Beck (1996) have assessed the new offshore safety regime on the basis of the model underlying the old indicates that these difficulties may well exist. It is already a problem if academic commentators fail to understand the nature of the new regime, but their concerns about the adequacy of that regime may nevertheless be justified if this lack of understanding penetrates further into the industry itself. And there is indeed a significant challenge in adequately conceptualising a regulatory approach which appears to have overturned many of the assumptions which underlie traditional understandings of what law is, what it can do and how it can do it.

Taking seriously Ladeur's ideas about the inherent instability of our causal models when they are confronted with complexity is one thing. Knowing what to do about it is quite another. Ladeur himself notes that the legal system in particular must be oriented towards uncertainty and must remove itself from the central position it assumes that it occupies (1989, 588). Instead it must seek to encourage the self-organisation of complex systems involving the continual transcendence of certainties and the devaluing of institutional knowledge (1989, 588-9). Only in this way can the risks associated with the masking effects of the only apparently stable models be addressed and minimised. In short, there must be a transition from 'universalistic law' to the 'law of uncertainty' (1989, 588-90). But while this appears sensible and understandable in the abstract, what can be done at a more practical level? Nor is this a question which affects only concrete regulatory mechanisms but, as was seen in the previous chapter, also concrete legal sociological methods. There is a need, then, to move from the general theoretical insights provided by Ladeur to more practical proposals for law in the context of complexity and uncertainty.

One step on this road is taken by Ulrich Beck, who describes the development of the 'risk society' in which the standard relationship of industrialisation is reversed. That is to say that the situation where the logic of wealth production dominates the logic of risk production is reversed. In this way, says Beck, society is gradually moving towards a state of 'reflexive modernity' (1992, 12). In particular, Beck highlights the fact that there is an increasing awareness of the *constructed* nature of problems and risks. There is nothing inherently fixed or certain about them. Rather they exist as constructs of science or of other disciplines (1992, 23). Thus, to understand risks, one must reconstruct them as 'a struggle among rationality claims, some competing and some overlapping' (1992, 59). This explains the need for reflection and there is a clear resonance with Ladeur's call for a continual transcendence of certainties and devaluing of institutional knowledge.

In order to move further along this road, then, there appears to be a need for an approach which can accommodate the constructivist insights of these writers, describe the competition among different rationalities and provide a model for law which can encourage the ongoing transcendence of 'certainties', thus offering something akin to 'reflexive modernity'. Such an approach would allow, firstly, a legal sociological description of the complexity of the field of offshore safety which reduced the risk of masking effects and, secondly, a conceptualisation of the legal form appropriate to such a situation which might put the new safety regime on a firmer foundation.

1.2 Standard Models of Law's Development

Amid a growing number of contemporary accounts of the problems facing law and the possible solutions, one in particular presents itself as especially resonant with the situation discussed so far in the field of offshore health and safety. We touched briefly on this approach in the first chapter when the possibility of a 'mismatch' between state law and the 'living law' of the regulated area was discussed. This is the account given by legal theorist Gunther Teubner which draws especially on the work of the social theorist Niklas Luhmann. Developed progressively in a series of papers during the 1980s (e.g. 1983, 1985, 1987, 1989) and culminating in the publication of *Law as an Autopoietic System* (1993a), this account is extremely thorough, not to say complex, but in its essentials it provides a compelling and thought-provoking view of both the development of law and the possibilities for its future orientation and deployment.

At the most fundamental level, Teubner's approach arises from a view of the development of the state and of law about which there is a fair measure of agreement among legal and social theorists. This view sees the recent past as characterised by the so-called crisis of the welfare state. Progressively developed out of the classical liberal state - characterised by its formal legal structures which sought to underpin the contractual relations among autonomous individuals - the welfare state witnessed ever-greater interventions on the part of government and consequently the ever-greater instrumentalisation of law by politics. As the state assumes responsibility for more and more aspects of social life, however, a situation of regulatory over-reach is eventually arrived at, the so-called crisis.

As was hinted at in the previous chapter, it is not difficult to perceive the development of the regulation of health and safety offshore along similar lines. At the outset, the state's role was minimal. A single clause in exploration and production licences required operators to abide by such instructions as might be forthcoming from the state and in practice they were told to follow an industry code of practice. The state engaged in no inspection or implementation with regard to this code. Evidence of the inadequacy of this approach, however, led to the state taking on an interventionist role in which it sought to prescribe all aspects of health and safety in the industry. Eventually, in the aftermath of the Piper Alpha disaster, the problems of that approach also became fully apparent. Not only was it impossible to prescribe everything, but where prescription was in place it often produced a false sense of security - compliance could itself be dangerous. An entirely new approach was, therefore, required.

Nor is the field of offshore occupational health and safety alone in facing the challenge of what comes next after both formal and substantive law have been tried and are perceived to have failed. Rather it is just one example of a broader difficulty. In general, however, the debate about the appropriate response to the crisis of the welfare state and of regulatory law tends to be dominated precisely by those two types of law. On the one hand, the deregulation movement is disturbed by the social and economic costs of regulation, hankers after the freedom and efficiency of the classical liberal state and consequently calls for a *reformalisation* of law. In other words, the demand is for the interventionist state to be dismantled and, in all but the most extreme versions, replaced with a more facilitative legal order which can provide a framework for the activity of autonomous actors. On the other hand, there are also those who see the crisis of regulatory law principally as arising from a problem of resources - whether material or cognitive. In other words, if only better information could be obtained about the area or activity to be regulated, if only the money or the manpower were available to implement and enforce regulations, then the desired ends could be achieved.[1] Thus, while the deregulation movement adheres to the formal model of law, the implementation movement retains faith in the substantive model (see e.g. Teubner 1985, 305-7).

While these models of law and views of the appropriate response to regulatory crisis exist at the theoretical level, they also dominate the debate about the new regime in offshore health and safety. Whatever Lord Cullen may have intended, the approach which emerged from his report is perceived to have become deregulation - not least by some in the industry - and the critics are adamant that more regulation, a return to prescription, is what is required (Woolfson *et al.* 1996, 346; 430). It is not difficult to see, however, that a debate premised on these polarised alternatives risks the creation of a vicious circle. If the economic theories underlying formal law produced the conditions favouring the development of the interventionist state (often characterised as 'market failures'), is it unreasonable to suspect that deregulation - reformalisation - may again produce similar conditions? In the case of the offshore industry, that means a return to the situation current at the time of the Sea Gem Inquiry. Similarly, if the lessons of the increasing interventions of the regulatory state are that failure to achieve desired ends is almost inevitable and is attended by both economic and social costs, is it unlikely that attempts at *further* intervention, *more* prescription, will make matters still worse rather than better? Offshore, that means a return to the situation applying in the immediate run-up to the Piper Alpha disaster. And while this characterisation of the debate is certainly something of a simplification, it is, nevertheless, not much of a simplification of the central assumptions of the two sides. There is a tendency for adherents to the implementation and deregulation schools to acknowledge the potential for risks and adverse side-effects arising from their recommendations but these acknowledgements in no way shake their faith in their favoured approaches. Indeed, the way to deal with any such problems is usually a further dose of the recommended medicine - more prescription, purer deregulation. It is a question, however, whether it is not time to see whether this polarised debate can be transcended along the lines hinted at by Ladeur and Beck, to see what Teubner's approach offers beyond an account of the development of law through formal and substantive rationalities.

1.3 A New Model

In order to understand the exact way in which Teubner's approach differs from those of the deregulation and implementation movements, it is necessary first of all to draw out some of the presuppositions which underlie those two approaches. At root, whether there is a belief in the superiority of regulatory intervention or in the greater efficiency and effectiveness of autonomous actors operating within a more minimal regulatory framework, there is a fundamental assumption that the world (physical and social) is ultimately understandable in terms of the causal relationships which constitute it and as a consequence is susceptible to interventions, whether by government or by private autonomous actors, that can produce predicted desired effects. Thus, it is assumed that information about the world can be gathered, processed and transferred in a way which does not affect the basic integrity of that information. Sometimes, no doubt, further or better information is required, causal models must be modified or better resources may be needed in order to process or act upon information more efficiently or effectively. But, in principle, there is no reason to suppose that these tasks are impossible, albeit that they may often prove difficult.

The view of the world held by Teubner, however, is significantly different. Drawing especially upon the work of Niklas Luhmann (e.g. 1995), this alternative view sees modern society as functionally differentiated into large social systems such as politics, law, science and economics. Up to this point, this approach is not particularly different from many others. One of the principal features characteristic of modern society is often said to be precisely this functional differentiation which is seen as permitting more rapid progress than would otherwise have been possible. But the approach of Luhmann and Teubner identifies these functionally differentiated systems as *communicative systems* (Luhmann 1995, 12ff). Thus, what distinguishes such a system are its individual communicative characteristics. In order that this distinctive feature of each system can be maintained, the system must be self-referentially closed. In other words, communication within such a system evolves on the basis of reference back to previous communication and in anticipation of future communication. The exact nature of this process will be considered more fully in due course but for the moment it is sufficient to note some basic implications of this view of society. First of all, the idea of systems being defined by features associated with communication means that not only must attention be focused on the large discourses such as law and politics, but equally on other systems, such as formal organisations, which similarly achieve this kind of self-referential closure on the basis of communicative processes (Teubner 1992a, 1454; 1993a, 133). Secondly, there are implications for regulation - or indeed for the intervention ambitions of any system in the workings of another. Most important is the fact that information can no longer be seen as being transferred between systems but rather as always *internally constructed* by a system. The causal assumptions underlying traditional regulatory strategies are, therefore, seriously compromised by this inevitable construction and reconstruction of information. And if information, indeed reality, is internally constructed by systems and organisations, it is possible to see that self-regulation takes on renewed importance and already the question arises as to how external regulation can influence it.

But does any of this make sense? Is it really helpful to speak of closed systems and constructed realities? Or is there a danger that this simply introduces unnecessary complications (see e.g. Lempert 1987, 157; Zolo 1992, 120)? That this approach is indeed helpful and, far from complicating matters, may actually help to illuminate the nature of regulatory problems, appears evident from many of the findings in the previous chapter - and included here are not just the more theoretical findings about the problems confronting legal, economic and scientific approaches but also those concretely related to the offshore industry. Consider the findings of the Sea Gem Inquiry, for example, with regard to the difficulty for law of understanding an industry code of practice (Ministry of Power 1967, para. 8.8). The solution to that problem, of course, was to replace the industry code with legal regulations. But then consider the evidence of the regulators to the Burgoyne Committee regarding the problems on the part of the industry in understanding regulations which met the requirements of the law (Burgoyne 1980, 228). Is there not, in other words, evidence that is highly suggestive of the sort of difficulties which the view of Teubner and Luhmann indicates will be present in a regulatory situation? Of course, it might be possible to argue that this evidence boils down to no more than 'the triviality that the legislator has to take into account certain facts about the addressees of his regulations' (Rottleuthner 1989, 274). But then what about Lord Cullen's concern regarding the limitations of prescriptive regulation in the face of a problem as diverse and complex as offshore safety (Cullen 1990, paras. 21.42 and 21.51)? His solution? Hand responsibility back to the industry and redefine the role of the regulators as one of auditing the mechanisms by which those operators run their safety management systems. That seems to indicate that in practice something more is required than just taking into account certain facts about the industry. We need, then, to see in greater detail what this new approach can offer both in terms of our understanding of regulation and in terms of how legal sociological research might be carried out.

1.4 Autopoiesis

Having gained an initial impression of the distinctive features of the approach of Teubner and Luhmann, it is necessary now to consider their ideas more closely. If society is composed of social systems which are themselves composed of communications, then society itself is a communicative system and it is to the nature of such systems that attention must be directed. In the field of law, many writers have noticed an inherent circularity in the fact that law ultimately refers to itself for its own authority. These writers have tended to regard this as a problem, as something to be straightened out or effectively masked, for example by the imposition of hierarchies of norms. But just as this circularity is evident in law, so does the realisation emerge that it is also present elsewhere. Thus Luhmann, as has been mentioned, has described the gradual emergence of other self-referentially closed systems in addition to law such as politics, economy and science. These systems he describes as *autopoietic* to denote the particular type of self-referential closure he has in mind. Autopoiesis (literally meaning 'self-making') represents the highest level of system independence and consequently the principal features of such a system are:

(i) All of its components are self-produced - that is to say, its elements, structures, boundaries, identity and unity.

(ii) The system itself maintains its self-maintaining cycles by means of a *hypercyclical* linkage. In other words, it provides the conditions for one self-producing cycle of communicative recursion by interlinking it with a second.

(iii) The process of self-production is regulated by a self-description - which means that the system proceeds on the basis of an internally constructed description of itself which distinguishes it from its internally constructed environment. (Teubner 1993a, 23-4).

Complex as this description undoubtedly is, it is not too difficult to begin to extract from it details which resonate with practical experience. Take the first part of the definition, for example, that autopoietic systems self-produce all of their components, which includes defining their own boundaries, their own processes, etc. Can these features not be discerned in the way in which systems such as, say, science or economics are typically referred to - both within and outside of these systems? And think also of the ways in which large organisations - not least multinational oil companies – 'think' about themselves. There is, however, more to the theory of autopoiesis.

The operation of these processes of self-production depends in each case upon the particular binary code specific to a system. The binary code for the legal system, for example, is thus legal/illegal and for science it is true/false (Teubner 1993a, 4; Luhmann 1995, 444). In this way, the system also produces its own internal construction of the external environment. While these *codes* are fixed points which serve to differentiate the system, it can nevertheless vary the *programme* by which it steers itself at any given time (Luhmann 1997, 52-3). Thus, the economy, for example, while always operating to its differentiating binary code (to have/not to have), may nevertheless vary its programme among those of, for example, profit maximisation and maximisation of market share. While autopoiesis is accordingly an evolutionary theory, its distinctive difference is that the evolutionary mechanisms of variation, selection and retention are now understood to be internal to the system (Teubner 1993a, 56ff).

The extent of the organisational closure of autopoietic systems is, therefore, clear. But if they are so apparently hermetically sealed, how do they perceive their environment? And if there is some element of openness, does this not mean that, despite their evident autonomy, they could nevertheless be steered? In answer to the first question, the proponents of autopoiesis insist that while such systems are organisationally closed, they are also cognitively open (1993a, 65). And in answer to the second question, they maintain that cognitive openness does not imply steerability (Luhmann 1997). These replies may appear confusing - and perhaps even contradictory - but they are no more than the logical result of what has been said above about autopoiesis.

Looking firstly at the relationship between closure and openness, Dupuy has suggested that there are three ways in which this 'dialectic' can be defined: firstly, by attributing openness and closure to different domains of the system; secondly, by holding that closure implies openness; and thirdly, by positing a form of self-transcendence (1987, 55). The difficulty with the first of these definitions is that it succeeds only in deferring the problem. Ultimately, the way in which the two *domains* are related would have to be addressed. The third definition has its somewhat esoteric origins in quantum theory and thus faces the difficulty that there is no evidence that such self-transcendence would be possible for communicative social systems occupying, as they do, the non-quantum world. That leaves the second possibility, that cognitive openness is implied by organisational closure, and this indeed is the definition preferred by Teubner. He points to the fact that in constructing its own environment, its own internal model of the external world, the system applies its own distinctions (such as legal/illegal, true/false) and thus achieves cognitive openness (1993a, 70). This is precisely because autopoietic systems are systems of communication whose basic units are communications and which thus only ever interact with their own communicative constructions. Since this openness is accordingly to a self-construction, it is clear that this is not openness in any conventional sense. Indeed, Teubner states that it 'is in fact not openness at all' (1993a, 89). But this is the implication of autopoiesis theory and is indeed its most significant contribution to an understanding of the possibilities for and limits to regulatory interventions. As a result, while concerns about this somewhat complex notion are understandable (e.g. Lempert 1987, 157; A. R. Edwards 1991; Zolo 1992, 120), the consequent temptation to modify the theory in ways which result in the loss of this significant feature should be resisted (see e.g. Kickert 1991; Koppenjan and Hufen 1991) as should the temptation to propose overly close links between autopoietic systems (see e.g. Bråten 1992, 52ff; Febbrajo 1992, 27-8).

1.5 Autopoiesis and Regulatory Failure

Given this intriguing idea of systems interacting only with their own internal constructions, however, it is equally not surprising to find that, whatever the doubts, the potential of autopoiesis in the description and explanation of regulatory failures has drawn much attention. Even those who remain uncertain about the theory as a whole are prepared to concede its utility at this level (e.g. Cotterrell 1992, 68; Bankowski 1994, 257). To understand this approach to regulatory failure, a practical example from offshore safety can be considered.

Accepting the autopoietic view of society means that the regulatory chain presupposed by the linear-causal models of regulatory law must be broken up into a series of self-referentially closed communicative systems. At the most basic level, we can consider the large social systems mentioned previously - politics, law, economics and science. Each system will operate according to its own binary code and programmes and on the basis of its internal model of the external world. Since these systems are consequently not directly accessible to each other, attempted interventions by one system in another confront what Teubner describes as the *regulatory trilemma* (1985, 386; 1987, 19). This suggests that insofar as a regulatory intervention over-reaches the self-referential limits of the system or systems it aims at, it risks being irrelevant, producing disintegrating effects on the regulated area or producing such effects on law itself.

If, for example, regulations are produced which require a particular approach to the design and construction of offshore installations but this approach is regarded by science as outdated, then the law will have failed to meet the *relevance criteria* of the regulated area and may simply be ignored. This approach to design and construction, while constructed by law as 'legal' is constructed by science as 'false', having been surpassed by a more recent approach which it now regards as 'true'. The regulated area will not, therefore, fail to abide by the law because it regards compliance as too expensive, for example, but rather because it does not see the regulations as relevant to the task they seek to regulate (see also Willke 1992, 354-5).

Alternatively, if the design and construction regulations represent what science regards as the current state of the art, they may be complied with without any hesitation. But this does not constitute regulatory success if the law continues to insist on compliance to the detriment of the further developments which the inner logic of science demands. In this scenario, law actually risks destroying the conditions of self-production of the regulated area and we can perceive echoes of this state of affairs in Lord Cullen's criticism of the compliance mentality encouraged by prescriptive regulations (1990, para. 21.51). In other words, left to its own devices, science would engage in an ongoing process of development of the best approach to the design and construction of offshore installations and would not hesitate to discard the previous approach when a new and better one was discovered. This consideration also provides an answer to those who might have responded to the first arm of the trilemma (indifference) by demanding tougher enforcement. It also raises the issue of the adequacy of law's internal construction of the regulated area, which we will return to shortly.

Finally, if the design and construction regulations have been produced on the basis of consultation with an industry that is experiencing low oil prices, costly financing or other conditions of economic stringency, then it is possible that the conditions of self-production of the law itself will be damaged. What may have been presented to the law as the state of the art may instead represent the currently least expensive approach to design and construction. Nor is the law under threat in this way only from the systems it attempts to regulate. The fact that it is required to develop and implement the means of achieving *politically* defined goals means that its integrity is in danger from that direction as well.

So far, of course, principally the relationship between law and the regulated area has been considered. By breaking the regulatory chain up into a series of autopoietic systems, however, this approach also reveals the possible relationships among those systems themselves which may be equally, if not indeed more, important to an understanding of the regulatory situation under investigation. Thus, it is possible, at this level, to postulate a 'trilemmatic' relationship between, for example, science and economics, between politics and economics, and so on.

The implications of these considerations for those who want more prescriptive law are clear. But this does not mean that deregulation is the inevitable response. As was mentioned before, a reformalisation of law risks recreating the problems which encouraged state intervention in the first place. Furthermore, it can now be seen how serious the problems of deregulation could be if self-referentially closed systems were to be left increasingly to their own devices. As the third arm of the regulatory trilemma in the example given above demonstrates, to allow efficiency to become the sole criterion of legal acceptability is a recipe for disaster (see Teubner 1987, 29-33).

So does a role remain for law? In answering this question, it is important first of all to recognise that adopting an autopoietic approach does not automatically mean that regulation must fail, as some commentators seem to imply. Nahamowitz, for example, appears to seek to undermine autopoiesis by pointing to an example of regulatory success, namely the intervention of the German Federal Bank in the foreign exchange market to force the dollar down, which proves for him that the economy is 'politically controllable' (1992, 550). But such a view can simply be challenged by considering the unsuccessful interventions of the Bank of England and the Treasury in September 1992 when they tried to keep sterling within its agreed band in the Exchange Rate Mechanism by pushing up interest rates and by buying currency to the tune of millions of pounds.[2] In other words, the 'appeal of post-interventionist steering concepts' (Nahamowitz 1992, 550) cannot be considered as justified or not on the basis of trading examples of successful or unsuccessful interventions. Autopoiesis is not in some sense the 'opposite' of regulatory success. Rather it accounts for that success in different ways just as it accounts for regulatory failure in different ways to traditional models. If the regulatory trilemma arises out of a failure on the part of law to recognise the limits imposed by the self-production and self-steering of the autopoietic systems it seeks to regulate, then regulatory success occurs when those limits are observed, when the relevance criteria of the other systems are taken into account. Not, however, that this constitutes the possibility that the interventionist dreams of regulators and politicians will be easily fulfilled.

1.6 The Limits of Law

In order ultimately to discover the extent of what may be hoped for regarding law, it is necessary to look more closely at the nature of the limits which autopoiesis imposes on interventionist strategies. So far, the closure of the system to be regulated has been stressed in order to introduce and clarify the nature of autopoietic limitations, but in order to understand their full extent the fact that law is also a closed autopoietic system needs to be considered. In this way, it is not simply the case that the regulated system may misunderstand legal regulations as it constructs them internally on the basis of its code and steers itself according to its own programmes. Rather it is also the case that the law itself has produced regulations in the first place, not on the basis of information from the area it seeks to regulate, but on the basis of its own internally-constructed information. The problem of regulation among autopoietically-closed systems is consequently not just one of closure but one of *double* closure (Teubner 1993a, 71). The opportunities for misunderstanding between law and the regulated area are accordingly multiplied. It is, therefore, necessary to see the regulatory chain of the implementation approach as replaced not simply by a similar *chain* of self-referential systems (politics - law - regulators - regulated systems) with each successive system constructively misunderstanding the signals of the previous system in the chain. Rather there is a much more complex array of potential misreadings among systems. We have a situation with a variety of different autopoietic systems, including law, evolving on the basis of their own internal versions of reality and continually constructively misunderstanding each other. It is, thus, possible to see a series of *path-dependent* evolutionary systems developing on the basis of their own codes and programmes, their own evolutionary mechanisms.[3]

In each case, the system seeks to produce order from the noise of complexity by constructing a reality on the basis of its own code. Its construction is thus contingent upon its own code, its own selections. But this very fact of having to observe on the basis of the code means that the system cannot, as it were, look at itself (see King and Schütz 1994, 280). As King and Schütz put it, autopoietic systems 'like eyes and ears, cameras, tape-recorders, and many other items, are *characterized* by the fact that they do what they do and nothing else' (1994, 277 emphasis in original). As a consequence, a blind spot is created that is precisely the location of the system's basic assumptions. From this, the nature of the masking effects which were discussed at the end of the last chapter becomes clearer: they are the inevitable result of the operation of the autopoietic systems of which society is composed. By observing on the basis of the code of the economic system, for example, it is impossible to see the reality constructed by the scientific code or the legal code and this holds true whether that observation is in the context of the practices of the offshore industry or of the legal sociological discussion of that industry. 'Behind the mask' thus becomes less of a metaphor and takes on a tangible and potentially disturbing meaning. What autopoiesis allows, however, is a second-order observation, an investigation of what it is that each system can see and equally what it is that it cannot - what is behind the mask that each system creates by its very operation and observation (see Luhmann 1993, 108).

That said, this awareness of the path-dependence of systems and the limitations of their constructed realities indicates more clearly than ever that, far from being able to speak of societal steering by law or politics, all steering must now be understood only as *self*-steering (Luhmann 1997, 46ff). Even if law, for example, directs its steering efforts at the environment, this too is only self-steering because they can be directed only at law's own environment which is, of course, internally constructed according to its own code. In the offshore situation, therefore, it is no longer possible to regard law as steering the industry by means of regulation in ways which will improve health and safety in accordance with politically-defined goals. Rather the law steers itself on the basis of its construction of the industry, of the safety situation and of the goals defined by politics. This indicates for Luhmann that steering can be seen as the *reduction of a difference* (1997, 46ff). Law, for example, seeks to reduce or minimise the difference between the current health and safety position and the position it desires - both of which are, of course, constructed by law itself. It does this by implementing and enforcing a regulatory programme. But if the systems in the area it is seeking to regulate are operating on the basis of different codes and, perhaps more significantly, steering themselves on the basis of different difference-minimising programmes, then the law may be failing completely to understand the nature of the problem it confronts. There is consequently no input and output as assumed by cybernetics or by previous forms of systems theory. Autopoietic systems are not trivial machines where the same input always produces the same output. This is not to say, however, that law produces *no* effects on the regulated area. But such effects as are produced are not steering. They arise from the legal construction of the difference between system and environment, between the current situation and the desired goal, but depend on the internal construction of differences by other systems according to their own codes and programmes. Law's self-steering may produce a *perturbation* in the system it seeks to regulate (1993a, 35) but it is not a direct effect. Instead, it too is constructed. As Teubner reminds us, we have to free our minds 'of any idea of information transportation' (1992a; 1455). Autopoietic systems are thus *non-trivial* in their operation. A given steering operation by law has no certainty of producing the same effect twice.[4] The full extent of the regulatory trilemma is now evident and the limits of law appear more daunting than ever.

1.7 Overcoming the Limits

But if autopoiesis insists on this irreducible separation between communicative systems and thus exposes the masking effect both of sociological models of law, economics, science, etc. which ignore this situation and of the communicative systems of which society is composed, it equally provides the means for a more adequate conceptualisation of regulatory problems. At a descriptive level, it raises the possibility of breaking up the traditional regulatory chain into a series of potentially path-dependent closed systems continually constructing and reconstructing their environments. The transfer of information from society via politics to law and the opposite transfer of regulatory information from law to society is thus complexified as the political construction of societal problems, the legal construction of political goals and the societal construction of regulation. At a normative level, autopoiesis indicates that even if direct steering is out of the question, nevertheless law can improve its chances of success if it observes how other systems operate, which codes they employ, which programmes they steer by. This observation will, of course, result in a *legal* construction of the self-production and self-steering mechanisms of the systems in question, but significantly it will be a construction based on an observation directed precisely at those mechanisms rather than a construction which ignores not only the autopoietic quality of those systems but also the autopoietic quality of the legal system and hence the fact that what it observes is no more than its own construction.

So far, then, the path-dependant nature of autopoietic systems has been stressed as a means of indicating the separation between communicative systems, but there are ways in which the impact of this separation can be moderated. Teubner, for example, points out that '[s]ocial interactions do not, as a rule, participate in the autopoietic cycle of one system only'. Rather, they involve and are involved in a variety of different systems. Thus, the regulatory trilemma discussed previously 'becomes apparent in the individual interaction' (1993a, 62). But just as the trilemma emerges when the limits of self-production and, as we have now seen, of self-steering are not observed, so the potential for a more fruitful - or at least less destructive or indifferent - interaction appears when those limits are observed, when there is what Teubner calls 'structural coupling' (1993a, 62). While care must be taken to avoid imputing information transfer to this situation, it does nevertheless raise the possibility of the *co-evolution* of different systems on the basis that, whatever the divergent nature of their world constructions, they have 'to be compatible with other expectations in actual interactions' (1993a, 62). In practice, this necessity can lead to the development of mechanisms which seek to avoid the dangers of the trilemma and it gives Teubner the foundation for the development of an orientation in law which can accommodate the problems raised by autopoiesis even if it must inevitably stop short of offering any strong hopes to politicians and regulators looking for fail-safe interventionist tools.

1.8 Reflexive Law

It was noted above that the social communicative systems described by autopoiesis are the result of functional differentiation. Teubner points out that this must be seen as the *internal* differentiation of society as a whole, which means that the structural coupling of these systems 'takes on certain specific qualities' which he describes under the heading 'interference' (1993a, 86). First of all, each autopoietic system (or *sub*system of society), because it is a communicative system, uses the same '"basic stuff", meaning'. Secondly, they all evolve on the basis of the same operations, namely communication. Lastly, every communication particular to, and on the basis of, the code and programme of a given system is simultaneously also a 'general societal communication' (1993a, 86). While Teubner insists that these conditions still mean that information is internally constructed rather than transferred between systems, interference adds another dimension: '[i]nformation is generated simultaneously and on the basis of the same communicative event in the subsystem concerned' (1993a, 87). While this does not mean that two systems will inevitably understand each other - they will still apply their own codes and programmes to the same utterance - it does allow us to see how 'independent pieces of information in different systems [are linked] through one and the same communicative event' (1993a, 89).

This definition of interference also allows Teubner to distinguish another possible form of relationship between systems - interpenetration. If we were to adhere to a linear-causal model of the regulatory process, we might be tempted to propose that the solution to a problem caused by the existence of closed systems is to bring them into direct contact - indeed to achieve an overlap - such that the elements of one system might be directly available to another and vice versa. What the above understanding of autopoiesis reveals, however, is that if such a 'solution' were to be attempted, each system would not in fact be presented with new and useful information but rather with 'a picture of unintelligible complexity, an internal Babel' (1993a, 89). That this is something more than just an academic categorisation becomes clear when we recall once again the law's difficulties with the industry Code of Practice at the Sea Gem Inquiry and the regulators' reports of industry confusion with legally perfect regulations at the Burgoyne Committee.

Teubner proposes instead that law must abandon the claims of command-and-control or prescriptive regulation and adopt a *reflexive* orientation. In such an orientation, law recognises the dual closure of the legal system and the system to be regulated and develops regulatory strategies on that basis. One possible approach might be the implementation of an 'option policy' (1993a, 93) which involves law in making alternatives available to regulated systems but not obliging them to accept them. Concern that such a policy might simply achieve the retention of the status quo - although recall that the options will have been developed on the basis of an observation of the self-production and the self-steering mechanisms of the regulated area and thus might be expected to be taken up more readily than regulations which ignore this dimension - leads him to suggest that all that law might stipulate is that one alternative must be chosen. Or it might offer privileges if certain options are chosen or more directly lock-in to the regulatory impulses of different systems (1993a, 95). Beyond these alternatives, Teubner points to the possibility of 'coupling through organisation' (1993a, 95). Formal organisations produce the opportunity for inter-system relations to emerge. These, once again, do not represent a crossing of boundaries, and indeed themselves become autonomous, but the 'interlocking structure multiplies...the operatively-closed relations of mutual observation' (1993a, 96). Such a development is, therefore, distinct from an interpenetration of systems. Interference is again the mechanism which provides the relations between system and organisation. And just as we noted that the advantage of autopoiesis in its descriptive aspect is that it directs attention to the self-production mechanisms of systems, so in this normative aspect, it opens up the possibility of providing one system with access to the mechanisms of another - albeit that for all the reasons we are now well aware of, this access is not direct (1993a, 96). Law in these circumstances withdraws from taking responsibility for substantive rule-making and seeks instead to adopt a stance which, while it respects the limits imposed by the self-production and self-steering mechanisms of social systems, encourages each system to take account of the mechanisms - the codes and programmes - by which others operate. This means that law, while it cannot overcome the difficulty of the blind spot created by a system's code, can encourage a system to consider the fact of its closure, the closure of other systems and the consequences of this situation. Just as reflexive law can only truly emerge when law becomes aware of its own contingency, so it is concerned to confront other systems with theirs. The ultimate achievement may be the development of a reflexive orientation also in other systems. To this extent, the limits of the path-dependence of autopoietic systems can be, if not precisely transcended, then significantly modified.

Concretely, law can seek to provide such formal organisations or 'linkage institutions' which can operate 'across' system boundaries in this way to regulate the 'duration, intensity and quality of structural coupling' (Teubner 1992a, 1458). The law remains interested in the production of norms but it no longer constructs social norms as legal norms, understanding as it now does in its reflexive orientation the limitations and dangers of such constructive misunderstanding. Instead it seeks to engage the processes of social self-production for law-production. It does not seek to tell other systems what to do, nor to determine inputs to or outputs from them, but seeks instead to 'foster mechanisms that systematically *further the development of reflexion structures within other social subsystems*' (Teubner 1983, 275 emphasis in original). Accordingly, laws are effectively self-produced by the social systems in the regulated area with law restricting its interventions to the installation and maintenance of procedures which constitute the formal organisation or linkage institutions. 'The idea is to make law "responsive" toward society by transforming social self-production processes into sources of law production' (Teubner 1992a, 1460). Most often this form of law is perceived as some form of proceduralisation. But we must be clear that not just any procedural law would fulfil the conditions of reflexivity. For example, many procedures could be described most adequately in terms of formal law (see also Teubner 1987, 33ff).[5]

So the question arises as to whether the new regime applying to health and safety in the offshore oil and gas industry is better seen as reflexive as opposed to a reformalisation as implied by recent commentators. But any rush to attach the label 'reflexive' to the new regime simply because it can be seen to have emerged from a development through formal and substantive legal rationalities and thus effectively to accord it a clean bill of regulatory health must be avoided. Instead, the regime will require to be studied to see whether the conditions of reflexivity can be said to have been fulfilled - especially the awareness by law of the problem of double closure, of double contingency. Equally, the potential offered by any reflexive features evident in the new regime should be recognised and developed. Without prejudging the issue, it is evident that certain features of the new regime can indeed be said to possess, at the very least, some reflexive potential. In this regard, the setting of general goals while leaving the means of their attainment to the discretion of the regulated area can be mentioned. Similarly, shifting from a system of detailed inspection and enforcement - albeit that this was a system that may have been more rhetorical than real - to one of auditing the safety management systems of individual operators manifests a certain reflexive potential. We have seen indications in the report of the Cullen Inquiry that both of these developments arose from an awareness about the limits of regulation which was distinctly different from the usual recognition of the effectiveness and efficiency failures of prescriptive regulation.

But before we are able properly to consider the character of the new regime, we need to reconsider the development of the regulated area on the basis of the autopoietic approach which has been discussed above in order to determine whether this is an approach which helps us to understand that development better. Only if it does will it make sense to go on to look at the reflexivity of the new offshore health and safety regime. This requirement, however, raises methodological questions about the autopoietic approach as an empirical tool which must be addressed first of all.

2 Mapping a Methodology

2.1 Getting the Bearings

In contrast to other legal sociological accounts, autopoiesis does not approach a regulatory situation with a ready-made rationality at hand with which to explain what it finds. Unlike economic approaches, therefore, it does not gather relevant data and test it with formulae to discover whether certain economic relationships are significant. Similarly, unlike capture theory approaches, it does not deploy political power relationships to demonstrate the dominance of regulated bodies or the weakness of regulatory authorities. And unlike any approach which accepts the standard implementation model of law, it cannot assume that more or better information (gathered on the basis of economic or political assessments, for example) or improved enforcement will ultimately produce desired effects. As autopoiesis demonstrates the limitations of the implementation model, so does it reveal that, far from *gathering* information, economic or political approaches *construct* the data they collect. Not only, therefore, are they unable to observe anything except that which is accessible on the basis of their distinctive codes, but even that which is made accessible in this way is not *directly* accessible but only constructed (see also Nelken 1987, 211; Jessop 1992, 188). But if autopoiesis reveals all of these problems, limitations, masking effects and blind spots, what can it do itself in examining a concrete regulatory situation? Some have, after all, pointed to the dearth of empirical autopoietic studies (Nelken 1987, 205; Rottleuthner 1989, 274; Rehbinder 1992, 584; Murphy 1994, 255) despite imprecations from others that sufficient theoretical work has now been done to allow such studies to be undertaken (S. C. Smith 1991, 337).

At the most basic level, it is possible to say that while the theory reveals the limitations of, say, economic analysis, it equally opens up opportunities. By being open to the possibility that more than one system, more than one rationality, may be significant in a regulatory problem, it is certainly open to the possibility that economics will be one of them. In this way, the theory can direct economic analysis to where observation suggests that the economic code is in play and where economic self-steering (difference-minimising) programmes are deployed. To be sure, economic analysis may attempt to resist this limitation on its scope, pointing out in its defence that it has already recognised the problems of a linear-causal approach to regulation. To this end, concepts such as co-effects and intervening variable causation, joint and co-causation, and reciprocal causation have been developed in an attempt to broaden the scope of analysis and minimise the masking effect on complexity (see Nagel and Neef 1978).[6] But while these developments do indeed increase the range of what economic analysis can see, they nevertheless do not address the problem that it can still only see - which means construct - economic relations. Similarly, they do not address the fact that information is also constructed in the area under investigation. Beyond this more appropriate deployment of different types of analysis, however, the question remains of discovering a methodology that can accommodate the definition and analysis of different systems operating on the basis of different codes and steering by distinct difference-minimising programmes.

Bearing in mind the discussion in the previous part of this chapter about the nature of autopoietic systems, what is required is a methodology that can identify the multitude of elementary acts (i.e. acts of communication and their recursive connection to what has gone before and their anticipation of communication to come) that constitute the autopoietic closure of the various processes involved (Paterson and Teubner 1998, 459). In other words, a methodology is sought that can identify and even reproduce the path-dependent evolutionary development of the systems involved in the regulatory situation to be investigated - in this case, offshore health and safety. Beyond this, of course, we must also be open to the possibility of communication between systems as distinct from the indifference or destructive tendencies suggested by the regulatory trilemma. Thus, the methodology must also be able to identify and reproduce the different types of mutual recontextualisation that would represent such communication (Paterson and Teubner 1998, 459; Teubner 1992b, Pt. IV; see also Heller 1987, 302).

2.2 *Maps of Misreading*

In trying to conceptualise both autopoietic systems in a regulatory situation and a possible methodology to study them, a particular metaphor for law presents itself as especially useful. This is the map metaphor employed by Santos in his consideration of law in post-modern conditions (1987; see also Teubner 1989, 730). Santos sees law as a 'map of misreading', distorting reality systematically through the mechanisms of scale, projection and symbolisation (1987, 283). Depending on the scale employed, different features of the landscape law attempts to map will appear or disappear; the particular projection used will emphasise some features over others; and the symbolisation says much about the cultural background of the law and its intended purpose. Whereas Santos believes that laws misread reality in order to establish their exclusivity (1987, 281), understanding law as an autopoietic system reveals that the misreading is not calculated in this way but is rather the *inevitable* result of law's nature as an autopoietic system. Whereas Santos's view implies that in principle it would be possible to read reality in a less distorted, even if not in an undistorted, way, autopoiesis denies any such direct access to reality. Instead reality is constructed on the basis of the selections made by law as it attempts to achieve order from complexity. In other words, it is impossible to avoid a misreading and law can only observe what its code allows it to construct. But the map metaphor remains useful since, in much the same way, a map, because it cannot reproduce the world, must offer a selective and incomplete view of that world and consequently there is a sense in which that which is not included on the map is not real (Wood 1993, 85-87). Indeed, there is in cartography a direct analogue of the binary code of autopoietic systems, namely the *tectonic code* 'which configures graphic space in a particular relation to geodesic space' (Wood 1993, 124). Thus the scale, projection and symbolisation of a map (its tectonic code) construct certain things on the map but equally produce a blind spot which masks other features of the landscape.

The map metaphor is a powerful one, also perhaps because according to neurologists our cognition itself depends upon a similar mapping function (Young 1988, 162-6; Edelman 1989, Chapter 5; Rosenfield 1992). Furthermore, a map enables 'the past to become part of the present...[its] effectiveness is a consequence of the selectivity with which it brings this past to bear upon the present' (Wood 1993, 1). There is accordingly a very close relationship between the map metaphor and the notion of an autopoietic system as a path-dependent evolutionary system developed in this chapter. Just as autopoiesis reveals how the rational understanding of reality is not so much dependent on 'how things really are' but rather is the consequence of selections (Rossbach 1993, para 131), so does a map reveal the consequences of selections on the observation it allows of the landscape. However, the true power of the map metaphor is only released for our present purposes when the following points are taken into account:

(i) law's map is but one of a potentially very large number of similar maps arising from the selections of different systems according to their own codes, their own attempts to achieve order from complex reality;

(ii) because law (and other systems or discourses or rationalities) are in a state of constant change, we must not see the map metaphor as introducing an unwarranted element of stasis but rather speak of evolving maps;

(iii) the second consideration should not, however, lead us so far away from the idea of a map that we lose the insight that maps are multiply-connected; once a particular tectonic code is in place, local changes cannot easily be made without having knock-on effects globally; there are, therefore, built-in constraints (analogous to path-dependencies) limiting the extent to which changes can unproblematically be made - a fact recognised by cartographers who concentrate on redundant information thus over-determining the main features (see Ziman 1978, 82).

These points taken together capture the nature of the path-dependent evolution of autopoietically closed systems. If we can, then, see the different autopoietic systems as maps evolving through time with the codes and programmes represented by different tectonic codes, constraining by this internal multiple connectivity the changes that can be made as the maps are recursively redrawn, then we can perhaps get a first idea of what the results of autopoiesis research might look like.[7] Such results would allow a comparison of the ways in which the same events (whether, for example, new regulations, a fall in the price of oil, or a major accident) appear on the maps of the different systems. Equally, they would allow examples of closer communication between systems to be identified. If such results could be attained then the second-order observation mentioned previously would be achieved - that is the observation of 'what others observe and what they cannot observe' (Luhmann 1993, 108) - and in this way the masking effects of the codes of different systems would be revealed. But can the map metaphor be made more concrete?

2.3 Cognitive Mapping

The stage has been reached, therefore, where consideration must be given to how data can be collected in a research programme informed by autopoiesis as discussed above. What sort of systematic observation might be involved? What sort of tools might be used? It is probably the case that only through consideration of individual concrete examples can researchers decide upon a methodology that is appropriate to each case. If a narrative style seems appropriate, then perhaps techniques such as multi-voice or reflexive texts (Woolgar and Ashmore 1988) may provide an answer. However, such an approach would appear to suffer from the inherent restrictions of text in that demonstration of the simultaneous processing of events by different systems will be difficult if not impossible. King and Piper (1990) successfully employ a very descriptive technique but in the work of both Heller (1987) and Clune (1992) it is possible to detect a desire for something which might represent more *graphically* what it is that autopoiesis claims to offer to legal sociology.

In addition to seeking such a graphic representation, it would be particularly helpful if a technique could be found which also allowed us to retain the map metaphor, which appears so useful in helping to conceptualise the insights of autopoiesis. In this regard, one existing technique (suitably 'stripped down') appears singularly appropriate to the sort of approach to empirical study implied by autopoiesis. It both maintains an insistence on systematic empirical observation and allows a representation of the multitude of autonomous but potentially interfering fields of action into which autopoiesis proposes to break the linear causality chain of traditional approaches: *cognitive mapping*.

This technique was developed from graph theory by Robert Axelrod (Axelrod (ed.) 1976)[8] primarily as a means of examining decision-making processes with a view to improving the performance of policy-makers, and it possesses many features which render it useful in the present context. The basic idea is extremely simple: in analysing, for example, a text or a series of texts, the concepts or constructs used by the writer(s) are represented as points, while the causal assertions used by them to link the concepts or constructs are represented as arrows between the points (1976a, 5). Positive and negative causal assertions are signified by the addition of a positive and negative sign respectively to the arrow concerned (1976b, 60). A positive assertion is one where one construct (A) reinforces another (B) and a negative assertion is one where A operates in the opposite direction to B (see Jones and Brooks 1994, 5). The basic format of the cognitive map is, therefore, as shown in Figure 2.1.

Figure 2.1 Format of Cognitive Map

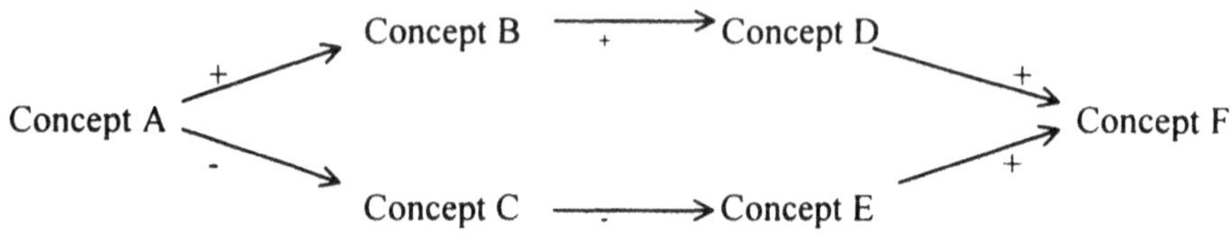

The cognitive map is thus for Axelrod and for Jones and Brooks a graphical representation of a belief system. In other words, concept or construct A is an explanation of B and is an answer to the question 'How or why did (or does) B happen?' Similarly, concept B is a consequence of A and answers the question 'What were (or are) the consequences of A?' (see Jones and Brooks 1994, 6). The details of the technique as developed by Axelrod (for example, the mathematical approach to the process) are not being discussed here because the value of the technique in the present context does not depend on the exact methodology proposed by him but rather on its ability to provide a graphical representation of autopoietic systems.[9] Indeed, the mathematical element of Axelrod's methodology implies a view of information and its transferability which is at odds with that of autopoiesis.

In the context of autopoiesis research, it provides a means of representing the world which a system has constructed, the concepts its code gives it access to as well as the causal relations which complete its model of reality. In other words, it allows a picture to be produced of the order that a system has created from the noise of complexity. In this way, one could imagine cognitive maps being produced in the context of offshore health and safety, for example, for legislators, regulators and for different sectors of the industry that would allow us to observe not only the economic and power relations which other approaches impose on the situation but rather the world construction of each system - what each can and cannot observe as a result of the application of its code. Similarly, perhaps even finer detail can be resolved in the form of the programmes by which each system steers itself, which differences it constructs and seeks to minimise. If this could be achieved then a potentially rich account of the development of health and safety offshore would emerge. Our explanation of regulatory success or failure would not be restricted to the dominant rationality of more traditional empirical tools but would depend much more upon what the regulated area itself could observe and what lay masked behind its inevitable blind spots. Furthermore, depending on what emerged, the range of prescriptions open to us would be similarly broadened along the lines of the reflexive orientation of law discussed previously.

2.4 Mapping Methodologies

In order to begin this process, it may be helpful to consider the cognitive maps of the approaches to law and legal sociological research which have been discussed so far themselves and to compare these with the cognitive map for autopoiesis. What is it that each of these can and cannot observe? Figure 2.2 presents cognitive maps for the implementation model of law, economic analysis, capture theory and autopoiesis.

As was discussed previously, the implementation model of law sees politics as defining a social problem and setting objectives which would constitute a solution. A legislative or regulatory programme is then developed and implemented in order to achieve the desired effects. The fundamental assumption is that information can be collected by politics with regard to the problem in question so that an adequate definition or stable model can be developed. The same assumption about the transfer of information also underlies the development of a regulatory programme on the basis of this model. Finally, the transfer of regulatory information to society is similarly seen as unproblematic - or at least achievable by means of enforcement - so that problems can be solved. If the predicted outcome is not achieved then further or better information is sought or better enforcement is attempted.

Economic analysis and capture theory both seek to improve the quality of information upon which implementation is based, revealing respectively the influence of economic and power relations in the regulatory situation. But as the cognitive maps for these approaches show, these economic and power relations are precisely what they can observe because that is what their codes give them access to. And because these relations are what they can observe, they cannot observe anything else. The risk, then, is that significant issues are masked.

By contrast, autopoiesis breaks the causal into a series of self-referentially closed systems and shows how each constructs reality according to its own code. The way in which politics initially understands social problems depends as much upon what its code fails to provide it with access to as upon what it allows it to observe. And similar considerations apply as regards law's understanding of politics, regulators'

Figure 2.2 Cognitive Map of Different Legal Sociological Approaches

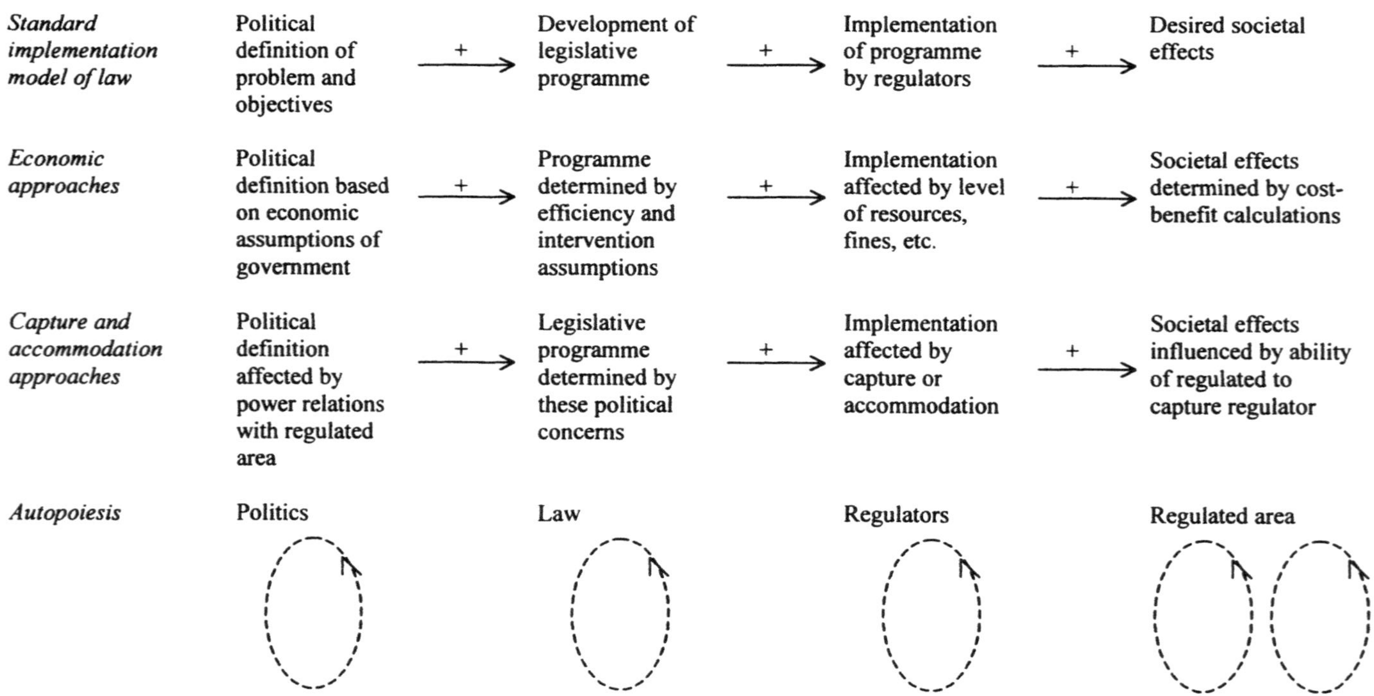

understanding of law and the regulated area, and the regulated area's understanding of regulatory 'interventions'.

While this cognitive map reveals some of the advantages of autopoiesis, a number of caveats should be noted. First of all, the systems described there are not decided in advance in a given empirical situation. The theory does not propose that society be viewed as 'a mechanical aggregate of several autopoietic systems' (Jessop 1992, 254). Rather they are defined upon the basis of empirical observation. In this sense autopoiesis can avoid the criticism levelled at deconstructive analysis that 'it can always be made to work' (Harland 1992, 218) insofar as it is involved rather in a process of reconstruction (see Marin 1992, 339). We need to ask: where are there indications of recursive closure, elements of communication linking up with previous communications to form relatively stable systems? In this way, autopoiesis and cognitive mapping can meet the requirement that an approach to legal sociology 'distils and respects local, partial perspectives rather than replaces them' (Cotterrell 1992, 310). Furthermore, the fact that the systems have been displayed on the cognitive map in a particular order does not mean that at different times, different systems will observe or fail to observe one or more systems. Regulators, for example, may not observe the law but rather politics and they may observe parts of the regulated area but not others. Lastly, the regulated area may be composed of any number of systems and it may be the case that different programmes may be evident at different times in the same system such that an adequate description of the system will require mention of each programme that is observed.

3 Some Technical Issues

So far, then, an alternative understanding of how social situations are composed and how regulation fares as a consequence has been described and a methodology outlined which can allow an empirical investigation based on that understanding. In producing this account, certain issues have been glossed over for the sake of clarity, both as regards the theory and the methodology, which are nevertheless extremely important. While it is not the intention to go into these in detail, nevertheless before proceeding with the study some of these issues will be briefly reviewed.

3.1 *Autopoiesis*

In describing the principal features of this theoretical account, the concentration so far has been on social systems. This is natural given that the theory describes the importance of functionally differentiated social systems of communication. But this does beg the question of what the theory has to say about everything else. Several writers have been worried about this issue and have asked, with varying degrees of concern, what has become of the individual (e.g. Ost 1987; Cotterrell 1992, 64; 1993; Beck 1992, 33; Bankowski 1994) and the organisational or institutional aspects of social life (e.g. Pokol 1990; Cotterrell 1992, 69; Clune 1992). While we have already seen that formal organisations can similarly achieve autopoietic closure on the basis of their decision-making processes, their relationship with social systems was not made clear, nor was the position of the individual. In the study that follows, the concentration will be on social systems but the following brief explanation is offered in order that the relevance for organisations and individuals can be appreciated.[10]

The theory of autopoiesis describes different levels of autopoietic system. In addition to social systems and organisations, individuals are also seen as such systems (Luhmann 1986a; 1986b). While this may appear somewhat odd at first, it becomes more understandable when we recall that, in common with the other levels, individuals also make use of the same basic stuff - meaning (see Luhmann 1995, chap. 2). This leads to the often misunderstood situation that, as far as systems and organisations are concerned, individuals are merely semantic artefacts (Teubner 1989, 730) and logically systems must have a similar understanding of organisations. Accordingly, each 'higher' level of system effectively 'parasitizes' the next level down (Hutter and Teubner 1994, 25; see also Luhmann 1993, 188). But as dreadful as this sounds, it is no more than the inevitable outcome of focusing on communication. And the position of the individual (and the organisation) is rendered less worrying when the 'hierarchy' is considered in the opposite direction. Individuals (or mental systems) can (indeed must) make use of (or construct) the rationalities of systems and organisations in order to make sense of the world (Hutter and Teubner 1994, 21). While this subjects them to the constraints and blind spots of these systems and organisations, they do have the advantage of being able to select other alternatives (King 1993, 228). And the same is true of organisations, albeit that somewhat less flexibility will often be evident.

It is possible to see, therefore, that the concerns about the individual and the organisational levels of social life can be accommodated by the theory and that it can indeed take account of the fact that these levels 'shade into each other and are interrelated in complex ways' (Cotterrell 1992, 47). And in this regard, it should be made clear (as has been hinted at in the discussion above about reflexive law) that the situation of the organisational level in autopoiesis is different from what is usually assumed. No longer is the organisation necessarily seen as some sort of mediator between individual and state but rather as having the potential to mediate between different systems. Thus, a vertically structured society is replaced by a horizontally structured one and notions of hierarchy give way to those of heterarchy (Teubner 1993b, 555-558). The theory does not, of course, assume this structuring of society but rather is open to its possibility. In this way, the potential for alternative prescriptions arises.

But even if concerns about autopoiesis and different levels of society can be answered, there remains the issue of *rate* of social change (Cotterrell 1992, 47). Snellen (1991) has attempted to deal with the problem of rate of change in autopoiesis by proposing a three level approach where each level is differentiated by a distinct rate. Unfortunately, this leads to inflexibility in any empirical orientation because it then becomes impossible to separate rate from level. Snellen is not unaware of such a problem but avoids it by insisting that meaning systems and organisations must be clearly differentiated. In other words, for him, organisations do not figure within an autopoietic schema. Not only does such a view jar with the reading of the theory presented in this chapter - especially with regard to the way in which the different levels are related *within* the theory - but equally it purports to solve a problem which does not exist in the first place. The fact is that the theory can deal with Cotterrell's concerns about rate of change without resorting to different 'levels of rates'. The fact that autopoietic systems are recursively closed means that a notion of a rate of change is already inherent in the theory. A concrete example may show how this might operate in practice. Jessop has described in some detail the idea of the economy as an autopoietic system (1992, 228-232) and he has also discussed how it is that the theory, while seeming to imply a heterarchical view of society, can accommodate the readily observable fact that the economic system is frequently in a dominant position, which would seem to imply a continuing hierarchy (1992, 258). He answers this problem by pointing to the fact that the economy has the greatest degree of organised complexity, meaning that it will tend to dominate. However, it is possible to go further than Jessop and state that an aspect of this organised complexity is the amount of opportunity which a system has for recursion within a given span of time.

Now it is simply the case that the flexibility of the economy in terms of, for example, the mobility of capital, the diversity of markets, even the computerisation of trading, means that it among other systems has a greater possibility of reacting *faster* to the same event, hence its frequent dominance. Such flexibility has its price, however. This very ability sometimes leads to a reaction, a perturbation or the construction of an event, which sooner or later comes to be regarded as an *over*-reaction. The main point in the current context, however, is that not only does autopoiesis provide an integrated analytical tool in terms of levels but also in terms of rates of change. It remains, however, to consider some potential difficulties with cognitive mapping.

3.2 Cognitive Mapping

Before proceeding to attempt to apply this methodology to the concrete study area, we should be clear about some of the limitations which have been identified regarding cognitive mapping and about the extent to which they are a problem for its use in the present context (see also Axelrod 1976c). The first point is that there is a stasis about cognitive maps which can be taken to imply a very deterministic nature in the autopoietic system which they represent - something which is entirely at odds with the theory (see e.g. Ladeur 1987, 257-8; Marin 1992, 296). And it is just this stasis which has already led some writers to abandon the method in favour of considerably more sophisticated and expensive computer techniques (e.g. Taber 1992, 889). However, while being aware of this limitation, it should be remembered that the approach outlined here involves looking for the codes and programmes *beyond* the cognitive maps which have produced and which continue to produce in a non-trivial way a particular version of reality. Thus, when Caroline Tuohy (1985) used a method similar to cognitive mapping based on the work of Herbert Simon to study the development of an occupational health standard in Ontario, she identified just such a limitation. She concluded that: '[i]n the decision frameworks presented...the decision points remain "black boxes"; we know which issues arose, but not how and why they were decided as they were' (1985, 370). The autopoietic approach to cognitive mapping is directed precisely at such issues. Further, this approach also depends on constructing different maps for different periods of time so that a diachronic comparison of the same system as well as a synchronic comparison between different systems can be made.

The second limitation to stress is that there is still a process of trivialisation going on here but the trivialisation (or simplification in order to understand or explain) is an attempt to present the non-trivial aspects of the systems involved. As King and Schütz put it: 'reduction is the very subject of the theory, its starting point...[a]ll system[s] are agents of and for reduction' (1994, 262). Autopoiesis research, as second-order observation, directs attention to what other systems can and cannot observe (Luhmann 1993, 21) and thus allows the second-order observer to look behind the mask created by each system's code. And, of course, the second-order observer is not immune from this feature of observation. The researcher cannot see what his particular code of observation cannot give him access to and must therefore remain open to the observer who, by offering an alternative code of observation, can reveal what lies behind this mask too. To this extent, autopoiesis can be 'a continually self-reflective and self-critical enterprise' of legal sociology (Cotterrell 1992, 310) with all the opportunities and limitations which it itself implies in this regard. In other words, the distance between complexity and traditional explanation is opened up (see Latour 1988) - to however limited an extent - a process only helped by the fact that the presuppositions which guide the researcher are manifest. In this regard it is worth noting that the technique of cognitive mapping in itself, unlike linear-causal models of law and society, contains no implicit stance on responsibility (Shapiro 1981, 194). This makes it a near ideal method in terms of the requirements of empirical discourse analysis (with which this particular use of cognitive mapping has certain similarities) in that it allows a closely-linked consideration of both form and content (Fairclough 1992, 194). If the result is not something so esoteric as a self-deconstructing text then at least the reader is able to see with some clarity the manner in which the researcher has proceeded.

3.3 Autopoiesis and Cognitive Mapping

In this regard, we find a relationship between the map metaphor and the nature of empirical data in the context of constructivist theories like autopoiesis. In cartography, the growing realisation of the contingency of maps leads to their being assessed not in terms of their 'accuracy or scientificity' but rather of their 'workability' (Wood 1993, 41). Similarly, autopoiesis because of its constructivist orientation identifies both theory and empirical data as constructed and hence notions of falsifiability become problematic (see Paterson and Teubner 1998). While this is an insurmountable obstacle to non-constructivist thinking, it produces a similar method of testing to that of maps insofar as it is no longer a question of deciding the validity of a theory on the basis of whether it is true or false but rather on whether it is 'profitable' (Ewald 1987, 42) or perhaps 'workable' at a given point in time (see also Febbrajo 1992, 28). Autopoietic empiricism, then, takes its validity from its 'performance' (Ewald 1987, 42; Frug 1989, 595-6) as much as from anything else, and its ability to orient us in an unfamiliar landscape or, perhaps better, to reorient us in a familiar one is the measure of its usefulness (see also King 1993, 222).

Notes

1 Some writers do not necessarily see this situation as a crisis but rather as part and parcel of what must be expected in implementing regulation and dealt with accordingly. See, for example, Lempert (1987, 154) and Rottleuthner (1989).

2 'It is well known, as the events leading up to Black Wednesday confirm, that the effectiveness of these signals is uneven, for it is beyond the capacity of any central bank to enforce actions or conditions they seek to induce merely by means of the weight of open market transactions' (Dodd 1995, 11).

3 Path-dependence in evolution refers to the fact that in many cases what survives depends not on current circumstances but rather on the history of problems that had to be solved in the past but which may now be irrelevant. For a discussion of this idea in law and economics see Roe (1996). It is also important to be clear that discussion of evolution in the context of autopoiesis does not imply evolution*ism* which would involve ideas of progress and perfection (Teubner 1993a, 48). See also Blankenburg (1984) and Teubner (1984).

4 For a discussion of these ideas of trivial and non-trivial machines, see von Foerster (1984, 305ff).

5 For a discussion of a reflexive orientation in environmental law, see Koppen (1991) and Orts (1995), in financial regulation, see Black (1996) and in utilities regulation, see Prosser (1999). While not identifying his conception of law as reflexive, Richard Stewart's ideas have much in common. In avoiding a reduction of social objectives to economic objectives, he is able to encourage law to create conditions in which economic objectives will tend towards socially desirable goals (see 1981; 1995). He describes this approach as 'reconstitutive law' where the aim is to reconstitute the regulatory field in order to encourage it in the general desired direction without specifying what must be done and how (see 1990).

6 See also the references cited in Chapter 1 note 57.

7 This also has a strong resonance with the idea of 'dynamic landscapes' mentioned by Francisco Varela and quoted in Ladeur (1989, 589).

8 Note, however, that Jones and Brooks (1994, 5) trace the technique to Kelly's (1955) Personal Construct Theory.

9 For an example of the application of the technique as proposed by Axelrod, see Savelsberg (1987).

10 For a fuller discussion, see especially Bankowski (1994) and Paterson (1995).

3 A Long Decade of Determinism

1 Introduction

In reading many of the commentaries on the development of the offshore oil and gas industry in the UK sector of the North Sea since the mid-1960s, a few frequently recurring themes are easily discernible. The work of the writers considered in the first chapter[1] very much fits into this tradition. As has been seen, there is a generally critical posture towards the industry, which is seen as having disregarded the safety of workers (at worst callously, at best carelessly or negligently) in a relentless drive for profits. Beyond this, there are suggestions of something akin to collusion on the part of successive governments for political ends and there is general lamenting about a lack of firm legal control - whether historically (Carson 1981; Wright 1986) or developing in the current post-Piper Alpha era (Tombs 1990; 1991; Woolfson *et al.* 1996). While the texts which have been considered have dealt principally with the question of health and safety at work, it is also the case that many more economically- or politically-oriented commentaries can be seen to reflect broadly similar views of industry and government, insofar as the former is characterised as single-mindedly concerned with profit while the latter, through a series of political interventions, sometimes encouraged this profit-drive in its attempts to secure for the nation an adequate share of the natural resources recovered (e.g. Odell & Rosing 1976; A. Jones 1981).

Given this broad agreement, it must be highly questionable for a new assessment to suggest that this version of events is entirely without foundation. In the first chapter, however, it was seen that there were some limitations to the existing evaluations of the regulation of health and safety at work offshore and indeed to regulation itself, while in Chapter 2 an attempt was made to demonstrate how an autopoietic approach might meet these limitations and thus provide a new perspective. It should be made clear at the outset that whatever an autopoietic evaluation of the situation produces, it is unlikely to be a radical reassessment or a turning upside-down of our current perceptions: the comparative modesty of the theory demonstrated in the second chapter leads rather to the expectation of an exposition of what the systems in play in the study area, as it were, already 'knew'. Nevertheless, this should equally not lead to an expectation that the results will be no more than bland confirmations of what has been said before: if the exposition is of what the systems already knew, it allows the second-order observer to see also what they did not know, what they did not observe.

In this chapter, then, this methodology will be used to consider the period from the beginnings of the UK offshore industry in the mid-1960s until the late 1970s. The choice of this period is not arbitrary. Rather, it constitutes a sufficiently long period for the development both of the industry and of its political and legal treatment. There should, therefore, be sufficient material to allow the construction of meaningful cognitive maps of the different rationalities in play in the study area. Furthermore, the end of this period coincides in particular with the second oil shock - an event which, as will be seen in the next chapter, was to prove a significant turning point. It will hopefully be possible to see how the rapid and extraordinary developments of these years were simultaneously constructed within the different systems or rationalities constituting the study area. Lastly, the fact that this period coincides broadly with that considered by Carson (1981) should allow some immediate comparisons to be made and perhaps some preliminary conclusions to be drawn. In what follows, it should not be a surprise if there is little mention of the law and regulation relating to occupational health and safety. The autopoietic approach attempts to discover the world constructions of the rationalities in the regulated area. The construction of the regulated area by law and regulation is but one on a potentially equal footing. Whether and how law and regulation appear on the maps of other systems remains to be seen and is not a forgone conclusion.

In deciding when and where to begin the study, it might be thought that this must be fairly uncontroversial. First of all, there was clearly a time before which the UK did not have an offshore oil and gas industry and a point after which it clearly did. Secondly, the study is concerned with health and safety at work in the UK sector of the North Sea. Time and location seem, therefore, to choose themselves. Similarly, in deciding how to present the study, a traditional linear-causal approach to law and regulation suggests a fairly clear and well-defined sequence of legislation, regulation, effects, assessment and reform.

An autopoietic approach, however, in breaking up the causal chain offers other possibilities of presentation and equally opens up the question of when and where to begin the study. In concentrating on the different communicative rationalities, it becomes a question (having identified these rationalities) of trying to determine the most appropriate starting point in each case - the point which seems to have played a significant role in shaping the world construction for the period the study is ultimately concerned with. These issues are abstractly expressed in autopoiesis by George Spencer Brown's injunction to 'draw a distinction' and 'divide the unmarked space' and by Luhmann's demand that the researcher must distinguish the distinction he draws from other distinctions (Luhmann 1997, 43). What this recognises is the fact that the researcher often presents findings as if his role has been a fairly neutral one of discovery, whereas in fact his decisions on where and when to begin and how to observe construct the field anew and may open up new possibilities or close off others. Explaining initial decisions may go some way towards opening up this process.

Research for this book was carried out by studying not only the usual sources of political debate, legislation, regulation and the statistics and other findings of regulators and academic commentators, but also, indeed predominantly, the literature produced within the industry itself. This latter research revealed two important systems with relevance to health and safety offshore: one which might be termed 'management' and the other being 'engineering'. In addition to this research (carried out mainly at the Institute of Petroleum Library in London), interviews were conducted with individuals across the whole range of the industry and its regulators, including representatives of the Health and Safety Executive, production companies (both onshore and offshore personnel), trade unions, surveyors, insurers, banks and external consultants.

In the presentation which follows, the sequence chosen is first of all to look at the political rationality which, as has already been seen in Chapter 1, attempted to deal with uncertainty and rapid change by means of a framework statute. A much fuller picture of this approach will be presented. Thereafter, industry management will be considered to see first of all how its view of offshore work differed from that of politics, and secondly, how political and legal activities were constructed. Then the engineering rationality will be examined from a similar perspective before finally the regulators themselves are considered. Looking at the regulators last will enable their construction of political and legal imperatives to be better appreciated in the light of a fuller understanding of the management and engineering rationalities which they not only encountered but to a great extent depended upon in their work. It is hoped also that examining in detail the world constructions of industry management and engineering without any preconceptions about regulatory success or failure will even at this early stage begin to shed light on the suitability of the political and legal approach to offshore health and safety and equally on the very preconceptions that tend to inform legal sociology. In each case, it will be seen that the points of departure may be different as the significant structural aspects of the different rationalities are sought.

2 Political Considerations

2.1 Introduction

It should already be clear from the discussion in Chapter 1 that the political interest in the oil and gas resources beneath the North Sea extended far beyond the health and safety of the workers involved in their extraction. It would thus be possible to construct a very extensive cognitive map of the political rationality covering all of these many issues. And indeed, it will be seen in due course that the political construction of the industry as a whole had a significant impact on issues which affected safety. Some of these points will be noted briefly here, although dealt with in more detail when industry management is considered. The concentration will then be on how politics constructed the issue of health and safety in particular so that an impression can be gained in due course of the adequacy or inadequacy of its approach.

With regard to the issue of energy as a whole, there is no question but that politics always faces considerable uncertainty in formulating policies and successive British governments from the outset in the North Sea have had to deal with gas and then oil as only component parts in a comprehensive policy covering additionally such sources as coal, nuclear power and hydro-electricity. Quite how these sources would develop in the future was subject to the vagaries of such issues as international politics, technological development within existing power industries, development of alternative sources of energy, changes in demand, and so forth. That the British government was well aware of these issues from the outset of the offshore industry is clear from its White Paper on Fuel Policy in 1965.[2]

Additionally, as the period of this study progressed, further uncertainty was added or the level of existing uncertainty intensified by such issues as greater doubts over the pace of economic development including those related to exchange rate fluctuations (paradoxically contributed to by the country's position as an oil producer); major changes in energy prices and doubts over long-term trends; and supply interruptions due to political developments, industrial action and, of course, major accidents (see D. Jones 1989, 1-2).

Thus, for any government the balance of energy sources may alter through time, perhaps even significantly advantaging or disadvantaging a given source, and the way in which these changes are brought about is by no means often (or indeed ever) in the direct control of government. Furthermore, throughout much of the period considered in this chapter, the government perceived a need to control the oil companies, because the scale of their business meant that too much speed could result in overheating of the economy (Noreng 1980, 25) whereas too slow a pace of development could result in the advantages of being a producer or self-sufficient country being delayed or lost. Government therefore sought to intervene in the offshore industry by way of taxation and in other even more direct ways as a means of ensuring that these macro-economic concerns were met. It has been suggested, however, that successive governments failed to understand the micro-economic realities of the industry (Noreng 1980, 15-16). At a general level, it will be a question for this study of how such political interventions were constructed by the industry. More particularly, some such macro-economic policies were directed to the long-term and some to the short and it will be a question how these temporal horizons interacted with those of the industry. Finally, it will be a question how all of these factors affected health and safety in the offshore industry.

From the outset, with the announcement of the factors to be taken into consideration for the grant of licences in the first licensing round in 1964, it was clear that of prime importance to the then Conservative government was 'the need to encourage rapid and thorough exploration and economical exploitation of the petroleum resources'[3] and this factor was immediately confirmed by the incoming Labour government later in the year.[4] Although other factors were also to be taken into account,[5] speed was the overriding concern. The addition of the applicant's contribution to the UK's balance of payments as a relevant consideration in the second round only served to reinforce this picture - although the simultaneous announcement of weight being given to proposals for the participation of public enterprise gave the first indication of troubled waters ahead.[6] With the fourth licensing round, oil entered the picture and the raising of £37 million from the experimental auctioning of 15 blocks indicated that this political interest in speed was wholeheartedly endorsed by the industry (Ellis Jones 1988, 286).

There is, therefore, much force in Carson's (1981) analysis of the 'political economy of speed' up to this point and the damning report of the Public Accounts Committee in 1973[7] further reinforced the impression of speed without thought for the consequences by politics. In particular, the Committee recommended that the government should act to increase greatly the tax yield from continental shelf operations, possibly by a system of quantity taxation, and should review all aspects of the licensing regime before any more licences were granted. In short, the impression created by this report was that in their haste to take advantage of the North Sea's resources, the Conservative and Labour governments which had presided over the early years had effectively 'given away' those resources (Corti 1983, 65).[8] This political construction of events was to influence policy significantly with regard to the taxation of the industry and to the possibility of state participation for a number of the North Sea's most troubled years. While these are issues seemingly remote from the question of health and safety at work, it is clear that they could have a significant impact on the industry and it will be seen in due course how they were constructed there in ways which affected the development and operation of oil and gas fields. Thus, while the political and legal approach explicitly to health and safety at work offshore (considered in the following section) is clearly of great importance, it is necessary also to bear in mind that other regulatory policies aimed at other aspects of the industry may have produced effects, due to their reconstruction there, which influenced operations in ways unintended by politics and law.

2.2 From Legal Formalism to Legal Instrumentalism

As was seen earlier,[9] safety in the initial period of development was dealt with from a legal point of view as part of the general licensing arrangements, but in the aftermath of the Sea Gem disaster the government moved to introduce the Mineral Workings (Offshore Installations) Bill. Again, as was seen previously, the Sea Gem Inquiry criticised the lack of a clear code of statutory authority regulating the question of safety offshore and this was precisely the issue which first the Labour government and then the subsequent Conservative government attempted to address in the drafting of the Bill. The legislative process which saw the passing of that Bill into law as the Mineral Workings (Offshore Installations) Act 1971 provides a valuable insight into the thinking of both the government and the opposition as regards the appropriate way to deal with the regulation of safety in what both sides saw as a technologically complex and rapidly developing industry operating in a hostile environment.

The Bill, as a relatively uncontentious item, began life in the House of Lords and passed ultimately to the Commons. The speeches of the government spokesmen in both Houses not surprisingly followed very similar patterns and were obviously heavily influenced by the findings of the Sea Gem Inquiry.[10] There was explicit mention of the difficulties with the previous licensing arrangement: Earl Ferrers in the Lords referred in particular to the inability to impose any sanction short of withdrawal of the licence; while Nicholas Ridley in the Commons spoke of the fact that the previous regime was contractual rather than mandatory. Instead a detailed code was envisaged which could be enforced but nevertheless in a more flexible way. Requirements were to be set out clearly and penalties were to be graded. The fact that the industry was comparatively new and developing rapidly was cited as a further reason for a flexible approach. The new regime would begin with registration of every installation. Thereafter control would be exercised in three ways: by certification as fit for use of all installations by Certifying Authorities (those already active in the certification of shipping were envisaged in this role); by the appointment of masters (later designated installation managers) as the focal point of responsibility; and by regulations to be made in due course within the framework of the Act. These regulations were seen as the way in which the regime could be kept flexible in the face of technological change and were envisaged as covering both the safety of the installation itself and of the operations on it and as providing the basis for detailed inspection and enforcement. The framework Act would allow coverage of both existing rigs and those not yet designed or built. Equally, concern was expressed that the regulations should not cramp development nor cause waste and extravagance for no good reason. Enforcement of the regulations was foreseen as 'benevolent' and 'advisory' with prosecution as a last resort. Stress was placed on the fact that ready co-operation had been forthcoming from the industry and was anticipated to continue - a point noted also by opposition spokesmen.

In keeping with expectations, this proved not to be a very contentious Bill and in both the Lords and the Commons opposition concern was largely restricted to the question of the qualifications of the master or manager of the installation. Equally, there were opposition members who were worried that certain items such as radio and radar requirements were not being included in the Bill but rather being left to regulations. There was concern also that Clause 6 of the Bill, which provided the authority for the making of many of the regulations, assumed a great deal and much greater specification was called for. It is interesting to note that these concerns were expressed alongside a recognition that it was difficult to regulate in advance and there appears to have been a tension between allowing flexibility in the regulations and restricting that flexibility by a more comprehensive Act. In all cases, the government response was to state that nothing must be included which might reduce the ultimate flexibility to be achieved by way of the regulations given the uncertainty relating to future developments. Indeed, given this aspect of flexibility, one opposition member foresaw the Act lasting up to 100 years. The result of this way of proceeding was seen by all sides ultimately as an improvement in the level of safety for those working offshore.

From these deliberations the cognitive map for legislators at the time of the passing of the 1971 Act shown in Figure 3.1 can be constructed. While this is obviously a simplification of the debates which took place and of necessity presents a unified view, it is probably a more representative picture of the basic assumptions underlying the passing of the Act than would often be possible given the cross-party support which was evident in this case. From the cognitive map emerges a fairly predictable view of regulation and its impact on the area of society at which it is aimed. The findings of the Sea Gem Inquiry as to the inadequacies of the existing formal regime are accepted along with the need for a detailed regulatory framework. The uncertainties regarding the future of the industry and its technology together with a desire not to cramp initiative mean that the legislation will be an enabling Act under which detailed regulations can be developed and renewed as required. The allocation of responsibility to the installation manager and the certification process are seen as underpinning the new regime. The expected result of this is greater safety. The whole approach is in keeping with the standard way of proceeding in situations where it is difficult if not impossible for the legislator to provide much in the way of detail, an approach outlined in any textbook on administrative law in discussing secondary or subordinate legislation (e.g. De Smith & Brazier 1994).

From the cognitive map emerges a fairly standard view of regulation and its impact on the area of society at which it is aimed. Perceiving a need to act on this issue as determined by the political power code, legislators

Figure 3.1 Cognitive Map: Politics (Mineral Workings (Offshore Installations) Act 1971)

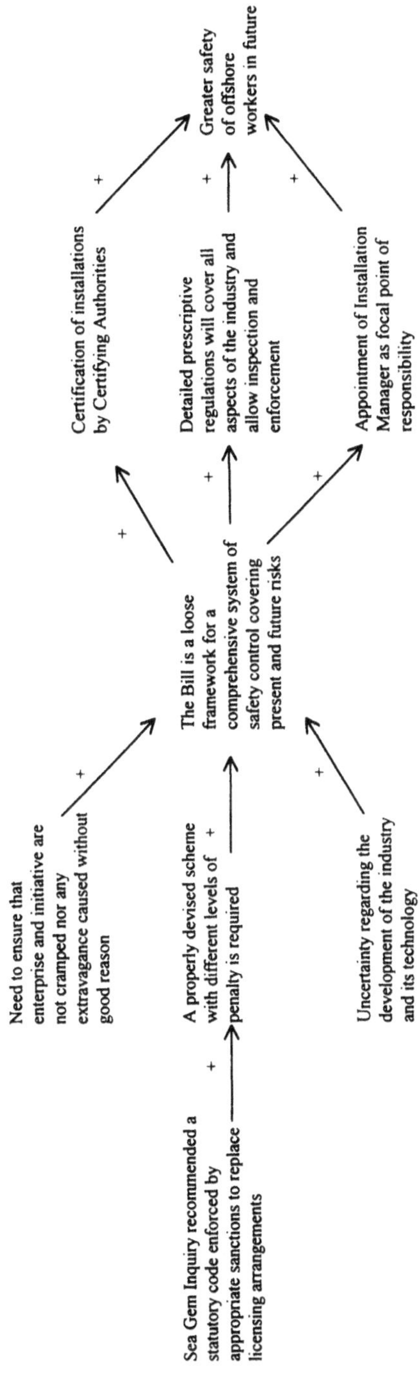

set up the framework for a detailed regulatory response. In other words, they deploy a programme of legal instrumentalism. A difference is constructed between the current unregulated situation where a number of accidents have occurred and the desired situation of improved occupational safety. The programme by which this difference is to be minimised is one of detailed regulatory intervention. Regulators will develop detailed norms of action which will tell the industry what to do. Provided these norms are followed - and if they are not then the regulators can impose sanctions - the difference between the current problematic safety situation and the desired situation can be minimised.

There is nothing particularly surprising here. Not only could we expect to find this basic code and programme repeated in many legislative chambers, but it is of course the code and programme which underlies many legal theoretical and sociological approaches. Thus, it is not surprising to find that in subsequent debates on the issue of offshore safety, legislators maintain very much the same code and programme and thus construct a relatively stable picture of the problems they confront and the range of appropriate solutions.

For example, when politicians next had an opportunity to debate offshore safety in 1974,[11] following the sinking of the Transocean 3 and the disabling of the Transworld 61 in the winter of 1972-73, the principal concern was the lack of regulations so far produced under the 1971 Act. In response, the Under-Secretary of State for Energy, Peter Emery, said

> [t]he problems have been considerable and the consultation that has taken place has been as great as with any legislation I have known, mainly because we are dealing with evolving technology and because, in construction and design, we are working with conditions never before faced when using rigs or building platforms - conditions which many Americans did not realise existed.[12]

And indeed there was little in the way of contention as regards the emphasis on the issue of design. As John Prescott for the opposition stated: '[c]learly, these accidents must raise important points of design problems'.[13] There was a practically unanimous call for regulations to be brought forward on construction and design while other safety issues, while discussed, were largely subordinated. Thus, two years after the passing of the Act which was to provide a framework for detailed regulations, no such regulations were yet in place. Politics was becoming aware of the difficulties involved, but significantly its faith that this approach was the right one was unshaken and the cognitive map (Figure 3.1) remained for politics an accurate picture of the offshore heath and safety landscape.

3 Mapping Management

3.1 The Essentials of Petroleum

The political construction of the question of offshore health and safety was, then, relatively straightforward and reveals no surprises. To begin to assess the appropriateness of that construction and how matters were seen in the regulated area it is necessary now to look at the way in which the same issue was constructed by the management of the oil industry, those responsible for both its strategic planning and its day-to-day operation. It must be stressed first of all that health and safety is not an issue which can be examined easily in isolation but is rather something which is inextricably linked up with the very activities of the offshore industry. In this way, it is necessary to understand how the industry saw its function and how that function could best be carried out in order to understand how the issue of health and safety was constructed. Starting out on such an ambitious project would be daunting indeed, but time and again in the literature on the oil industry one name and one seminal work continually reappear: Paul Frankel and *The Essentials of Petroleum*. It is safe to say that this book represents a sound starting point in the construction of a cognitive map for the industry management which first entered the North Sea in the mid-1960s and for an understanding of its world construction.

Frankel's book, which first appeared in 1946,[14] has been described as a framework within which the industry has operated for much of its history and which has influenced generations of oilmen (Roeber 1993, 17).[15] His analysis perhaps derives much of its force from the fact that it begins with the product at the centre of the industry - the oil itself - and demonstrates how certain characteristics of that product determine the structure of the industry which sets out to extract, transport, process, distribute and sell it.[16] He also stresses the importance of viewing the industry as a whole rather than trying to separate out individual parts:

> there exist certain traits which permeate through the whole of the oil industry, and only by appreciating their common denominators can we understand properly how vital it is to think always in terms of the *whole*

> industry rather than to try to solve the problems of any one of its component parts as if it were self-contained. (1946, 11; emphasis in original)

The first important characteristic of the product for Frankel is its *concealment*: it is simply not clear where the oil is, albeit that certain search techniques (especially seismic techniques) can give indications as to geological features favouring the formation of hydrocarbon deposits. There is, however, no alternative ultimately to the mechanical process of drilling exploratory wells, which is expensive and offers no guarantee of success. It is not impossible for an oil company to drill half a dozen, ten or even twenty exploratory wells at a cost of many millions of dollars only to find them all dry. Oil companies, therefore, need to recover the costs of unsuccessful exploration out of the income from successful ventures.[17] Even after oil or gas has been struck the find must be appraised, usually by further drilling, with regard to the extent and the nature of the reservoir. At all stages of drilling, both exploratory and appraisal, there is pressure to drill continuously since in the offshore arena rig hire costs are payable whether the rig is operating or idle due to bad weather or supply delays.[18] As a general rule of thumb, the ratio of the cost of drilling between offshore and onshore is approximately 25:1 (Abdel-Aal & Schmelzee 1976, 179-80). Every reservoir is physically different, flows naturally at different rates and will require varying degrees of intervention (in the form of secondary or even tertiary recovery techniques including water or gas injection in the case of oil fields) to sustain a viable flow. Appraisal of the reservoir allows the company to decide whether or not the field is commercial and what production facilities will be required to take best advantage of the size and nature of the reservoir. Although a fair degree of certainty about future production can be achieved at this stage, allowing the modelling of the build up of production to the peak followed by the decline curve - and hence of the economics of the field - there is still a degree of risk (Abdel-Aal & Schmelzee 1976, 151-2, 166). As production proceeds, the appraisal is continually updated on the basis of whether there has been any decline in production capacity or pressure, or whether there has been any water flooding or changes in the ratio of gas to oil (Connolly 1978, 79).[19] As to the arrangement of production facilities, it is a question of balancing an increased number of wells and perhaps even platforms, which might improve ultimate recovery, against the greater fixed and operating costs which each well and platform entails. For Frankel, the uncertainty and expense of this initial process before production can begin leads to an imperative to produce quickly in order to recover the heavy investment as quickly as possible (1946, 18-19). In situations where companies are short of cash this becomes a necessity (Abdel-Aal & Schmelzee 1976, 93-4).

In order to assess a find and develop a project, a variety of indicators can be used including the following: *payback* (the length of time required to recover the investment cost); *average rate of return on investment* (a measure of funds invested and the anticipated return); *time-adjusted rate of return*; and *net present value* (discounted cash flow less compounded capital expenditure) (Rimell 1975; Abdel-Aal & Schmelzee 1976, 93-101; Johnson 1979 (I), 132-3). The last two indicators are regarded as the most useful because of their ability to take account of the effects of inflation, but uncertainty then lies in the appropriate rate to add into the calculation.[20] In general, although payback is seen as an inferior analysis in terms of the long-term interests of the company, because of its inability to take account of actual income beyond the payback period and to allow for the costs of unrequited capital expenditure in the years before first oil (Johnson 1979 (I), 132-3), its relatively short reach into the future means that it exercises a powerful influence on field economics. Equally, its ability to provide the greatest degree of 'certainty' in terms of cash recouped produces a weighty influence in the choice of capital projects. Each of these indicators, however, is *deterministic* in that they each produce a construction of the future which is in a sense absolute. Each requires a fixed assumption of certain variables (including the timely and enduring availability of equipment and services) and produces a fixed result in terms of return.

Frankel was writing in 1946, just before the first offshore well out of sight of land was sunk off Louisiana in the Gulf of Mexico (Lumsden 1978, 142). The differences in the degree of investment required for production offshore as compared to onshore are immense and the need to build and install offshore platforms significantly increases the lead-time before income can be received. So although even Frankel stressed the technical complexity of the industry at all stages and its influence on lead-time, this has in fact been greatly magnified in the offshore environment, reinforcing the eventual need for rapid production (see Roeber 1993, 17ff).

The second characteristic of the product stressed by Frankel is the fact that its *ownership and/or control* are in the hands of a party other than the company seeking to produce it. This introduces the concept of licensing. The owner of land or of the mineral itself issues a licence which imposes certain obligations on the explorer or producer. In many jurisdictions the owner of the land charges a royalty for every unit of production while in the UK the state as owner of the mineral in the ground charges such a royalty.[21] Both production licences and the foregoing exploration licence contain conditions related to the speed at which work must be carried out and may require a certain amount of the licensed area to be relinquished after given periods.[22] A party other than the operator directly concerned with the technical and commercial aspects of the search for and production of oil therefore has a direct say in the rate of exploration and production. In the case of state-owned mineral resources, it is clearly in the interests of the state that exploration be carried out as thoroughly and as quickly as possible so that it can have an indication of the amount of resources (and the consequent royalties and revenues) it can count on. In the case of production licences, the owner will want the mineral produced sooner rather than later in order that an income will be received.[23] These factors 'make for swift action, especially in the case of operators with limited resources' (Frankel 1946, 19).

The third characteristic of the product which for Frankel produces an influence on the ultimate structure of the industry is that crude oil is a *fluid*.[24] As a related point, it is a fluid which must be processed before it can be used. These factors lead to a situation where continuous production is favoured. Not only is this a result of the need to recoup the investment in exploration, appraisal and production facilities as quickly as possible but also because of the investment required in pipeline and refinery facilities. Regarding transport, Frankel points out that:

> [w]hereas other trades can rely upon means of transport catering for a host of materials and are thus not compelled to provide machinery of their own, the oil industry has always had to consider transport as being a major problem to be solved within its own orbit. (1946, 34)

The major forms of transport are of course tankers and pipelines, with the latter being favoured in the offshore in many cases because of their ability to be used irrespective of weather conditions.[25] However, the choice of a 'pipe-line transportation system is economically feasible only if there is a continuous flow on a considerable scale' and it is a highly significant fact that pipelines are limited to one product in one direction from a diminishing source of supply (1946, 40-41). As regards refining, the high capital cost and the continuous nature of the production process means that this sector of the industry is 'hurried by unavoidable technical forces towards working to capacity and concentration in big units' (1946, 31-2).

Frankel reduces these factors to the following basic feature of the petroleum industry, namely, 'that it is not self-adjusting' (1946, 67) and therefore has an inherent tendency to extreme crises, there either being too much or too little oil. In more technical terms there is *low price elasticity of supply* (meaning a low ability on the part of the industry to respond in terms of production to a change in the price) and a *limited price elasticity of demand* (meaning a limited capacity on the part of consumers to respond to changes in price) (1946, 51-6; 57-66). The industry has to produce continuously and a broad range of consumers cannot easily alter consumption in response to a change in price.[26] This lack of self-adjustment again favours rapid production as, with such an uncertain future, the value of money today is greater than the value of money tomorrow - a factor with particular significance in the case of an oil reservoir, which is a diminishing, finite resource (Abdel-Aal & Schmelzee 1976, 166).[27] A further aspect of this is that a sufficient margin of profit must be achieved on current production so that capital will be available in the future for continued exploration (Abdel-Aal & Schmelzee 1976, 138). This rationale of 'feast or famine' has been found to be an enduring aspect of upstream management where low prices lead to cost considerations taking a higher priority and high prices produce an emphasis on discovery and getting the oil out of the ground as quickly as possible (Ellis Jones 1988, 122).

Some 20 years later, Frankel produced an update of his analysis entitled *Essentials Revisited 1968* in which he stated that he found his initial assessment unaltered in its significant details and he once again stressed the need for speed:

> there is an overwhelming inducement to recoup one's investment to the maximum possible extent as quickly as possible since, within certain limits, the prime cost of every barrel is low and, in many cases, lower than that of the previous one - a case of decreasing costs. These circumstances ...influence the oil producer at all times. (1968, 75)

In addition to speed, one other way in which the industry had developed to cope with the risk of failure inherent in exploration and in the limited elasticity situation was integration: that is, the involvement of single corporate actors in more than one level of the industry from exploration through production to processing and retail of end products. Initially the risk of failure in exploration can be spread by exploring in different regions[28] but this requires significant resources and hence 'very large economic units within the industry.' This growth into different levels also helps to absorb risk: 'by operating on more than one level of the industry, i.e. by integration, the investment in each one of them is made more secure' (1968, 75-6). Supplies to the downstream are secured by having access to production and outlets for production are secured by having access to transport, refining and retail facilities. The significant conclusion of Frankel's detailed assessment is that in order for the whole system to work the individual enterprise of the industry must be untouched: '[w]hereas decisions of a strategic kind cannot be taken but on the highest level, tactical decisions are best left to the industry itself' (1968, 144). In other words, the industry should be allowed to self-regulate.[29]

3.2 Mapping the Essentials

The cognitive map at Figure 3.2 can be derived from Frankel's analysis as a representation of the fundamental concepts on which the industry management world construction was based at the time when it first embarked upon the exploration and development of the North Sea.

This graphic representation reveals that speed as purely a headlong rush for profits must be seen in the context of industry management rather as the product of a reasoned and internally coherent economic system. Furthermore, while profit is clearly and unquestionably a major motive for the industry, it is considerably more than an end in itself, but is rather part of a programme of minimising economic risk so that the industry can continue to operate. Rapid production is, therefore, seen as vital to the continuation of the industry and as the inevitable consequence of the nature of the product the industry is concerned with. At all times the industry is concerned to manage, spread and minimise economic risk. It is concerned to maximise the return on capital with a view to creating conditions of long-term stability - something which implies maximising the share of gains and the degree of control it can exercise (see also Noreng 1980, 21).

In autopoietic terms, the system operates on the basis of the economic code where 'to have' is preferred to 'not to have' but the precise programme by which this is achieved is one of rapidity of production aimed at minimising economic risk. In other words, the self-steering programme of industry management is not related to two situations of occupational safety but to two situations of economic safety. In order to guarantee the freedom required to operate in this optimal rapid mode, self-regulation is regarded as the appropriate regulatory form. To clarify further, profit is not so much an end in itself as the factor which allows the continuation of the system and thus effectively could be said to 'close the

Figure 3.2 Cognitive Map: Industry Management (Essentials of Petroleum)

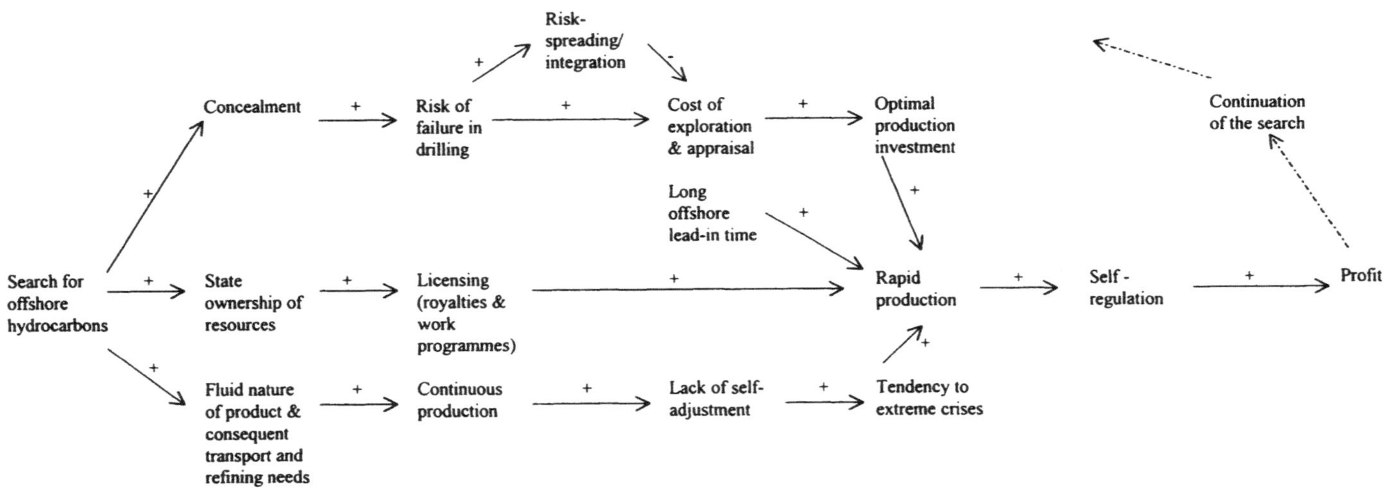

loop'. It is immediately clear that this world construction presents a significant obstacle to the political programme of detailed prescription as regards matters of health and safety at work envisaged by the legislators of the 1971 Act. It can be said even on the basis of this initial picture of the industry management rationality that regulatory interventions which fail to take account of its world construction, its relevance criteria, will be reconstructed according to its code and programme as fundamentally incompatible with the very essence of what it is that the industry is about.

This sort of analysis provides a different emphasis from the assumed profit-driven cost-benefit calculation which the economic analysis of law approach reviewed above[30] applies to the conduct of industry. Such an approach can be seen on the one hand to mask out too much of what counts as important in the reasoning of the industry and on the other hand to assume that precise calculations can determine how decisions are taken. At this stage, then, it can be suggested tentatively that the standard economic analysis assumption that safety regulations are obeyed or disobeyed on the basis of a calculation similar to:

COST OF IMPLEMENTATION < COST OF NON-IMPLEMENTATION = OBEY
COST OF IMPLEMENTATION > COST OF NON-IMPLEMENTATION = DISOBEY

with refinements to take account of perceptions of the likelihood of discovery, prosecution and sentencing in the event of non-compliance, is too simplistic. To the contrary, it can now be seen that it is more instructive to try to understand the essentials of the industry's world construction *across the whole industry* rather than selecting individual parts and subjecting them to an equation which may have little relevance or meaning in that context. Thus, it would appear that the implementation of a safety regulation will depend upon whether it is perceived by the industry in a given situation as contributing to the minimisation of the general level of economic risk. Whether this happens in practice remains to be seen. Nevertheless, the current approach is more open to the possibility that the construction of the magnitude of risk and its effects on the operation of the field is not something which can be easily represented by equations. Some impression of what this statement means in practice can be gained from the following graph of costs and benefits at different stages in the development of an oilfield (Figure 3.3).

Figure 3.3 Costs and Benefits of an Oilfield Development[31]

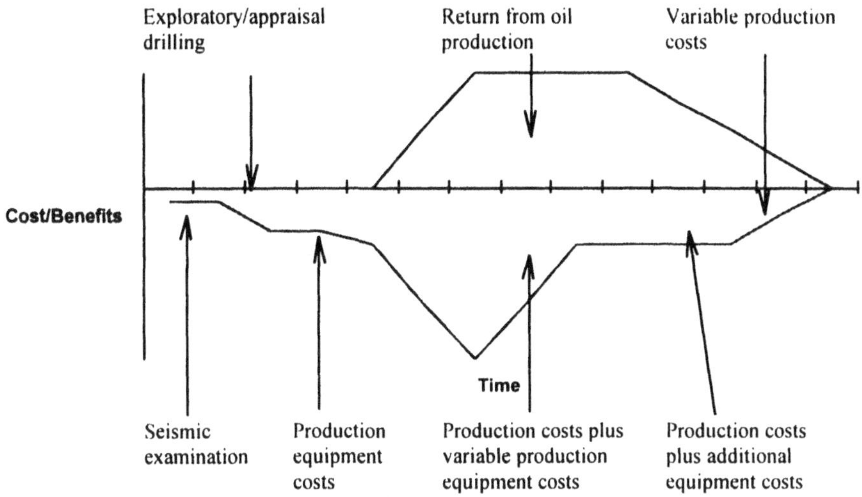

Clear from this graph is the heavy front-end loading of capital investment in a field at a time when oil has not yet actually flowed in anything other than exploration and appraisal drilling and the extent, therefore, to which the companies investing and their financial backers are exposed to risk. This factor is, of course, of much greater importance in the offshore context where costs are exponentially higher. In other words, we have a graphic representation of the notion that the

> 'front end loading' of Nort', Sea development...causes financial problems rather than the size of the sums required. The fact that the expenditure is concentrated into a relatively short period for each field may make it bulk larger in the imagination. (Johnson 1979 (II) 53)

From a legal sociological point of view, an awareness of the industry's reality construction, its communicative system, makes it clear that the retrospective application of 'objective' measures, whether economic or regulatory, risks being a pointless exercise in the 'discovery' of what those measures are bound to produce. Thus, as regards economic analysis it can be seen that the *impression* of cost was of greater importance than the *actual* cost and we are therefore confronted with a need for analysis which is more qualitative than quantitative. Equally, checking to see whether regulations were adhered to assumes, firstly, that they made any sense to the industry and secondly, that they could be accommodated within the time-horizon which the reality construction produced. Of great importance in this construction of reality is the idea that time is more important than cost. While profit is the end point, since any income is in the future the sooner it is received the greater and more certain will be the profit. It has been noted in this regard that the offshore industry displays a willingness to accept cost increases rather than time delays (Hamilton 1978, 71).

The autopoietic approach, therefore, demonstrates the way in which industry management constitutes a communicative system operating on the basis of a particular construction of reality. The product of a particular code and steering to a programme of rapid production aimed at the minimisation of economic risk, this version of reality is coherent and logical in its own terms. But for the very same reasons, there are things that the system cannot observe, which will become evident in due course as we consider other versions of North Sea reality.

3.3 Essentials in Action

The analysis so far has drawn heavily on the work of Frankel with support from other writers on the economics of the oil industry and some examples from experience in the North Sea. While Frankel occupies a special position as both a chronicler of the industry world construction and a writer whose work has helped to pass on that construction, it remains to be seen whether and to what extent the cognitive map produced is a reasonable representation of the world construction of the industry in day-to-day action. In this section, the writings of some of those directly involved at the level of management in the development of the North Sea will be considered. Starting with the exploration phase, we can consider a paper produced by a manager from Conoco (one of the major companies which has operated throughout the history of the province) at the time when the search for hydrocarbons had moved from the gasfields of the shallower and comparatively less hostile waters of the southern North Sea to the prospects of oil in the deeper and climatically more problematic northern waters (Wilson 1973). Figure 3.4 is a cognitive map prepared from this paper.

Figure 3.4 Cognitive Map: Industry Management (Exploration Phase 1970s)

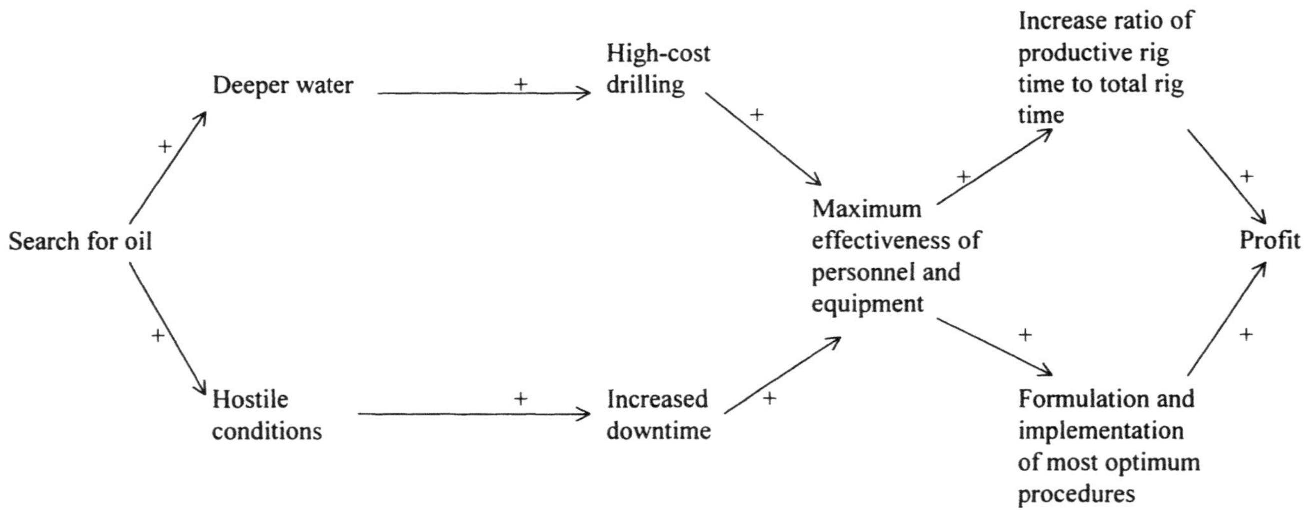

It can be seen, then, that, as Frankel identified, exploration is uncertain and expensive. Indeed, costs in the North Sea were higher than expected and the amount of time when work could not be carried out due to bad weather was posing a problem. There is pressure to keep costs low especially at this stage when there is no certainty of a return. The preferred method of achieving this end is maximising the effectiveness of the operation by increasing the amount of time that the drill is turning. The solutions are, therefore, technological or related to operating procedures and it is then a question of determining whether or not to install new equipment or adopt new procedures for this purpose. It is worth noting that in the early stages of exploration both for gas and then for oil in the North Sea, a world shortage of drilling units also increased the pressure on those available.[32] Wilson gives us some insight into the way in which this decision-making process is carried out when he points to the use of a mathematical formula by which the benefit to be had from a new piece of equipment or procedure can be measured:

$$C_o T_o > (C_o + \Delta C)(T_o - \Delta T)$$

Where:
C_o =total daily operating cost, \$/day before time-saving devices, etc.
ΔC =incremental daily cost, \$/day, required by adding a device, etc.
T_o =total time, rig days/well, required without additional devices, etc.
ΔT =net time, rig days/well, saved by adding devices, etc.

But the formula in practice is not deployed as a straightforward comparison between the existing product of cost and time against the new product of cost and time but rather is reformulated to produce the time that must be saved for a particular item or procedure to be economically advantageous, thus:

$$\Delta T > \frac{\Delta C T_o}{C_o \Delta C}$$

So again we see firstly, the prime importance of time and speed in the behaviour of the industry and secondly, the deployment of a deterministic formula which will produce a definite answer for every modification. In this way, the complexity of the entire operation is reduced to a single formula which models only selected aspects of the whole: the product of cost and time for the operation as it stands and the assumed saving in time together with the additional cost of the new equipment or procedure. There is, however, some limited recognition of this shortcoming when it is stated that the uncertainty inherent in the actual time which will be saved with each modification cannot be taken into account in such a calculation. Thus, Wilson admits that 'any item selected for installation' must be 'unquestionably advantageous' (1973, 354). Ultimately, then, there is an apparent bias towards a conservative approach but it is by no means clear whether this happened in practice or indeed whether other operators and contractors adopted a similarly cautious approach or whether the drive for time savings prevailed.[33] The lack of any mention of safety or of whether modifications meet regulatory requirements is significant. The tightness of time schedules meant that regulation was extremely problematic and it is not surprising to find those within the industry (even at this early stage when the UK regime was very much in the development stages) stating that only by self-regulation can the industry meet all of its objectives (see Biewer & Wallin 1970). The conflict between the industry's self-steering programme of minimising economic risk by using equipment and procedures that will save time and the programme of politics of minimising risks to health and safety by prescribing appropriate equipment and procedures is clear.

If we move forward to the stage where exploration has been successful and a field has been discovered, appraised and a development plan produced, we find a similar situation when it comes to the installation of the production platform. Holter & Hagen (1976), for example, detail the experience of the industry at the stage of the installation of the first generation production platforms in the oilfields of the northern North Sea and Figure 3.5 is the corresponding cognitive map.

Although similar pressures apply as to the exploration stage, they note that problems have led to installation having to be delayed for up to six or eight months until conditions are again suitable for the extremely weather-sensitive operations involved in placing the jacket and lifting the modules. This, on the one hand, increases the demand for innovative technologies and, on the other, increases the pressure on the whole project as field economics have to be recalculated. Again we can see the logic of the cognitive map at Figure 3.2 and again we can see that the imperative for rapid production is given new force in the conditions of delay in the North Sea. The fact that exploration and installation costs are higher than expected puts even more pressure on the economics of the field in its production phase as well as adding pressure to the installation phase itself,

Figure 3.5 Cognitive Map: Industry Management (Installation Phase 1970s)

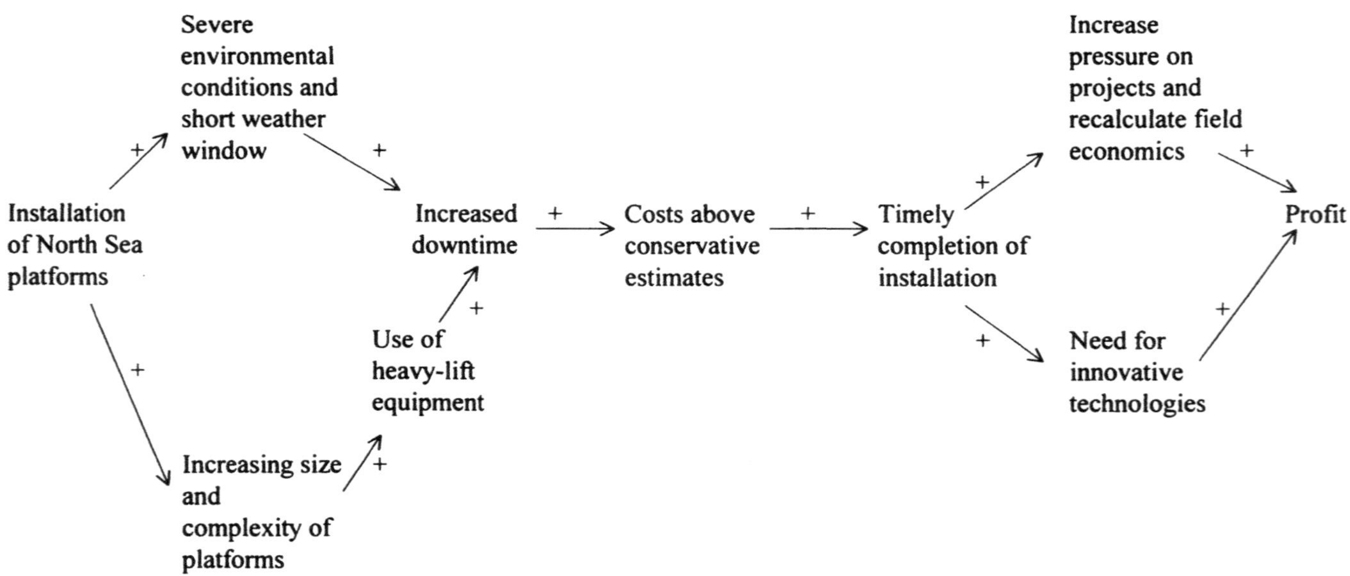

as in both cases the appropriate method of reducing costs in operations is improvement in time efficiency - speed.[34]

The issue of costs greater than expectations is by no means an isolated feature. Rather, throughout the 1970s there is a recurring lament about increasing costs coupled to an expectation that difficulties in this regard may in fact become more severe. In 1974, for example, the chief executive of Shell-Mex and BP told the *Financial Times* conference on the North Sea that costs in the previous year had risen dramatically and cited a doubling in the cost of production platforms, the fact that an exploration well now cost up to £3m without guarantee of success and that in that period the investment required for one barrel of production per day had risen by 50%. He pointed to the 'obvious moral' that the oil industry must make adequate profits in order to be able to finance the huge investments required and to ensure continued exploration for future production.[35] Two years later with more experience of production behind them, all fields then onstream reported operating costs much higher then expected. The Heather, Claymore, Piper and Thistle fields had all shown particularly large increases and capital costs had continued to rise to a point where some fields were now showing a negative net present value.[36] Just one year later, the managing director of Mobil indicated that operating conditions in the North Sea had raised investment for one barrel of production per day (at peak rates) to between £3,500 and £5,300 and contrasted this with the historical development cost for existing world oilfields of between £120 and £240.[37] Cost rises were associated with a number of factors including the realisation of engineering problems, which in some cases necessitated design changes at a very late stage in projects. In the mid 1970s this led to as much as a 90% increase in capital spending over an 18 month period - equivalent to a nearly 150% increase once inflation is taken account of. As noted previously, there is evidence that some cost increases were deliberate and chosen in preference to further delays. Given our understanding of the way in which the industry constructed its world, we can see the reasons for such choices - when operating according to net present value in a situation of high front-end expenditure, cost increases are preferable to time delays (Hamilton 1978, 71; Johnson 1979 (I), 137-8; Noreng 1980, 92; 96-7). An example of the way in which the retrospective application of an apparently objective measure can mask out the construction of reality at the time is the point that if the fact of the industry's willingness to accept cost increases over delays is taken into account, it can be said that costs escalated in real terms in line with major innovative projects onshore (Johnson 1979 (I) 138) and thus were nothing out of the ordinary. Of more significance, however, is the point that the industry did not generally perceive the issue of cost in this way and operated to a much shorter temporal horizon in terms of the recovery of capital outlays. As a result, the question of cost takes on a predominance which the argument cited here by Johnson does not address. Indeed, Johnson himself deploys elsewhere the contrary argument (1979 (II), 53) and points to the conditions of alarm in the industry especially in 1975 when cost increases coincided with financing difficulties (1979 (II) 48).

Added to this pressure on existing operations, companies were, by 1978, becoming aware of the difficulties they would encounter in developing the next generation of fields. At the higher end, wells were now costing £5m to drill (Quinlan 1978) but of more concern was the fact that the new discoveries were more difficult in all respects. A BP spokesman pointed to the fact that these fields had an average of 40% less reserves, were in deeper water and had poorer rock characteristics, which were harder to define and develop (see Lumsden 1978, 142). Companies were therefore looking for reduced costs and greater certainty of profits (Quinlan 1978). The impact of such issues was again perhaps greater than could easily be measured by straightforward economic means in that the fear of increased costs became an acceptance of their inevitability throughout the 1970s in the industry's world construction: '[t]he pessimistic view that North Sea capital costs are bound to continue rising even faster than the general rate of inflation is widely held' (Johnson 1979 (I) 137). Thus, again, time was the factor which was perceived as more easily controllable.

An interesting feature of papers produced by industry managers at this time is the fact that explicit references to law and regulation are rare, although it must be remembered that despite the passing of the enabling legislation in 1971, the first regulations having a direct impact on physical aspects of the industry were not in operation until 1976. When regulations are discussed (e.g. R. J. Robinson 1975), the preference for self-regulation and a fear of the negative effects of government intervention, which was a feature of the general cognitive map at Figure 3.2, is clear. Legislation is seen as imposing technical requirements which may not be commercially justified and it is said to be more prudent if regulation takes account of individual field requirements.[38] Thus, it is contended that the aim of the industry must be to provide regulators with the basic information required for good regulations. Regulations must not preclude the use of the most appropriate technology for a given situation. Further, industry must ensure prudent operations to avoid 'precipitate action by government'. The twin aims of safety regulation are adequate safety and no imposition of economic hardship that could lead to reserves not being developed (R. J. Robinson 1975, 761).

This is a very revealing picture of the industry construction of law and regulation. Far from regulation itself ensuring safety, the industry can achieve this without regulation. Regulation is seen as a necessary fact of life which government introduces precipitately in response to perceived difficulties. The motivation for the industry to ensure safe operations is *not* the content and enforcement of regulations. Rather it is, on the one hand, the contribution that safe operations make to the achievement of immediate industry goals (rapid and continuous production which in turn produces profit which in turn ensures continuation of the search for and development of new reserves) and, on the other hand, the belief that unsafe operations will lead to greater government intervention which will have negative effects on the ability of the industry to operate. For so long as there is regulation, however, the industry aims to ensure that it does not restrict developments and can achieve this by the provision of information to regulators - information which the regulators must to a great extent rely on the industry for (see also SREA 1989, 21).

The process of regulation, then, faces considerable difficulties in the context of an industry which firstly, is both so complex and so remote from the regulator that the latter is at an information disadvantage and secondly, has a very well-defined construction of reality which by no means includes regulation as necessarily a positive factor. Equally, the industry's construction of its task as being made much more difficult by the nature of the product it seeks was very much reinforced by the environmental conditions which were encountered in the North Sea. However, we will see in the next section that this reinforcement of the construction went far beyond environmental factors. In particular, its dislike of outside intervention was tested by financial backers and by government as well as by its own workforce and those it contracted with for equipment and services. The demands of these parties, understandable in their own world constructions, take on a quite different appearance on the cognitive map of the industry as it steers according to its programme of speed aimed at the minimisation of economic risk.

3.4 Mapping Interventions

(a) Finance In this map of the oil industry's communicative system which drives towards rapid production and greater certainty of profit, one of the most significant factors in the move into the North Sea was the

source of financing. In the traditional Frankel analysis, the source of finance in many cases was internal, with companies funding especially the exploration stage themselves and thereafter perhaps seeking equity finance for development (Merkey 1978). This payment for exploration out of reserves was of course very closely linked with the overwhelming concern for rapid development and production to recover those costs. As regards the equity market, the pressures were somewhat less immediate but nevertheless present. Equity would only be forthcoming if investors considered that the company was a good risk and thus the impetus on the company was to produce a good return quickly in order to be able to distribute a dividend so that when it next needed to go to the market equity capital would be available (Abdel-Aal & Schmelzee 1976, 138). While this picture also accounts for some of the developments in the North Sea, the sheer scale of the investments required meant that other innovative sources of finance appeared. There were certainly companies who looked to the stock market, but this was a fairly insignificant feature of the North Sea after the exploration stage (Tempest 1979, 33) and indeed at that time the stock prices of the oil companies were generally depressed and thus equity was not an attractive option (Carlisle 1978, 48). Equally there were examples of major oil companies funding entire developments from internal reserves[39] and in such cases the drive for rapid production is clear. The third general form of financing which appeared was a variation of the production payment method where the source of funding was usually a group of banks.

This last form of funding developed especially after the first oil shock in 1973 when prices rose sharply and when the industry and governments worldwide were forced to consider security of supply more seriously than they had done at any time since the Israeli occupation of Egyptian oilfields during the 1967 war.[40] The consequent search for and development of new reserves put a huge strain on the financial resources of the industry and its traditional backers as the demand for project finance grew exponentially. One banker described the position for companies at this time in the following dramatic terms: 'there is simply very little room for error and an idle facility can literally bring a company to its financial knees' (Merkey 1978, 36). The price rise also brought other difficulties for companies. Whereas the massive price rises in 1973-74 following the already rising price during 1970-72 were viewed by politicians as a reason for increased taxation to take account of surplus or windfall profits, the internal industry view was somewhat different. Although the value of oil reserves increased, there was a concomitant requirement to build up central funds in order to provide the same level of protection from contingencies as had existed at the old price, especially in view of the effects of inflation at this time (Carlisle 1978). The profits of these years did not appear as excess to the industry but rather as a relief to internal pressures as it began to adjust to OPEC's increasingly interventionist stance and moved the search for oil to more difficult environments.[41] The cumulative effect of these circumstances was an increase in gearing (the ratio of long-term debt to total capital employed) from the historical industry maximum prevailing throughout the 1950s and 1960s of some 15% to a mid-1970s figure of 25% (Carlisle 1978, 48).[42] The rise in costs over this period mentioned in the previous section is well exemplified by the experience of BP in the Forties field and the strain on financing which such cost increases threatened is clear.[43] Forties was ultimately saved by price rises ahead of expectations[44] together with the fact that, firstly, the loan had been calculated so that it could be repaid out of 60% of production (with cash from production available as early as 1976) and, secondly, the field then produced at a rate substantially better than expected. Cost rises at Piper and Claymore necessitated further loans while BP bridged the gap itself at Forties (Johnson 1979 (II) 48).

The industry's view of high front-end costs was, therefore, being confirmed and reinforced by events in the North Sea and, bearing this in mind, let us consider the details of the external funding which the operators encountered. Much of the attitude of banks towards lending to the industry is explained by the fact that, as was shown in the graph at Figure 3.3, a large amount of money must be advanced before any oil has flowed - except through exploration and appraisal wells. Given the unprecedented sums of money involved in the North Sea, the risks for lenders were high and their approach was, therefore, extremely cautious.[45] The lender's decision about the value and period of the loan was based on the reservoir analysis being used by the company to reach economic and technical decisions about the field. Although the Volumetric and Performance analysis techniques had often proved very accurate, engineers employed or consulted by banks to make assessments on which loans would be based exercised extreme conservatism (Connolly 1978, 79). The lack of historical data and hence the uncertainty of performance in the North Sea was a major problem for banks (Elwes 1978, 63).[46] The bank then applied a safety factor representing the number of times the loan was to be covered by the expected revenue of the field after all expenses including taxation had been paid. Normally the factor was 2:1 but in the North Sea it rose to 2.5:1. Thereafter, the period of the loan and the payback schedule were calculated (Connolly 1978, 79). Whereas onshore production might actually be policed by banking engineers so that field profiles could be checked and updated, in the North Sea the banks had to rely on company data, protecting themselves with more 'stringent loan default provisions' (Connolly 1978, 80). Much of the finance was advanced as production payment loans, which meant that the assets of the company were unaffected, the loan being secured on the proven reserves. This, of course, created a very direct link between repayment of the loan and production in the industry's world construction (Elwes 1978, 63).

The hostile climate and the use of untested technology in the North Sea were the factors which led to the introduction of the technical or completion guarantee as a means of the bank covering the uncertainties of project timing and cost (Connolly 1978, 80; Elwes 1978, 64). This was the case for BP's development of the Forties field where the borrower had to guarantee the technical or engineering completion of the field as a means of providing for the risk accepted by the lender with regard to the technical uncertainties of the project in addition to the 'normal' risk that the reservoir would not perform as predicted (Connolly 1978, 81). Notwithstanding this significant modification of the already stringent production payment method, it has been suggested that only the financial strength of BP allowed the loan to proceed, the general security situation in the North Sea falling 'some way short of the bankers' requirements' (Elwes 1978, 64-5). The higher safety factor mentioned above reflected the banks' continuing fears over the technical risk of offshore production as much as concern about reservoir performance in the new province. It is worth mentioning also that once Petroleum Revenue Tax was introduced[47] pressure was increased on debt-financed as opposed to equity-financed developments since interest payments and other financing charges could not be offset against profits (see Robinson & Morgan 1976).

The political policy of the wide involvement of different licensees as a means of ensuring rapid and thorough exploration and exploitation provided more uncertainties for lenders, resulting in yet further tightening of lending procedures. The presence in licensee partnerships of companies new to the industry, especially some who were unable to contribute sufficient equity to their intended projects led to banks seeking guarantees from major partners or from the government.[48] Banks would also on occasion seek guarantees in the form of long-term sales contracts, which was a further spur to continued production. In addition, banks would sometimes seek protective covenants which would provide for accelerating repayment, additional security, minimum acceptable working capital levels, debt limitations, management changes, salary limitations and insurance cover. As a final safeguard, banks also began to charge a royalty in addition to interest. Banks justified their tough stance on the basis of the risk accepted and pointed out that their funds belonged ultimately to depositors and not to stockholders and that the former anticipate a lower risk than the latter (Houseman 1970; Connolly 1978; Elwes 1978).

In retrospect, the risks involved in this way of proceeding for both the industry and the banks are clear. While this approach generally prevailed, there were indications that some involved in the management of the industry in the North Sea were becoming concerned. A step-by-step approach to field development was proposed, for example, as a means of restricting the massive cash draw-downs and of allowing more complete appraisal and proving of a field before a total commitment was made.[49] While this would have served to reduce economic risk in a way which did not rely on the self-steering programme of speed, the cognitive map at Figure 3.2 demonstrates that such an approach would have represented a significant departure from the prevailing industry understanding of what it did and how it did it. And indeed the general view, put forward by UKOOA, was that such a step-by-step approach would be impractical in the North Sea given the technological factors where investments could only be made on the basis of a total production plan.[50] Equally, in retrospect it can be seen that a further means of reducing the enormous pressures for production being built up by the industry's own world construction became available in the mid 1970s with the opening of oil futures markets in New York and Amsterdam.[51] But, so long as the price of oil continued to rise, producers in particular saw no need to resort to them and their traditional economic risk reduction programme - rapid production - prevailed.

The industry's view of the high front-end loading of costs was, therefore, reinforced in the North Sea by high-cost external finance coupled with a high degree of intervention on the part of banks with regard to technical matters and time-scales. The paradox is that while the banks' activities were aimed at reducing the risk of default, and while this was reconstructed by the industry also in terms of the minimisation of economic risk, this construction masked other risks and the programme of rapid production served to exacerbate them. These further risks in the relatively uncharted waters of northern North Sea production (in terms of technology failure and industrial accidents) could ultimately have backfired on the bankers and few will now dispute that luck rather than judgement prevented such an outcome. As a final example of this point, the financing situation of the Piper field can be considered. In this case the operator, Occidental, provided a technical completion guarantee with respect to the field but the banks providing the loan (a risk-spreading consortium, the International Energy Bank) accepted the risk of repayment only from Thomson, one of the minor partners in the venture which had no previous oil industry experience - although the latter had to accept 'stiff terms' in return. Further, extensive reservoir data were required by the banks for Piper, resulting in 'considerable "front-end" investment' which was then followed by a requirement that 'field performance...meet certain minimum parameters stipulated by the lenders'. To add to this pressure on Piper, its cash flow was then used as collateral for loan finance for the nearby Claymore field - providing additional cover for the service of its debt (Elwes 1978, 66).[52] The impact on the 'optimal production programme' of the industry's logic is clear. Not surprisingly, the Piper and Claymore loans have been described as the 'two most risky and controversial loans' in the North Sea (Johnson 1979(II), 56).

In terms of the different rationalities at work here, the logic of each must be admitted while at the same time the inherent dangers must be pointed out. The industry management rationality has been discussed at some length and its internal coherence has been seen. But there are now more signs of its weaknesses which were already apparent as regards the environmental factors of the North Sea. For one thing, it constructed technology, engineering and operational issues as absolutes which could be counted on irrespective of the time and cost pressures placed upon them. Similarly, banking, in seeking to minimise the risk of default, was effectively blind to the increased technological and operational risks its demands and interventions could create. In short, both industry management and its bankers operated to deterministic world constructions when it came to technology and operations.

In conclusion, it should not be forgotten either that for a period in the mid 1970s there were serious problems in trying to convince banks to lend at all for North Sea projects due to political uncertainties with regard to such issues as taxation, the possibility of depletion controls and especially state participation, the exact format of which could have had significant effects on field economics.[53] While such political uncertainties led to worries on the part of bankers, the industry itself viewed these issues with even greater concern. These are all topics of considerable complexity and it is not proposed to go into them in detail here. Rather, the important point is that these are all issues which retain a high profile on the cognitive map of industry management throughout the period under consideration in this chapter and were constructed by the industry not as the understandable attempts of political actors to secure the best advantage of the North Sea's hydrocarbon resources for the nation, but rather as continuing uncertainties which had a profound impact on the modelling of field economics and hence on every aspect of its plans for the North Sea from exploration through assessment, development, finance and operation. Insofar as this is the case, the effect on health and safety at work can also be perceived. It is too easy to see the industry as being concerned only to ensure lowest tax and minimum state participation but, as we shall see, while this would undoubtedly have been the preferred outcome, the principal concern was rather for decision, any decision, on these matters followed by consistency.

(b) Taxation As regards taxation, it is ironic that one of the factors affecting the decision of UK-based companies to invest in the North Sea was the fact that their overseas investments were adversely affected by the introduction of Corporation Tax with effect from FY1964-65, which was designed to deal with balance of payment problems.[54] As a result, they regarded future changes in taxation of oil and gas with particular disfavour and saw it as the government 'moving the goal posts' or 'changing the rules' after the game had started. Noreng has described this problem in terms of the difference between the *technical* and the *political* approach to taxation (1980, 160ff). The industry saw taxation in the former, technical, sense as a static framework within which it could function on the basis of fiscal certainty in a way which encouraged efficiency. Government on the other hand saw taxation as a dynamic political tool to be used differentially according to changing circumstances. In what follows we will see how these contradictory viewpoints worked out in practice.

In the early days, when hydrocarbon production from the North Sea was of natural gas, the profits available to the industry were effectively controlled by the state buyer of natural gas, the Gas Council. The need for the industry to dispose of gas into the national grid meant that it was not in a very strong position to object to imposed prices. Nevertheless, the battle over price was long and acrimonious with the industry insisting on the arguments which formed its world construction (Figure 3.2): that successful developments must not only pay for themselves but must equally absorb the costs of both failed exploration and ongoing exploration to ensure continuity of supply both for the consumer and for the industry; and that the industry faced uncertain costs due to environmental and technological factors. Further, it was stressed that a fixed price took no account of field variabilities. The argument raged from 1966 until 1973, with continual warnings that the price on offer was not sufficient to sustain development. Despite this, Philips agreed a price with the Council in 1968 which was widely felt by the rest of the industry to be too low. If this agreement encouraged the Gas Council then the celebration was short-lived, as in 1970 some three quarters of the originally licensed area was surrendered at the expiry of the first period of the licences. This was seen as a vote of no confidence in the North Sea as a gas province and in the following year a higher price was negotiated. In 1973, the Gas Council finally acknowledged that a higher price was necessary. This history was somewhat overshadowed by the advent of oil at about this time, but it serves to demonstrate once again the force of the industry's construction of reality on its own behaviour as well as the uneasy balance in its relations with government (see Odell 1975, 51-52). Richard Marsh, appointed Minister of Power in 1966, later wrote that:

> [o]ne of the chastening experiences of that period was to discover just how ill-equipped a Ministry is to intervene in detailed administration. This was nowhere more evident than when we came to negotiate North Sea gas prices with the oil companies. (quoted in Harvie 1995, 84)

This relationship took on much greater significance when the North Sea became an oil province and government realised that its control of profits had gone, as oil did not need to be disposed of to a monopoly state buyer. With the stern words of the Public Accounts Committee[55] ringing in its ears, the government intervened to ensure that no excess profits were made by the oil companies (by means of their taking advantage of domestic tax law provisions which allowed them to offset artificial Middle East losses against UK profits) and to ensure that a greater share of the hydrocarbon resources were secured for the nation, factors which took on additional urgency in the wake of the 1973 price rise. These intentions were intimated as early as the 1973 Budget speech[56] and reiterated by the incoming Labour government in the following year's Budget.[57] The industry responded that despite the price rises around this time, taxation and participation could 'make or break' the North Sea.[58] The intervention took the form initially of the Oil Taxation Act 1975, which introduced a 'ring fence' around the North Sea to prevent the offsetting of foreign losses (see Hayllar & Pleasance 1977, 148), and a new tax on the industry (on top of the existing royalty payment and Corporation Tax) - Petroleum Revenue Tax (PRT). In addition, the Finance (No. 2) Act 1975 contained provisions to limit the carryforward of losses accumulated by oil companies.

Before discussing the tax itself, the point should be made that the ring fence was an innovation as far as the industry was concerned and ran counter to the traditional risk-spreading practice of offsetting losses incurred in one sector against profits in another (L. Turner 1975, 102). From a government point of view such a practice led to an unacceptable loss of economic rent, but our understanding of the risk-minimisation thinking of the industry based on Figure 3.2 which demonstrates the need for the costs of failed exploration and development to be absorbed by successes renders the industry activity somewhat less sinister. Such a government response is probably inevitable, but the side-effects of such interventions may have included an unintended pressure on the industry's operations.

PRT operated as a prior charge on Corporation Tax and was initially set at a rate of 45%. It was charged on an artificial 'assessable profit' calculated on the production from each individual field. What is interesting about the introduction of this tax was the industry reaction. Undoubtedly happier without the tax, the industry nevertheless expressed relief that the uncertainties which had surrounded the tax were finally over.[59] This fits the industry desire to be able to calculate with as much certainty as possible what the costs associated with a field will be in order that the technological requirements as well as the production profile can be assessed. However, this relief was short-lived when the widely varying impact of the tax on different fields was appreciated (Robinson & Morgan 1976, 170). While the introduction of a modified quantity tax had been intended to take account of field-to-field differences, the impact of the tax was ultimately not related to field requirements and differed, for example, according to whether the field development was debt- or equity-financed, there being no deduction allowed for interest paid. On the one hand, the removal of uncertainty meant that field development could be modelled. On the other hand, the arbitrary effect of the tax tightened the economics of some fields which prior to the imposition of the tax may already have been marginal projects.[60] In short, the new tax failed to 'offer the industry the stability needed for the implementation of long-term projects'. Ironically, this lack of stability turned out to be the one certain feature of the tax as it subsequently underwent 'annual and sometimes more frequent amendment' (Daintith & Willoughby 1984, I-1103) in response to price increases, as will be seen in the next chapter.[61]

Apart from the direct and economically measurable effects of this taxation debacle on field developments,[62] other less easily determinable effects have been identified. Robinson & Rowland (1978) point to the different temporal horizons of the industry as compared to politics. The former is involved in field projects of at least 25 years' duration where the sort of PRT changes which had at that time been suggested (and which, of course, materialised in due course) can have a much larger impact than the simple effect on rate of return. They stress the need for certainty and criticise short-term political tinkering. In other words, the point at which costs are recovered disappears further into the future and, in terms of the industry management cognitive map (Figure 3.2), can only be brought nearer by increasing operational pressures. Equally, Quinlan (1978, 522) points to the damaging effects of the uncertainty produced by the PRT changes and describes a deteriorating level of confidence between government and industry. These commentators suggest that, by making such frequent changes to the tax regime, politics sets up the expectation in the industry that such uncertainty would be a continuing feature, with the unpredictable effects this can have on existing and future developments. Again, the industry cognitive map contains only one solution for the uncertain future. The point is put most pithily by MacKay & Mackay when they state that

> although oil companies may be risk-takers rather than risk-averters by nature, the number of risk-takers tends to decline when the bookmaker reserves the right to change the starting prices after the race has been run! (1975, 45)

And this is the general concern of many commentators, namely that if the risk is seen to be too great then oil companies will not commit investment to the North Sea but will move their capital to areas of the world where taxation conditions (in terms at least of certainty) are seen to be more favourable. However, if this uncertainty is considered in terms of our model of the industry reality construction we can see that, as regards *existing* developments as opposed to the question of new capital, it is constructed as yet another factor increasing economic risk and hence as yet another factor requiring the application of the industry's difference-minimising programme of rapid production. The taxation situation has been summed up as follows:

> [i]n times of need the Government has not hesitated to extract additional revenues from North Sea activities to meet short-term objectives and without regard to a coherent policy for the exploitation of the nation's resources. (Daintith & Willoughby 1984, I-1103)

No doubt if the idea put forward by MacKay & Mackay (1975, 45) of pegging taxation to 'an adequate target internal rate of return' of something in the region of 25% for any given field could have been achieved, then this would have been much more acceptable to the companies and would have suited the government as well - a point incidentally supported by Garnaut & Clunies Ross (1975) who find that the unintended side-effect of increasing tax in response to price rises and changing perceptions of costs has been income lost to government through reduced investment. It would seem that as regards taxation the industry, whether considering new investment or engaging in the continuing appraisal of ongoing projects, adheres to its construction of the essentials of petroleum whatever government may think it is actually doing - the difficulty being that its exact behaviour does not appear to be easily reducible to external economic assessment given the degree to which internal constructions of costs and the need to recoup them quickly weigh in operational decisions. To return to the terminology with which this discussion began, it is possible to see both the force of government's legitimate interest in a dynamic political approach to taxation as the price of oil rose during the 1970s with a dramatic jump in 1973 and equally industry's concern to have a static framework in a situation of considerable technical and environmental uncertainty and the expectation of rising costs. Unfortunately, the 'dynamic political tool' used throughout this period became more of a blunt instrument as far as the industry was concerned which, as the self-steering programme of speed continued to operate, inevitably produced many unintended side-effects at an operational level with significance for health and safety at work.

(c) Participation Of potentially much greater concern to the industry throughout the 1970s were rumours of the government's intentions for state participation. While there were elements of participation through the National Coal Board and the British Gas Corporation from the outset, this was on a largely equal footing with the private sector (Daintith & Willoughby 1984, I-303). First indications of a more thoroughgoing and systematic participation emerged at the Labour Party Conference in 1967 and a study group report was published in 1968.[63] There was early concern in the industry that this idea introduced a major uncertainty into their plans although the Parliamentary Labour Party's apparent lack of interest in the idea at the time was seen as encouraging.[64] The landmark Public Accounts Committee report of 1973, of course, did much to focus the attention of politics on the dangers of

allowing too much leeway to the industry and just as it prompted new taxation provisions so it forced the government to think more seriously about participation in the form of a state oil company. Equally, the impact of the 1973 oil shock is evident here as well: the extra cost of importing oil as a result of the price rise accounted in large part for the the balance of payments deficit for 1973. The interest of the government in taking as big a share of the resources as possible and in exercising as much control as possible is clear. The industry, sensing what was coming, stressed that all had an interest in rapid and extensive development - something which could only be guaranteed if the North Sea remained attractive to investment.[65] But the government felt that greater intervention was required and proposals were issued in mid-1974[66] which included the idea of majority participation in new licences together with negotiations with existing licensees for participation.[67] It has been suggested that despite the attempted unilateral action with regard to existing licences, the net result of the eventual 1975 changes (including participation, with the setting up of the British National Oil Corporation on 1 January 1976, and taxation) was a secure level environment for oil company activities (Daintith & Gault 1979, 67). There is no doubt that UKOOA was instrumental in many of the amendments to the Petroleum and Submarine Pipelines Bill during its parliamentary passage,[68] but it is highly doubtful whether in the longer run the industry construction of that event and the succeeding changes to taxation was quite so sanguine (see Park 1979, 96). As Tom King for the Conservative opposition put it in 1978: 'oil companies do not know whether they are dealing with a competitor, a partner or a boss'.[69] Equally, the proposal to amend the conditions of existing licences granted in the first place at the discretion of the government has been described by one commentator as creating a 'crisis of legality' (Cameron 1983, 92ff). Whereas the traditional feeling in the industry was that licences allocated after auction involved a higher risk because they were more easily subject to state repudiation, the behaviour of the British government at this time indicated that that risk attached also to discretionary allocation licences - in other words, companies were simply unable to trust the state (Dam 1976, 178-9; see also Elwes 1978, 71).[70]

The major problem for the industry, however, was the fact that such participation could take a variety of forms - the worst-case scenario being that of the 'carried interest', where the State took no risks, paying nothing until it chose to do so but reaping any benefit to the full. The government's intention to achieve a carried interest was clear in the initial document containing the proposals and in the consultative document setting out proposals for the fifth licensing round conditions which were implemented in due course.[71] During the delay between the announcement of the fifth round and its conclusion, the industry response to these proposals was to reiterate the logic of petroleum production shown in Figure 3.2. The chairman of Esso, for example, warned that the effect of government taking powers which went beyond what the industry saw as good oilfield practice was to introduce a major uncertainty into planning. He stressed that field economics involved careful calculation of the production rate and any interference with this would introduce a significant economic penalty. Once again, there was the threat of delayed projects as companies were forced to reassess developments. In particular, Burmah went ahead with its platform for the Thistle field only with 'great hesitancy' and expressing the hope that future government policy would not affect the operation and financing of the project.[72] These sentiments were echoed by Shell who described uncertainty about freedom to plan for optimum production as one of the most restrictive and damaging limitations from the producer's standpoint.[73] This was linked explicitly to the uncertainties relating to costs and technology, which as we have seen were becoming all too apparent as the companies moved north. The appointment of the left-wing Tony Benn as the new Secretary of State for Energy during this period[74] merely added uncertainty as far as the industry was concerned, not least because he wanted to enter participation negotiations 'with no pledge on petroleum revenue tax or future policy' (Harvie 1995, 206) and did not invite UKOOA to join the Energy Commission set up in June 1977 to consider future policy until the following year (Harvie 1995, 180; 210). Eventually, however, participation was accepted in principle by many of the companies operating in the North Sea: amendments to the Petroleum and Submarine Pipelines Bill in Parliament at the Committee Stage which provided *inter alia* for arbitration in case of disputes over depletion rates, activity programmes and the like provided some reassurance in a situation where most discoveries in the sector now had to be considered marginal.[75] When the Bill became law in November 1975, the participation question was still open but the government was by now stressing a no gain, no loss situation which dispelled fears of the worst case 'carried interest' scenario.[76]

The spectre of participation looms large in industry thinking at this time and taken together with doubts over future taxation discussed above can be seen to have led the industry on the one hand to delay new developments - either from choice or due to lack of external funds where bankers were equally concerned about uncertainties - and on the other to intensify existing operations because more than ever it saw the value of money today as greater than its highly uncertain value tomorrow (see Lucas 1976, 346). The impact of the uncertainty is evident from the fact that as soon as the government made it clear that participation would not affect discounted cash-flow estimates, several hundred million pounds of funding immediately became available.[77] While the delaying of new developments due to these uncertainties is very public, their impact on existing operations can be inferred. Equally, the pressure on delayed developments when they finally go ahead must be seen to have increased in terms of industry management's self-steering programme.

When consultation began for sixth round licences, it was suggested that bidders should offer even more participation to BNOC and pay all appraisal and exploration costs - the suggestion which had ultimately been dropped from the fifth round.[78] This drew the predictable warning from UKOOA about the effect on field planning.[79] The introduction of more uncertainty in the sixth round was criticised especially as regarded the intentions of BNOC with regard to retail - a number of companies foresaw the state company becoming a major player in the downstream and for those who needed certainty over ultimate disposal of oil this was an unsettling time (Quinlan 1978, 337). Almost on cue, the situation was further confused by the adoption of the objectives of full state ownership of North Sea oil by Labour's Executive Committee, albeit that Cabinet Ministers were less enthusiastic.[80]

(d) Depletion policy That politics was aware of industry thinking about such uncertainties is nevertheless clear from the so-called Varley Assurances of 6 December 1974 which laid down certain guarantees about depletion policy.[81] The eventual expiry of these assurances in the early 1980s was an issue continually present in the thinking of industry management. The power conferred on the Secretary of State by the Petroleum and Submarine Pipelines Act 1975 to fix depletion rates was criticised by academic commentators who stressed the rationale shown in Figure 3.2 and questioned whether the public interest would be served by political intervention in this area of policy (Robinson and Morgan 1976). Equally, the point that depletion policy increased industry uncertainty was made.[82] The vast divergence of view on this question between industry and politics is seen in the writing of a Conservative Member of Parliament who put the political viewpoint as follows:

> [i]f a country has indigenous production or the prospect of it, the government must decide how it should be treated. Its development cannot

> simply be left to the commercial self interest of the companies but must be considered in the context of the overall national interest. The speed of development, the location of the refining capacity, and the availability of crude and products for export are all subjects on which the government should have the last word. (Tugendhat 1976, 253-255)

The conflict with the industry rationale could not be more stark or more comprehensive and again, as with the issue of taxation and participation in a more general sense, the question of depletion control was to linger on for a number of years, with the concomitant production of uncertainty for the industry. In late 1977 a joint TUC-Labour meeting saw the TUC calling for depletion controls[83] and in 1978 discussions began between the DEn and UKOOA on the subject.[84] During these latter negotiations, differences emerged as regards what was and what was not feasible. The government proposed a stepped approach to the approval of future developments, which was, of course, completely at odds with the industry's ideas of how field developments were assessed and operated.[85] There were also proposals to affect licences granted under earlier rounds. Ultimately, however, there was little movement on the issue before the 1979 general election.

Although not strictly an issue of depletion policy, the question of the treatment of associated gas from oilfields can be seen to be a related issue in terms of the intervention of government in the ability of an operator to decide production speed. At first, no provision was made in this regard but eventually the government began to take a tougher line on the flaring of associated gas. It ordered, for example, the shutdown of Brent B from June 1977 to the late summer of 1978 to allow the installation of gas reinjection plant one year ahead of what had previously been agreed.[86] While the government clearly had a legitimate interest in conserving gas, its decision to demand gas reinjection rather than flaring after the approval of the work programme - and after indeed production had started - resulted in serious delay which had a substantial impact on field economics: £57m in revenue postponed with all the significance this had for the industry in terms of the value of that money at the end of the field's life (Johnson 1979 (I), 51). It is worth noting, however, that in 1979, the DEn allowed the flaring of some 450-500cf/d of gas at the field in preference to cutting oil production following difficulties with the installation of the plant (Quinlan 1980, 16).

(e) Contractors and trade unions High on the agenda for some of the critics reviewed in the first chapter (especially Wright 1986) were the problems perceived to have been caused by the industry's reliance on

contractors and also the failure of the industry to encourage unionisation offshore (Carson 1981; Tombs 1990; Woolfson *et al.* 1996). It has already been suggested that to propose that the level of contracting should be reduced is perhaps rather naive when the matter is viewed as a response to complexity rather than as creating complexity and in view of the degree of restructuring it would entail. While the industry saw contracting as the only way to ensure that specialist services could be obtained economically, it is interesting to consider how it dealt with the contracting question in practice. Fundamentally, as is now familiar, of prime importance to the industry was the length of time between commencement of a project and the payback point and thus the prime consideration in contracting out work was whether or not a contractor could bring the project, or their section of it, in on time. As has been mentioned, the failure to appreciate adequately the magnitude of the problems about to be faced in the North Sea led to serious difficulties as late design changes were made and contractors delivered late.[87] Both had a knock-on and potentially exponential effect on project timing as other orders were held back and as annual weather windows were missed. It is significant that while industry management certainly stressed the importance of cost as regards the selection of contractors, again this took a secondary position in the final analysis to time (e.g. Holloway 1983, 47-49).

Once again, however, the question of contracting was somewhat complicated by the intervention of government in an attempt to ensure that UK companies were given a 'fair share' of the work on offer. To this end, a Memorandum of Understanding was signed by the DEn and the members of UKOOA on 3 November 1975.[88] In this document the government 'made it clear that UK industry should be given full and fair opportunity to compete' and the Members of UKOOA signified their full support for this policy.[89] The Members agreed to 'use goods and services of British origin...whenever they are competitive in regard to specification, service, delivery and price'.[90] So that the government could assess the implementation and effectiveness of this programme, the Members agreed in a Code of Practice annexed to the Memorandum to supply such information as the Offshore Supplies Office of the DEn might reasonably require. The situation was further complicated, however, in that if a factor other than price was to be used in the decision against a British company, the government was to be informed so as to allow time for tripartite meetings between government, unions and management (Benn 1990, 174). The interest of the government in such a move is obvious and despite industry agreement it is clear that a tension was set up by this initiative. In particular, the very problem of delay was seen by the industry as potentially being exacerbated by this requirement to offer work in the initial stages to UK companies who had no proven record in the offshore environment (Frihagen 1983a, 11-12). Far preferable was the existing system of closed invitations to tender intimated to so-called 'prequalified' contractors. In other words, operators had lists of contractors who had a proven record with regard to technical expertise, cost and, of course, ability to meet required deadlines. The prospect of opening up tender invitations to new and untried contractors was basically seen as firstly, imposing an actual delay while qualifications were checked and while a greater number of tenders were examined and secondly, as creating a potential for further delay as they had their first chance to prove themselves (Holloway 1983, 49ff).

Unfortunately, in some cases, including some in the period before the Memorandum was signed, the industry had fairly bad experiences with British contractors especially in the construction phase. For a start, '[d]espite nearly five years of North Sea gas, UK firms had little experience of platform construction' with much of the work for the southern North Sea being carried out in the Netherlands (Harvie 1995, 79). There were delays during the construction phase caused by faulty workmanship - in some cases work which had been passed onshore was judged inadequate once the platform was floated. Equally there were delays at this stage due to labour disputes and, to the embarrassment of the UK contracting sector, platforms which had been ordered abroad were completed on schedule whereas the local product was often late. In some cases orders were switched to non-British yards to avoid further delays (Johnson 1979 (I) 145). There is, however, probably an element of 'passing the buck' in some of the industry pronouncements at this time. While contracting and labour problems undoubtedly played a significant part, many of the difficulties had their origins in a failure to appreciate the scale of the problems in the first place - an issue which could only be solved at the level of project management.[91] Nevertheless, it appears that delays were compounded by contractor and labour issues. BP's first two Forties platforms, for example, were initially delayed by design changes but late subcontract deliveries and labour disputes meant that the 1973 weather window was missed.[92] Occidental blamed labour problems for their missing the 1974 weather window for Piper Alpha[93] and we can recall the pressures already facing that field in terms of its finance arrangements.[94] In addition, a government commissioned report identified labour disputes as one of the problems standing in the way of UK companies getting a good share of

North Sea orders.[95] It is hardly surprising then that a Shell-Expro spokesman mentions the question of labour relations as an explicit consideration when selecting a contractor (Holloway 1983, 56).

In this section in general we have seen how industry management concentrated on the timely technical completion of projects and thereafter their operation according to schedule to achieve payback in line with NPV calculations. The issue of occupational safety does not appear on their cognitive maps except perhaps as a side-effect of concern for technical integrity of equipment with a view to general project success. In the next section we will see how engineering demonstrates a similar 'blindness' to this issue. One way in which the occupational safety problem and its potential impact on major accidents could have been given a higher profile and perhaps thus figured more prominently in the thinking of the engineers and the industry as a whole would have been through better trade union representation - as Carson (1981), Tombs (1990) and Woolfson, Foster and Beck (1996) correctly point out. Now whereas the analysis of these commentators - and that of the trade unions until comparatively recently (e.g. OILC 1991) - sees a simple blind hostility in the industry attitude towards trade unions, what we have seen in this subsection may suggest a more complex reason. There is, for example, certainly no evidence to suggest that oil companies were hostile to trade unions in the early days of the search for hydrocarbons in the North Sea. At this time, indeed, certain oil companies were at the forefront in the development of new employment arrangements onshore, including collective bargaining to reach productivity agreements.[96]

The question, then, is why this attitude did not continue into the offshore environment. Carson (1981, 214-5) has conceded that workforce attitudes may have been part of the story but places greater emphasis on company hostility which manifested itself in open victimisation of workers who were active trade unionists.[97] However, the analysis of the industry reality construction in this section may hold the key. Basically, just at the time when the early North Sea operators were getting a first taste of the particular problems of the new environment with all the consequences this had for schedules, costs and finance arrangements, an added difficulty was the occurrence of industrial disputes at fabrication yards where first generation production platforms were being built. In some cases, as we have seen, these disputes contributed materially to delays in float-out and, because of the weather problems, produced costly knock-on effects in installation and ultimately in the start of production. At a more abstract level, the general labour situation in the UK at this time was extremely serious with the miners' strike ultimately bringing down the Conservative government of Edward Heath. The impact of this onshore situation on the oil industry was felt in its contribution to the shortage and consequent expense of steel as the first generation northern North Sea platforms were being built.[98] Equally, the issue of disputes *between* unions at that time in other industries created problems which the oil industry took note of (Johnson 1979 (I) 152).[99] The difficulties of the industry at this time were of course much more complex, but it would appear that thereafter trade unions were constructed in the industry management rationale as productive of delay and equally as one factor which it was possible with comparative ease to remove from the equation. The emphasis in the industry management system on continuous production makes the possibility of strike action something it is unable to countenance.

In conclusion, it has been suggested that the government failed to support the unions offshore at this time. It may be true that the 'government needed the oil to flow too urgently to contemplate any union complications' (Arnold 1978, 289) but it equally succeeded in creating in management thinking all manner of other complications and uncertainties, all of which were constructed as increasing economic risk and thus as reasons for the intensification of production and none of which, therefore, helped the cause of health and safety offshore.

3.5 The Essentials Confirmed

An autopoietic approach to safety in the early stages of development in the North Sea has, then, isolated first of all the communicative system of industry management and it has revealed some rather disturbing issues. Of greatest significance is the fact that occupational safety is simply not an issue which appears to any great extent. And worryingly, given the prescriptive regime which politics has set in motion, industry management understands such an approach as problematic, preferring self-regulation. The reasons for this are, however, relatively clear. Constructing its reality according to an economic code, industry management can only observe events in economic terms. And steering itself according to a programme of rapid production aimed at reducing economic risk - understood principally in terms of NPV - its range of responses to problems from whatever source and of whatever nature is fairly restricted.

The cognitive map for industry management by the late 1970s (Figure 3.6), therefore, retains very much the same appearance as the initial map (Figure 3.2). Significant changes are shown in italics.

Figure 3.6 Cognitive Map: Industry Management (First Decade, North Sea)

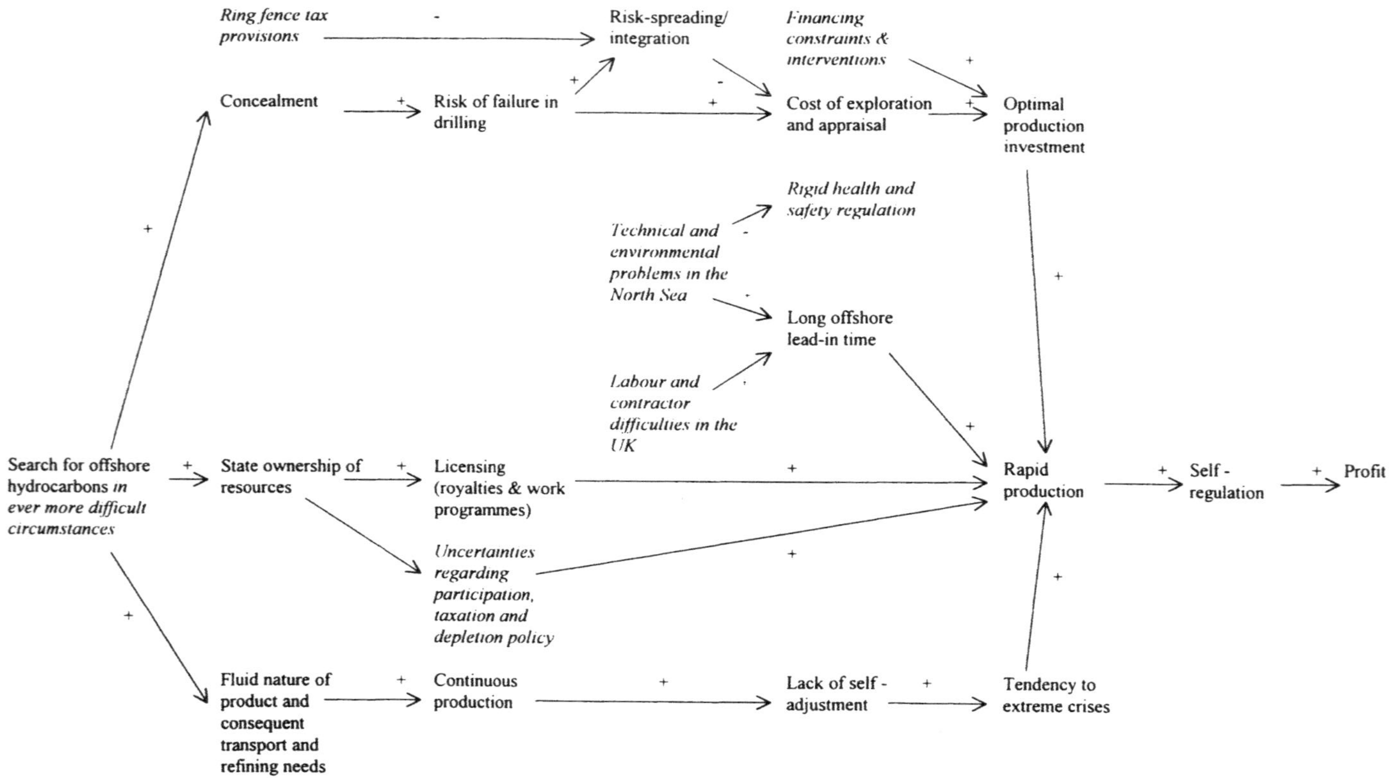

The influence of path-dependence is, therefore, clear. The reality construction with which the industry entered the North Sea is still very much in evidence and the issues it has faced have not so much resulted in any fundamental change as been constructed in its terms. Thus, the interventions (actual and proposed) by politics regarding taxation, participation and depletion policy were not observed as they were by politics, as attempts to maximise the nation's share of its natural resources, but rather as further pressures on field economics. Both interventions which were carried through and produced measurable effects on cash flow and the many uncertainties regarding other proposals served to increase economic risk according to the industry code and the way to minimise that was to intensify operations to ensure that production was achieved as quickly as possible. And, of course, once production was underway, the same logic balked at any interruption - the paradox being that such an interruption merely increased economic risk and thus a spiral of pressure on operations ensued. The additional pressures from financial backers only added to the picture of increased economic risk.

Similarly, when problems arose with contractors and labour disputes, this economic code only observed the effect on economic risk and only offered one programme in response. The same was true when engineering problems produced delays - and here we see one of the problems for safety regulation. The fact that early experience was beginning to feed back regarding installation performance in this new environment meant that design changes were having to be made. This militated against rigid prescriptive regulations and the supposed flexibility of the approach envisaged by politics is already in doubt when it is considered that changes to assumptions were already underway before the first set of regulations were issued. These are matters to be considered more fully in the next section, however. For the moment, the point to stress is that whatever the problems facing engineering, management could only see the impact in terms of increased economic risk. This inability to observe risk in other terms meant that its difference-minimising programme (intensified operations and rapid production) could operate to increase technological and operational risks without management being able to observe it.

In other words, industry management's world construction was essentially *deterministic*. New events and experiences in the new environment were constructed according to a model of the world it had brought with it from other oil provinces. Even if the industry continually repeated that it was at the cutting edge of technology in the deepest water and worst conditions yet encountered, it understood all of this as a simplistic scaled-up version of what it had done before and thus could not see the greater complexity it now had to deal with. In these circumstances, its construction of every outside event as a further increase in economic risk and as calling for further intensification of operations could hardly have been worse from the point of view of occupational health and safety. To get a better idea of what management could not observe, however, we need to consider the experience of engineering.

4 Engineering in the North Sea

4.1 Introduction

In the previous section, it was seen that difficulties emerged for industry management during the first decade in the North Sea as a result of construction and installation delays as regards equipment and technology. It was also seen that management understood these difficulties in terms of increased economic risk and tried to minimise it by intensifying operations. In this section, the same period will be considered from the perspective of engineering.

As was mentioned earlier, offshore production out of sight of land began in 1948 and by the mid-1960s the practice was well established, especially in the Gulf of Mexico. However, from the outset it was recognised that the North Sea, especially the northern part, represented a very different offshore environment.[100] Even a fairly cursory glance at the developing situation identifies the platforms (in terms of their scale and cost) as the novelty in an otherwise well-known picture of oil exploration and production and hence accounts for the amount of attention that was devoted to them both within and outside the industry.[101] Carson, of course, was at pains to play down the comparisons with 'space age' technology which were so easily taken up by the media and thus entered the public consciousness (1981, 47ff). Adopting the methodology developed in Chapter 2, however, and attempting to construct a cognitive map for the engineers responsible for the design and construction of the platforms, we can perhaps discover whether mere novelty is sufficient to account for this preponderance of attention.

The very earliest stages of the search for oil and gas in the North Sea had not been a test for technology as the initial seismic search techniques are actually easier (and cheaper) to carry out offshore and no innovative equipment was required.[102] The nascent UK offshore production industry concentrated around the newly-discovered gas fields of the southern North Sea. Environmental conditions there are less severe than in the central and northern areas but, as mentioned above, there was early recognition that there was a dearth of data on the precise situation and early experience of technical problems, delays and unforeseen difficulties at the drilling stage.[103] Despite this recognition, the industry proceeded on the assumption that technology proved in the Gulf of Mexico could be transferred directly to the North Sea.[104] This transfer and the problems that arose are often quoted in the history of the North Sea (e.g. Mackay 1974; Rye *et al.* 1974; Lowe & Odone 1980) but the deeper reasons are never explored outside technical papers. Furthermore, the legacy of this experience is probably too easily underestimated.

The environmental conditions in the Gulf of Mexico are in general much less severe than those encountered in the North Sea and the water in areas developed or in contemplation at that time is shallower. The area is at risk from hurricanes, however, with the result that offshore platforms must be designed and built to withstand significant forces over the normal loadings for short periods of time. This resulted in a method of engineering which was aimed at an estimation of the maximum expected wave and equally at an ever-better understanding of the effect of that maximum wave. Efforts were therefore concentrated on the collection of data and extrapolation from that to such concepts as the 25 year wave or the 100 year wave - that is, the maximum wave that could be expected to occur within that period. Usually it was accepted that it was not possible to design for the worst conditions but rather for severe conditions with a low chance of occurrence (Durning 1971). Engineers were certainly aware of the importance of design criteria with respect to function and the operation of equipment but the predominance of the question of strength and stability under adverse environmental conditions is marked (e.g. Freudenthal & Gaither 1969). The background to this emphasis was the severe losses suffered in the Gulf of Mexico in the mid 1960s to Hurricanes Camille, Hilda and Betsy (see McKay 1970, 663-4). More than twenty platforms were lost or rendered unusable and the problems were attributed to structural underdesign (Visser 1993, 347). The result was an alteration of the entire basis of the then prevailing 25 year wave approach (Tannahill 1971). The subsequent loss of the Sea Gem and several other rigs in the North Sea in the mid to late 1960s due to structural problems merely served to intensify the effort towards improved structural integrity.[105] Whatever the Sea Gem Inquiry thought about the need for strict regulation, as far as engineering was concerned the problem was a structural one which could only be addressed by its methods.

But, of course, purely 'scientific' questions such as this are not the only issues of concern to engineers. The 'well-engineered platform' has been described as 'one that will serve the intended purpose in a safe and efficient manner under the environmental conditions involved at minimum cost' (Carter *et al.* 1969, 444). Similarly, another engineer points to two guiding principles: suitability for a particular environment and economics (Brader 1970). There is, then, an inherent tension in the production of such (and indeed any) technology, a tension which is particularly interesting and problematic when viewed in terms of autopoiesis theory. Autopoiesis would see engineering, as the producer of technology, operating principally at the interface between the meaning systems of science and economics. And while engineering might dispute an autopoietic interpretation of its work in terms of the potential influence of the closure of these discourses, the actual location would not appear to be so controversial. In the words of one engineer:

> it is...engineering that makes a reality of the potential value of science...to marshal tools, resources [and] labour, and bring them into the service of man...Economics is particularly important in engineering because it provides the analytical mechanism for determining the relative participation of these three factors and the value of a new technology to society. (Sporn 1969, 8, 11)

The nature of this balancing act between science and economics is not universally viewed in such optimistic terms, especially by those who perceive a lost opportunity in technology and who believe that the balance always tips in favour of economics (e.g. Feenberg 1991). To consider the influence of these two rationalities from the point of view of autopoiesis, it is necessary to consider what is inherent in them, what it is about them that produces a distinct construction of the system and its environment. In the case of economics it is said that it operates on the basis of a binary code of 'to have/not to have' and in the foregoing discussion of oil industry management it was seen how this code operated and equally how it was operationalised in the context of a particular difference-minimising programme. In the case of science, autopoiesis suggests that this system operates on the basis of the binary code 'true/false' - it is the social system which, in a differentiated society, is the ultimate arbiter of questions of what is true. What is interesting, however, about this aspect of science are the different ways in which 'truth' is constructed both within and outside the system of science. Within science, certainly since Popper,[106] there is an understanding of truth as, at best, provisional. Any finding of science is, within the terms of science itself, immediately open to a finding that it is 'in fact' false and can be replaced with a new 'truth' which is itself as solid and as precarious as the foregoing 'truth'. The search for truth in science on any given subject is, therefore, inherently never-ending. On the other hand, when science is called to provide truths for other systems such as law or economics, the truth so produced is reconstructed by those systems as something more absolute than the internal construction of science. Thus, when law seeks scientific information on the appropriate level at which to set, for example, the maximum wave height which a platform must be designed and built to withstand, the figure which is put forward is constructed as absolute by law and as such capable of grounding the distinction legal/illegal in relation to any platform which the law is called upon to consider. Similarly for economics, at the point at which a field has been appraised and scientific information provided as to the profile of the reservoir, this is constructed by economics in absolute terms and forms the basis of the equipment requirements which are then given to engineers. Again, a point is reached when the required technology must be delivered and at that point the provisional truth of science becomes the absolute truth of economics or industry management.

To put this differently, it could be suggested that while the temporal horizons of law and economics are determinate, that of science is indeterminate and thus any situation which is decided on the basis of a legal or economic reconstruction of science carries with it an inherent risk that the provisional truth of science will be falsified not in the laboratory but in the context demanded of it by law or economics. Collingridge & Reeve (1986), following the work of, among others, Popper, characterise this as a threat to the 'essentials' of science in its interactions especially with economics. Firstly, its autonomy is threatened, and secondly, a low level of criticism associated with the low error cost of scientific conjectures disappears as the level of criticism is potentially high and the error cost potentially astronomical. Our methodology should enable us to consider this tension between science and economics in the development of technology for the North Sea and to discover whether viewing the situation in this way provides a different light on the question of the regulation of health and safety at work.

4.2 Conservative Determinism

The cognitive map at Figure 3.7 can be offered as a representation of engineering thinking at this early stage derived from the published papers in that field.

Basically, there is very static, deterministic approach to the design process. The major factors in the equation are the maximum life of the platform (the period for which it is designed to operate) and the maximum wave height that could be expected during that period, as there is an explicit assumption that overload is more likely to cause structural failure than fatigue (see Cannel & Stasmore 1980). The fact that different locations provide very different conditions in terms of water depth and the severity of expected waves means that platform design is not uniform but rather location-specific (McIntyre 1973). This factor plus the lack of sufficient historical data for the North Sea means that there is a degree of uncertainty. This uncertainty is dealt with by the application of engineering judgement and intuition to produce factors of safety in order that the design requirements of suitability and economic viability can be achieved and thus a well-engineered platform.

Despite the use of such terms as 'factors of safety', engineers were aware that beyond their judgement they were effectively meaningless (McIntyre 1973; Bea 1973). Equally, engineers were criticised because their deterministic methodology completely failed to take account of the effects of waves both larger and smaller than the design wave whilst their conservative response to uncertainty resulted potentially in over-design and hence in increased costs. Both confirming the magnitude of the problem and justifying the emphasis on structural safety in the world of engineering, the winter of 1972-73 saw the sinking of the Transocean 3, a rig only a few months old, and the disabling of the Transworld 61. The suggested solution even at this early stage by a small number of engineers was the use of probabilistic techniques aimed at assessing both reliability and the probability of failure (e.g. Bea 1973; Ingram & Dee 1973). There was, however, hostility at this time to such techniques because of their relative immaturity and because of their heavy reliance on historical data, leading to a perception among engineers that in the context of a dearth of such data they must inevitably produce different results for different people. A proponent of these methods described this conservative attitude as understandable if a scientific design solution was required but not where an engineering solution was wanted (Bea 1973).

Figure 3.7 Cognitive Map: Engineering (late 1960s - early 1970s)

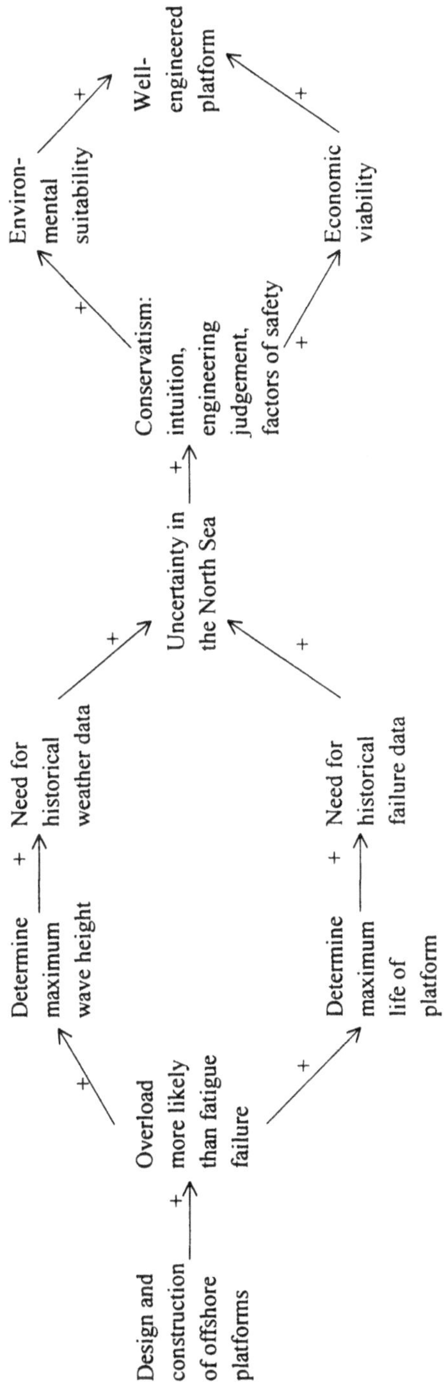

It can be suggested, then, that at this time the tension between the demands of science and the demands of economics was resolved in favour of the former as a programme of scientific conservatism dominated. That is, where there is doubt following the application of scientific methods, a wide margin for error is added in order to minimise risk. This conclusion is supported by the assertion that at this time available technology was actually far in advance of that being applied (Craven 1973). In other words, engineers were aware that they faced uncertainties but felt that they lacked any adequate means of assessing the degree of uncertainty. Whereas the scientific approach to such a problem would have been further research and collection of data in an ongoing process of refinement of the appropriate values to be fed into deterministic equations of structural integrity, the fact of economic imperatives, especially at this stage in terms of time as was seen very clearly in the preceding section, meant that final answers had to be produced. The response was to err on the side of caution without much idea of how much caution was being exercised. The impact on costs of such an approach is clear but equally, as was seen in the preceding section, the industry was quite prepared to accept cost increases if time was saved - especially in the wake of oil price rises after 1973 which modified the economics of developments then in contemplation.

Nevertheless, conservative though the approach of engineering may have been, it constructed risk in terms of technological factors as opposed to occupational ones and its inherent determinism was about to be profoundly shaken. Indeed, the prevailing situation was described as the 'design criterion muddle' (Bea 1973), with there being calls for industry and regulators to 'thoroughly define the parameters' (McIntyre 1973).

4.3 Pressures towards a Probabilistic Approach

The cause of the problems for the deterministic approach was a growing awareness that the effect of the use of lifetime and maximum wave height was that too many other variables were masked out, simply could not be observed. Indeed, at the extreme, the net effect of the deterministic approach was that gross failure could be 'discounted as a non-credible effect' (SREA 1989, 42). Deliberate though this choice had been, it was becoming clear that in the North Sea, *fatigue* played a much greater role than had been anticipated. Thus, the effect of the maximum wave was not as important as the cumulative effect of much smaller waves and the current (Hallam & Heaf 1978; Nolte 1978). The extent of this problem is seen clearly in the statement that 'engineering experts have confessed that they do not fully understand the dynamic forces that the North Sea puts on offshore platforms'.[107] Significant also is the fact that by this time a number of platforms were either already installed or in an advanced stage of design or construction. One platform where fatigue had arisen as a problem was Piper Alpha. Three years after installation, routine inspection revealed fatigue cracks and even after repair the possibility of future problems was acknowledged. Worryingly for the engineers, the original design analysis based on deterministic techniques revealed no part of the structure with a life less than the intended operating period of the platform (Green 1983). Concurrent with this realisation was industry concern about rapidly spiralling costs. Engineering was thus under considerable pressure - its rationale had been undermined by experience and this increased uncertainty coincided with demands for either lower costs or at least greater certainty of timely completion of projects. This cost issue was further complicated by the fact that while the industry wanted reduced overall costs, there was also pressure to reduce the costs of insurance premiums (Baird 1976). As early as 1968 there were complaints from the industry about the cost of insurance, complaints to which the insurers responded at this time by pointing to the loss of three rigs in quick succession, all of which were supposed to have been the 'last word' in rig design.[108] The difficulty for engineers operating to a programme of conservative determinism was that in order to reduce the risk of loss, which in turn was felt to be the best way to reduce insurance premiums, they appeared to have to incur greater overall costs. Conversely, attempting to reduce costs within a similar framework appeared to be possible only at the expense of increased risk and thus potentially higher insurance costs.[109]

In these circumstances, it is not surprising that a large number of engineering papers at this time took up the earlier theme of Bea (1973) and it is clear that hostility to probabilistic techniques began to disappear. Now they were hailed as the only sound way of achieving optimal design in terms of safety and cost (Schüeller & Choi 1977), as the only way of producing meaningful safety factors to deal with random error (Fjeld 1977) compared to the hidden safety factors of the deterministic approach which led to over-design (Planeix *et al.* 1979), as the only means of achieving consistent levels of safety (Pavia *et al.* 1977), as compared to the realisation that earlier designs had over-estimated waves by up to 50 or even 100% (Ramberg & Niedzwecki 1979). There was a clear admission that the reliability and integrity of platforms in the North Sea was based on more complex phenomena than had been previously realised or anticipated (Moses & Stahl 1978). Then, as if on cue, in the midst of this concern about fatigue, the Alexander L. Kielland was lost on 27 March 1980 with 123 lives. Carson, writing just as the Inquiry into the loss was concluding, pointed to human error in the welding (1981, 287-9). For engineering, however, with its cognitive map of reality recently reconstructed to show fatigue as an important factor, the proximate cause of this loss was indeed fatigue and its worst fears seemed confirmed (see Almar-Naess *et al.* 1982).

The change in attitude to probabilistic techniques, however, met with the same problem as Bea (1973) reported earlier, namely a lack of historical data (Tveit *et al.* 1980) and then a lack of agreement about which techniques were suitable (Nolte 1978; Rodrigues *et al.* 1980).[110] Difficulties were further compounded when doubts began to arise about the nature of the data on which fatigue calculations were being carried out - in particular there was a reliance on constant amplitude information which was said to be too far removed from in-service conditions (Holmes 1980). To make matters still worse, just as the realisation of the fatigue problem was dawning, it was discovered that platforms in deeper water were also affected by their own dynamic response to wave and current loadings rather than just the static force itself (Ansquer & Carton 1980; Cannel & Stasmore 1980).[111] One of the paradoxical findings at this time, however, was that the conservative approach which was so criticised in terms of cost increases had actually operated in many platforms to compensate for the lack of awareness of complex factors masked by deterministic design approaches (Holmes 1980; Ansquer & Carton 1980). This overdesign in turn ironically contributed to the 'lack' of failure data, which compounded the difficulties of applying more sensitive probabilistic design techniques (Tveit *et al.* 1980).

Beyond these complications, there was some initial awareness of the other factors which could contribute to accidents, including the human element. It was recognised that probabilistic techniques were the only ones capable of accommodating this factor and some moves were made in this direction but ultimately the uncertainty involved and the relative newness of modelling the contribution of the human factor led those engineers concerned to recommend that the reduction of risk lay in design and the addition of double safety features (see Haun *et al.* 1979; Tveit *et al.* 1980). Thus, the cognitive map for this period towards the end of the 1970s shown at Figure 3.8 reflects a different construction of the situation of technology in the North Sea. Gone is the deterministic certainty of the past about which features could be slotted into a platform strength equation, and coupled with this new awareness of complexity is the move into ever more

Figure 3.8 Cognitive Map: Engineering (late 1970s)

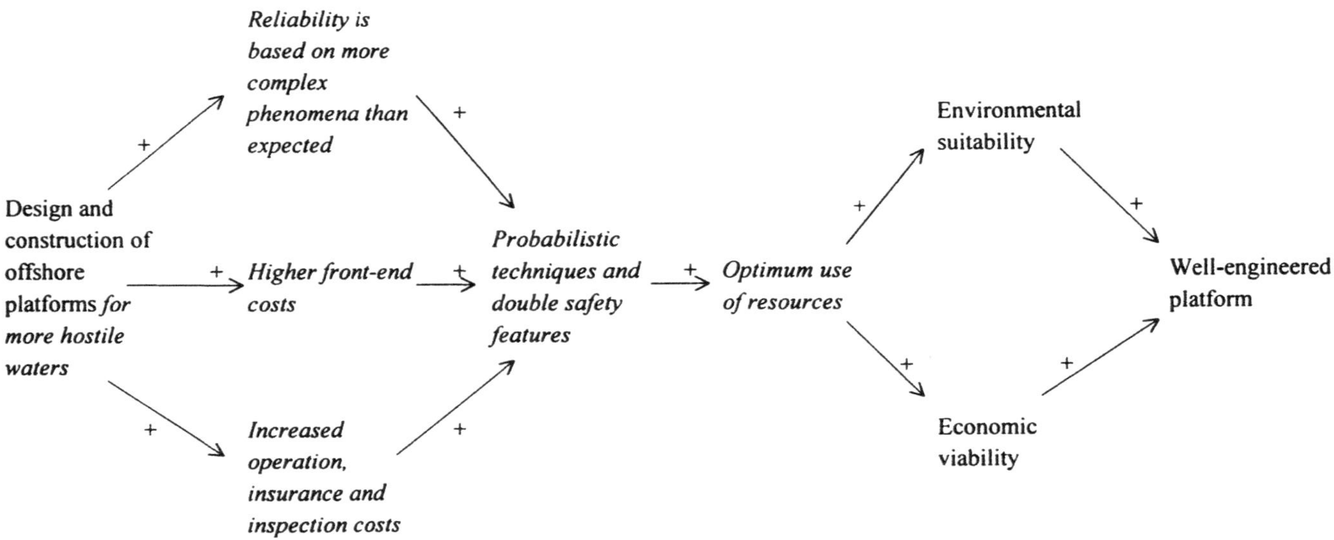

hostile waters and the continuing cost push. Gone also is the absolute faith in engineering judgement, and probabilistic techniques now rank alongside some continuing elements of conservatism.

In short, there was an increasing awareness of the complexity of the task in hand together with the need to deal with complex demands in terms of cost (both immediate and more distant in terms of operation and insurance) and of time. This level of complexity was beyond the capabilities of the conservative risk-minimisation programme and encouraged the adoption of a probabilisitic programme which could accommodate more factors. The intention was that such techniques would produce more 'rational' designs, which would be more responsive not only to the maximum wave force but also to fatigue and dynamic forces while at the same time reflecting a closer approximation of the factor of safety to the risk involved. In this way it was felt that the cost of the platform would be as low as possible consistent with safety. The fact that some elements of conservatism remained, however, demonstrates that the step towards the probabilistic programme was tentative.

It is noteworthy that whereas Carson (1981) and Wright (1986) pointed to the number of accidents resulting from failures of *occupational* safety, it is clear that these do not figure largely on the cognitive maps of engineering at any stage throughout this period compared to issues of *technological* safety. What this approach reveals, however, by concentrating on the reality construction of engineering, rather than imputing failures to it, is the degree of risk it was aware of in the realm of technological safety and the knowledge that problems here could result in catastrophic failure with the loss of entire platforms. There is, then, something of a systemic blindness to occupational health and safety but it is not the product of indifference or a lack of understanding but rather the rational product of a reality construction which saw the principal risks existing in a different order of magnitude at a different location.[112] In seeking to minimise technological risk, engineering simply could not observe occupational risk.

It is significant, however, that, in contrast to industry management at this time, engineering had begun to develop a rationale which was less deterministic and more open to the possibility of other risks. It was, nevertheless, in the very early stages and, as will be seen in the next chapter, the development was not to be smooth or unambiguous. It should also be noted that just as industry management felt itself subject to political interventions at odds with how it understood its task, so there were times when the decision on the appropriate technology for a field was taken out of the hands of engineering completely and decided according to political criteria.[113]

5 Developing and Implementing the Regulations

5.1 Introduction

In the previous two sections, the rationalities of industry management and of engineering during the first decade of North Sea development have been considered. With this in mind, it is possible to get some impression of the adequacy of the political construction of offshore health and safety at work. It will be recalled that politics saw the issue as amenable to a programme of detailed regulation to be developed progressively within the framework of an enabling statute. Given the fact that health and safety simply did not feature prominently on the cognitive map of industry management during this period, it would seem that intervention was definitely called for. However, experience with other regulatory interventions and such mention as was made about safety regulation suggests that intervention would be constructed according to the industry code and programme and thus be accepted only insofar as it was consistent with rapid production and the consequent minimisation of economic risk. Of course, given the difficulties in engineering which we are now aware of, both law's requirement for certainty about technical and operational requirements and management's requirement for the most appropriate technology for a given task appear very optimistic. With this background, what was the approach of the regulators during the first decade?

5.2 Adapting to Complexity

In this regard, we are fortunate to have an early insight into the regulators' operations (beyond the regulations they produced) in a paper presented by the DEn to the Offshore Technology Conference in 1975 (Street 1975).[114] At that time, the major set of regulations which was in force was that relating to Construction and Survey (which politics had been so anxious to see enacted) and the most important in preparation related to Occupational Safety and Health and to Emergency Equipment and Procedures. The DEn outlines how, with the drafting of the Construction and Survey regulations, the regulators learned at an early stage just how difficult was the process of preparing regulations for the offshore industry. For one thing, it was an industry which had managed for a long time without external regulation (see also Eri 1975) and which therefore remained to be convinced of the need for it. Additionally, there was a dearth of environmental data for the North Sea with which to inform the regulations. As a result, committees had to be set up to conduct and supervise research with a view to obtaining the relevant data. In the meantime a draft set of Construction and Survey regulations was circulated to both oil companies and to foreign governments. The response is described by the DEn as 'anguished'. Basically, there was concern that rigid interpretation of such rules would effectively strangle the industry. However, it seems that once both sides, industry and regulators, had met there was a realisation that they had a common interest in safety: the industry understood that regulators were not tied to an inflexible rulebook, while the regulators understood that the industry was concerned with safety as a priority. The DEn describes a 'mutual respect' developing. With continuing difficulties regarding the collection of definitive environmental data (an issue which has already been seen in the cognitive maps of engineering), the regulators realised that it was impossible to codify many issues in the regulations. As a result, the decision was taken to produce functional regulations which laid down only the broad principles which must be complied with. The technical detail would be filled in by guidance notes which could be amended easily in the light of experience in a way which even regulations could not.

At this point, the regulators operated on an assumption which would probably trouble legislators and lawyers alike. The point is made that the need for rapid adaptation to experience in the form of guidance notes means that recourse cannot be had to Parliament. While the recourse to Parliament envisaged by the 1971 Act was in any event minimal given that the regulations were to be subject to negative resolution procedure, the very fact that the detail was to be at the level of guidance notes meant that failure to comply with such a requirement would not constitute a breach of the law unless it could be shown that the failure to comply also contravened the broad principle laid down in the regulation. Furthermore, even this statement may be putting the position of the law too strongly in that the DEn describes the guidance notes as merely 'indicating' standards which, if complied with, would be acceptable to the regulators. There is perhaps some evidence here of a somewhat more 'benevolent' or 'advisory' enforcement than politics had envisaged. Dubious though this might have appeared to legislators or to lawyers, it can be seen to be a step which was based on the same sort of rationale which motivated the legislators. In other words, in the same way that the legislators were unable to provide the degree of detail at the level of the 1971 Act, so the regulators, faced with a rapidly developing technological industry and ever greater refinement of models based on the ongoing collection of environmental data, found that even the relatively broad confines of negative resolution procedure were not suited to the speed and flexibility which they required. Their response was to develop detail at the yet lower level of guidance notes.

A further point of concern no doubt to legislators and to lawyers might be the fact that, as a result of the concern which the industry had felt in the face of the draft Construction and Survey regulations circulated by the DEn, it was the industry itself which produced a new draft which formed the basis of the regulations ultimately brought into force. The DEn at this point is keen to stress that it was not their intention to impose arbitrary regulations on the industry but rather to develop them in consultation. There then follows a very revealing statement by the regulators, namely that the

> sole justification for the regulations is the assistance of the men working in the North Sea and the provision for them of a reasonably safe working environment in which to conduct their work providing the energy necessary to sustain our civilisation. (Street 1975)

This is no doubt expressed in rather high-flown terms, but the 'sole justification' is very evidently composed of the tension between safety and production which critics in Parliament and outside were later to express concern about for as long as the DEn remained in control of the safety regulators. The cognitive map at Figure 3.9 is a graphic representation of this rationale in the early days of the formulation and implementation of the regulations envisaged by the legislators at the time of the passing of the 1971 Act.

Support for this view of the best way to proceed came from the Certifying Authorities (see e.g. C. A. Bainbridge 1975; Eri 1975). They stressed that the design of installations in the North Sea is so dependent on local conditions that each is unique. As a result, rigid rules gave way to 'generalised acceptable standards' and, equally, the certification procedure was in a continual stage of development in order to take account of new technology and experience (C. A. Bainbridge 1975). A positive attitude from the industry could only be expected if the regulations were not unnecessarily stringent but were rather as flexible as possible. The fact that most regulations designed to ensure safe and clean operations also led to

Figure 3.9 Cognitive Map: Regulators (mid 1970s)

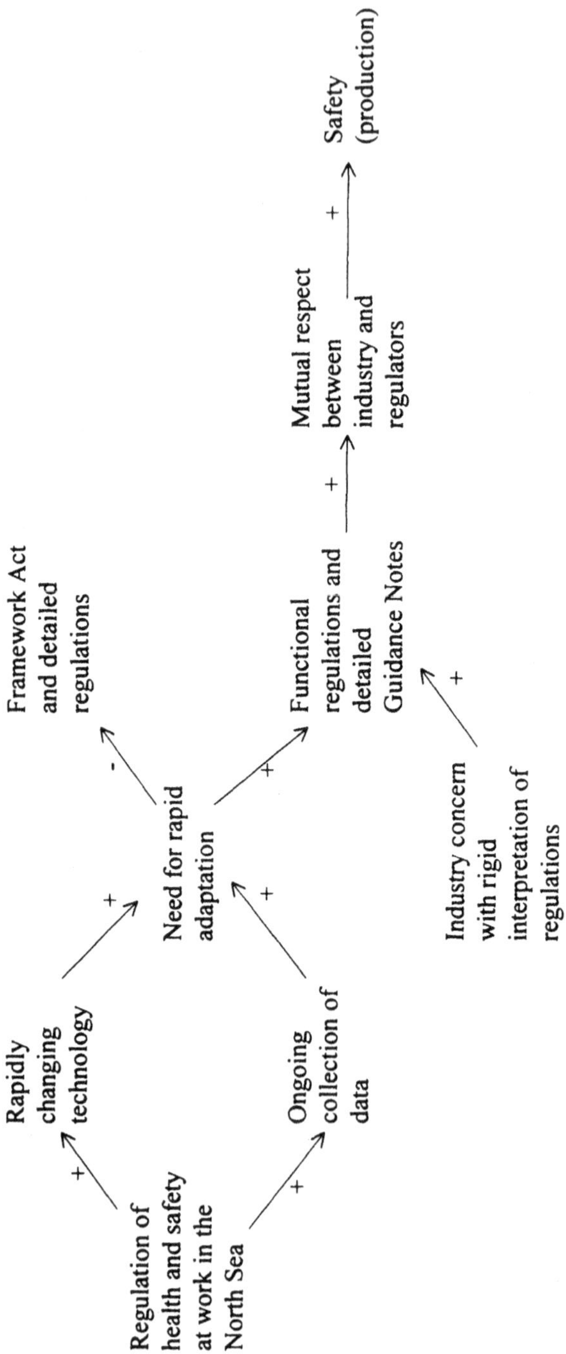

steady production meant that there was no essential conflict between regulator and industry (Eri 1975).

But the programme of legal instrumentalism envisaged by the legislators has very clearly become something quite different in the hands of the regulators. Faced with technical problems in the form of a lack of data and rapidly developing technology, the regulators are also trying to minimise the difference between two safety situations (the current and an improved one) but the programme of legal instrumentalism no longer appears appropriate. Instead, lacking the cognitive resources to develop regulations with any degree of certainty and in any event unable to keep pace with developments, they adopt a programme of fostering the respect of the industry as a means of ensuring that the requirements of guidance notes are complied with.

Given the level of confusion in engineering and the intense pressure for production in management thinking, this flexible approach to regulation becomes much more understandable. The 'technological negotiability' of the detailed application of legal rules criticised by Carson (1981, 179) appears now not as a sign of regulatory weakness but rather as a pragmatic response to developments in engineering. The downside, however, is undoubtedly the fact that just as engineering concentrated on technical factors as a result of ongoing doubts about the adequacy of models, and just as management constructed technology as an absolute in its field programmes and thus put ever greater pressure on it and its operators, so it is evident that the regulators were also preoccupied with technical issues as opposed to occupational health and safety. While this is a point noted and criticised by Carson, it is possible to see that this regulatory approach may have been a much more rational risk-reduction programme than otherwise acknowledged. If flexibility is an indication that regulation was aware of the rapid reassessments taking place in engineering and of the pressures produced by management on technology, then it is possible that a concentration on technical integrity was an approach which indicated an awareness of the location of the greatest magnitude of risk.

While the Sea Gem inquiry had specifically referred to the American regulatory system as a model of what they were recommending for the UK, the view of the developing UK regime from the other side of the Atlantic - of both industry and regulators - was not positive. Rather the system was seen as having the potential for delay and rigidity which was not suited to the offshore industry (Brannon 1977; Gerwick 1977; Lee 1977). It seems clear that the regulators in practice were equally well aware of this potential and saw the difficulty of trying to apply a rigid regulatory regime to the industry - not just from the point of view of costly delay but equally from the point of view of producing regulations of sufficient detail to implement political and legal requirements which would have any significance in the regulated area where what counted as the state of the art one day was regarded as deficient the next.

In conclusion, it is possible to agree with Carson insofar as it is clear that the regulators operated to a programme aimed at minimising technical risk. And albeit that this also suited the goal of continuous production, it is now possible to see that this, whether deliberately or otherwise, took account of a rapidly developing and in retrospect highly disturbing situation in engineering. Nevertheless, whatever the extent of this realisation, whatever the extent of a flexibility aimed at coping with change and whatever the extent of a recognition of significant technical risk, the regulatory approach remained prescriptive. Even if there was a problem of enforcing the requirements of guidance notes, the expressed aim of the regulators was still to prescribe all aspects of safety. In this regard, the regulators were as deterministic as politics, as industry management and as certain aspects of engineering, and as systemically blind to other dimensions of risk. Thus, the regulators operated on the basis that ultimately the code legal/illegal could be applied to all aspects of the industry albeit that their exact approach envisaged an enforcement procedure some way short of the full rigour available by law.

6 Conclusions

In this chapter, the methodology developed in Chapter 2 has been used to examine the rationalities in play in different sectors of the regulated area of the North Sea offshore oil and gas industry from its inception until the late 1970s. An attempt has been made to demonstrate how the issue of health and safety at work offshore was observed or constructed (or not) in politics, industry management, engineering and by the regulators. Of course, in the space of relatively few pages such a demonstration must be a simplification, but the aim of the methodology relying on an autopoietic view of the regulated area was to bring out not every detail but rather the significant features, the codes which formed the reality constructions and the difference-minimisation programmes by which the systems steered themselves.

Perhaps the most significant finding of this second-order observation emerged from the examination of the reality construction of engineering throughout this period. It was shown that a considerable degree of uncertainty was effectively masked by the initial approach to the design and construction of the technology to be deployed in the North Sea. As a result, a number of serious problems emerged as experience was gained which revealed that the behaviour of installations was much more complex than had been assumed. The way in which engineering had initially sought to minimise risk, however, a programme of scientific conservatism, in some cases served to accommodate the emergent problems. Nevertheless, the scale of the difficulties meant that platforms under construction were often redesigned at a late stage and hence delays arose which put further pressure on the economics of projects. The realisation by engineering that previous deterministic techniques had been responsible for masking complexity led to an acceptance that probabilistic techniques were better able to accommodate both this complexity and equally the need for cost control, which was a major concern by 1978. The fact that probabilistic techniques co-existed with continuing elements of conservatism demonstrates, however, that this was by no means a total shift. Nevertheless, the fact remained that in engineering at a comparatively early stage, the blind spot of the initial world construction had been revealed and considered and from that revelation there could really be no way back in the longer term. What this examination also revealed was the non-existent or at best very minimal appearance of questions of occupational safety on the cognitive maps of engineering. While there is, then, evidence of an institutionalised blindness to the ongoing toll of accidents of a more mundane nature, it can now be seen that this blindness does not arise out of indifference but rather out of the recognition by engineers of the location of risk of a higher order of magnitude at the level of the structural integrity of entire installations. The scale of this problem is perhaps also evident from the fact that it preoccupied engineering to the exclusion of practically any consideration of regulation.

The world construction of industry management also threw a new light on the situation. Again, little recognition of occupational health and safety issues was evident from the cognitive maps produced. Equally, however, a different picture emerged from the typical allegation of an almost mindless drive for profits. Instead, the study revealed how the industry operated according to a clear logic related to its identification of certain features of the product it was concerned with as fixed points determining a certain way of organising and of operating. In particular, the programme of intensified operations and rapid production was a 'given' which the rationale of the industry rendered practically sacrosanct - it was the programme by which the industry sought to minimise economic risk. The problems encountered in engineering, with labour disputes, with the interventions of financial backers, all effectively increased economic risk in the reality construction of the industry. Equally, it was shown how a whole range of political interventions in the industry were also reconstructed as increasing economic risk. The only way the industry could respond in terms of its construction of reality was by means of its programme for risk-minimisation: rapid production.

The situation which the regulators confronted, then, was extremely complex. The engineers upon whom they relied to a great extent for information were in a state of some confusion about the task in hand and were under considerable pressures from customers variously as regards time and cost. The industry itself constructed outside intervention in a very negative way and was clearly more influenced by concerns about taxation, depletion controls and state participation than it was by health and safety regulation. The regulators had been handed a framework statute by legislators who expected that negative resolution procedure would be sufficiently flexible to respond to a complex and fast-changing industry with regulations but quickly found that they needed to be able to adapt more quickly and at a higher degree of complexity than the legislative and regulatory scheme allowed. Significantly, however, it seems that for all their flexibility, they continued to operate on the basis of a fundamentally prescriptive model. Flexibility was only required to the extent that it enabled solutions to be prescribed at the level of guidance notes. And even if the programme of legal instrumentalism envisaged by politics became the less easily definable 'fostering of mutual respect', the regulators still in principle believed that it was possible to tell the industry what to do and how to do it.

In short, it can be seen from the cognitive maps of the various sectors that the determinism of engineering and of industry managers was a significant factor in producing an industry which operated in such a way that *occupational* risk was increased while this risk remained masked from view by steering programmes aimed at the minimisation of *technological* and *economic* risk respectively. While the industry's own construction of the world around it served in its own terms to 'confirm' the map and vindicate the drive for rapid production, it can be seen that this construction of reality served equally to make this response inevitable. With only one way of reducing economic risk, any outside intervention or event which ran counter to a pre-determined projection for an oil or gas field could effectively only be responded to by improvements in the speed of production. The difficulty is, of course, that this very determinism makes it ever more likely that occupational safety problems will arise which may in turn become so serious that they impact on operations, thus compounding the problem. The same form of blindness to risk applied also to those rationalities which produced the interventions which troubled management so much. Finance and politics equally adopted programmes which were aimed at the minimisation of economic risk without being able to see the possible concomitant increase in technical, operational or occupational risk - even if the long-term impact of the realisation of these risks might equally be economic loss.

It can of course be suggested that the development of the North Sea during the 1960s and 1970s followed a familiar pattern of the host nation acting initially to attract investment and once resources had been proved and were under development getting tougher in order to extract a larger proportion of the benefits for itself (Daintith & Gault 1979, 64). With this in mind, it could be argued that the industry was disingenuous in being surprised by the actions of the UK government. It would have to be said to the contrary, however, that nowhere else had the industry encountered quite the degree of attempted intervention or of political uncertainty that it did on the UK continental shelf. It was even said that the developments in the North Sea had 'given a substantial impetus to dirigiste thinking within Europe' (L. Turner 1975, 107).

Equally, the engineering determinism produced technology which in some cases required remedial work either at a late stage of design or construction or once *in situ* to accommodate new problems which were masked by original assumptions. In the context of the management risk-minimisation programme, these problems and consequent delays could again only be dealt with by intensifying operations to increase the speed of production.

In other words, neither industry management nor engineering was well set up to deal with the complexity of the situation they were entering in the North Sea and the masking effects of deterministic rationalities merely served to increase the risk that the assumptions of such world constructions would be found wanting. With only limited responses available in terms of these rationalities, the possibility of vicious circles increased. In the case of engineering the response was a hesitant move towards probabilistic methods of modelling complexity while industry management stuck steadfastly to the only risk-minimisation programme it knew. In the case of management, existing models of project management and technical operations were applied to the new environment with little appreciation of the complexity confronted and significantly little ability to incorporate and model uncertainty beyond basic techniques of scaling up and ultimately of trying to move faster. In both cases, and especially that of management, the influence of the path-dependency of the systems is evident - constructing reality in the North Sea on the basis of codes and programmes developed particularly in the Gulf of Mexico.

What this chapter has also shown is the importance of the wider picture of the offshore industry and its impact on health and safety. It is not enough to look at the question of health and safety in terms simply of a set of given regulations which are then considered in terms of whether they are being obeyed or not. Not only is the construction of the regulatory process important but equally the rationales - the codes and programmes - upon which the regulated area operates. While Carson, for example, has provided such a linkage between occupational health and safety and the broader political and economic picture, he nevertheless ultimately saw the solutions to the problems of regulating health and safety in a tougher application of rules and in the removal of responsibility from the DEn. What the methodology and the theorctical background employed here reveal is that, far from having to restrict our attention to political or legal interventions with direct application to health and safety, we must also look at the way in which the industry as a whole is treated by politics and law. It has been seen that possibly of far greater importance during the period studied in this chapter in terms of the way in which the industry operated was its response to interventions which were not in any way concerned with health and safety matters. These issues appear on the cognitive maps of the industry in a way which interventions regarding health and safety do not. As a consequence, the *absence* of these issues from the cognitive map of the regulators becomes significant - indicative of their inability to observe these problems. Indeed, in such circumstances, a programme of fostering mutual respect appears to hold particular risks. But just as the regulators' self-steering programme manifests these shortcomings, so this approach has also revealed that the rationalities in force in industry management, in engineering as well as in politics were so oriented as to mask complexity and as to prevent an adequate response to it. These issues present more serious problems for law than can be easily addressed by the standard legal sociological recommendations. In the next chapter, the succeeding period will be considered to see how these issues developed.

Notes

1 See Chapter 1, Section 2.

2 Ministry of Power, 1965 *Fuel Policy* (Cmnd. 2798) London: HMSO para. 36.

3 Hansard HC (Debs) 28 January 1964 col. 218.

4 Hansard HC (Debs) 7 April 1964 col. 897. See also Harvie (1995, 85).

5 The other factors were as follows:
(i) The requirement that an applicant should be incorporated in the United Kingdom.
(ii) The extent to which British oil companies receive equitable treatment in the country of any foreign owned applicants.
(iii) The programme of work, ability and resources of the applicant.
(iv) The applicant's past contributions to the development of resources on the British Continental Shelf and in the British fuel economy generally.
(See Corti 1983, 59-61)

6 *PPS* 1965, 313.

7 Public Accounts Committee *North Sea Oil and Gas* (1972-73) HC 122.

8 *Ibid.* para. 97.

9 Chapter 1, Section 1.2

10 Earl Ferrers Hansard HL (Debs) 18 Feb. 1971, cols. 741-746; Hon. Nicholas Ridley (Under Secretary of State for Trade and Industry) Hansard HC (Debs) 28 April 1971, cols. 645-649.

11 Hansard HC (Debs) 16 January 1974 cols. 669-696.

12 *ibid.* col. 691.

13 *ibid.* col. 685.

14 *Essentials of Petroleum* was reissued in 1968 bound together with an update entitled *Essentials Revisited 1968*. I have used the reissued version of *Essentials of Petroleum* but for clarity will refer to it in the text as Frankel (1946) and to the updated work as Frankel (1968).

15 For an impression of Frankel's importance to the oil industry, see Skeet (ed.) (1989).

16 Although Frankel concentrates on crude oil, much of his analysis is applicable also to natural gas, the product with which the earliest years of the UK's offshore history were primarily concerned.

17 For example, BP, agreeing the first contract for the supply of natural gas from the West Sole field to the state-owned Gas Council in 1966, stressed that economic principles must be right, that this success had to pay for a number of failures; *Petroleum Press Service* (*PPS*) 1966, 63. Perhaps the most dramatic example of expensive failure in the North Sea has been Shell-Esso's bid of £21m for block 211/21 which ultimately yielded nothing (Harvie 1995, 87).

18 Even in 1966 rig hire costs were in the region of $5,000-$10,000 per day plus support costs of $2,000-$3,000 per day and mobilisation/demobilisation costs of up to $2m depending on the distance the rig had to be brought and returned. The cost of drilling a well was in the region of $1.5m-$3m; *PPS* 1966, 58. By the late 1960s the impact of weather conditions on drilling schedules was becoming apparent. For example, one operator reported that downtime for a drilling barge averaged 52% for the year, never falling below 15.7% even in mid-summer and peaking at 87% in March; *PPS* 1969, 134. By the early 1970s drilling costs for the northern North Sea were quoted at £11,000 per day plus £9,000 per day in support costs with the price

for a single well falling in the region of £0.5m-£2m; *PPS* 1972, 409. Throughout the book, monetary values are quoted in pounds sterling and in dollars as reported at the time. No attempt has been made to convert values or to adjust them to a fixed date. Rather, the values are offered solely to give an impression of the magnitude of costs involved.

19 It was announced in 1977 that the Argyll field, for example, was expected to run dry two years earlier than previously anticipated due to water flooding. Estimated recoverable reserves were reduced by around one-third from 35m barrels to 22m; *Petroleum Economist* (*PE*) 1977, 371. The field was eventually shut down in 1992; *PE* April 1993. Further, in the period 1980-1981, Chevron reduced the estimate for Ninian from 1,200m to 1,000-1,100m barrels while Conoco indicated that reserves at Murchison initially estimated of 350-400m barrels now appeared to be at the lower end of that assessment. The converse could also happen - at the same time BP revised its estimate for Forties upwards from 1,800 to 2,000m barrels (Quinlan 1981, 248).

20 For an example of the dramatically different effects of using different discount rates on production policy see the rather bad-tempered exchange between Odell & Rosing (1977) and W. Jones (1977).

21 It is ironic that the exact legal status of the state's interest in the mineral resources of the UK continental shelf - the basis upon which the whole regulatory structure is built - has been the subject of some debate. The arguments are reviewed by Cameron (1983, 48-9) who goes on to make the cogent point that the legal debate is not really an important matter because '[t]here is, after all, sufficient clarity about some of the rights [the state] "has" for it to establish a licensing regime'. Whatever lawyers have made of the issue, on this basis the companies have regarded the matter as closed.

22 Petroleum (Production) Regulations 1966 (SI 1966, No. 898); Petroleum (Production) Regulations 1976 (SI 1976, No. 1129); Petroleum (Production) Regulations 1982 (SI 1982, No. 1000). See now Petroleum (Production) (Seaward Areas) Regulations 1988 as amended by the Petroleum (Production) (Seaward Areas) Amendment Regulations 1990, 1992, 1995 and 1996.

23 In the case of state-owned minerals (as in the UK) there will of course come a point, especially after self-sufficiency has been achieved, when there may be an interest in slowing production through the imposition of depletion controls to sustain the period of self-sufficiency for as long as possible. Frankel's model as regards this issue, however, holds good certainly up to this point. As will be seen later (Section 3.4(iv)) the *possibility* of depletion controls if left undefined can produce an impetus towards faster production while their later imposition can interfere with field projections.

24 Again, the main points of the analysis which follows hold good for natural gas.

25 As was mentioned above, Frankel was writing before the development of the industry offshore but his point about the need for continuous production and the negative effects of interruptions can be applied to the use of tankers to remove oil from an offshore production facility. If weather conditions are sufficiently bad as to prevent tanker loading then eventually it is possible that field storage facilities may be filled and production must be shut down until removal can be achieved. For example, production from such fields in the North Sea was badly affected by adverse weather in 1977; *PE* 1977, 89. In addition, even where field economics indicate tanker removal, an operator may be required to install a pipeline if, for example,

regulators feel that the pollution risk is thereby reduced. This was the case for the Beatrice field lying comparatively close to the Moray Firth coast; see *PE* 1978, 32 and Hay *et al.* (1982).

26 The situation of the industry in this conclusion should be clear from the foregoing discussion. To clarify the situation of the consumer we might take the example of the oil-fired power station. Its production of electricity depends upon the demand from consumers of electricity - a demand which might be assumed to remain relatively stable over a reasonably broad range of prices. If oil prices are low, the production of electricity is unlikely to increase and the power station will only have limited storage capacity with which to take advantage of the low price. If prices are high, production is unlikely to fall and it cannot risk running stocks down too far in the hope of an eventual price fall for fear of being caught short. A long period of high or low prices might persuade governments to take strategic decisions respectively to add oil-fired power stations to the production grid or to invest in alternatives hence affecting demand, and similarly, it might persuade consumers of electricity to alter, for example, forms of cooking and heating, but these are not decisions which can be taken in response to every price shift (see also Tucker 1987; Ellis Jones 1988, 304).

27 As an example of the great importance of this factor in the context of the scale of the industry, Wingate & Taylor (1980) reported that, at that time, lost production at peak rates deferred revenue of approximately $200,000 per hour until later in the life of an oil field.

28 Indeed, it has been said of the oil industry that 'in a dynamic competitive internationally volatile activity, the ability to make major shifts in exploration and production strategy on short notice is...an economic necessity' (Craven 1973, 943).

29 It is clear that some of what has been said above applies only to the major multinational oil companies - for example, the development of vertical integration. Further, it has been said that it is impossible to generalise about the behaviour of players in the industry, even between different majors let alone between majors and independents (Park 1979, 72-3). However, on the one hand, the importance of the majors in the North Sea is significant and, on the other, the 'essentials' can be seen to have a direct relevance to all players in the industry at whatever level. Equally, the point was made in Chapter 2 that an autopoietic approach stresses the futility of trying to obtain and deploy ever greater detail and instead concentrates on structural issues.

30 Chapter 1, Section 3.1.

31 Based on Banks (1980, 52).

32 See *PPS* 1965, 404; *PPS* 1971, 283.

33 One manager's admission to me that during this period he had experience of an OIM having to be forcibly talked out of pushing a broken-down helicopter overboard from an installation rather than holding up operations for one day while it was repaired may indicate the likely approach in many cases.

34 As examples of delayed installation during the initial phase of work in the northern North Sea we can consider the first two Forties platforms, scheduled to be in place in the summer of 1973 but installed only a year later; the Piper platform due in place in June 1974 but installed only during the summer of 1975; and the first Brent platform due in place in July 1974 but installed only in the summer of 1976.

Furthermore, as evidence that installation was much more difficult than had been anticipated we have the total loss of one of the platforms intended for the Frigg field, which sank in the wrong place and could not be refloated (see Hamilton 1978, 71-2). A further list of development delays is provided by Castle (1985).

35 *PE* 1974, 230.

36 *PE* 1976, 457 citing the annual report by Wood Mackenzie.

37 *PE* 1977, 457.

38 *PE* 1974, 446 quoting a paper 'Economics of North Sea Ventures' by A. Hols of Shell given at the Stavanger North Sea Conference, September 1974.

39 For example, Shell and Exxon self-financed the Brent field and their other North Sea ventures at a cost of some $8 billion up to 1978 (see Symonds 1978).

40 See the Appendix for a graph of oil prices.

41 The opposing views are well and concisely summarised in the public exchange between Lord Balogh - an adviser to the previous Labour government - and Frank McFadzean - the then chairman-designate of Shell Transport - over whether oil companies were making exorbitant profits in the North Sea (*Sunday Times* 13 February 1972 'The Scandal of the Great North Sea Giveaway' and 27 February 1972 'Has Lord Balogh Mistaken the Hole for the Doughnut?'). Lord Balogh accused the industry *inter alia* of downplaying the amount of reserves, an issue conversely described by McFadzean as conservatism in the face of uncertainty. Allegations of excess profits by Balogh were described by McFadzean as having been based on one company which had struck oil early and in response he repeated the familiar argument that the failures must be paid for by the successes. See also, of course, the Public Accounts Committee report *North Sea Oil and Gas* (1972-73) HC 122.

42 This, of course, is the average figure. As examples of individual gearing figures by the end of 1977, BP's stood at 42%, Shell's at 31% and Exxon's at 21% (Johnson 1979 (II) 53).

43 At the outset in 1972, Forties had a projected cost of £300m and was the largest single project ever undertaken by BP. Eventually it was financed by the world's largest ever bank loan at that time: £360m to be repaid with interest over a five year period after the start of production. In the event of unforeseen delays, repayment could be postponed for three years until the end of 1982. By the following year delays in construction caused by design changes, late delivery by subcontractors and labour disputes had forced BP to postpone until spring 1974 the installation of two platforms - previously due for completion in late summer 1973. Estimated costs thereafter spiralled to £630m in 1974, £745m in 1975, £1 billion in 1978 and £1.3 billion in 1979; *PPS* 1972, 121; *PE* 1974, 415; 1975, 451; 1979, 146; (Quinlan 1978).

44 Lord Kearton, Chairman of BNOC, in (1977-78) HC 198 iii s 202 - quoted in Johnson (1979 (II) 49-50).

45 See Harvie (1995, 107-110) on the relative unwillingness of London-based banks to get involved in the North Sea as compared with their Edinburgh-based counterparts.

46 There were also indications that the high cost of drilling appraisal wells was leading companies to commit resources to field development on the basis of much less information than ever before; see *PE* 1975, 301 and also Hamilton (1978, 69).

47 See Section 2.4(ii) below.

48 For example, Tricentrol issued a warning in 1974 that a lack of clear government policy was delaying the development of the North Sea. They had been told by banks that receiving finance for their share of the Thistle field was dependent on this issue. Shortly thereafter it was announced that the government was guaranteeing loans of up to £38.8m for Tricentrol to pay for its 8.4% share in developing this field. This was followed by announcements that the government was providing interim guarantees of £3m and £7m to expire in mid 1976. In return the company conceded a 51% government participation in its holding and agreed to pay an additional royalty of 5% either in cash or oil. A similar arrangement was concluded with Ranger Oil where the government guaranteed a $20m advance for its development of the Ninian field in return for 51% participation. Such guarantees were made under s.42 of the Petroleum and Submarine Pipelines Act 1975; *PE* 1974, 252; *PE* 1975, 232; *PE* 1975, 272; 352.

49 The step-by-step approach was proposed at the Spring 1974 meeting of the Society of Petroleum Engineers in Amsterdam by engineers from Shell; *PE* 1974, 301.

50 For the UKOOA view see *PE* 1978, 72. See also Hamilton (1978, 69).

51 See *PE* 1974, 364.

52 See also *PE* 1974, 415.

53 For example, a spokesman for the Bank of Scotland at the Offshore Scotland conference in 1975 expressed extreme pessimism in this regard: see *PE* 1975, 364.

54 *PPS* 1965, 164. Finance Act 1965 ss46ff.

55 Public Accounts Committee *North Sea Oil and Gas* (1972-73) HC 122.

56 Hansard HC (Debs) Vol. 852 6 March 1973 cols. 262-265 (Anthony Barber).

57 Hansard HC (Debs) Vol. 871 26 March 1974 col. 320 (Denis Healey).

58 *PE* 1974, 415; see also Brown (1975, 115, 123).

59 The Bill was greatly amended during its passage through Parliament (Daintith & Gault 1979, 62). For the industry view see *PE* 1975, 98, 163.

60 As an example of the widely differing costs per barrel across North Sea oilfields, Professor Colin Robinson published figures in late 1979 which showed costs for the cheapest field (Dunlin) approximately one third of those for the most expensive (Magnus); quoted in *PE* 1980, 18.

61 See Finance Act 1976, s130; Finance Act 1977, s54.

62 For example, the announcement of an intention in 1977 to increase the PRT rate from 45% to 60%, to reduce allowances from 75% to 35% and to cut tax-free oil from 1 million long tons to 500,000 tonnes (eventually enacted in the Finance (No. 2) Act 1979, ss. 18ff) was assessed by Robinson & Rowland (1978). They discovered that profitability was reduced and government take increased - in line with intentions - but the size of the changes was 'highly variable', with the greatest effect on the middle range of profitable fields.

63 *PE* 1968, 326.

64 *PE* 1969, 5.

65 *PE* 1974, 122.

66 Department of Energy *United Kingdom Oil and Gas Policy* (Cmnd. 5696) (1974).

67 The range of opinions within government ranks at this time with regard to participation is well summarised in Tony Benn's diary (1989, 417-8) as also is Benn's view of the oil companies at this time (1989, 420). See also (1989, 447-450).

68 Hansard HL (Debs) Vol. 365 31 October 1975 col. 775 - Lord Balogh 'It is fair to say that no comparable piece of legislation has ever been so fully discussed with the industry that is affected by it. We are proud of the fact that a number of government Amendments are to a very large extent the outcome of consultations with the industry'. Note also that even the US government intervened directly to stress the adverse effect of UK proposals on the pace of development (see Benn 1989, 427).

69 Quoted by the Earl of Limerick Hansard HL (Debs) Vol. 392 22 May 1978 col. 766.

70 While provisions for new licences were included in the Petroleum (Production) Regulations 1976 (SI 1976, 1129), the point has been made, contrary to Dam (1976) and Cameron (1983), that new terms for existing licences were included in the 1975 Act so that they were at least debated in Parliament (see Daintith & Gault 1979, 60-61).

71 *PE* 1976, 258; 343; Hansard HC (Debs) Vol. 925 9 February 1977 cols. 1442-54.

72 *PE* 1974, 384.

73 *PE* 1974, 446.

74 *PE* 1975, 253.

75 *PE* 1975, 311; Hansard HL (Debs) Vol. 365 31 October 1975 col. 775.

76 *PE* 1975, 451; 1976, 82; Benn (1990, 4).

77 *PE* 1976, 82.

78 *PE* 1978, 261. Indeed, this sixth round was delayed while BNOC's position was strengthened (Benn 1990, 171).

79 *PE* 1978, 307.

80 *The Times* 6 October 1978.

81 Hansard HC (Written Answers) 6 December 1974 Vol. 882, cols 649-650.

82 Professor Colin Robinson quoted in *PE* 1978, 72.

83 *PE* 1977, 499.

84 *PE* 1978, 72.

85 See above in Section 3.4(i).

86 *PE* 1977, 324.

87 This will be considered in greater detail below in Section 4.

88 The text of this Memorandum is reproduced in Frihagen (1983b, 155ff).

89 Paragraph 1 of the Memorandum.

90 Paragraph 3 of the Memorandum.

91 *North Sea Cost Escalation Study* Department of Energy, Peat Marwick, Mitchell & Co., and Atkins Planning 1976 London: HMSO quoted in *PE* 1976, 316.

92 *PPS* 1973, 264. See also Harvie (1995, 159): 'Much of the welding on the Forties platforms carried out at Nigg had to be re-done'.

93 *PE* 1974, 294.

94 See Section 3.4(ii) above.

95 *PPS* 1973, 52.

96 *PPS* 1969, 19.

97 However much the companies deny this sort of allegation, the fact that the Offshore Safety (Protection Against Victimisation) Act 1992 was passed in the aftermath of Piper Alpha is clearly significant. See also SREA (1989, 34). The concerns of both industry and government about the security of installations also plays a role here. Indications of these concerns surface in Tony Benn's diary (1990, 470). See also Harvie (1995, 153) for industry concerns about subversion.

98 *PPS* 1973, 14.

99 As will be seen in Chapter 5, Section 6, the history of unionisation in the North Sea has indeed been marked by inter-union rivalries, a situation perhaps only now beginning to be resolved.

100 Dr. T. F. Gaskell of the British Petroleum Company speaking at the Institute of Petroleum in London in early 1965 pointed out that the weather hazards were particularly great and asked for the setting up of special forecasting offices to supplement the general forecasts available for the area; *PPS* 1965, 127-8.

101 'The bulk of the attention, and consequently of the fears of those whose business it is to imagine what might go wrong, is focused on the platforms, the novelty element in the extraction process'; *PE* 1974, 419. Platforms accounted for anywhere between 50% and 70% of total development costs (Noreng 1980, 77).

102 *PPS* 1965, 128.

103 *PPS* 1965, 404.

104 Gaskell, despite his fears about weather data, explicitly felt that the discovery of the Groningen field's offshore potential at that time meant that the North Sea had not been exploited too soon thus allowing the employment of the most up-to-date tools. See footnote 100 *supra*.

105 Other rigs lost in the North Sea include the Conoco I off Grimsby in April 1967, the Ocean Prince off Flamborough Head in March 1968 and the Constellation also off Flamborough Head in November 1969. Further, it was reported that two rigs, Mr. Cap and Glomar IV, were moved out of the North Sea due to fears about their ability to survive there. Reported to Parliament by Kevin MacNamara MP, Hansard HC (Debs) 28 April 1971, col. 656.

106 As was seen in Chapter 1, Section 4.

107 See *PE* 1976, 152. Government and industry did take a number of steps to deal with this situation. In 1974, a joint government/industry project to gather weather/wave information in the North Sea had been set up; *PE* 1974, 68. In 1975, the Offshore Energy Technology Board was set up as an advisory body to the Department of Energy on research and development into safety and efficiency in offshore operations; *PE* 1975, 271. And in 1976 it was announced that the DEn was to provide £2.6m over the next three years on research into fixed offshore structures with the bulk (£2.3m) going on research into steel platforms *PE* 1976, 152.

108 *PPS* 1968, 219 and see also Thaler & Geminder (1972).

109 It is worth noting that while the pressure put on the industry by insurers was taken up relatively directly by engineering in its approach to technological questions (albeit in conjunction with certain other issues), the reason for a lack of any similar impact from insurance on thinking about occupational safety at a more individual level can perhaps be traced to the differential insurance arrangements. While companies bought insurance against construction and installation risk and against collision and catastrophe risk, they carried the risk of injury to third parties, including workers, themselves (Thaler & Geminder 1972; Johnson 1979 (II) 59).

110 Some work, however, was carried out on the basis of such techniques (see e.g. Chen 1980).

111 A good overview of the growing awareness of these problems is provided by Howe (1986).

112 Despite a tendency for the UK to be contrasted unfavourably with Norway in the matter of offshore health and safety, precisely this finding is also made by Graver with regard to the latter at more or less the same time (1979, 57).

113 An example of this type of political intervention occurred in the SE Forties field which BP wanted to develop with seabed templates but which the DEn wanted to develop with platforms, as these would create employment (Harvie 1995, 220).

114 For the complicated administrative history of the regulators, see Chapter 1, note 28.

4 The Road to a New Rationality

1 Introduction

In the preceding chapter, the theory of autopoiesis was used to inform a cognitive mapping based study of the health and safety at work situation in the North Sea oil and gas industry from the mid-1960s to the late 1970s. The value of this approach was its ability to identify the codes and programmes of the varying rationalities involved across politics, management, engineering and regulation which influenced their world constructions and their self-steering. As regards industry management, the study revealed a world construction dominated by economics and explicitly concerned with the minimisation of economic risk. However, the programme, the steering mechanism of the system, which prevailed throughout this period was largely deterministic, with speed being the method by which the risk of future adverse price and cost movements was dealt with. The programme was deterministic in that while it sought to minimise economic risk it did so by reference to calculations of NPV, lead-times and the suchlike which were unable to model consequent technical and operational risks. Instead, the product of engineering was constructed in industry management as an absolute answer to technical problems, as a fixed point. It was shown how regulatory interventions in the industry (or the possibility of them) across a range of issues from taxation to state participation appeared in this world construction as political uncertainties which also threatened to adversely affect project projections thus increasing economic risk. By comparison, health and safety interventions made little impact - although in such a context that may have been no bad thing.

The comparison of the management world construction with that of engineering during the period considered demonstrated the way in which this demand for speed jarred with the scientific rationale in engineering and forced the production of absolute answers to technical questions which engineers were not in a position to provide with such certainty. The deterministic rationality prevailing in engineering at the time was ill-equipped to provide an indication of degrees of uncertainty in any event. Thus, in the rush to production, engineering operated a programme of minimising technical risk by means of conservatism. While this was shown in some cases to have accommodated emerging problems as experience was accumulated, in other cases platforms in position behaved in ways which transcended even conservative expectations. Equally, the pressure on engineering to provide absolute answers to problems of a magnitude not previously encountered led to delays which further exacerbated the economics of fields for which the only management method of improving the situation was speed. The pre-existing path-dependent industry models of economic and technical management entered the North Sea with an inadequate appreciation of the degree to which it differed from other offshore areas and more significantly without an adequate ability to incorporate either the uncertainty or newly produced information. Furthermore, in many cases, the sheer scale of the vertically integrated majors provided sufficient cash or sufficient creditworthiness to drive projects forward through financial difficulties - even as there occurred the beginning of deintegration during this period. The bottom line was that while the systems of industry management and engineering mutually reinforced the speed of operations, simultaneously their deterministic rationalities masked the level of technical and operational risk thus produced. In these circumstances, it was seen also that the continuing faith of politics in substantive regulation and a programme of legal instrumentalism was similarly flawed in so far as it was too constraining. The much-criticised PED practice of the use of guidance notes and the issuing of waivers from regulations takes on a less sinister appearance when seen in this light. It served to remove pressures from the situation rather than increasing them as many other regulatory interventions did. That said, the regulators held faith in an ability to prescribe in detail and, perhaps influenced by the dominant concerns of engineering, tended to concentrate on technical safety.

But while it seems clear that the rationalities at work in the industry were inadequate in that they were continually, as it were, 'surprised' by emergent difficulties, there were equally attempts to transcend these problems. In the last chapter, it was seen how engineering in particular over a period of years made tentative moves towards probabilistic techniques albeit that by the late 1970s the shift to such techniques was not uniform. It was also mentioned in the last chapter, however, that the experience of engineering during the 1970s in terms of the emergence of fatigue and dynamic response problems constituted in autopoietic terms a confrontation with the blind spot - a realisation that the prevailing world construction effectively masked risks which simple over-design might not always accommodate and might even exacerbate. In this chapter, the study of the different rationalities identified previously will be continued. Clearly, the next major event for industry and government alike was the second oil shock of 1979 and it will be seen that this was to prove a significant turning point in the way in which engineering and management were to develop.

2 Prices and Markets

2.1 After the Second Shock

Like the 1973 oil shock, the price rise of 1979 had its source in the activities of OPEC. The history of the rise is beyond the scope of this study but the following short summary is offered as background to what concerns us here, namely the way in which the rise was reconstructed within industry management in the North Sea - and, as we will see later, within politics. After the rise of 1973, crude oil prices remained fairly stable for the next five years, showing only a moderate rise from around $11 to around $13 per barrel.[1] With the Iranian Revolution in 1979, OPEC saw the opportunity to raise prices as the world market immediately feared a shortage given the cutting off of the Iranian supply. Retrospectively, the market reaction was out of all proportion to the drop in supply but fears of a shortage and the disproportionate effect on the supply to certain buyers who were consequently in the market for immediate alternative sources to fulfil long-term supply contracts meant that there was little in the way of calm reflection. The barrel price hit a high of $40 and averaged over $35 for the year. The strategy backfired on OPEC, however, in the longer term as the world became wary of future dependence on the cartel's oil and its market share fell sharply over the next few years with the North Sea high on the list of those areas benefiting as a result. Equally, a high oil price had a detrimental effect on consumer economies and costs rose. While this thumbnail sketch of the global picture shows the way in which the rise was viewed negatively by most parties, the construction of the price rise by industry management in the North Sea was altogether more rosy. The rise coincided with the period when the pressures on new projects in the North Sea were becoming unbearable, with costs spiralling beyond all expectation as technical difficulties and environmental problems emerged.

While there has been little in the way of public acknowledgement of the scale of difficulties at this time, such details as are available reveal the extent to which the 1979 rise provided the potential for serious reflection by the North Sea industry on the way it conducted its business. There can be no doubt that a barrel price in excess of $35 was not a factor in any of the field projections produced before that date and yet it required that price to ease the pressure on many fields. Some indication of the extent of the pressures on field operations at this time can be found in the graphs at Figures 4.1 and 4.2.[2]

Figure 4.1 shows the percentage cost overrun in 19 UKCS fields through 1983. Two fields, Tartan and Fulmar, were operating within projected costs but the others surveyed were running at costs ahead of projections, half of them by more than 50%. The average cost overrun (including the underrunning fields and excluding the Cormorant figure of 974%) was just in excess of 50%. The high oil price was nothing short of manna from heaven for the North Sea in these circumstances and the internal pressures revealed by the industry management cognitive map at Figure 3.6 take on greater and disturbing clarity.

Of greater significance, however, is Figure 4.2 which compares the original projected rate of return for the same fields with the revised projection in 1984 and the rate of return which could have been expected assuming there had been no price increase in 1979 but rather a constant price. The last set of figures takes account only of royalty payments but no other taxation and so may even be optimistic. It can be seen that the revised projections of ten of the fields show improvements over the original figures. In many cases the 1979 rise has fully absorbed cost increases and allowed returns above initial expectations - although in some cases revised reservoir profiles also played a role. In the remaining fields even the rise does not improve original projections and instead expectations are down. Most significant of all, however, is the fact that in all but two fields the result of no price rise is a rate of return below both the original and the revised projections. In some cases the difference is dramatic and a number of fields no longer show a positive rate of return. In other words, without the price rise some fields would have been in serious difficulties. Jahnke & Webb (1983) confirm that there were no major losses in the North Sea because cost overruns, delays and reservoir estimate reductions were offset by price rises. Castle is somewhat more forceful: 'most fields would be "underwater" if they had not been "bailed out" by the price increases' (1985, 358).

Figure 4.1 Cost Overruns Through 1983 for a Range of North Sea Fields

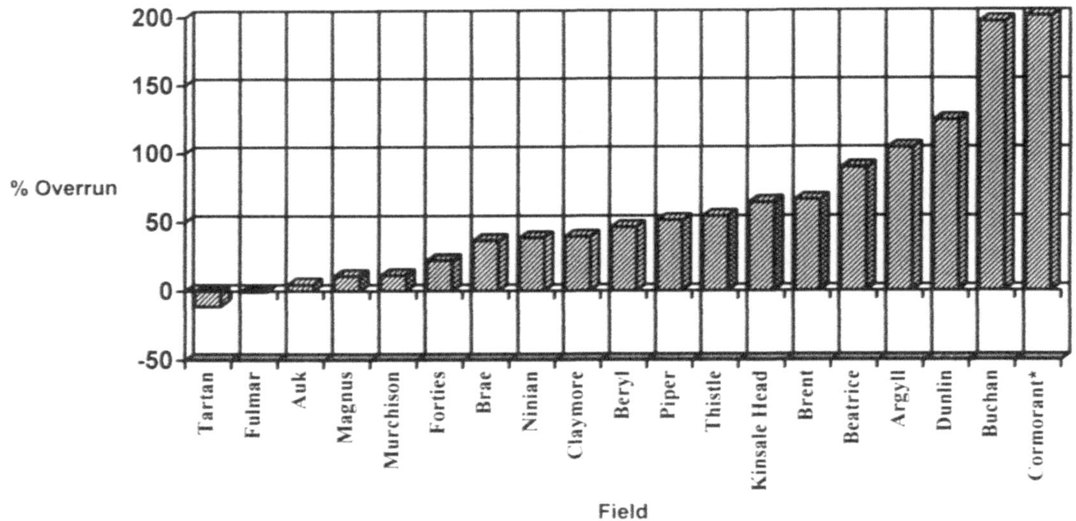

* Cormorant overrun 974%.

Source: Drawn from figures in Castle (1985, 358)

Figure 4.2 Comparison of Rates of Return for a Range of North Sea Fields

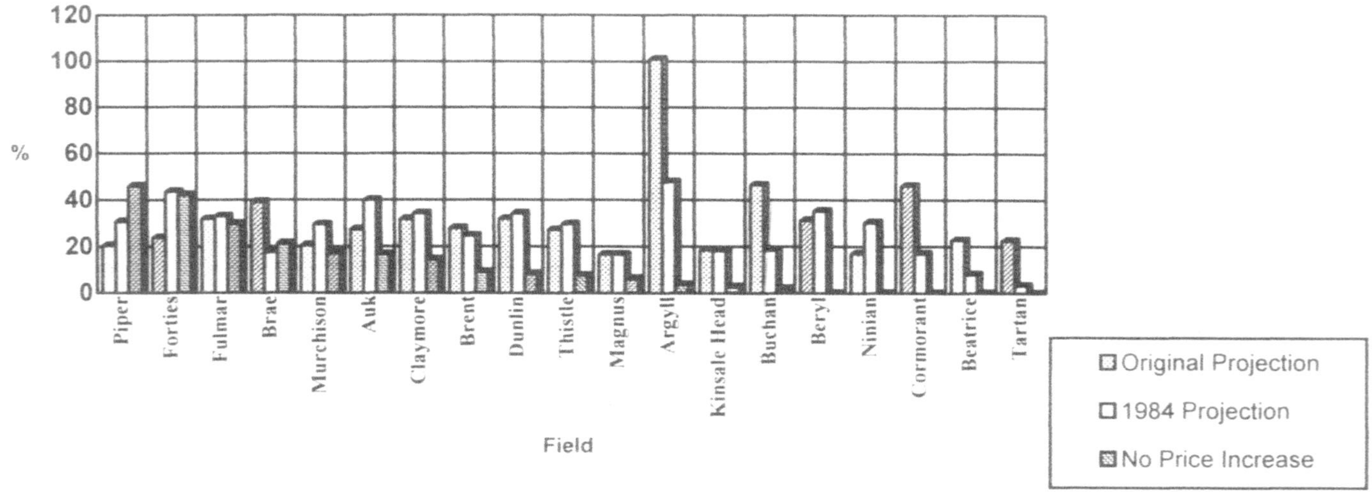

Source: Drawn from figures in Castle (1985, 359)

Calculations such as these were of considerable concern to the industry and it is from this point that the first signs of a new rationality, a new programme, begin to emerge. In a certain sense, what these figures revealed was the blind spot of the previous rationality. Operating on the basis of an economic code with a specific programme of risk-minimisation which depended on speed and calculated success on net present value, the industry had masked the increased technological and operational risks which arose as a consequence. In other words, the programme was in danger of producing a vicious circle of increased technological and operational risk - which in turn increased economic risk - precisely as it sought to minimise economic risk. While this realisation arose, there was, nevertheless, a concomitant reinforcement of existing practices. The rise in the price of oil was so dramatic that there was an element in the industry and especially its financiers which saw oil as an extremely safe bet and as a commodity for which the price could only rise - certainly in the longer term. This latter view lasted at least from 1979 until the first sign of a more serious decline in the price in 1982, but during that period the level of optimism was so high as to appear incomprehensible in retrospect. Project funding arranged during that period was in some cases calculated on the basis of an expected barrel price in 1990 of $95. Even after 1982, when optimism was somewhat more subdued, there were lenders who expected $65 per barrel in 1995. Equally, during the 1979-82 period, banks began to relax their previously very stringent stance on loan terms with reductions in discount rates and credit given also to probable as well as proven reserves.[3] These latter practices halted in 1982 when even the moderate price fall left banks exposed and companies cut their budgets for the first time (Jahnke & Webb 1983). There was criticism of the calculation of future oil industry budgets on the basis of a rising price in the context of a world which was now significantly different from that of the 1970s (Odell 1983).

While the redeeming effects of the 1979 rise exposed the blind spot of the former rationality and while the price declined slowly after that (though remaining historically very high), it was probably the slightly greater fall of 1982 which brought about greater change in the industry's construction of the world it operated in. Now the industry was confronted both with the blind spot and by the possibility that the price might continue to fall or at least enter a period of greater volatility. The previous 'given' of a rising price was now seriously in doubt (Kemp & Rose 1983a, 81) and there were even warnings that a price crash was not out of the question (Odell 1983).

2.2 The Possibility of Price Risk

Whereas in the 1970s the industry had attempted to minimise the risk of not recovering costs principally by speed, the price had always risen and it was not until it began to fall, together with the realisation of all the other difficulties discussed above, that the inadequacy of speed alone in dealing with economic risk became evident. More sophisticated techniques were required if projects were not to be fatally exposed to falling prices. The pressure in this direction was greatest for projects funded during the heady days of 1979-82, which were based on price assumptions which were by the end of that period looking increasingly doubtful. As will be seen in due course, matters were somewhat improved by changes in engineering, but industry management had to make its own contribution.

As was mentioned above, the rise of 1979 produced major changes in the global oil industry and contributed to others. The growing supply of non-OPEC oil meant that there was more oil on the spot market and buyers could shop between this market and OPEC oil with its administered prices. While the spot price was responsive to market forces it was also influenced by the administered OPEC value. This complicated system of pricing between two separate but interdependent sources meant that purchasers of oil faced a significant risk, for example, of a price fall during the transportation of a cargo. Another new feature of the oil industry in the early 1980s was the extent to which stocks of oil were being built up as deintegration proceeded. This for the first time allowed more traditional supply and demand forces to influence short-term prices. Both producers and purchasers, then, had to deal with the new situation of an oil price which could fall significantly in contrast to the historical rise and it was said that for the first time the market believed that prices were fragile (Krapels 1983, 211). The traditional assumption about the limited price elasticity of demand had to be modified.[4] It was increasingly clear that the high price of oil was not justified by the real costs of production (Odell 1983), although this was less true of high cost provinces such as the North Sea which were accordingly most exposed to a price cut. The way in which all parties concerned began to manage this problem was to add a time dimension to the market with the introduction of forward transactions both in the physical commodity and increasingly in paper instruments in order to hedge (Horsnell & Mabro 1993, 73-4).

In the UK, a spot market had existed since the 1970s as major companies sought to discover prices, for example, for tax reasons, while the small companies which were a feature of the North Sea's diversified ownership sought to dispose of oil as quickly as possible and the state-owned BNOC diversified its transactions. First forward transactions occurred on the UK market in 1981 in a number of the major crudes before trading concentrated on Brent from 1983 onwards (Horsnell & Mabro 1993, 77-9). The significant feature of this development from the point of view of politics and law is that it occurred without any direct intervention and continued without any regulatory intervention. The only aspect of law involved in the developing market was contract law and the standard forms which were used to regularise transactions were developed and accepted by the market without any regulatory intervention. Rather, we have here a situation where economics developed a new programme of risk-minimisation as it came to terms with the shortcomings of previous programmes and sought to accommodate an uncertain price future. The consensus in favour of hedging and risk-management existing in the industry was a significant feature in the maintenance of an orderly market (Horsnell & Mabro 1993, 79).

It was not only the Brent market, however, which experienced growth and the development of forward trading. At the same time and in response to the uncertainties introduced to the market by the circumstances surrounding the rise of 1979, the futures markets for oil products in New York and London also began to grow (Niering 1983). Initially, crude oil futures were not offered by the exchanges but within a couple of years such instruments became available. Despite this development, it seems that oil producers were slow to get involved, with some explicitly advising that they should concentrate on observing rather than on using the new markets.[5] While the potential of futures trading for hedging and risk-management had been a feature of the markets for other commodities for some time, a continuing reluctance in the industry meant that it had not been realised for oil. At least part of the industry's reluctance from a production point of view was due to the world construction which saw the price of oil as something which would remain stable - a view which was increasingly out of step with ever-growing OPEC control of supplies during the 1970s. Paradoxically, when this view was most seriously challenged in 1979, it was replaced, as we have seen, with an initial expectation of an increasing price. In both cases the industry view left it exposed to a decline or to volatility and operated effectively to deny these possibilities. We have already seen the influence of this view in the period from 1979-82 when, despite falling prices, projects were funded and operations continued on the assumption of a significant rise even 10 to 15 years out. By 1983, however, it seems clear that major producers who before the 1979 rise would have had no thought of becoming involved in futures were at the very least 'shadowing' the market with a view to later participation or were indirectly involved through subsidiary companies (Niering 1983). It is significant that at this time market research carried out for the International Petroleum Exchange (the London futures market) concluded that the traditional assumptions and structure of the oil industry were not appropriate to the new world and equally that:

> [t]he opportunities presented by futures contracts can only be seized by companies prepared to reconsider their assumptions and radically to alter their methods of working.[6]

It would, however, be going too far to suggest that even the beginnings of growth in the Brent and futures markets indicated a thoroughgoing acceptance of the 'reality' of price risk. There are indications that even after the sharper decline in price during 1982, the more moderate decline in the following three years was constructed by the industry as an indication of a more stable price. To this end, reductions in costs were called for as a means of ensuring that new fields could be brought on stream and that existing fields continued to return a profit as no price hikes of the order of 1973 or 1979 could be counted on.[7] Equally, despite the discussion of a further possible advantage of the use of futures markets at this time in addition to the provision of security against price falls - namely that by providing a means for buyers to express a forward view of their willingness to pay such markets would help to produce price stability in the long term - the industry was still largely reluctant to enter them to any significant degree (Niering 1983; Verleger 1984). Thus, while industry management took steps aimed at ensuring that projects were brought in on time and within budget they were not similarly oriented to the possibility of significant price reductions. This lack of full support meant that exchanges were in turn unable to provide the full range of instruments and contracts which would be required by the market for full hedging cover (Verleger 1984).

By 1985, however, there is evidence of growing concern about prices. At the Shell AGM, the chairman indicated that despite renewed confidence in the North Sea at this time the major uncertainty was with regard to price.[8] There was a growing awareness that trying to predict oil price movements was an extremely difficult process - something which the continuing decline from 1979 contrasted with the expectations of the early 1980s had reinforced. Industry management was hampered by deterministic reasoning which sought to understand in ever greater detail the intricacies of the forecasting process and thus failed to realise that despite a high degree of technical accuracy such forecasts could nevertheless turn out to be wrong. One report[9] indicated that the way forward was for the assumptions underlying the forecast to be examined - in other words the blind spot - a process most easily accomplished by providing different scenarios rather than just one forecast. In this way, decisions about, for example, capital spending could be tested against different scenarios and some measure of the probability of their occurrence considered. In other words, a form of economic risk analysis was developing which allowed a more rational choice of projects and of operations and showed the sensitivity of each to, for example, different price and tax situations. While such an approach did not make the future more certain it did allow and even encourage different possibilities to be considered rather than submerged by one dominant version of the future.[10] The report indicated that the difficulties in predicting prices called 'for a new orientation in forecasting, strategic planning and decision-making'. It is significant, however, that while the report also noted that the experience of forecasting oil prices over the past 15 years had been one of 'continual and costly surprise', this had not of course been the experience of industry managers in the North Sea where an inability to predict accurately the level of prices through 1980 may even have prevented worse cost overruns than actually occurred. Yet again we have an indication that in the North Sea the dominant rationality in management was still oriented towards at least relative price stability and that decisions about both operational and new projects were based on that world construction,[11] albeit that steps away from this position were beginning to be taken.

3 Health and Safety at Work

If there were at least some tentative developments towards more sophisticated management of economic risk in the aftermath of the 1979 price rise, the same cannot be said about the management approach to health and safety at work. An excellent insight into industry management thinking on safety at this time is provided by the UKOOA submission to the Burgoyne Committee.[12] In this submission, the organisation representing the offshore operators presented a view of the safety situation which is at odds with the picture which has been built up in the previous chapter of the problems in engineering. Yet again, then, there is evidence that management was simply blind to the difficulties there and constructed technology as effectively a fixed point in its calculations of field economics. UKOOA was concerned mainly to stress that the existing arrangements for ensuring the integrity of technology were satisfactory as was the existing system for controlling drilling and production. In reaching these conclusions, UKOOA pointed to the industry's own extensive experience in both areas as well as to the fact that the codes of practice to which the industry operated were evolutionary and thus not easily amenable to traditional regulation. Instead, the system of Certifying Authorities and guidance notes was seen as appropriate. To the contrary, the developing regulatory situation where other government agencies in addition to the PED were becoming involved in the offshore area (the Health and Safety Executive and the Department of Transport) was seen as likely to cause confusion. By comparison, the 1971 Act and its regulations were adequate and comprehensible to the industry - a contention which accords with the evidence of the regulators to the Burgoyne Committee, albeit that they had also pointed to earlier difficulties of comprehension.[13] Regulation was also implicitly attacked when UKOOA stressed that while legally only annual inspections of installations were required, the industry in fact carried out more frequent checks precisely because it needed 100% reliability. Similarly, the use of monitoring equipment during production meant that there had never been any serious problem arising from this phase of operations. As to simultaneous activities, these were explicitly considered to present no additional hazard since tight Permit to Work systems were operated. On the design and layout of installations, it was contended that these must always represent a compromise between competing objectives and while the risks involved were unquantifiable the sheer weight of experience of the industry was the surest safeguard against problems. Finally, in the event that something should go wrong, UKOOA pointed to the industry's own arrangements as being the best way to ensure the best response. To this end so-called Sector Clubs had been established so that operators could share equipment and resources and count on each other in the event of an emergency.

The preference of industry management for self-regulation and its distrust of external agencies is very evident in this summary. Even as it stresses its preference for the existing situation with the PED as the main government agency and expresses concern about the possibility of others becoming involved, it prioritises its own expertise, experience and arrangements over any external alternative. Unfortunately, while this difference in expertise and experience as compared with the regulators undoubtedly existed, the limitations of the industry's construction of the risks is all too clear. Simultaneous operations 'present no additional hazard'. There have never been any problems with production because monitoring equipment is in place. In the event of an emergency, the industry is best able to respond. The very fact that the industry was prepared to make these assertions alongside an admission that the risks involved in the layout of installations were 'unquantifiable' speaks volumes for the state of industry management thinking at this time. To a great extent, the world construction of the industry relied on the fact that nothing major had actually gone wrong and it extrapolated from that to a belief that nothing therefore would go wrong. The Alexander L. Kielland had been lost but the engineers now had fatigue problems under control. There had been a blow-out on Ekofisk Bravo in the Norwegian Sector but it did not turn into a disaster because emergency procedures were effective. This kind of thinking was utterly blind to the possibility of impending disaster arising from any number of sources because it did not seek to consider or quantify those risks. Equally it was blind to the ongoing fatalities and casualties simply because they did not impact on the integrity of entire structures, which was clearly the major concern of the industry.

The limitations of industry management risk-minimisation programmes were, however, to be exposed a few years later. After 1986, the industry would never view the North Sea in quite the same way again. Before discussing this event, however, the political and engineering developments of the period from the second oil shock until the middle of 1985 will be considered.

4 Taxation, Participation and Depletion Policy

4.1 Introduction

In the last chapter it was seen how the Labour government in power from 1974 to 1979 progressively implemented a variety of taxation measures and introduced legislation which opened up the possibility of state participation and depletion controls. While the political construction of these interventions was as legitimate moves to ensure a 'fair share' of the hydrocarbon reserves for the nation, they were conversely constructed by the industry as interventions which heightened the already significant economic risk which it confronted. It was suggested that the industry response to these interventions was in terms of its risk-minimisation programme of rapid production and that health and safety regulation fell victim to the unintended side-effects of other regulatory measures. It is not surprising that the incoming Conservative government of 1979 was greeted with more enthusiasm by the industry and it did indeed appear initially to adopt a stance much more favourable to the industry. Regarding participation, for example, the industry was reassured as the new government immediately announced the removal of certain of BNOC's privileges.[14] It then proceeded with a small seventh licensing round at which an industry proposal to allow companies to choose their own blocks was followed - albeit that when this was implemented the companies were charged £5 million per bid.[15] But this industry joy was short-lived as further tax changes followed. In this section, these changes together with the Conservative government's attitude towards participation and depletion controls will be considered in more detail with particular emphasis once again on how these issues were constructed by the industry and how it responded in terms of its operational decisions.

4.2 The 1979 Oil Shock

The meteoric rise in the price of oil during 1979-80, which is shown graphically in the Appendix, gave rise to fears in the new Conservative government (echoed by the opposition) that windfall or surplus profits would accrue to the oil industry in the North Sea and that unless the tax regime was appropriately set up the nation risked losing its 'fair share' of those profits. As a result, a range of changes to the regime was introduced over the course of the next few years. The rate of PRT was raised from 45% to 60% in 1979, to 70% in 1980 and finally to 75% in 1982. An additional tax on hydrocarbon production, the fourth, was introduced in 1981 - Supplementary Petroleum Duty.[16] This was viewed with particular alarm by the industry because it was charged at a rate of 20% on gross revenues and thus effectively took no account of whether a field was in profit or not (Kemp & Rose 1981, 147). The government, however, made it clear that it wanted an extra £1bn in revenue from the industry in Financial Year 1981/82.[17] One problem with the tax as far as the industry was concerned was the unfairness to new fields which had to bear the tax from the outset as compared to older fields which had enjoyed several years without it. The major problem with SPD, however, was that it was a tax which was explicitly insensitive to field differences and which was being added to a regime which already had one other explicitly insensitive tax (royalty) and one other tax which despite being designed to be sensitive to field differences had proved to be otherwise in practice. One effect of the tax was for reservoir depletion rates to be reassessed by the industry in order to minimise liability rather than according to normal reservoir engineering practice (Kemp & Cohen 1981, 16). The extent of industry concern about the potential for disproportionate effects on marginal fields is perhaps evident from the field differences shown above in Figures 4.1 and 4.2 and equally in the fact that it attempted to prevent the imposition of the tax by offering a payment of £1bn.[18] The willingness of the industry to produce this amount of money, however, was viewed by politics as a sign that it had indeed made windfall profits and that the tougher tax stance was necessary. The effect of these tax measures, however, was a continuation of what was seen in the last chapter - the tax burden falling differentially on different fields with no necessary connection to their profitability. Once again, the expectation of an ever tougher and more complicated tax regime and the impact of the changes on cash-flow produced pressures on operations in terms of speed and cost. An indication of the pressure on existing operations at this time can be gained from the field postponements which were reported following the implementation of the new tax regime. The Andrew field was shelved and, but for the level of existing investment, the same fate would have befallen Montrose.[19]

As a result of the problems encountered, the industry began to lobby intensively for a relaxation of the regime. At about this time, both the Institute of Fiscal Studies and researchers at Aberdeen University brought forward proposals for a radical revision of the system that recalled the ideas of MacKay & Mackay (1975) for taxation to be related to the rate of return on investment.[20] The benefit of the proposals (for a petroleum profits tax and for a progressive profits tax respectively) was that a specified rate of return was guaranteed before a tax liability arose - something which clearly fitted the cognitive map of the industry's managers and removed part of the pressure on the front-end loading of project costs imposed especially by royalty and SPD. Additionally, such a tax automatically accommodated changes in capital and operating costs and in the price of oil. Lastly, the situation of satellite developments from existing fields which was beginning to concern the industry was not affected by such a tax as compared to PRT where the feasibility of such developments had to be judged on other than purely technical criteria. Despite these advantages, the 1982 Budget saw no relaxation in the taxation of oil production. For the government, the short-term losses implied by a move to a tax based on rate of return on investment were unacceptable, while for the industry the upheavals involved in changing to the new system were too great (Bland

1988, 6-7). Instead, while the industry pressure brought about the abolition of SPD,[21] it was replaced by Advance Petroleum Revenue Tax (APRT) which was charged in a similar way to SPD but allowable as a credit against PRT.[22] The downside for some fields, however, was the fact that whereas SPD was immediately deductible against Corporation Tax (CT),[23] APRT was not deductible until it had been credited against PRT. Some new fields and some declining fields were badly affected as regards cash-flow (Kemp & Cohen 1982). Additionally, of course, the PRT rate was raised to 75%. As regards extra capital expenditure, it was noted that the tax regime encouraged it early in the life of a field when it was not necessarily required and discouraged it later when improvements, life-extension, satellite developments and the suchlike might well be required (Kemp & Cohen 1982). The major concern for the industry, however, was the fact that while the recent changes to the tax system were a response to the 1979 price hike, which loomed large in the political cognitive map at a time when means were being sought to finance income tax cuts, the trend in prices since that high point had been a steady decline. The combination of tougher taxes and falling prices impacted strongly on field revenues and operations, with individual fields - sometimes the most marginal - bearing a disproportionate burden. Once again tax as a dynamic tool of political intervention had become a blunt instrument in the cognitive map of industry management. To make matters worse, projects planned and financed on the basis of 1979 prices were beginning to look particularly problematic (Jahnke & Webb 1983).

With the tax changes coinciding with the development of more remote and more marginal fields, the industry response to the 1982 Budget was immediate. BP began looking for a buyer for its 15% stake in the Beatrice field which was now showing a rate of return of only 3%[24] while Shell shelved plans for the Tern field and Phillips those for the T-Block. The new North Cormorant, Fulmar and Magnus fields were also adversely affected with their higher costs (Quinlan 1982b). The impact on the operation of existing fields can again be inferred from this response even if the industry has been coy at revealing the extent of cuts in operating costs during this period. Regulatory interventions designed to cream off windfall profits and to meet short-term revenue demands (and thus appearing as reasonable, indeed necessary, in the reality construction of politics) appeared to industry management as grossly inappropriate to the prevailing situation of rising costs and falling prices as technical and environmental aspects of new developments tightened margins and older platforms began to require remedial work.[25] In this context, it is not surprising to find that health and safety regulations do not figure prominently on the cognitive map of industry management and that the pressure on operations again adversely affected technical and occupational risk. Ironically, the government itself was a victim of the new situation as it struggled to sell off Britoil before the estimated £1bn development costs for the ever-more marginal Clyde field were incurred.[26] In these circumstances, the government announced tax concessions to ease the effects of APRT on the working capital of marginal fields (Kemp & Rose 1983b).

As regards depletion policy, there was early concern for the industry in the approach of the new government when it announced the intention to introduce depletion controls after 1982 when the Varley Assurances expired. This especially concerned the industry as there was specific mention of a 'greater emphasis to the need to limit the sharpness of the peak in production', which conflicted directly with the industry's view of field production.[27] The government gradually moved to allay industry fears, however, with the announcement that there would be no depletion controls at least until the end of 1984.[28] This was viewed positively by the industry and continuing concerns that control might in any event be exercised through development delays disappeared when the government tried instead to stimulate activity by processing the application from Total and Elf for the North Alwyn field in only fifteen days.[29]

4.3 Converging Constructions

The trend of a relaxation in the government's stance towards oil taxation continued in the 1983 Budget with APRT being phased out over a 4 year period[30] and with new fields being exempt from royalty.[31] The removal of these two taxes, which had applied immediately to new fields whether or not in profit, produced a significant easing in cash-flow and thus reduced pressure on operations. As regards PRT, the oil allowance for new fields was doubled to 500,000 tonnes[32] with a doubled cumulative total of 10m tonnes. The position regarding reliefs was also improved[33] (see also Kemp & Rose 1983b; Bland 1988, 7-8). Many of these changes were in response to industry demands although the call for a reduction in the rate of PRT was ignored. Nevertheless, the removal of regressive taxes leaving only PRT and CT on new fields which, whatever their imperfections, were at least nominally related to profit, was a major encouragement to the industry, albeit that part of the decision for new development may have been based on the desire to offset PRT and CT payable on maturing fields (Jahnke & Webb 1983). The reluctance of the industry prior to these changes can, however, be overstated as the auction blocks in the 8th licensing round raised £33m,[34] though a further increase in development was expected after the Budget.

The new concern of the industry, however, was how far prices were going to fall. At this time, companies were operating on the basis that a price of at least $25 per barrel was needed to support developments in prospect and the price was already sliding below $30.[35] As a result a number of companies, including Britoil and Chevron, were looking for further tax concessions.[36]

Meanwhile, the difference in the tax-efficiency of companies with production and those without was becoming stark when it came to exploration and development under the existing tax regime. One study suggested that the company with production and paying CT and PRT could use offsets to reduce exploration costs to a mere 12% of those facing a company without production and reduce development costs to about one-half (Lovegrove 1983). The demand for shares in BP's giant producing Forties field was therefore not surprising - although the government moved quickly to close what it saw as a loophole (Bland 1988, 8). From a health and safety point of view, however, maintaining a substantial differential in the relative pressures on field economics between companies appears more questionable. The tax regime was continuing to impose varying financial pressures on operators whose concern with economic risk minimisation meant that technical and operational decisions were inevitably taken on other than technical and operational grounds.

There is evidence, nevertheless, that the government was increasingly inclined to view the need for certainty about depletion controls in precisely the same way as the industry. Responding to OPEC criticism of production levels in the North Sea, a government spokesman stated that in order for the required investment to be made, the industry needed to be confident that it would not be prevented from producing at the agreed rate.[37] Furthermore, the trend of relaxing the tax regime continued in 1984 with a phased reduction of CT to 35% over a period of years.[38] Even though first year capital allowances were to be reduced and then abolished,[39] the reduced tax rate suited mature fields and new fields would benefit from more years at the lower rate. Pressures on cash-flow being eased, expenditure on capital projects and new exploration was seen as encouraged (Kemp & Rose 1984, 148-150). And the changes in the regime were constructed as encouraging by the industry, with an upturn in drilling and exploration, the raising of £120m for 13 auction blocks in the 9th licensing round and the allocation of eighty discretionary blocks including some in deep water frontier territory to the north and west of Scotland.[40] But if new work was encouraged, the industry was increasingly concerned by mature fields and work that would need to be carried out to lengthen life and allow step-out developments. Some form of incremental allowance against PRT was called for by UKOOA and while independent commentators echoed this they equally warned of the possible side-effect of encouraging 'gold-plating'.[41] The picture was blurred somewhat by figures from Wood McKenzie suggesting that the rate of return from step-out developments was massive compared with new stand-alone fields - although the industry had seen projected rates of return disappear before. The government took the view that the regime was favourable enough and removed immediate relief for exploration and development[42] without making any provision for incremental development (Bland 1988, 8-9).

A further concern of the industry - state participation - was removed in late 1984/early 1985 as the government announced that the BNOC was to be abolished. Following the sale of Britoil, the state company had limited functions and once it began losing money on its purchase (at an official price) and sale (on the open market) of 51% of North Sea production in the context of a declining price its position became untenable.[43] The political view was now that an open market was preferable, that depletion controls were inappropriate and that the strategic importance of oil could be covered by a new agency, the government Oil and Pipeline Agency, which could reactivate previous participation agreements in the event of a supply crisis.

In summary, after an initial continuation (and indeed intensification) of the construction of its situation by industry management in terms of the cognitive map at Figure 3.6, an easing of political pressures, the revelation which the 1979 price hike provided about previous practices, and the growing awareness of price uncertainty are all apparent on the cognitive map by 1985 as shown in Figure 4.3.

Pressures towards rapid production produced by political uncertainties have all but disappeared and while that programme is still present, it is now accompanied by other risk-minimisation programmes associated with price risk and a better appreciation of the problems caused in the 1970s by putting too much pressure on engineering. The extra uncertainties associated with price are seen as amenable to a programme of risk-minimisation involving financial instruments while a more rational approach to project planning aims at dealing with the knock-on effects on economic risk of pushing too hard on technology.

Figure 4.3 Cognitive Map: Industry Management (after 1979)

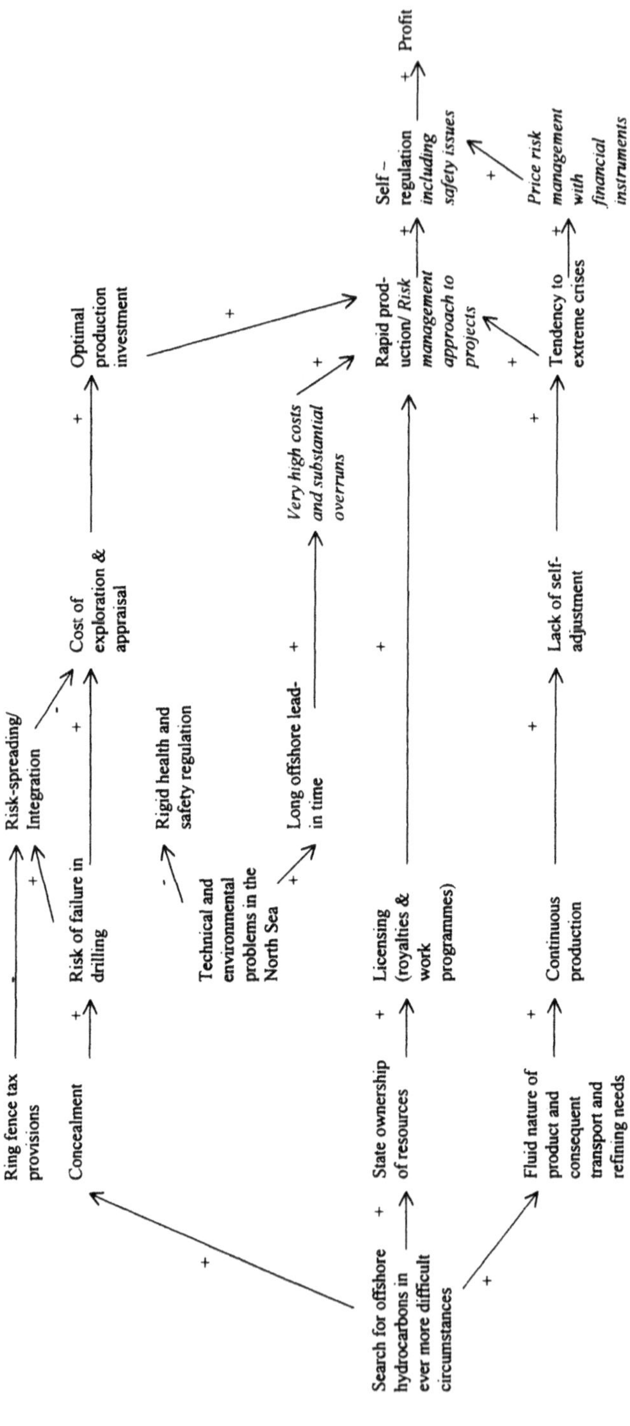

But while these alternative programmes were evident at this time, it must be emphasised that they were by no means well-developed and there must be severe doubts about how much headway they had achieved in the face of the traditional programme by which the industry steered itself. Significantly, whatever the greater awareness of other dimensions of risk as they impacted on economic risk, this does not seem to have extended to issues of occupational safety. In any event, all programmes were about to be severely tested.

5 Politics and Health and Safety

While the political approach to certain aspects of the regulation of the offshore industry (taxation, participation and depletion policy) appears to have become progressively more sensitive to the nature of that industry during the first half of the 1980s - in other words, that politics was beginning to observe how the industry operated, what differences it constructed and sought to minimise - the same cannot be said of its approach to health and safety. As compared to those more economic issues, health and safety makes only one significant appearance on the cognitive map of politics during the same period, namely the debate on the Report of the Burgoyne Committee in 1980.

The findings of the Burgoyne Committee have been discussed previously[44] and, as was seen, there was some appreciation there of certain difficulties confronting the regulators. The orientation of law intended by the legislators was proving difficult to implement in that the regulators were unable to keep pace with developments using regulations and had been experiencing problems in communicating legal requirements to the industry. However, issues such as these do not appear on the cognitive map of politics in the aftermath of that report. Instead, the extensive parliamentary debate which followed publication of the report of the Committee[45] focused very largely on the point which mainly divided the majority of the Committee from the Trade Union dissenters, namely the question of where ultimate responsibility for the safety regulators should lie: with the DEn or with the HSE. The government line was to accept the ideas of the majority report that responsibility should remain with the DEn and the reasoning behind this was based very much on the view that the offshore situation presented a unique challenge to the regulation of safety. Those involved in administering safety regulations should therefore have an intimate knowledge of the complicated field. Further, it was felt that the

PED needed direct and immediate access to the geological and reservoir engineers in other parts of the DEn. Nevertheless, it was explicitly recognised that there was a danger in isolating the offshore from health and safety developments onshore and therefore the Secretary of State for Energy was to take over the responsibilities of the Employment Secretary under the HSWA 1974 - the matters which had previously been the subject of the Agency Agreement between the two Departments. The former would still seek the advice of the HSE but ultimate responsibility would now rest with him. In direct opposition to the Trade Union concern as to the risk of a conflict of interest, the government expressed itself concerned about the risk of splitting these responsibilities having regard to the limited number of experts at the government's disposal. The claim was that, while there was no doubt room for new safety initiatives in such a technologically fast moving industry, the new administrative arrangements would be able to respond to this in an efficient and effective manner.

The opposition, however, regarded the new arrangements rather as a 'dog's breakfast' and was concerned that the Burgoyne Committee found that nonc of the safety committees visited during their investigations had ever been spoken to by the PED and equally that the PED's view was that they had never had the need to speak to such a committee. They were adamant that the responsibility for offshore safety must go to the HSE. There was, then, at this stage in politics a change in stance by the Labour Party from the situation in 1971 as to where ultimate responsibility for safety ought to lie while the Conservative government remained content with the DEn together with certain administrative modifications. Nevertheless, and this is the significant point, politics across the board remained convinced of the fundamental ability of prescriptive regulation to ensure that greater safety could be achieved. Labour saw the conflict of interest within the DEn between safety and production as having the potential to reduce overall safety whereas the Conservatives saw any increase in the distance between the technical experts of the DEn and the safety regulators as having the potential to reduce overall safety. But crucially the cognitive map of politics from 1971 remained the rationale on which politics constructed the regulatory situation. It could be objected that the Robens approach upon which the 1974 Act is based would have resulted in a move away from prescriptive regulation and hence that the Labour programme must be seen as fundamentally different,[46] but neither side once mentioned this point during the course of the debate. The *orientation* of the law (prescriptive or tripartite/self-regulatory) was not an issue for politics whereas the location of responsibility was. Whatever the

Burgoyne Committee had discovered about difficulties of communication and about the limitations of prescription, politics could not see. It is ironic that if the opposition had focused on these aspects of the Burgoyne Committee's findings, the government would have found it much more difficult to resist the calls for a transfer of responsibility to the HSE. But politics could not observe law except in terms of prescription and enforcement as its instrumental tool.

6 Engineering

6.1 The Second Oil Shock

In the last chapter, it was seen that in the period up to 1978, engineering became increasingly aware of the limitations of its deterministic and conservative approach to the development of technology in the North Sea. It was beginning to understand the limits of the path-dependency which had imposed Gulf of Mexico concepts on the North Sea and the range of issues it was unable to observe as a result. Thus, tentative but increasingly optimistic steps towards probabilistic techniques were taken, but the immediate concern in doing so may in many cases have been as a means of dealing with the extraordinary cost pressures which were building up in the industry at that time rather than a more abstract concern with an appropriate rationality. It is not surprising, then, that when the 1979 price hike relieved the cost pressures on North Sea developments, one response in engineering was a re-embracing of conservatism (see e.g. Praught 1983) with the new risk-oriented techniques simply disappearing from the cognitive map. The other cost pressure which had been very directly of concern to engineering before 1979, namely the size of insurance premiums, also receded in the period after the price rise with insurers beginning to express satisfaction that offshore installations were now a better long-term risk (Peterson *et al.* 1981). The cognitive map for the period immediately after 1979 is shown in Figure 4.4.

While risk-oriented techniques no longer appear, it is highly significant that for the first time there is a recognition of the potential for other causes of accidents, including human factors. Nevertheless, these are seen as rare and productive of infrequent and severe accidents. It is significant also that at this period the regulations, particularly the Construction and Survey Regulations, had been in force for a few years and engineering had by this time had some experience of them. The

Figure 4.4 Cognitive Map: Engineering Determinism (after 1979)

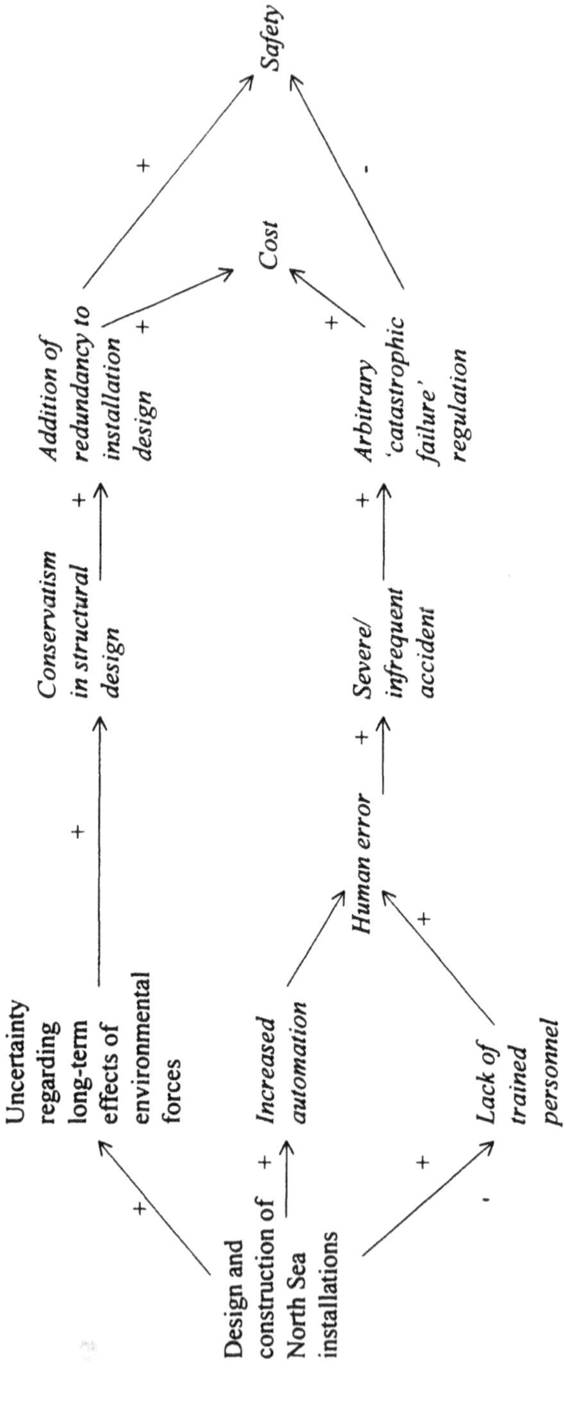

construction of these regulations by engineering is not, however, positive. Rather they are seen as a political response to the sort of severe accident caused by human error and in effect arbitrary. The similarity with the attitude of management to regulation before the UK regime was in force is striking (see Chapter 3, Section 3.3). In addition, regulations are seen as adding cost without improving safety. Conversely, the preferred engineering approach of conservatism in structural design, while it also increases cost, is seen equally as increasing safety. Paradoxically, while human error is blamed for some severe accidents, one of the reasons for the increased incidence and effects of human error identified by engineering is the increased automation on offshore platforms. This indicates the extent to which the deterministic blind spot is back in position for some areas of engineering and the extent to which the previous tentative move to a probabilistic programme of risk-minimisation had been influenced by cost concerns.

Nevertheless, as was mentioned before, the very fact that engineering had confronted its blind spot in the 1970s with the emergence of fatigue and then dynamic response as problems masked by initial design techniques, meant that it was impossible for there to be a complete return to the old ways of operating. Thus, simultaneous with the post 1979 return to conservatism, there was a continuing development of risk-oriented and probabilistic techniques. As in management, this development was given some added impetus by the slightly steeper fall in oil prices after 1982, when the industry began once again to be more concerned about costs.

6.2 The Advent of Risk Assessment

The most significant development of the early 1980s in this regard was that the probabilistic techniques, which had previously only been applied tentatively to the behaviour of structures, were in some quarters being applied to the whole range of risks which could endanger an offshore platform including human factors and process problems (e.g. Tveit *et al.* 1980). The technique was now specifically referred to as risk assessment, a term which opened up the recognition of other possible problems.

The process of risk assessment had its earliest and most systematic use in the NASA space programme of the late 1950s and 1960s (Cooke 1991). Throughout the 1970s, there was in science and engineering in general a growing interest in such ideas as hazard identification, risk assessment or evaluation and consequence analysis in response to the perceived exponential development of technology and growing public concern with hazardous consequences, including '[n]ew evidence of latency, irreversibility and catastrophe' (Kates 1977, 16). At this time, however, the 'underlying scientific specialization' was described as 'still emergent' (Kates 1977, 15) and '[m]any of the major issues of risk assessment' were said to be 'as yet unresolved' (Slovic *et al.* 1977, 83). It was noted, for example, that a major problem with 'almost all methods' of hazard identification was their 'dependence...on the suffering of consequences' (Kates 1977, 20). In other words, they were not well set-up to be proactive or to incorporate uncertainties, rather responding to actual events or perhaps 'near-misses' which drew attention to a hazard and allowed a response in terms of assessment and regulation. A possible reason for this was that the growth of technology had effectively overloaded societal capacity to identify and respond to hazards (Kasperson 1977). In other words, the management of hazards depended very much on the hazard actually arising. An example of this offshore, of course, was the emergence of first fatigue and then dynamic response problems, neither of which had been foreseen.

The perceived magnitude of the problem of technological risk, however, meant that development of such techniques continued to try to meet these difficulties. In general, such techniques make use of probability theory to take account of the uncertainties involved, in the case of technology, in design and operation. Thus, for an offshore installation as a whole or for a particular component or event relating to it, a probability value, whether of failure or occurrence, can be calculated for a given period of time. Broadly, two approaches are available within probability theory - the classical and the Bayesian. An analysis of the relative merits of these approaches is well beyond the scope of this study but it is sufficient for present purposes to note that the latter is regarded as much less restrictive and allows the incorporation of more uncertainties (Cooke 1991). It thus closes down less distance between explained and explanation in the sense discussed above in Chapter 2.[47] The interaction of different failures and events can also be modelled using the probability values in the context of fault and event trees, an example of which is shown at Figure 4.5.

Such a process by no means guarantees that a better solution to engineering or operational problems is reached. Firstly, the process of identifying risks may be hampered by the latency of risks, especially in new technologies, such that significant faults and events may be omitted from the assessment. Secondly, the assessment of the probability of a failure or event is always difficult, but especially so in the case of rare

Figure 4.5 Diagram: Fault Tree/Event Tree Methodology

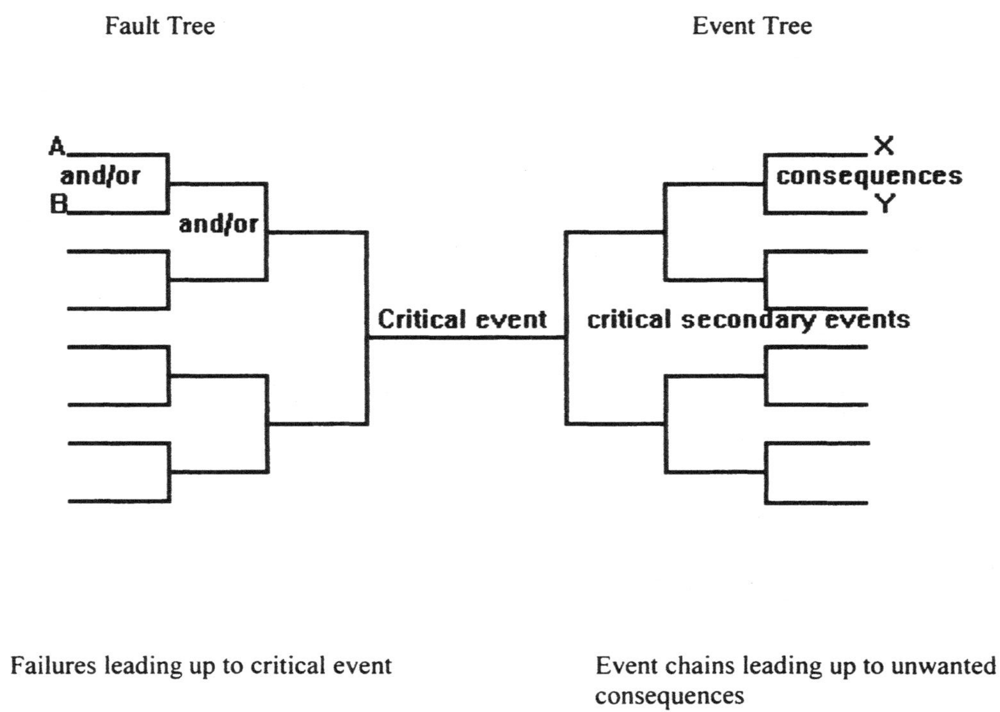

events where by their nature there is little historical data (Slovic *et al.* 1977, 85-87). Whatever the problems, however, risk assessment in general was presented as the best means of dealing with the issue of technological risk insofar as it constituted a rational process for considering that risk. In contrast to often emotionally charged discussion, it provided a quantitative means of communicating risk. Whereas both engineers and their critics frequently employed intuitive judgements, risk assessment required an explicit and comprehensive justification of decisions. While uncertainty remained a significant problem, risk assessment provided a rational means of expressing uncertainty and equally of incorporating new findings. Finally, risk assessment allowed decisions to be taken openly on the basis of best available data rather than waiting for the outcome of research which would never perhaps produce an absolute result. Whereas deterministic methods achieved this last objective by conservatism and factors of safety, risk assessment forced an opening up of the decision process and the revelation of assumptions (see Slovic *et al.* 1977, 98).

Techniques such as these gained early acceptance in the Norwegian sector of the North Sea (especially in the aftermath of the Ekofisk Bravo blow-out) where they were used to help in the planning and control of simultaneous activities - for example, simultaneous construction and drilling or simultaneous drilling and production. Simultaneous activities are part of the industry management programme of minimising economic risk by reducing lead time to production and allowing early access to reservoir performance data. The use of risk assessment indicated an awareness that unless the technical and operational risks of simultaneous activities were also minimised then the goal of minimising economic risk would be compromised (Rundt & Luppens 1981).[48]

The advent of such techniques, however, put demands on safety regulation. As soon as equipment and procedures were open to risk evaluation, the fact that they might be regarded as unacceptably risky or not the best alternative though still demanded by regulation became problematic. The industry was still highly critical of regulation which attempted to prescribe in what it saw as too much detail and pointed to the fact that a wide variety of design criteria were specified by different national codes and by certifying authorities with no two agreeing on what was required. In some cases, it was noted that criteria seemed to have no 'firm theoretical or empirical basis' (Bunce & Wyatt 1982). Self-regulation was favoured in order that each operating unit could develop and apply its own strategies to meet safety objectives (Patterson 1983, 37-8). It was said that even if motivated by nothing other than economic considerations, the industry would not ignore the possible risks to extremely expensive assets (Gordon 1983). As failures of technology which complied with regulatory requirements mounted, some operators developed their own more rigorous testing and inspection regimes (even when this meant increased costs and what were described as 'nebulous' benefits (Joosten & Robinson 1983)), and risk assessment techniques with the consequent realisation of the risks masked by deterministic techniques and the discovery of the 'hidden' costs of the former rationality.[49] Equally, both evacuation procedures and the employment of stand-by vessels were criticised for 'meeting regulations but not reality' (Benedict *et al.* 1982; Daniel 1982). Not only, therefore, was there a move in engineering, however tentative, towards a new rationality - a new risk-minimisation programme based on probabilistic risk assessment - but there was also a demand that law 'keep up' with such a development.

In the Norwegian sector, the answer was arrived at jointly between the Norwegian Petroleum Directorate and the industry with regard to the issue of simultaneous activities mentioned above. Instead of providing a detailed code of how simultaneous activities were to be managed, a basic philosophy was worked out within which operations could be conducted. This philosophy stated that simultaneous activities would only be carried out with a minimum of two tested 'safety barriers' in place for each activity. The responsible operators were therefore free to respond as they thought best in any given situation provided that this basic philosophy was followed (Rundt & Luppens 1981).

In the UK, while as was seen in Figure 4.4 there was concern about regulations in force, there was also optimism that the regime offered the potential for accommodation of new techniques and the attitude of the PED was viewed as favourable (e.g. Patterson 1983, 42). Here the system, consisting of broad principles contained in regulations with guidance notes providing a flexible means of adding detail and the Certifying Authorities carrying out an auditing function, was seen as providing a framework within which the industry could operate to consider the probability of certain problems rather than being required by detailed regulations to act in ways which might ultimately prove inappropriate. The continuing experience of problems with older conservatively designed platforms was specifically mentioned as a reason why such a flexible approach was desirable (Faulds 1982). Thus, after 1979, and especially after 1982, an alternative cognitive map, shown at Figure 4.6, with an alternative programme for dealing with risk was available in engineering alongside that shown at Figure 4.4.

Figure 4.6 Cognitive Map: Engineering (mid 1980s)

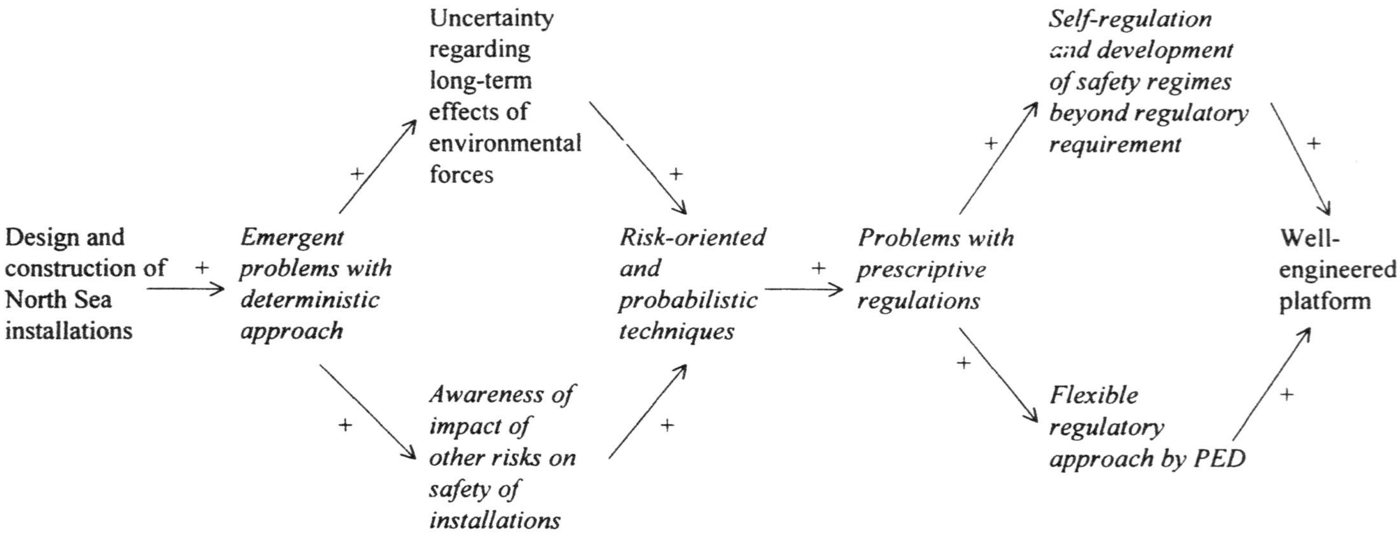

Not least of significance in this cognitive map is the greater openness to regulation - provided it was flexibly applied and accommodating of new techniques - than that apparent in the more conservative Figure 4.4.

6.3 *Competing Constructions*

To view this picture as a complete break with previous determinism encouraged by enlightened regulatory regimes, especially in the UK, would be going too far, however. We have already seen how in some cases there was an open embracing of the programme of conservative determinism once again after 1979 (Figure 4.4) and whereas there was now in other cases greater confidence in the use of the programme based on probabilistic techniques (with the full range of risk assessment tools including fault tree and consequence analysis being applied to certain projects) once again concern arose about the lack of appropriate data. Engineering, therefore, turned to analogous onshore process industries for data but noted that this served to introduce further uncertainty. It also warned that including human factors in risk calculations had a similar effect (Tveit *et al.* 1980). What can now be seen in comparing this and previous oil engineering critiques of probabilistic techniques with the brief outline of these techniques given above is that there was and had been something of a misapprehension on the part of oil engineering about just how they should be used. Instead of their being used to allow an expression on the part of engineering *about* degrees of uncertainty there was instead a deterministic desire to use them to *remove* uncertainties. In other words, the former dominant rationality was still in play in some areas and probabilistic or risk assessment techniques were reconstructed in those terms rather than forming part of a rationality oriented towards uncertainty. What this might mean in practice can be seen by looking in comparison at the developing management approach of economic risk assessment which was referred to briefly above (Faeke *et al.* 1981). There the magnitude of the uncertainties confronting the industry (in terms of future price and inflation figures and in terms of alternative technological field development concepts in addition to those relating to reservoir performance) were the stated reason for the use of risk assessment techniques. By *including* the uncertainties in economic evaluations the field concept with the highest NPV and the lowest economic risk could be discovered. Significantly, in this approach, the possibility now existed to calculate economic risk in terms of the magnitudes of economic, technical and operational uncertainties in contrast to the previous situation where these risks were masked.

Despite the new awareness of the possible impact of human factors in major accidents, the tension between the different rationalities is clear from the different views of how this should be dealt with. There was a recognition on the one hand that the expansion of the offshore industry had outstripped the supply of properly qualified personnel and that even where individuals knew how to act safely, organisational practices often prevented them from doing so (Gentile *et al.* 1983; Chapman 1983). On the other hand, the deterministic approach saw the greater potential for more severe consequences as a result of human error and believed that '[f]ew accidents are caused wholly by technical failure, even fewer by administrative factors' (Gentile *et al.* 1983; Roxburgh 1983). Training was the common response to the problem, but the risk-oriented rationality saw the need also for management changes while the more deterministic rationality saw the need instead for conservative technology to accommodate human error.

Equally, as regards the regulatory approach, while the UK regime as developed by the PED certainly possessed the flexibility to accommodate a probabilistic approach it did not really assist in developing such a risk-minimisation programme as compared to the Norwegian regime. This is evident not only from the reconstruction by sections of engineering of probabilistic techniques in deterministic terms but also from the fact that the broader consideration of risk and the attempt at least to measure probabilities did not always extend beyond structural issues. There is thus a tendency to consider the safety of personnel only in terms of the safety of the whole structure with the legal requirements for personnel safety, health and welfare described as being defined by Construction and Survey Regulations (e.g. Faulds 1982). Again, however, engineering saw unfolding events as confirmation of the need for this emphasis. Just as the loss of the Alexander L. Kielland in 1980 had confirmed engineering in its emphasis on structural integrity so did the sinking of the Ocean Ranger off the east coast of Canada on 15 February 1982 with the loss of 84 lives. In contrast to the concern of trade unions and academic commentators with the ongoing problem of more 'mundane' accidents and individual fatalities, engineering continued in large part to construct these as being at an acceptable level. It saw the injury and death rates as lower than for other extraction industries and as 'good' when compared with the amount of new wealth generated per fatality. In contrast to trade union and academic concerns, the point was made that more men died on the Ocean Ranger than on the UK Continental Shelf as a whole between 1970 and 1979 (Benedict *et al.* 1982). Thus, engineering was more concerned about risk at the level of the entire installation both because accidents at that level were occurring with huge loss of life and because the scale of the problem there was potentially very significant. Again at this time there was the admission that even in 1982 'the actual stress history experienced by offshore structures is a major unknown' (Kenley 1982).

Development of new techniques continued, therefore, and as the problems caused by deterministic design criteria (both scientific, in terms of the masking of significant factors, and economic, in terms of over-design and consequent cost) continued to emerge, so the impetus towards risk assessment grew. For example, the technique was used to assess the risk to platforms during installation - a period not well accounted for by deterministic techniques which depended upon discrete values for soil strength and wave height. The risk assessment approach rather considered uncertainties in these values and attempted to produce a platform which offered acceptable risk for the minimum cost (Kriger *et al.* 1983). A similar approach was evident in the assessment of critical subsystems in new technological approaches such as the Tension Leg Platform used in the Hutton field (Stahl & Geyer 1985). Similarly, the Tern platform for a smaller, 'marginal' field was the product of a design process which set out to re-examine 'conventional practices'. The platform achieved considerable weight and cost savings while retaining global structural redundancy and increased fatigue lives (Henderson *et al.* 1986).

Further development of these techniques took place in response to the needs of platforms *in situ*. Firstly, as has been noted previously, such platforms were often the subject of emergent fatigue and dynamic response problems which initial design criteria did not allow engineering to observe. Secondly, there was often the need to retrofit equipment associated with revised production profiles, secondary recovery or step-out developments - all of which would alter deck loadings and hence the total weight and the weight distribution which the structure would have to support (Nehring 1985).[50] In all cases there was a need to reassess the structural strength of the platform which required either the application of deterministic criteria brought up to date in the light of data collected *in situ*, the retrospective application of probabilistic techniques or the application of risk assessment techniques. This last alternative sought to achieve a more thorough picture of the viability of the platform by taking account not only of structural issues - even calculated probabilistically - but also of the risk inherent in inspection, maintenance and repair operations and the uncertainties inherent in the calculation process (Bea *et al.* 1985). The significant advance here was that this process depended not simply on the adjustment of key variables for a given solution but on the comparison of solutions. In this way, for the first time, an explicit recognition is evident of the value of risk assessment in the comparison of alternatives and not in the production of a risk figure which is regarded as acceptable or unacceptable for a given solution. Significant also was the linking of the process directly to economic criteria of NPV and cash-flow with the point made that these figures would be best in the ideally-built, operated and maintained platform which had the lowest amount of downtime and unserviceable behaviour. Thus, the reduction of economic risk was directly linked to the reduction of technical and operational risk. The application of such an approach not only revealed problems caused by the masking effects of deterministic techniques but also examples where regulatory demands for repairs based on prescriptive codes led to accidents producing significant losses which a risk assessment approach would have been able to avoid (Bea *et al.* 1985).

The proposed and enacted changes relating to the stability of Mobile Offshore Drilling Units (MODUs) at this time provide another example of the continuing tension in engineering regarding the appropriateness of employing probabilistic and risk-based techniques. The loss of the Alexander L. Kielland and the Ocean Ranger had prompted reconsideration of this issue and changes were made to Norwegian regulations at this time with proposals for further change which would introduce a requirement for the design of MODUs to be based on the new techniques - all of which was likely to be followed by the UK (see Praught *et al.* 1985; Dahle 1985). The then current regulations and guidance in the UK set a variety of parameters within which a structure had to be designed and which possessed the advantage of being easy to use and to check. These parameters, however, were felt also to operate as a restraint on design such that, given the wide variety of structures which they covered, it would have been possible in many cases to design a better structure without referring to the regulations. Thus, a structure might fulfil regulatory requirements but be catastrophically sensitive to situations only marginally beyond them.

Up to a certain point, the two competing programmes in engineering were in agreement. Both were keen on self-regulation, believing that left to itself engineering would do the best job. When it came, however, to deciding what engineering should do to improve the situation in the aftermath of the Alexander L. Kielland and Ocean Ranger disasters there was complete disagreement.

On the one hand, the recognition that operating conservatively and deterministically in the past had been part of the reason for the problems now encountered led the developing programme to propose a risk-assessment solution. In other words, the proposed regulatory changes were seen as reasonable and rational. The question of stability would not then simply be a matter of complying with regulatory parameters but of considering it in the light of all possible events and failures which could effect stability changes. Such a risk assessment would cover hardware issues, software issues (procedures and maintenance) and also human factors. These would be prioritised in descending order with the aim being to solve most problems at the design stage and removing as much sensitivity to software and human failures as possible. One reason for this order of priorities was the difficulty in assigning probabilities to human factors (Dahle 1985), although even this issue was being addressed as simulators were used to help collect data and provide feedback to the design process (Kumar & Michael 1985).

On the other hand, the deterministic programme saw this response as simply a typical over-reaction to the Alexander L. Kielland and Ocean Ranger accidents on the part of politics and regulators who needed to be seen to be doing something with regard to the stability of MODUs. This view conversely saw the industry itself as reacting promptly and effectively without taking costly and time-consuming measures which did not in any case lead to significant improvements in safety. When it came to the point, however, of deciding what changes should be made to design parameters there was a reluctance within this rationality to move to dynamic as opposed to static analysis even if it was conceded that the computer technology was available. The reason given was that the existing design process was in any event conservative and the new techniques would only serve to complicate matters (Praught *et al.* 1985). The impact of the deterministic blind spot is very evident in this approach. Even though conservatism had clearly not availed the Alexander L. Kielland or the Ocean Ranger, the proposed solution to these problems was more conservatism.

A similar divergence can be seen in the reassessment of platforms. Even in 1986, when meteorological, wave and current databases were much more extensive than they had been when first generation platforms were built, there was 'still considerable uncertainty about the method of estimating actual forces' (Tebbett & Lalani 1986). While there was a growing belief that non-linear, probabilistic techniques could offer significant advantages in this respect and a growing emphasis on the dynamic response of platforms and the non-linear nature of wave-loading processes (Spidsoe *et al.* 1986), reassessment work was carried out on the Thistle platform using conventional static and fatigue analysis (Bond & Shaw 1986).

The new rationality in engineering had also produced other changes in the way platforms were designed and constructed. There were changes, for example, in the project management of platform construction, with emphasis on trying to transcend customs and practices in the industry which were unacceptable as regards the assurance of quality and on improving communications between all parties, including subcontractors, concerned with specification, design and construction (Saunders 1983; Salama *et al.* 1985; Bradshaw *et al.* 1985). In many cases, the development of new technologies (such as the Tension Leg Platform) represented a degree of complexity never before encountered and which required new management techniques if the problems of the first generation platforms were not to be repeated. Equally, the advent of the integrated deck - itself made possible by developments in heavy-lift technology - allowed engineers to design decks for the first time according to criteria other than the weight limits of anywhere between eight and twenty modules. For the first time, engineering began to consider the layout of facilities on the basis of safety with, for example, production equipment being located away from accommodation rather than on the basis of the constraints of offshore lifting and construction. Another significant safety advantage of the integrated deck was the fact that the offshore hook-up time - previously an average of one million man hours over a period of 10 months - was reduced by over 90%. This factor, together with an onshore construction process which was much less sensitive to subcontractor delays, reduced the pressure on field economics - the heavy front-end loading that so dominated management thinking - as production could begin much earlier in the total life of the project (Abbot *et al.* 1980; McDonnell & Hasz 1985).[51] Developments such as these indicated a new awareness in engineering about the impact of previous assumptions and the previous deterministic risk-reduction programme of conservatism - all of which had operated to mask other dimensions of risk including occupational risk. As in industry management, there was an awareness in engineering that first generation projects had only been saved by price rises the scale of which could not be expected to come to the aid of current projects (Nehring 1985).

Most striking of all, however, from the point of view of health and safety at work, was the growing awareness at around this time (as a consequence of the application of risk assessment techniques) of the shortcomings in platform evacuation procedures and in fire protection (Bengtsson & Thulin 1985; Peters 1985). These were issues which had previously not figured largely on the cognitive map of engineering in comparison with the over-riding concern with structural safety but now there was a recognition of shortcomings in existing regulations, which had been based on assumptions and calculations which were now revealed to have masked significant risks. Notwithstanding all the developments towards and involving the new programme, however, there was equally a recognition that a basic change in engineering attitude might still be required before they were widely adopted (G. Edwards 1984) and that such a process required 'a substantial shifting of gears in an engineering sense' (Bea *et al.* 1985, 168).

In summary, both industry management and engineering up to this point demonstrated a growing awareness of the inadequacies of the risk-minimisation programmes which had produced so many problems during the 1970s. Alongside this awareness, there were definite attempts at a reorientation towards alternative programmes which would be more open to the dimensions of risk that had previously been masked. We can see in economic risk assessment (esp. Faeke *et al.* 1991) and in engineering risk assessment (esp. Bea *et al.* 1985) clear signs of an observation by one system of how other systems were observing, which differences they constructed and sought to minimise. That these developments might even have been leading to a firmer structural coupling of management and engineering on this basis is evident from the formation of QUASCO (Quality Appraisal Service Company) by the major operators in 1985 to carry out assessments of quality control procedures in contractors supplying services, materials and equipment to the industry (Passemard 1988). In both systems, however, as has been noted above, the developments were by no means complete and had to compete with the original deterministic programmes. And however much headway had been made by the new programmes, they were about to be subjected to a severe test.

7 Regulation

In contrast to management and engineering, sources for the approach of the regulators during this period are limited although the evidence of the PED to the Burgoyne Committee is instructive.[52] Very broadly, this evidence suggests that the cognitive map for the regulators changed little between the mid 1970s (Figure 3.9) and 1980 (Figure 4.7). The basic issue remains that the complexity of the regulated area leads to a need for flexibility and the ability to react rapidly to new circumstances. Whereas previously the regulators had been sensitive to industry concern with rigid interpretation of regulations, they now complain of difficulties in drafting regulations which meet legal requirements and which are understandable by the industry. This, together with the finding that detail at the level of regulation is impossible, leads to detail being provided at the level of guidance notes and individual interpretation by inspectors. The programme is still one of fostering mutual respect between the industry and the regulators which was a feature also of the previous cognitive map (Figure 3.9) and the basic approach is still prescriptive: the regulators are still, in the final analysis, seeking to tell the industry what to do and how to do it. Interestingly, the rather awkward formulation of the 'sole justification' present in the previous cognitive map is now dispensed with in favour of an open statement of the twin aims which are secured by this approach: safety and continuity of production.

The problem with such an approach is that it cannot observe safety problems which do not affect continuity of production - a blindness which has obvious implications for occupational as opposed to technical safety. In the light of such a world construction, the concern of many to see the HSWA 1974 fully applied offshore is very understandable. While the PED stated at this time that it was 'becoming aware of the need for Inspectors to acquire additional expertise in the field of occupational safety' (Burgoyne 1980, 230) and that the training of inspectors 'could perhaps be augmented in one or two areas, for example, on general occupational safety and legal enforcement matters' (Burgoyne 1980, 231), it did not see the HSWA as part of that process and even perceived dangers in its application. Pointing to the need to take account of both on-duty *and* off-duty workers on an offshore installation, the PED demonstrated that the 1971 Act was preferable to the 1974 Act which they characterised as 'deficient' (Burgoyne 1980, 228). In view of the previous point about continuity of production, the ability of the regulators to take adequate account of the safety of workers beyond the technical integrity of the installation must be in doubt. Even the undoubted concern with technical integrity must be qualified, however, as the adequacy of fire-fighting arrangements was judged solely on the basis than 'none of the 22 fires on offshore installations in 1978 developed into a major disaster' (1980, 232). Similarly, on the question of 'blast walls between the accommodation

Figure 4.7 Cognitive Map: Regulators (early 1980s)

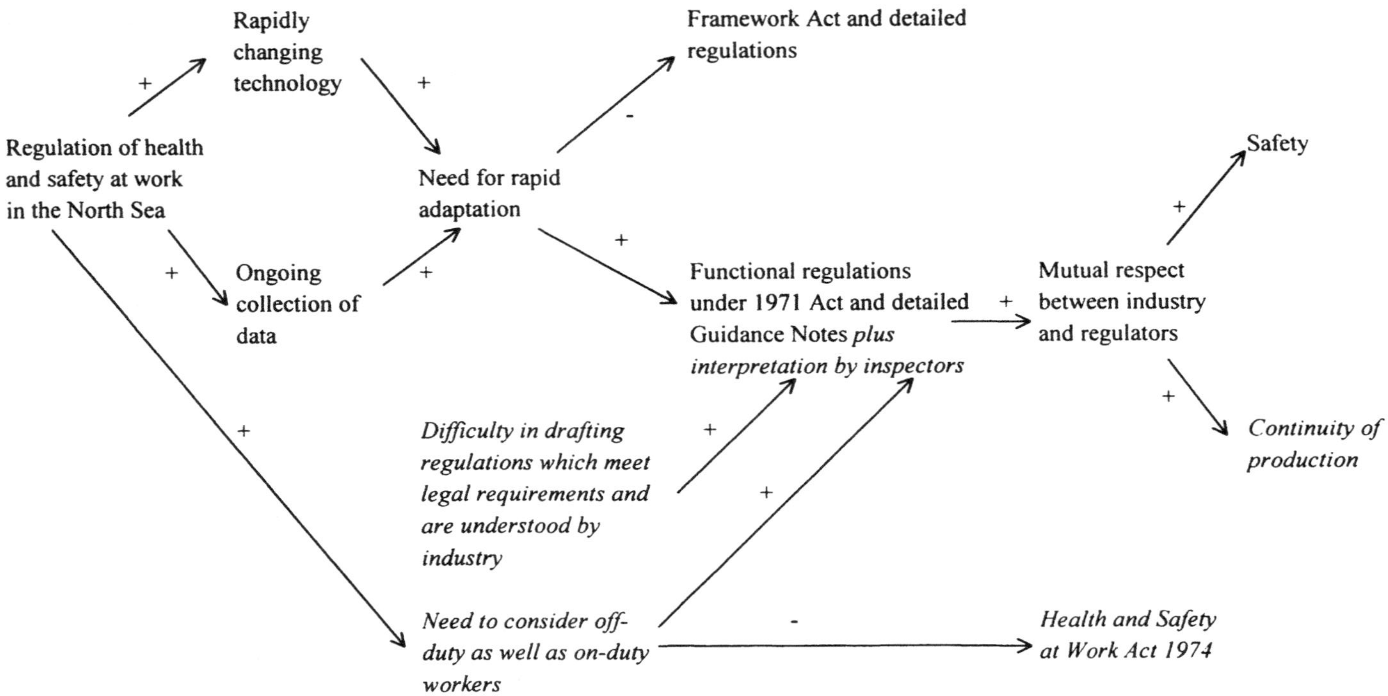

block and the rest of the platform', while it was conceded that it was possible that this 'would improve safety' this had 'not proved necessary' (1980, 233). It seems clear that the regulators were still operating to a very deterministic programme of risk reduction implemented by detailed guidance.

Once again, it is possible to characterise the approach of the regulators as admirably flexible in the face of a challenging and rapidly developing regulated area. However, there is by now clear evidence that the focus on technical issues, which appeared justified in the light of the earlier concerns in engineering, is woefully inadequate in terms of the relative appreciation of technical risks. The contrast between the regulators' approach to the measurement of risk and that developing in engineering is striking. In common with the UKOOA evidence to the Burgoyne Committee discussed above, the regulators' view is that if nothing has gone wrong so far then everything must be in order. The stark lesson being learned in other parts of the industry at this time, however, as has been seen, was that this attitude to risk was fundamentally flawed. Equally, it seems reasonable to suggest that the explicit mention of twin aims of safety and continuity of production indicates that safety issues which did not impact on the question of continuity were not accorded a similar weight. It would be wrong to say that the regulators prioritised production over safety but it seems clear that their understanding of safety was quite different from that intended, for example, by the Health and Safety at Work Act 1974. And while that Act was available as a source of authority for a focus on occupational issues, the regulators paradoxically regarded it as a hindrance to that very purpose because of confusion about its coverage of off-duty workers. Thus, those charged with the regulation of offshore safety operated according to a programme and on the basis of a world construction which was dangerously restricted in the observation it allowed of both occupational safety and the relative risks of certain technical issues. Nevertheless, in its own terms, this approach appeared as a rational approach to a complex problem. In the light of what was about to happen, the relatively restricted observation provided by this approach was nothing short of disastrous.

8 The 1986 Price Collapse

> The tangibility of need suppresses the perception of risks, but only their perception, not their reality or their effects; risks denied grow especially quickly and well. (Beck 1992, 45)

8.1 Introduction

The regulators apart, the picture presented in the foregoing sections of this chapter is one of comparative optimism for the development of new rationalities, new risk-reduction programmes, both in the management of the offshore oil industry and in the engineering world. In both cases, despite tensions with the pre-existing rationalities, the developing rationalities were more explicitly concerned with assessing the risk of offshore activities and with overcoming the restricted vision previously available. By the middle of 1985 we have seen evidence of a quite detailed understanding of the uses and limitations of risk assessment methods in helping to manage both economic and technical or operational risk. Industry management and offshore engineering had by this time become more aware of the blind spots of the previous deterministic programmes and of the more complex environment they confronted which therefore required a more responsive and less deterministic approach. It would be going too far, however, to suggest that these developments constituted a complete transcendence of the old programmes. Equally, what was discussed in Chapter 2 revealed the impossibility of ever transcending at least some blind spot. If the industry had seen the problems caused by its former determinism, it was equally now operating on the basis of a world construction which, if it was not so restricted as the previous one, nevertheless did not leave it the room to deal with the event which overtook it between November 1985 and February 1986. Now open to the idea that projects could not expect to be saved by fortuitous price hikes and that the ongoing decline after 1979 might end in stability, the cognitive maps of both management and engineering were showing risk-management and minimisation strategies which took account of this possibility. They did not, however, take account of the risk of a significant price *fall* despite the warnings which were mentioned earlier (e.g. Odell 1983).

The dramatic collapse in the price of crude oil which occurred at this time had its origins, as did the price hikes of 1973 and 1979, in the activities of OPEC. In response to these rises, there had been a growing movement by Western governments to reduce, firstly, their dependence on crude oil and, secondly, their dependence on crude oil from the Middle East. Thus, as OPEC received a greater price for each barrel, they sold in turn fewer barrels. Saudi Arabia as the strongest and largest of the OPEC producers adopted a 'swing' position in order to allow the other cartel members to maintain their production levels. This situation persisted only for a certain period of time, however, as both the continuing development of non-OPEC oil (especially in the North Sea) and a lack of discipline in the cartel (with members doing secret deals beyond their agreed quotas) led to a halving of the level of Saudi production and export - a level which the Saudis were not willing to accept. Instead, they introduced a new form of oil pricing to replace the previously administered system: netback pricing. This system meant that the price of a barrel of oil at the time of its sale was not fixed but depended on the final value of the products which were refined and sold from it. In effect, the full extent of price risk was passed from the buyer of crude oil to the seller. The aim of this strategy was to put pressure on high-cost oil provinces like the North Sea where a quick sale of oil at a certain price was more important than in onshore areas where costs were often negligible in comparison. Pressure was increased by OPEC producers offering buyers overt or covert price concessions. The Saudis wanted non-OPEC producers to agree to a market shares arrangement where production would be controlled in relation to demand and each party to the agreement would be guaranteed a specified share of that demand. Whereas it was seen that politics originally in the 1970s was by no means hostile to the idea of production controls whether in the form of participation or of depletion policy, it was seen equally that by 1985 the political world construction had changed and there now appeared to be a convergence of view with the industry on this point. Thus, the UK response to the Saudi request was a firm refusal. The Saudis had banked on the fact that the government would not be prepared to accept the cut in revenues which a lower oil price implied nor to run the risks of weakening sterling and raising interest rates, but it seems instead that the government took the view that the interests of the economy as a whole were better served by lower priced oil. Even if the oil industry felt the pressure from a price fall, the rest of the economy as consumers of oil could only benefit (Ellis Jones 1988, 53-7; Horsnell & Mabro 1993, 79-81; Harvie 1995, 301).

If politics was relatively unconcerned by the prospect of a price fall then it seems that the Saudi expectation was that the industry in the North Sea at least would respond in a way which they viewed as more favourable. In particular, they calculated that with new North Sea fields being developed on the expectation of a barrel price of $28 any fall significantly below that level would drive fields out of production. There was, however, an alternative argument which suggested that while projects might have been planned on the basis of such an expectation, nevertheless, if much of the costs had already been incurred in the form of capital investment then the actual cost per barrel of production would only be in the region of $5 to $8. Thus, even if at a level below, say, $28 an operator might be showing a loss on the annual profit and loss account, nevertheless it would not drive it out of business because cash-flow could still be positive right down to a barrel price of around $10. Further, if loans which were accruing interest whether the field was in production or not had to be serviced then again there was another reason for staying in production (Ellis Jones 1988, 305-6).[53]

The price of oil immediately before the collapse in November 1985 was just over $30 although for most of the year it had been between $26 and $28. When the fall came, however, it was dramatic, with a steady decline right down to a low point of around $10. This low was momentary, however, and despite another slump in July 1986 down to nearer $8 following OPEC's indecisive June meeting, the average price for 1986 was around $15.[54] Thus, on the immediately foregoing analysis, the price fall which occurred between November 1985 and February 1986, which politics was prepared to accept, perhaps ought not to have troubled the industry much either. Insofar as North Sea production was not cut this analysis is correct. To suggest that the industry carried on as before, however, would be quite wrong. The way in which the industry constructed this event both at the level of management and within engineering requires closer scrutiny.

8.2 The Response of Industry Management

The immediate response of industry management to the price collapse was to announce major reductions in expenditure with regard to exploration.[55] As a result, small exploration companies ran into serious trouble and within a very short time were in many cases technically bankrupt. If such companies had any production income at all then it was likely to be from small shares they had bought in the Forties and Claymore fields and the price of a barrel was now less than half of what it had been only a few months before.[56] By the end of the year, around half of the drilling rigs in the North Sea were without work.[57] The other major casualty to emerge within a short time of the price fall was the development of new fields. The small fields which were in prospect before the fall simply did not appear viable at a price less than $15. Thus, a number of delays were announced[58] and fields going ahead were described as having to be 'low-cost lean developments, making use of finely-tuned engineering' (Sanderson 1988, 7-8).

But while these problems were well-publicised at the time, perhaps especially because of the redistribution of assets which occurred as large companies bought up the smaller ones which could not survive in the new conditions, the impact on existing fields was less visible. The prevailing view seems to have been that most existing developments would be unaffected by the fall for the very reason mentioned above that where capital costs had already been incurred the importance of maintaining cash flow meant that production would continue down to a barrel price of around $10 - a price which had not yet been experienced for more than very short periods at the end of March and in July 1986. There was some analysis at the time, however, which suggested that even at a price of $15 - much closer to what was being experienced - only 13 of the 39 fields then either in production or under development had a positive remaining net present value.[59] Similarly, the warning was issued that even mature fields which had already passed payback point were severely affected by the fall as regarded ongoing expenditure related to maintenance, satellite developments and so on (Kemp 1986, 289). The position of companies which had taken on extraordinary levels of debt just before the price fall should also be remembered.[60] The level of concern in some quarters of the industry can be well imagined. In these circumstances, industry management responded in a number of ways which reflected the ongoing tension we saw in the preceding sections between the deterministic programme and the emerging risk-oriented programme.

(a) The risk-oriented response In Section 2.2 above, it was noted that despite growth in the Brent forward market after 1981 and a growing interest in futures (if not always their actual use), the industry in the period up to the price fall of 1985-86 was if anything more convinced of price stability with an eventual rise in due course, meaning that it was not well-adjusted to the possibility of a fall. When the price fall came, therefore, it revealed a significant blind spot - even in the more risk-oriented rationality. Equally, the scope of the 15 day market for sophisticated risk management was limited as it was principally used for setting prices - especially for tax purposes. The scale of the 1986 slump put immense pressure on the forward market, and fears about clearing and performance arising from a

'serious set of defaults' (Sas 1989a, 4) led to further fears of withdrawals from the market and a consequent reduction in liquidity. While the ending of netback pricing by Saudi Arabia in early 1987 shortly after an OPEC decision to set a marker price of $18 eased the situation and confidence returned to the market with large finance houses entering and bringing both increased liquidity and expertise, the period of doubt had led more in the industry to the futures market as a means of coping with price risk (Horsnell & Mabro 1993, 79-81; Roeber 1993, 48-9). Among other reasons for this shift was the fact that in a forward contract there are only two parties and thus companies with financial problems caused by the fall found it difficult to continue trading, as others viewed them as too high a credit risk. On the futures market, by comparison, the exchange operates as an intermediary and guarantees performance, allowing companies to continue trading so long as they can provide the initial margin and meet subsequent daily calls to cover adverse price movements (Horsnell & Mabro 1993, 198-203).

The degree of development in futures in the two years following the price fall can be exaggerated, however, and a good picture of the situation can be gained from the words of the BP chairman in mid-1986 when he said that there was really no well-developed long-term futures market.

> If everybody really believes that future oil prices are going to be stronger than those at present, why hasn't a financial way of taking that punt been devised?
>
> We ought to establish some form of hedging technique because the reality is that future oil prices are still uncertain. (Simon 1988, 58)

The need to protect projects from price volatility was recognised, but statistics from IPE and NYMEX indicate that while volumes traded increased after the fall, development was initially slow.[61] It would also be wrong to suggest that the forward market played no role in price risk management after the shaky period in mid-1986. Despite greater legal complexity (Sas 1989a; 1989b) and the fact that in a forward contract 'it is impossible to have the same degree of security as is offered by a cleared system' (Sas 1989a, 33), the forward market continued to play such a role, not least because of the costs and labour-intensive requirements of a cleared or futures market. Similarly, it would be wrong to suggest that forward and futures contracts were the only price risk management tools available to the industry at that time. Standard Oil, for example, issued bonds linked to the price of oil, thus reducing the cost of its debt by linking the rate of return on the debt to the price of oil forecast in the 1990s. This involved being prepared to give up potential future value to reduce costs in a period of low prices (Simon 1988, 58). That this risk management tool was designed to reduce current costs as much as anything else points, however, to the dominant concern of the industry at the time - cost reduction. A move into futures after the slump would take some time to have an impact on projects whereas the industry saw a need for action with an immediate effect.

(b) The deterministic response The issue of cost reduction in ongoing operations in the aftermath of the 1986 price fall is well exemplified by the continuing debate between industry and politics about the tax regime. Despite the convergence of world constructions noted in Section 4.3 above, the fall was of such a magnitude that the appropriateness of the system of taxation was again put in doubt. While all concerned in the industry were agreed that the pressure on the profits from current production should be reduced so as to improve cash flows (Simon 1988, 59), they were unable to reach a consensus about how this should best be done. Despite the improvements in the tax regime over the preceding few years, the underlying issue of a system which was always unable adequately to take account of field-to-field differences came to the forefront with a vengeance in the context of a dramatic change in one of the key variables. Thus, it was pointed out that while a cut in the rate of PRT might help mature fields it would do nothing for newer and smaller fields which were perhaps years away from paying this tax. Similarly, the abolition of royalties would help the older fields but not the post-1983 start-ups which were not subject to royalty payments in any case. The alternative most favoured was, therefore, that of changes to expenditure allowances to encourage ongoing expenditure (Quinlan 1986, 205).

For its part, the government saw the position somewhat differently. It regarded the current regime as still sufficiently attractive even after the fall and was wary of making changes which would improve company cash flows without simultaneously encouraging further development. In particular, the tax regime for newer fields was seen as more sensitive to the price change than that for older fields (Quinlan 1986, 205; Kemp 1986, 289; Simon 1988, 59). The 1986 Budget, admittedly occurring relatively soon after the fall, saw no changes in the taxation of the industry related to the new price situation but the year closed with the introduction of legislation designed to speed up repayments of APRT which discriminated against fields with low profitability.[62] This trend continued somewhat in

1987 with the introduction of two reliefs against PRT. One was specifically aimed at encouraging new developments by allowing these costs to be set against the income from other fields.[63] The other allowed research costs not related to any particular field to be offset against income for PRT purposes after three years - the idea being to encourage the development of new technologies to exploit hydrocarbon reserves in the context of lower prices.[64]

While the APRT changes of late 1986 indicate a political sensitivity to the pressures on existing fields, the Budget changes of 1987 show that the principal political concern was with ensuring that new developments were brought on-stream and that the industry did not respond to lower prices in ways which threatened production in the longer term. This seems to have been effective as the immediate response of the industry was to announce that shelved projects were to go ahead.[65] Concerns remained, however, about the tax impact on producing fields and the Institute of Fiscal Studies again made proposals to counteract the fact of varying rates of tax applying to different fields unrelated in large part to profitability. Two alternatives were offered, both abolishing royalties to improve the profitability of older fields and both attempting to provide incentives to make incremental investments and incur new capital expenditure. While Budget changes over a period of years had sought to improve the neutrality of the tax system, the Institute found continuing problems which could only ultimately be solved by relating tax to cash flow (Bond, Devereux & Saunders 1987). That there was some political sensitivity to this issue can be seen from the 1988 Budget which again sought to link tax more closely to profits. The changes, however, applied only to onshore fields and Southern Basin gas fields to bring them into line with changes applied to other areas in 1983.[66] There were no new reliefs or tax reductions for the Central North Sea or the Northern North Sea (Kemp & Kellas 1988; Bland 1988). The Institute of Fiscal Studies had, however, precisely identified a serious problem relating to the industry's response to the 1986 price fall with regard to ongoing operations.

It is difficult to be certain about the exact impact of the price cut on individual operators. Some figures are available, however, with BP, for example, estimating that every dollar reduction in the price of a barrel cost the company as a whole some $100m in cash flow (Simon 1988, 52-3). There was a renewed pressure on the front-end costs of projects, with these once more being described as 'crucial', and an increased drive to get maximum value out of the earliest part of projects. Conversely, however, the idea of ongoing investment or the stepped approach to production which had previously been ruled out by the industry was now under serious consideration (Simon 1988, 54). For existing projects, however, where the operating plan was already in place, the options were somewhat more limited and the typical response was to look for efficiencies at every level of operations from the drill floor to the financial structure of a company:

> each additional investment must contribute to project economics. This simple approach is not new but bears restating in a climate where it is essential to separate wants from needs. (Rule & Huddleston 1988)

The explicit aim was to maintain the highest possible positive cash flow and net present value - something which could be done either by raising income or by reducing costs. In the context of relatively fixed opportunities for receiving income in operating fields, the preferred course was to look for cost reductions. While exact figures differ from field to field, it is clear that the impact of a fall in the price of oil from around $30 to around $15 with periods below that level had a dramatic impact on field income. The pressure on operating costs and on ongoing capital expenditure to retain anything like the same positive cash flow was immense - both in the case of newer, smaller fields which had been regarded as 'marginal' even before the fall and in the case of older fields where remedial work was required. The industry management construction of a price 'crisis' is more important for our purposes than the exact figures for any given field.

As was noted above, while the cutting of exploration expenditure and the deferral of new projects was immediately noticeable, the exact impact on existing fields was less clear. There are indications, however, that cost-reduction measures were implemented immediately and indeed that even within a couple of years it was felt that these measures in some cases had gone too far (Sanderson 1988, 3).[67] Some indication of the scale of the cuts can be gained from figures published in 1989 which suggested that in the previous ten years the average cost of producing a barrel of North Sea oil had fallen by two-thirds with most of the reduction being achieved after the price fall of 1986.[68] There was evidence of a new attitude of 'increased efficiency and cost-consciousness throughout operations' (Sanderson 1988, 8) with the aim being the optimisation of the field without loss of production or reduction in safety standards (1988, 11). The measures implemented, however, reveal in retrospect a reimposition of the old deterministic rationality which disregarded the multiple connectivity of technical and operational risks in its concentration on minimising economic risk.

Whereas previously the risk-minimisation programme had been rapid production, the programme in place now was one of straightforward cost-reduction. For example, maintenance intervals were increased, topsides painting was reduced with the imposition of a strict upper limit on spending, a backlog of 'non-urgent' maintenance was allowed to build up to higher levels,[69] subsea inspections (previously the subject of industry criticism for their inadequacy as required by regulations)[70] were reduced to the 'statutory minimum', emergency support vessels were used for diving support rather than contracting specialised diving support vessels, and there were examples of the imposition of a criterion of payback of capital investment within one year for 'any project not strictly required for safety or operational reasons' (Sanderson 1988, 10). Despite this assurance, a survey of offshore workers suggested that they suffered high stress levels and expressed the view that safety received less attention following the price slump.[71] In some cases, work shifts were increased from 12 hours to 15 hours with no days off on a 15 day tour of duty (Harvie 1995, 322). The OILC's assessment of a 'dramatic panic reaction by the operators' does not seem wide of the mark (1991, 33).

Despite the explicit mention of production and safety, the major concern was that cost-reduction should not constitute a withdrawal of investment of a magnitude which would increase the risk of not receiving the benefits of the price upturn as quickly as possible. It is worth noting that at this time there was no doubt in the industry mind that it was only a question of *when* the price upturn came and not *if* (see G. H. Robinson 1986; Sanderson 1988; Simon 1988). The cost-reduction measures were specifically aimed at maintaining a posture such that positive cash flows and NPVs were achieved and capacity was maintained ready for the price upturn. Bearing in mind the tax changes of 1987 mentioned above, it can be seen that this intervention served to encourage this industry posture. Rather than relieving cost reduction pressures on operations, it intensified them. The reiteration of the logic we first saw in Figure 3.2 is complete and even intensified as shown in the cognitive map at Figure 4.8.

The programme of economic risk minimisation is different (cost-reduction in place of rapid production) but its effect is similarly to mask technical and operational risks. The completeness of the return to the old rationality can be seen in the fact that although the risks of, for example, new technological approaches aimed at cost-reduction were mentioned, these were specifically the economic risks of cost and time over-runs associated with unforeseen difficulties inherent in any untried equipment (Hall 1988, 13).

Figure 4.8 Cognitive Map: Industry Management (after 1986 Price Collapse)

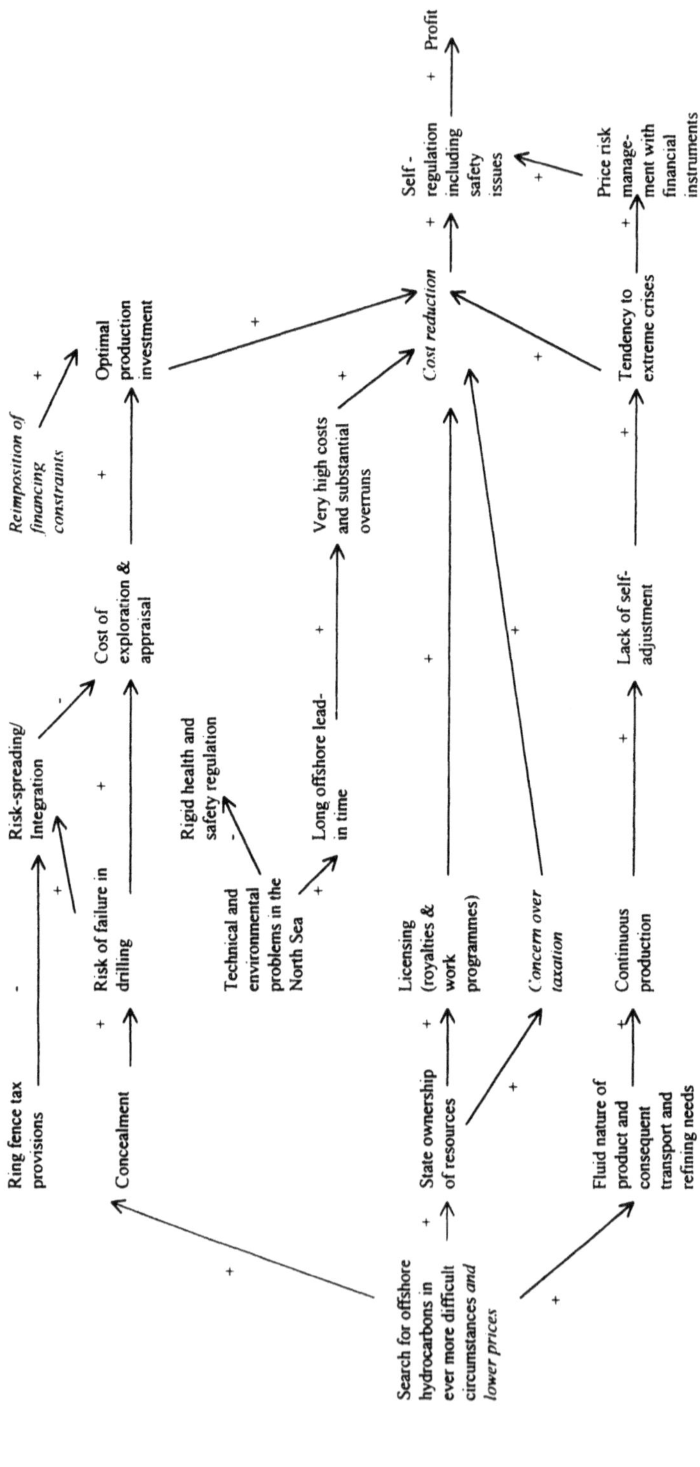

The impact of the new programme of economic risk-minimisation on the industry's construction of the most appropriate contractors is also interesting. In contrast to previous concerns about competitive tendering and the use of contractors without a proven track record,[72] the emphasis is now on the 'passive' opportunities for cost reduction as contractors compete for diminishing business as operators cut budgets (Sanderson 1988, 3-4) and on encouraging competition to ensure the best product at the lowest cost (Hall 1988, 14). The impact on contractor operations is clear - cut costs or go out of business.

As regards the availability of finance, after the days of plenty from 1979-82 and the days of relative plenty thereafter, the price fall produced the reimposition of pressures from banks on projects. Again banks were explicitly concerned to minimise risks but again these were economic risks narrowly understood and the added pressures on operations is clear. At the most basic level, as the possibility to receive income diminished as the price of oil fell, the cost of borrowing increased as banks took a dimmer view of the industry and were indeed unimpressed by claims that the price would rise again in the future. This was especially the case for smaller companies - often the contractors who had to reduce rates to stay in business and retain any kind of positive cash flow - as opposed to the integrated majors (Simon 1988, 56-7). Banks were more than ever concerned that borrowers should provide equity for the early and most risky stages of ventures and thus confined their lending to the most secure stages of the cash flow. Further, they would only allow a borrower to extract profits after they had ensured that the whole repayment schedule could be met. The level of security required was the borrower's total interest in the assets of the project and similar interventions in the operation of the project to those seen previously reappeared (Radford 1988, 25-6). Significantly, the use of new technology was considered as a potentially negative feature of a project which was likely to attract higher borrowing costs as it was seen as increasing the economic risks in terms of unforeseen costs and delays (Radford 1988, 28). In short, this was a time when 'the operators were particularly vulnerable with commissioning deadlines to meet and massive short-term cash borrowings to service' (OILC 1991, 43).

The deterministic response to the price fall is well exemplified by the reaction of Shell and British International Helicopters to the crash of a Chinook helicopter in the North Sea on 6 November 1986 which killed 45 of the 47 men on board. Unpopular with passengers since its introduction in 1981, perhaps significantly not certified for civilian use in the United

States where it was designed, and the subject of greater controversy since a ditching incident in 1984, there was no question of a withdrawal from service or a reassessment of its use on the part of the operator following the crash. With its huge capacity, the Chinook was quite simply a cost-effective way of transferring personnel. Only in June 1987 in the face of sustained criticism from all sides did Shell discontinue use of Chinooks (OILC 1991, 39-41). They have never been used since in the North Sea. Worse, however, was to come.

8.3 The Response of Engineering

It was seen above that, in the period from the 1979 price rise until immediately before the 1985-86 price collapse, engineering demonstrated both an ongoing development of a more risk-oriented rationality and a continuation of the more deterministic rationality which continued to regard the new developments with scepticism. Among factors appearing in the cognitive map of engineering at this time, however, was the issue of the development of smaller more marginal fields which the use of probabilistic techniques was seen as aiding. While to an extent, therefore, new developments under way at the time of the price fall represented a considerable advance over first generation platforms, not least in the control of costs, the size of the fall resulted in a need to reassess their viability completely.

The pressure to cut costs which we saw in the cognitive map of industry management after the fall appears directly and immediately in the cognitive map of engineering (e.g. G. H. Robinson 1986). There are reports of demands from managers for platforms which are 'leaner and meaner' (Boyd 1986) or 'lean and pared to the bone' (Passemard 1988, 107). Thus, while engineering had always had to produce technology which was 'robust' over a range of expected crude oil prices, for the first time it now had to come to terms with a '"disaster" scenario' of a price as low as $10 (Passemard 1988, 107). Just as even the risk-oriented rationality in management before 1986 had still not considered the possibility of a significant price fall, it can be seen that the same was true in the world construction of engineering. The emphasis was now, therefore, on 'eliminating any fat' and on 'getting it "right first time"' in order to comply with the prevailing tighter margins (Passemard 1988, 107).[73] Once again there was an increase in the tension between economics and science in engineering and the way in which the tension was resolved is interesting. On the one hand, the emphasis remained on probabilistic techniques but, on the other, the developing risk orientation which had seen the use of these techniques extended to other risk factors before 1986 suffered a set-back.

Thus, one of the immediate responses of engineering was to return its concentration to the structure as the most expensive single item in a development (Heaf 1988, 41). The principal aim was to use less structural steel and the way to do that was to reduce the weight of the topside equipment. In general, it was seen that reducing topside equipment by one tonne would allow the reduction of topside structural steel, jacket and piles by a further three tonnes (Boyd 1986). Recommendations for ways to achieve weight reductions in topsides included, however, items which demonstrated that the risk orientation evident before the fall had disappeared. For example, it was suggested that 'double safety factors' and 'unnecessary contingencies' be eliminated from the design (Heaf 1988, 50). Where new design techniques were to be used, it was to aid in removing over-estimates associated with 'opinion engineering' (Heaf 1988, 43; 50). Conservatism, previously criticised by the risk-oriented rationality for having masked unforeseen factors as well as producing increased costs, was now criticised solely on the basis of cost and thus of going beyond what was actually required for a safe platform. The removal of remaining conservative factors from future designs was aimed at reducing costs (Svehla & Elliot 1988; Visser 1988). The choice of technology for field development was once again considered very much in terms of economic risk without regard to the technical and operational risks associated with different alternatives. For example, in contrast to the earlier concerns with simultaneous activities on the grounds of safety, comparisons were now drawn between approaches which involved simultaneous drilling and production and those which minimised topside weight by pre-drilling through a template solely on the basis of economic indicators such as relative return on investment and profit to investment ratios where the choice depended on the relative significance of such indicators (Grecco 1987).

As regards inspection, maintenance and repair of platforms, engineering noted 'the necessity to minimise these expenses' and the problem of defining the principles upon which this process should be based. Once again the use of 'predetermined general code type recommendations' was not favoured given their inability to deal with the 'complete spectrum of conditions' (Buslov *et al.* 1987). Engineering, however, also saw difficulties in organising inspection, maintenance and repair in the context of depressed prices, reduced contract rates and increasing maintenance costs. Fixed prescriptive codes were simply not flexible enough and instead risk-assessment procedures were used to produce both an acceptable level of risk and an affordable inspection, maintenance and repair programme (Bea *et al.* 1988). While cost was the motivation, the procedures were nevertheless used to compare alternative programmes rather than to produce an absolute assessment of one programme. Significant at this time was a recognition by engineering of a role for public regulatory input, but nevertheless its construction was in largely negative terms as having the potential for delay, forcing the abandonment of viable alternatives and of producing litigation (Bea *et al.* 1988).

Perhaps the clearest indication of this new concentration on cost emerges from the fact that even as the development of probabilistic techniques continued, albeit in a much more restricted area than before, the period after the fall saw the *cost* of using these techniques coming under scrutiny. Thus, there are examples of the complexity of the techniques being reduced by 'reducing the number of parameters and the size of the element model' in order 'to minimise the cost of the...analysis' (Søreide *et al.* 1986).

While this section began with the point that the impetus to develop smaller, marginal fields before 1986 had resulted in a new cost-saving outlook by management and engineers, later attempts to claim that developments after the price fall were no more than a continuation of this process (e.g. Carter *et al.* 1992) sit unhappily with earlier identifications of the event as a significant watershed in the industry (Rule & Huddleston 1988). It is probably not insignificant that these two assessments date respectively from after and before the Piper Alpha disaster. One of the most striking aspects of this and the previous chapter has been the extent to which health and safety at work as a distinct issue has not figured on the cognitive maps of management and engineering. Equally, it has been seen that even when risk has been a concern, it has been constructed in terms of one aspect only and thus its reduction has often been at the expense of an increase in other aspects of risk. If the price hike of 1979 served to expose to some extent the blind spots of the industry rationalities, the price fall of 1986 effectively served to reinstate them. The observation of other dimensions of risk could only develop when cost pressures were absent. An event two years later, however, was to change profoundly the way in which the industry constructed its world. If health and safety had been invisible before, it was about to attain an unprecedented degree of visibility which has barely diminished in the years since the Piper Alpha disaster.

9 Piper Alpha

> [T]he British authorities' complacent belief in the superiority of their own regulatory approach will retain even the semblance of credibility only as long as a similar tragedy does not overtake an installation operating in the British sector of the North Sea. (Carson 1981, 289, discussing the loss of the Alexander L. Kielland)

9.1 Management and Engineering

The immediate causes of the Piper Alpha disaster as determined by the Cullen Inquiry were outlined in the first chapter.[74] It was seen that a concatenation of in many cases relatively minor events and circumstances produced a disaster of unprecedented scale. At least one trade union has pointed to the price collapse of 1985-86 and the 'dramatic panic reaction' of the industry followed by a gradual 'realisation that the over-reaction in terms of cost-cutting had been ill-advised' as the context within which the disaster occurred (OILC 1991, 33, 41). Occidental, the platform's operators, were sensitive to this sort of contention and vigorously denied in their closing submission to the Cullen Inquiry that there had been reductions in planned maintenance due to the drop in oil prices.[75] The company contended that the reduction in the maintenance budget which had undoubtedly occurred could be explained by the replacement of the previous 'tear down and inspect' method of maintenance, with a more efficient system based on predictive condition monitoring. Equally, the company's extensive closing submission was adamant that they had had in place effective safety systems with clear lines of responsibility, adequate and appropriate staffing at all levels, a positive management attitude to safety, full and frequent communication, training and instruction, incentives to support a positive safety attitude in all personnel, an 'open door' attitude to the raising of safety concerns, constant review and updating of procedures both as regards equipment and operations, and monitoring of activities on the platform.

As was seen in Chapter 1, Lord Cullen disagreed profoundly with this assessment of Occidental's safety arrangements. If his findings are considered in the light of the background which has emerged in this chapter, a number of interesting points emerge. Regarding the permit to work (PTW) system, ten examples were listed 'to demonstrate that the operating staff had no commitment to working to the written procedure; and that the procedure was knowingly and flagrantly disregarded' (Cullen

1990, para 11.3). Discussing the informality of the system, it was stated that a failure of communication of the sort which occurred on the night of the disaster 'can well be understood against the background of informal and unsafe practices...outlined' (para 11.4). Both the training of personnel in the system and its monitoring were regarded as inadequate (paras. 11.9, 11.11). Occidental's approach to 'potentially dangerous jobs' was described as having 'grave shortcomings' (para 11.14). As a result, management were surprised at the number of deficiencies identified by the Inquiry in the PTW system and could not understand why they had not been aware of them. Lord Cullen pointed out, however, that '[i]f there had been adequate monitoring and auditing it is likely that these deficiencies in the PTW system would have been corrected' (para 14.29).

With regard to the operability of the fire-water deluge system, problems had been identified by Occidental necessitating the replacement of the pipework for modules A, B and C on the platform. By the time of the accident, however, only the module B work had been carried out taking a period of some two years up to mid-1987 and the remainder had been deferred. Lord Cullen questioned whether the work had been given a sufficiently high priority but stopped short of agreeing with the contention that the lengthy period involved was due to a desire to save or spread cost (para 12.23). Rather, he noted that the

> prolonged process appears...to have stemmed from the failure of senior management to manage the rectification with the urgency which such a vital safety system warranted...They too readily accepted the advice of more junior staff that the system would still be effective in handling an emergency; whereas in reality by at least February 1988 it was clear that it would not. (para 14.51)

At this time, a memorandum from Occidental's Facilities Engineering Manager mentioned that 'on Piper...we have no structural fireproofing...and all structural members are highly stressed. Structural integrity would be lost within 10-15 minutes if a fire was fed from a large pressurised hydrocarbon inventory' (para 12.2). It is easy to see in Occidental's admitted change in approach to maintenance (the move to 'predictive condition monitoring') the adoption of the sort of probabilistic techniques for cost reasons discussed in the preceding section which ultimately masked technical and operational risks.

Regarding response to emergencies, Lord Cullen concluded that he was 'not satisfied that the system operated on Piper came close to achieving the necessary understanding on the part of all personnel as to how to react in an emergency' (para 13.12). This state of affairs was considered all the more surprising since there had been an opportunity to consider the suitability of the response to emergencies following an earlier incident. On 24 March 1984, there was an explosion and release of gas on Piper Alpha resulting in a fire. Alarms, the deluge system and the fire pumps all functioned properly. The fire was brought under control in two hours and 179 personnel were evacuated in 50 minutes to the *Tharos* lying some 500 feet away by helicopters which were in the area at the time. Despite the apparent success of emergency systems and procedures on this occasion, the Safety Superintendent afterwards postulated what would have happened if helicopters and the *Tharos* had not been available and the weather had been too severe to allow evacuation by sea. It would have taken two-and-a-half hours to scramble helicopters from land and he therefore called for offshore-based helicopters and a shift in bias to air evacuation. The response from management, however, was to regard this as a worst-case scenario and to assume that even if both air and sea evacuation were to prove impossible in a given situation then, nevertheless, the platform would be self-sufficient in coping with any contingency. The tension between the deterministic and risk-oriented rationalities at this time identified earlier is clear in this exchange. On the one hand there was a growing awareness of the other risk factors affecting the safety of the platform and personnel while on the other there was a belief in the suitability of the built-in technological solutions without, significantly, any risk assessment being carried out to support this belief (para 14.12ff). The discovery of problems with the very technological 'solutions' considered as sufficient to meet any contingency and the long period accepted for their rectification demonstrates the extent to which an inability to observe risks other than economic risk was reinforced in the cognitive maps following the oil price fall in 1986. As Lord Cullen described it '[t]he type of scenario that happened in the disaster had never been considered' by Occidental's Loss Prevention Department. They had not used their expertise to determine the probability of failure in circumstances specific to Piper Alpha (para 14.22). As regards the management response, Lord Cullen stated that:

> the attitude of management witnesses to the assessment of risk was...unsatisfactory...the witnesses reliance on a merely qualitative opinion showed a dangerously superficial approach to a major hazard...management were remiss in not enquiring further into the risks of a rupture of one of the

> gas risers and in such an event the risk of structural damage and injury to personnel. (para 14.23)

Another consequence of this attitude was that despite the fact that an 'unusually high level of work...was proceeding on Piper in the period leading up to the time of the disaster' including major construction work, additional maintenance work, the changeout of the gas conservation module and the consequent change in the operating mode of the platform to greatly increased flaring (para 14.37), it did not appear that adequate account had been taken of the need to ensure a higher level of supervision and control. Evidence of the greater risks involved could be drawn from the fact that in the days leading up to the disaster there had been a number of gas leaks (para 14.39). The total shutdown of the platform had originally been contemplated for June 1988, but following the deferral until 1989 of the only work which was considered to require a shutdown - the maintenance of electrical switchgear - phase 1 operation which allowed production to continue with increased flaring was chosen instead (para 14.41). At the Inquiry, Occidental agreed that there was more scope for mistakes to occur at the time of the disaster than in normal circumstances. Managers maintained, however, that had OIMs been concerned that there was too much work they could have requested a total shutdown. The surviving OIM, on the other hand, indicated that he had not been involved in the decision to allow production to continue and could not explain it (para 14.42). Of similar significance was the fact that despite the 'substantial and diverse' programme of work and the need for strengthened management and supervision, two senior posts (including the lead safety operator) were vacant and three posts had been filled by temporarily upgraded staff at the time of the disaster (para 14.43).

Despite all of these problems, Occidental's statement of general policy under s2(3) of the HSWA 1974 stated *inter alia* that '[t]he promotion of health and safety is an integral part of the duties of line management and should be afforded the same priority as other key responsibilities' (para 14.3). According to the surviving OIM, this was commonly interpreted on Piper Alpha as meaning that the safety of personnel came first at all times - a point reiterated by the shore-based Production and Pipeline Manager (para 14.5). There was evidence, nevertheless, at the Inquiry that another set of priorities was possible. Presented with evidence that a large number of 'hot work' permits were issued rather than saving such work for a shutdown, the DEn inspector who had visited the platform in the month before the disaster concluded that

Occidental 'considered production more important than safety' (para 15.29). Significantly, however, this had not been his finding at the time of the inspection. It is possible to see, then, that Occidental operated very much according to the deterministic programme of cost-reduction which aimed at the reduction of economic risk and which as a consequence could not observe other dimensions of risk.

9.2 Regulation and Piper Alpha

In the immediate aftermath of the Piper Alpha disaster, the PED were required to produce a further account of their role in a submission to the Cullen Inquiry.[76] Whereas at the Burgoyne Committee the world construction revealed by the PED's submission showed a perceived fundamental tension between the HSWA 1974 and the MWA 1971 which the regulator's resolved by favouring the latter (Figure 4.7), the position in 1988 was somewhat different. Perhaps influenced by the administrative changes made after the Report of the Burgoyne Committee was produced, the PED now viewed the 1974 Act as complementary to their favoured 1971 Act. Now the regulators saw the statutes as allowing the choice of the most appropriate response to any given hazard. While the 1974 Act puts general duties on employers and employees, the 1971 Act creates a structure of duties and responsibilities which is not related to the employment relationship and thus applies to all on an installation whoever they are and whether or not they are on duty. The PED described this choice of Acts as having allowed the enactment of a wide range of regulations which had to address diverse environments, complex technology and a wide range of activities and which was supported by non-mandatory guidance.

Up to the Piper Alpha disaster, guidance had been published by the PED on design and construction, life-saving appliances and firefighting equipment and on issues of selection, training and qualifications for a number of different jobs. In addition, some 120 Safety Notices had been published on more detailed issues, a somewhat greater number of Diving Safety Memoranda and between 40 and 50 Offshore Technology Reports. Despite this apparently high degree of regulatory and guidance activity, the PED stressed that the government had no direct legal responsibility for safety offshore but rather

> develops, administers and enforces the statutory framework and seeks by guidance and advice to assist those responsible, and seeks to promote progressive improvements in standards of safety.

Apart from the publication of guidance and safety notices, the most direct method employed by the PED in this regard was physical inspection of offshore installations. This function was carried out by the Inspection and Operations branch, which sought 'primarily...to secure the health and safety of offshore workers', but the precise approach to inspections looked in the aftermath of the Piper Alpha disaster tragically inadequate.

The PED's own position was that its work depended on the professional skills of its inspectors. These were predominantly qualified mechanical, structural, electrical or petroleum engineers who also received some specialised training in health and safety. The actual inspection in any given case had the potential to cover all aspects of the installation and the work environment and in more detail the mechanical, structural, electrical or petroleum engineering aspects according to the specialisation of the particular inspector involved. The frequency of inspections depended *inter alia* upon the installation in question, the number of personnel on board and the rotation of different disciplines in the inspectorate.

As to the process of the inspection itself, the PED stated that its purpose was 'not exclusively to seek out cases of non-compliance, but more to assess the adequacy of the safety of the installation as a whole'. This was essentially a 'selective procedure' since 'total supervision' was never possible. The purpose was rather to provide 'stimulus and support'. Inspection also took account of working procedures and of management resources and performance, while the Certifying Authorities looked in detail at specified aspects of structure and equipment. If an inspector was dissatisfied with what he found, then he had three options open to him: firstly, he could simply indicate the need for improvement; secondly, he could serve an improvement or prohibition notice under the HSWA 1974 or use powers under the Inspectors and Casualties Regulations to require owners or OIMs to do or refrain from doing something; or thirdly, he could recommend prosecution. Prosecution was not a frequently used option and even the second alternative was described as having been 'used sparingly'.

While, then, the comprehensive prescription aimed at by the regulators from the outset was still present in the vast range of documents they had produced, there was by this time clearly no attempt to achieve similarly comprehensive compliance. The extent to which inspection was selective can be seen in the statement of a PED witness to the Cullen

Inquiry that whether a particular issue would be included in an inspection depended on 'whether they catch the eye during the visit or not' (Cullen 1990, para 15.32). That said, when a dangerous situation occurred or was noticed during an inspection, the PED would disseminate information to the industry as a whole on how it had arisen and how it could be avoided. But this selective or rather haphazard approach to inspection and reactive approach to problems means that by this time it is not clear what programme the regulators were operating to. Never adopting a tough stance, they by now appear to have lost sight even of their 'fostering mutual respect' programme in an attempt to minimise risk. It is consequently impossible to produce a cognitive map for the regulators at this time as there is a lack of coherence in their pronouncements to the inquiry.

It is no surprise to find, then, that, as was noted in Chapter 1, the regulators were severely criticised by Lord Cullen in his report. There could be no more damning indictment of the PED than the finding that their inspections were 'superficial to the point of being of little use as a test of safety on the platform' (Cullen 1990, para 15.48) and not really an effective means of assessing the management of safety (para 15.50). The bottom line was that the regulators had persisted in a prescriptive approach to regulation (for all that they professed flexibility and adaptability) long after the Burgoyne Committee's recommendations of a shift towards objective-setting. This prescription, however, was not the result of any assessment of risk and not subject to any form of adequate inspection. There was consequently no ability on the part of the regulators to observe what was happening in the industry as it preoccupied itself with cost-reduction.

In the light of these findings, Lord Cullen's recommendations, as was seen in Chapter 1, went right to the heart of how the industry operated and how it would be regulated. The HSE would take over responsibility from the PED. Individual operators would have to make out the case that each installation was safe and that an adequate auditable Safety Management System was in place. A demonstration would be required that major hazards had been identified, that the risks had been assessed and that these were being or would be managed. In the event of an emergency, a temporary safe refuge would be provided along with the means of evacuation and escape.

10 Conclusions

In this chapter, the construction of two significant oil price events in the systems of engineering and industry management have principally been examined. In both communicative systems, the 1979 price rise provided an occasion for, on the one hand, a reappraisal of how the industry operated and how it had got itself into the dire situation it found itself in 1978, and, on the other, a belief to take hold that oil prices could only rise - possibly even to quite extraordinary levels - over the coming decades. In both communicative systems, therefore, there was evidence of an ongoing and developing rationality which was more oriented to risk in terms broader than had been the case in the 1970s and which sought to minimise risk in ways which did not thereby mask or even increase other aspects of risk. In management, there was a growth of forward contracts on the Brent market and a developing, albeit tentative, interest in more sophisticated techniques for managing price risk by means of derivatives markets. In engineering, there was a steady development of probabilistic techniques which had appeared in the late 1970s as a means of dealing with cost pressures in structural engineering but which were now applied to all aspects of risk in design, construction, operation and maintenance. Equally, however, there was evidence in both systems of continuing determinism which applied the traditional programmes and fought shy of more sophisticated techniques for managing risk. In other words, different programmes were simultaneously available within each system.

Significantly, however, even in the more risk-oriented programmes, those which began to observe other dimensions of risk as constructed in other systems, the possibility of a price fall does not appear to have been considered. Thus, when the crash came, while it was an event which was ultimately constructed by management as necessitating full use of price risk-management instruments, it was equally constructed as necessitating immediate and drastic cost-cutting across the board. Whatever more sophisticated risk minimisation had been employed by management before 1986, it could not absorb such a fall. Here the limitations of even the risk-oriented programme in engineering became evident as measures were taken which, while they were explicitly regarded as safe, appeared in retrospect as rash and as having increased risk.

This account set out the context within which the Piper Alpha disaster occurred. While the 1986 price collapse was not mentioned as a significant issue by Lord Cullen despite allegations made at the Inquiry, the extent to which Occidental management's view of its actions fits with the management cognitive map for the period after the price collapse (which served to mask significant risks while explicitly mentioning safety) is striking. That we are not focusing too much on a single event rather than on structural issues is clear from the abundance of evidence reviewed which points to a wholesale return to deterministic programmes across the industry at this time.

As regards politics, the debate about the government's acceptance of the Burgoyne Report demonstrated the continuing political belief in the prescriptive regulatory approach to health and safety and indicated a political misunderstanding of what had been revealed at the hearings of the Committee. Thereafter, the issue of health and safety at work offshore largely disappeared from the concerns of politics - albeit that there was a steady trickle of questions from MPs concerned largely with safety equipment, training and Stand-by Vessels.[77] On the other hand, there was much greater political interest in other aspects of the offshore industry. The political response to industry concerns about other interventions regarding taxation, depletion and participation developed after the early 1980s so as to remove in large part the pressures which these issues had produced in the previous decade when they were constructed by the industry as productive of economic risk and uncertainty. Crucially, of course, the dynamic political tool of taxation was never quite dynamic enough to keep pace with the developing situation in the North Sea. With Piper Alpha, however, politics could not remain indifferent to health and safety nor could it so easily misunderstand the import of what the public inquiry had discovered and what it recommended. Its response, however, was not the one which has been characterised by industry management as little more than a knee-jerk over-reaction to public opinion. Public opinion undoubtedly played a part - Piper Alpha made for dramatic news coverage, it was in the UK sector and people were shocked. But for politics this was much worse than Alexander L. Kielland or Ocean Ranger, even if the loss of life was of the same magnitude and not just because Piper Alpha was under UK jurisdiction. The economic impact of the disaster was enormous and of a quite different order of magnitude to the other two rig disasters. Piper Alpha was a production platform and one of the most significant in the North Sea. The loss of production resulted in some £2 billion in lost revenue. The effect on the London insurance market and on oil exports affected the balance of payments and there have even been suggestions of a knock-on effect on the strength of the pound and on interest rates. Politics became very interested in health and safety at work offshore but not least because it simply could not afford another Piper Alpha.

When it came to the implementation of the prescriptive regulatory regime which had been envisaged by politics in 1971, the regulators undoubtedly attempted to deal with the complexity of the situation they confronted by means of what they saw as a flexible and adaptive approach. While such an approach in the period before 1986 undoubtedly allowed the development of risk-oriented techniques in engineering, it is significant that this development occurred in large part without explicit regulatory encouragement or support. The opportunity which existed before 1986 to develop and extend the risk-oriented approach in engineering and even to link it to the equivalent programme in management was entirely missed by the regulators because they themselves were essentially operating to a deterministic, prescriptive programme in the last analysis. Thus, when the price fall came, there was no regulatory response to the shift to a more deterministic and inherently riskier programme on the part of engineering. Similarly, there was no regulatory connection with the management of price risk and again in the aftermath of 1986, no regulatory response to the cost-cutting orgy which took place. Operating at best to a deterministic, prescriptive programme and at worst in a haphazard way that defies coherent definition, none of these shifts and changes was easily observable by the regulators.

The use of framework statutes, functional regulations which set out general principles and guidance notes which filled in the detail was a response to complexity which undoubtedly avoided the difficulties of over-prescription at the level of regulations and which was intended to allow best individual solutions to be developed. It did nothing, however, to ensure that best individual solutions were in fact being developed and nothing to ensure that the problems of a compliance mentality were not occurring at the level of guidance. Indeed, compliance with guidance could not appear as a problem in the regulatory communicative system which at root was prescriptive. The Piper Alpha disaster exposed the extent to which this response to complexity simply assumed that flexibility would allow best individual solutions to be developed without providing a mechanism at the level of management to ensure that they were.

It is highly significant that the price rise of 1979 and the price collapse of 1986 which figure so prominently on the cognitive maps of management and of engineering and which were constructed there in ways which profoundly influenced the way in which the industry understood what it did and how it did it, simply do not appear on the cognitive maps of the regulators. Their programme for minimising risk and improving offshore health and safety for all its professed flexibility was simply blind to the impact of significant economic events on the way in which the industry conducted its business. For Piper Alpha, this blindness and the blindness of management and engineering to the risks being run in the period after 1986 was to prove as fatal as the concatenation of events which were the immediate cause of the disaster.

It might be regarded as pushing the issue too far to rely only on this 'one-off' accident as significant or as 'proof' that the autopoietic and cognitive mapping approach is useful or to suggest that the findings of the cognitive maps in the period after the 1986 price collapse have been vindicated or proved by this event. In response to such criticism, two points must be made. Firstly, this sort of approach does not rely on statistics or actual occurrences to prove or disprove a theory. Rather it sets out to examine the world constructions of systems making up the study area. By looking at the codes by which these world constructions are arrived at and the programmes by which systems steer themselves - the differences they construct and minimise - this approach seeks to discover what each system can and cannot observe. In other words, it seeks to discover what lies behind the mask created by the very operations of these systems. Thus, even if Piper Alpha had not happened, such a study would have value in having exposed potentially dangerous blind spots in the wake of the 1986 price collapse. Secondly, while Piper Alpha can be easily characterised as a dramatic, one-off event, engineers from another major company have admitted that the potential for a similar event existed on other platforms at that time as a result of the post-1986 deferral of maintenance. In particular, it has been admitted that a gas leak on another platform just days before Piper Alpha could have escalated to similar proportions. That engineer told me simply: 'It could have been us.' This admission is perhaps a more honest assessment than another statement which was made to me on several occasions during the course of this research that: 'No one was surprised it was Piper Alpha.'[78]

More striking still was the number of times I heard from a wide variety of sources the phrase: 'No one actually thought that could happen.' This phrase sums up well the systemic blindness to risk which existed in the industry prior to Piper Alpha.[79] Both the industry and the regulators were convinced of the adequacy of existing arrangements to ensure safety and the communicative systems by which they operated effectively masked the potential for this sort of disaster. Just as with the price crash of 1986 which had such a significant effect on the way the industry conducted its operations, Piper Alpha actually had to happen before anyone could accept that it *could* happen. With this in mind, the *current* thinking of the industry and its regulators is clearly of great importance. There has been an inability in the past to come to terms with severe events until they actually occur or to take account of the masking effects of prior codes and programmes or the consequent instability of models of reality. It will be a question, therefore, whether the aftermath of Piper Alpha has produced a regulatory regime which is sensitive to that finding.

Notes

1 See the Appendix for a graph of oil prices.

2 Both graphs are based on figures contained in Castle (1985).

3 Marathon's funding arrangements for its share in the development costs of the South Brae field serve as an example of the new attitudes of banks towards the industry in the North Sea. A loan of $650m was provided by an international consortium of twenty banks with the option for the borrower to request the consortium's assumption of 50% of the project risk before the field came on-stream. Further, the banks could also be asked to assume non-recourse risk for the full amount of the loan after a certain level of production had been achieved; *PE* 1982, 31.

4 See Chapter 3, Section 3.1.

5 See Niering (1983) quoting a Conoco spokesman.

6 This research, carried out by Joe Roeber Associates for the IPE with specific reference to the gasoil contract, was not published but a summary appeared in *PE* 1983, 227-229.

7 An example of this thinking is the Economist Intelligence Unit report prepared for Shell *The North Sea and British Industry: the new opportunities* discussed in *PE* 1984, 188.

8 *PE* 1985, 179.

9 See the report prepared by Arthur Anderson & Co. and Cambridge Energy Research Associates *The Future of Oil Prices: The Perils of Prophecy* discussed in *PE* 1985, 190.

10 An example of this sort of rationality in project planning is Faeke *et al.* (1981) where there is an early reference to economic risk analysis.

11 As evidence of this view of the future oil price, one can consider the amount of debt which certain major oil companies (notably Mobil, Texaco and Chevron) accumulated at this time. All show considerable increases in their debt/equity ratios in the period up to 1985/86 (Simon 1988, 51-53). Even if banks were more wary about the industry in terms of the conditions imposed on borrowers, there was certainly still money to be had (see Cockburn 1985).

12 See Burgoyne (1980, 241-266).

13 See Chapter 1, Section 1.3.

14 *PE* 1979, 299.

15 *PE* 1980, 7 & 238.

16 Finance (No. 2) Act 1979, ss18-22; Petroleum Revenue Tax Act 1980; Finance Act 1980 ss104-109; Finance Act 1981, s111-121; Finance Act 1982, s132.

17 *PE* 1981, 537.
18 *PE* 1981, 123.
19 *PE* 1981, 401. Occidental and BNOC also announced postponements: *PE* 1981, 147.
20 *PE* 1982, 31; Quinlan (1982a).
21 FA 1982 s132.
22 FA 1982 ss139-142.
23 FA 1981 s127.
24 Note that this figure assumed a constant $31 barrel, the figure then prevailing. Similarly, the post-Budget rate of return for Heather was down to 2.5%. See *PE* 1982, 205.
25 See footnote 50 below.
26 Quinlan (1982c, 449); *PE* 1982, 385-6.
27 Hansard HC (Written Answers) 23 July 1980 Vol. 989 cols. 226-227; David Howell (Secretary of State for Energy).
28 Hansard HC (Debs) 8 June 1982 col. 6.
29 *PE* 1982, 296.
30 FA 1983 s35.
31 Petroleum Royalties (Relief) Act 1983.
32 FA 1983 s36.
33 Oil Taxation Act 1983 s36; FA 1983 s37.
34 *PE* 1983, 100.
35 *PE* 1983, 186.
36 *PE* 1983, 279.
37 *PE* 1984, 39 quoting Alick Buchanan-Smith MP.
38 FA 1984 s18.
39 FA 1984 s58.
40 *PE* 1984, 211, 390; 1985, 31, 220.
41 *PE* 1985, 99.
42 FA 1985 s90.
43 *PE* 1985, 18.
44 Chapter 1, Section 1.3.
45 Hansard HC (Debs) 6 November 1980, cols. 1472-1546.
46 Although it should be noted that this point can be overstated. There is evidence that even up to the mid 1980s the development of the approach to regulation onshore proposed by Robens and provided for by the HSWA 1974 was still relatively in its infancy. See Baldwin (1987, 145).
47 Section 3.2.
48 See also Visser (1993) for a discussion of the NPD's 'Guidelines for Safety Evaluation of Platform Conceptional Design' published in May 1981.
49 An example of this approach can be seen during this period in Shell's development of a 'comprehensive assessment procedure...to appraise the adequacy of jack-up units from a structural and foundation point of view'. The procedure was quite independent of regulatory requirements and revealed a number of shortcomings with recommendations made by manufacturers of jack-ups in the operating manuals and some 'fundamental weakness of jack-up design'. Such recommendations showed

little awareness of the practical issues involved in operating the units and the hope was expressed that improved analysis would replace the deterministic approach to provide a clearer answer to the question of the response of platforms (Pascoe *et al.* 1987). Similarly, the incidence of 'two repairs of note to fatigue damage in main members away from welds' during this period served to highlight the tendency of inspections to concentrate on joints on the assumption that problems would only arise there (Tebbett 1987).

50 For example, Piper Alpha had experience both of early fatigue damage and retrofit of equipment which would have overloaded the structure without modification (Green 1983; Foerster 1985). Thistle needed new equipment because of under-capacity in the initial specification and to cope with production profiles different from those originally envisaged (Bond & Shaw 1986).

51 Examples of integrated deck platforms are Maureen and the Hutton TLP.

52 See Burgoyne (1980, 227-238) Submission 37 Department of Energy - Petroleum Engineering Division.

53 See also 'Living with a buyer's market' *PE* 1986 74-5.

54 See the Appendix.

55 For example, Exxon announced a 26% reduction in exploration spending as a result of the price fall while Amoco announced the deferral of all North Sea spending. Other companies announced drastic cuts of between 40% and 50%. Shell, meanwhile, announced that it would not reduce either exploration or capital expenditures although it ultimately did so (*PE* 1986, 147; 161).

56 *PE* 1986, 161.

57 *PE* 1986, 423 quoting figures from UKOOA.

58 For example, Shell's plan for the Gannet cluster of five small fields was reduced to the development of Kittiwake alone at this point; *PE* 1986, 161. BP announced a one year postponement of the Miller field; *PE* 1986, 198. Amerada Hess were allowed to postpone the development of the Ivanhoe/Rob Roy project for one year; *PE* 1986, 307.

59 Figures from Wood Mackenzie quoted in *PE* 1986, 161 &198. The Den's Brown Book for 1986 indicated that fields commenced during the 1980s required at least $15 per barrel while those under development at that time required over $21 on average.

60 See footnote 11 above.

61 The average daily volume at the IPE from 1982 to 1985 varied between 1,000 and 4,000 contracts. The figure rose above 5,000 in 1986 and 1987, was nearer 10,000 in 1988 and then grew dramatically: 16,000 in 1989 and more than 25,000 in 1990. See *PE* November 1990 Special Supplement. At NYMEX, the Average daily volume in crude oil futures increased as follows: 1983 - 1,692; 1984 - 7,361; 1985 - 15,923; 1986 - 33,254; 1987 - 57,864; 1988 - 74,837; 1989 - 81,812; 1990 - 94,370. See *PE* November 1991, 21.

62 Advance Petroleum Revenue Tax Act 1986.

63 FA 1987 s. 65.

64 FA 1987 s. 64.

65 For example, Sun Oil announced that it was going ahead with Arbroath and seeking development consent for Glamis. Shell said it was going ahead with Kittiwake-

Osprey. Conoco announced that it was re-evaluating three fields in the light of the tax changes and Amoco, Shell-Esso and Esso all announced new exploration drilling; *PE* 1987, 200.

66 FA 1988 s. 138; Petroleum Royalties (Relief) and Continental Shelf Act 1989 ss1&2; Continental Shelf Act 1989.

67 Interviews with engineers carried out in the post-Piper Alpha period confirmed this assessment with the point being made that operators were ultimately 'caught out' by the degree of cost-cutting implemented in the immediate aftermath of the price fall.

68 *PE* 1989, 230 quoting figures from County Woodmac.

69 The OILC view is that maintenance programmes were in some cases not only curtailed but completely shelved (1991, 33).

70 See Section 6.2 above.

71 'Occupational Stress and Accidents in the Offshore Oil and Gas Industry' C. Cooper & V. Sutherland, Manchester School of Management, UMIST, quoted in SREA (1989, 15).

72 See Chapter 3, Section 3.4(v) above.

73 An example of the dramatic impact of the price fall on a project is the Eider platform ordered by Shell. When the project team was formed in early 1984, the estimated cost was £900m. 3-D seismic studies shortly thereafter resulted in a downgrading of the reservoir, however, and the project was substantially reassessed and redesigned resulting in a new cost estimate of £625m. Following the price fall, the project was again reassessed and the idea of a pre-drilling template was scrapped. The estimated cost in 1988 was £480m (Smulders *et al.* 1987).

74 Chapter 1, Section 1.4.

75 The account which follows is based on this submission by Occidental to the Cullen Inquiry which has not been published.

76 The account which follows is based on this submission by the PED to the Cullen Inquiry which has not been published.

77 About 40 questions were asked by around a dozen MPs between 1980 and the Piper Alpha disaster in July 1988. Two members of the House of Lords also raised some four questions during that period relating to the Ocean Ranger disaster and training issues.

78 While the immediate causes are many and various, it is worth noting also the other accidents which occurred at around the same time: a fatal accident on the Ocean Odyssey; the loss of the Fulmar floating storage facility in winter storms, an equipment failure at Brent Alpha, the discovery of defects at the St. Fergus gas treatment plant leading to a shutdown, and a gas explosion on Cormorant Alpha during work to install an Emergency Shutdown Valve as required following the Piper Alpha disaster. See *PE* 1989, 161; 175.

79 There is, nevertheless, a prophetic statement in Tony Benn's, then Secretary of State for Energy, diary entry detailing a meeting prior to the establishment of the Burgoyne Committee and quoting Frank Kearton: 'rigs [are] desperately dangerous installations because they compress gas at 6000 atmospheres in confined spaces, and...a leak would cause a massive explosion killing up to 200 people' (1990, 265).

5 Reflexivity and Risk

1 Introduction

> [I]f an 'alternative' is to *compete* with an established system it must be presented in terms which cannot be disregarded as totally foreign, permanently outside and of no concern to the system itself. (Carson 1981, 301; emphasis in original)

1.1 Reflexivity

This study has examined the issue of offshore health and safety from the perspective of a constructivist theory. This has had the advantage of not imposing one legal sociological perspective on the empirical material but rather has allowed to a greater extent the perspectives or world constructions of different sectors of the study area to emerge. While it can be objected that such an approach is bound to produce this picture of a differentiated study area, it can be argued in reply, first, that offering more maps is likely to allow a more adequately complex picture of the study area to emerge, and second, that this approach must be judged according to the utility of the maps it produces.

In this regard, it may not be possible to conclude that concepts such as autopoietic closure or the internal construction of information by communicative systems have been 'proved', but it is possible to see that different communicative systems do appear to offer very different constructions of reality, very different accounts of which are the important causal relationships and, significantly, very different opportunities for communicating about concepts such as health and safety. Thus, whether one can finally say that industry management or engineering as the two main communicative systems identified in the study area are autopoietically closed or not is less important than the fact that understanding them in terms of their construction of reality on the basis of stable differentiating codes and their self-steering according to variable difference-minimising programmes produces a useful and suggestive account of the evolving situation. The persistent path-dependency of both systems appears clear from the extent to which pre-existing assumptions influenced their constructions of reality in the new province and from the extent to which developments which constituted a closer structural coupling, an observation of how other systems observed, were never able to make unhindered progress. The shortcomings of the regulators in this regard, of course, became especially problematic in the aftermath of the 1986 price collapse.

But if the analysis of the situation points to the significance of these different reality constructions, the normative question of how, in some sense, to reconcile them in accordance with the needs of regulation rapidly arises. If it has been found that different systems operate according to different codes and programmes, on the basis of different internally constructed environments, then what hope is there for regulation in trying to produce some kind of order? One thing appears clear: a prescriptive orientation for law in which an attempt is made to regulate the health and safety aspects of the industry in detail is not an option. Apart from anything else, the study has shown that many more factors than the technical and even the operational aspects of the industry have an impact on health and safety. Most striking in this regard has been the extent to which health and safety and its regulation have been constructed in terms of their possible contribution to delay and also the extent to which other regulatory interventions concerned with taxation, participation and so on have had a greater impact on the cognitive map of industry management and consequently on the safety of its operations. Similar issues arise from consideration of the cognitive maps of engineering, where technical preoccupations created a blindness to occupational safety irrespective of the potential risk to installations. This multiple connectivity and this inability to 'break in', as it were, to the communicative systems of the regulated area suggests that the task of prescriptive regulation is even more complex than both politics and regulators readily admitted throughout the history of the industry in the North Sea. To this extent, then, the study is (not surprisingly) in agreement with the findings of the Cullen Inquiry. Beyond that, it becomes a question of considering alternatives to detailed prescriptive regulation.

The frequently mentioned possibility of deregulation is a clear contender in such circumstances and, as was mentioned in the first two chapters, was a recurring theme of government policy in the UK under the Conservatives from 1979 to 1997. Furthermore, Woolfson, Foster and Beck (1996) appear to characterise the post-Piper Alpha offshore health and safety regime as just such an example of deregulation where the industry has been given substantial freedom to do what it wants - with the added complication that this has been achieved under the pretext of increasing regulatory control. More recently, a study carried out on behalf of the HSE has concluded that there is 'some evidence to support the "Gradual Erosion Scenario"' proposed by Wolfson, Foster and Beck in which 'the HSE's initially enthusiastic approach to offshore safety is gradually being eroded and...the industry is gradually reasserting its hegemony' (AUPEC 1999, 34).

If, on the other hand, the findings of this study are taken seriously, that the closure of communicative systems is a significant feature of the regulated area, then, as was discussed in the second chapter, the theory of autopoiesis has its own suggestions for the appropriate response by the law. If the direct interventionist desires of politics and regulation are thwarted by closure then law must adopt a *reflexive* orientation. While the self-regulation and decentralisation which are a feature of deregulation are certainly also a feature of reflexive law, they by no means represent the totality of this orientation. Reflexive law, unlike deregulation, does not arise from views based on economics that things run more efficiently in the absence of big government or regulatory intervention. Rather it emerges from a recognition that in a world constituted by closed communicative systems, law must come to terms both with the fact of its own closure and that of the closure of the systems it would attempt to regulate. Law's own closure implies that it constructs the reality it attempts to regulate rather than having certain and direct access to it. The closure of other systems implies that law cannot count on other systems understanding its utterances (in the form of regulations, for example) in the way in which it intended and in which, to a great extent, the whole process of regulation implicitly assumes. It would not be going too far to suggest that in Chapters 3 and 4 we have seen clear indications of both aspects of this closure.

Thus, while reflexive law would certainly shy away from the sort of prescriptive regulation envisaged under the MWA 1971, it would not suggest that deregulating is an adequate answer. Leaving engineering and management to do their own thing does not appear to be a strategy with a high probability of success in terms of achieving a particularly high level of health and safety. For long periods of their history, both communicative systems operated very much on the assumption that they would be best left to do exactly that and yet it has been seen how quite extraordinary risks were run as a consequence, risks which the regulators and their detailed prescriptive approach - even in the context of their programme of fostering mutual respect - were significantly at a complete loss either to comprehend or to deal with.

Neither prescriptive nor deregulatory, reflexive law instead shifts the emphasis away from the legal production of substantive norms towards an interest in the processes by which social norms are produced within the different social systems. Analytically, reflexive law suggests that there is evidence that such an orientation can be perceived in recent legal developments. Normatively, it proposes strategies by which law can adapt to cope with the closure of communicative systems.

The situation in which closed systems 'communicate' with each other becomes in autopoiesis, as was seen in Chapter 2, a process of reciprocal observation. Utterances on the part of one system are constructed (or not) as information and understood by another on the basis of its own code and programmes. A greater potential for mutual understanding exists when 'interference' occurs, that is, when information is constructed within different systems simultaneously on the basis of the same communicative event. This can occur in a random fashion: thus, law can in some instances apply the legal/illegal distinction to social utterances because it happens to have detected those utterances or because its attention has been directed towards them by politics, while in other instances it is effectively unaware of them. Alternatively, however, the random element associated with such interference can be removed by providing organisational structures or 'linkage institutions' which operate across the boundaries of the systems with which the law is interested and effectively seek to regulate the 'duration, intensity and quality of structural coupling' (Teubner 1992a, 1458). In this way, the law remains interested in the production of norms but it no longer constructs the resulting self-produced social norms as legal norms in order that it can then prescribe behaviours on the basis of them. Rather it aims to employ the processes of social self-production for law production. Laws are thus effectively self-produced by the social systems with law restricting its 'interventions' to the installation and maintenance of certain procedures. 'The idea is to make law "responsive" toward society by transforming social self-production processes into sources of law production' (1992a, 1460). Implied in that, of course, is the idea that law aims to 'foster mechanisms that systematically *further the development of reflexion structures within other social subsystems*' (Teubner 1983, 275 emphasis in original). In that way, law can aim to deal with the situation which arises when systems assume the validity and stability of their own constructions and thus fail to recognise their contingency and the possibility that risks are being masked.

The importance of the foregoing discussion lies not only in outlining the regulatory stance implied by autopoiesis, but also in providing a somewhat richer set of concepts with which to consider the regime which has emerged in the wake of Lord Cullen's report. At present, there would appear to be an overly restricted debate if the only concepts available are deregulation and reregulation. The Cullen report itself implied a sophisticated transcendence of prescription which had little in common with deregulation. It will be a question, therefore, of examining the new regime in this light to see whether it possesses reflexive potential and whether concerns which emerge when it is considered as deregulation can thus be allayed.

1.2 Risk

The orientation of the law, however, is only one issue to have emerged as significant from this study. The other key finding has been the extent to which the different systems have over time been preoccupied with questions of risk. Management, for example, has been concerned to minimise economic risk and has operated on the basis that rapid production minimises the impact of an uncertain future and increases the value of the income from the reservoir. As was seen, this concern with only one dimension of risk created blind spots which exposed the industry to other risks, which in turn had an adverse effect on the very risk that management was most concerned about. Similarly, the preoccupation of engineering with the risk of structural failure and its further preoccupation within that area with overload was later seen to have masked both other structural risks and other (for example, operational and occupational) risks which had a potentially greater impact on the integrity of installations. Thus, although risk has been an ever present concern for the offshore industry, its communicative systems have constructed it in deterministic ways which have effectively masked other aspects and dimensions of risk. The advantage of the autopoietic approach has been that it provided the conceptual apparatus with which to account for this phenomenon. The blind spots created by the binary codes by which the systems were differentiated and by their deterministic programmes were precisely the location of the risks which ultimately emerged.

It was significant, nevertheless, that programmes were emerging in both management and engineering, especially after the 1979 price hike bailed out the early North Sea projects, which attempted to deal with this situation. Thus, industry management moved increasingly towards sophisticated financial instruments for dealing with price risk and engineering developed probabilistic techniques to cope with the risks associated with technology. In both cases, however, it would be impossible to say that these new approaches were widely accepted or well-developed before the mid-1980s. In the case of management, it took the actual occurrence of the price crash in 1986 to convince many of the possibility of significant price risk - and even then the response was not only a greater acceptance of price risk management instruments but also a cost-cutting drive which heightened technical and operational risk. In both engineering and management it has taken the destruction of a platform to produce the conviction that a more all-embracing approach to risk is required.

Irrespective, then, of any regulatory efforts, risk has become since the late 1980s a major issue in the cognitive maps of management and engineering. The question arises in an autopoietic perspective, however, of how precisely risk is being understood. Two broad perspectives are available in this regard, both of which accept that risk depends in some sense on the 'world view' within which it emerges, whether economic, scientific, political and so on. The first perspective, while accepting this contingent view of risk, nevertheless seems to assume that some form of democratic forum, suitably enhanced by social science perspectives, can serve to allow 'a common understanding of the problem and the potential solutions' to be reached (Renn 1992, 78). The idea is that a 'meta-perspective' can be reached which will provide a 'semantic framework that allows a comparative analysis across the various perspectives' (Renn 1992, 79). It is not surprising to find the early Habermas co-opted in support of this suggestion. To the contrary, however, others argue that the search for an objective method of risk assessment is 'doomed to failure' on the basis that problems of risk are 'decision problems' (Slovic, Fischhoff & Lichtenstein 1985, 273-4). Thus, risk is not something which is out there to be discovered in some tangible and objectively agreeable sense. Rather risk emerges as a result of decisions within communicative systems, whether social or organisational (see Beck 1992, 23).

The implications for law are clear. The legal norm, effectively presupposed as a risk-free structure inasmuch as it implies that there is no risk in being guided by it for as long as it is valid, appears singularly vulnerable in this context (see Luhmann 1993, 55). Upon questions of risk, the prescriptive legal norm will continue to insist on a particular issue, even after experience suggests that it is wrong, for so long as it continues to be valid. But it is not simply a question of speeding up the production of legal norms - as the PED attempted to do by using more informal techniques such as guidance notes. Rather it is a question of the appropriateness of the form of the prescriptive legal norm in situations of complexity and uncertainty. The shift from a deterministic to a probabilistic or risk-aware programme has profound implications for the rationality underlying law. In a context where the engineering rationality upon which regulation depends no longer operates according to a calculus of certainty but rather a calculus of probability, a legal approach which implies the former is redundant. Luhmann points out that in such circumstances the law *can* help with procedures for amending the law and coming to a new decision but this does not alter the fact that the original rule was simply wrong and that in the context of uncertainty its replacement will probably be wrong in the future (1993, 59).

In these circumstances it no longer makes sense for the law to continue in a prescriptive mode where it effectively places an imprimatur on a given decision, stating that it is right beyond all question. Instead, the law must withdraw to a position where it guarantees procedures for reaching decisions which are in principle and *ab initio* mutable in the context of experience. In other words, the issue of risk lends support to a legal orientation which shifts the emphasis to the processes of social norm production for law production and which is more concerned to support procedures which are open to risk than to insist on finality - a finality which simply is not there.

The challenge for law in such circumstances is not simply to take account of the dual autonomy affecting regulator and regulated but also - crucially in the field of offshore health and safety - the mutual closure of significant systems in the regulated area itself. Thus, reflexivity in the sense implied by autopoiesis must be fostered in those systems as well if risk is not to be systematically masked. As soon as the uncertain is reconstructed as certain or is communicated (under compulsion perhaps) as certain, the risks which threaten health and safety are once again behind the mask. Autopoiesis, then, can help the movement towards reflexive modernity in which the logic of risk production gains ground against the logic of wealth production (Beck 1992, 12).

With these considerations in mind, we can turn to the regulatory approach to health and safety at work offshore which has emerged from the Cullen Inquiry into the Piper Alpha disaster.

2 The Political Context

It was seen in the previous chapter that politics was not as exercised by health and safety during the early and mid 1980s as it was about other aspects of the offshore industry, notably taxation and the encouragement of future development. When it was compelled to debate the issue in the aftermath of the Burgoyne Report, it was seen that attention was focused on the location of responsibility for the regulations - either with the PED or the HSE - and largely ignored other issues.[1] Significantly, the orientation of the law, identified as an issue both by the regulators and by the Committee, was not a matter which appeared on the cognitive map of politics. Thus, the fact that the regulators pointed to difficulties of keeping pace with developments and of communicating legal requirements to the industry, and the fact that the Committee recommended a shift towards regulations which set objectives as a means of dealing with this problem were issues which were quite simply ignored by politics, operating as it was on the basis of a very traditional view of the development and implementation of regulation and accordingly unable to observe any alternative.

It is not surprising to find, therefore, that when the issue was next debated in the wake of the Cullen Report into the Piper Alpha disaster[2] there were recriminations about why the government had done nothing to ensure that this particular recommendation of the Burgoyne Committee was implemented.[3] Perhaps the magnitude of this oversight, this failure to understand the import of this significant recommendation of the Committee, contributed to the vigour with which the government now stressed the extent to which the orientation of the law must change. It was keen to stress that the approach recommended by Lord Cullen went beyond even the Robens philosophy and the requirements of the HSWA 1974.[4] The prescriptive approach was completely rejected and the central responsibility of the individual operators was emphasised. The role of the regulator would shift from being one of physical inspection to become one of reviewing the safety management system of the operator.[5]

Cullen's findings in relation to the shortcomings of the prescriptive approach and the inspection system based on it and his recommendations as regards their replacement with a goal-setting and auditing approach were now wholeheartedly endorsed by politics, with only one exception where concern was expressed about a possible dilution of detailed regulations.[6] Again, the approach was justified on the basis of the flexibility required for a dynamic and complex industry[7] but whereas the aim previously had been to regulate in detail for every aspect of the industry by means of secondary legislation, now politics was convinced of the need to shift detailed responsibility to the operator with the preparation of a 'living' safety case and with the regulators ensuring that the operator's management system was adequate to the task.[8]

Beyond these issues, the major point of political debate was the role of trade unions in offshore health and safety. Opposition members quoted selections from Lord Cullen which supported their contention that union involvement in Safety Committees and union support for Safety Representatives would benefit the safety situation,[9] while government members responded by quoting Lord Cullen's conclusion on this point which was that he considered 'that it would be inappropriate...to recommend any change in the method by which safety representatives are chosen' (Cullen 1990, para 21.85).[10] In contrast to the opposition view that trade union involvement is indispensable for safety,[11] the government view was that to equate union recognition with safety is simplistic.[12] While the opposition cited examples from the period after the Piper Alpha disaster of alleged victimisation (and even sacking) of workers who raised safety concerns and called for trade union involvement to support such workers,[13] the government insisted that applying the onshore system offshore would disadvantage non-union workers in an industry where union recognition was low.[14] In view of figures quoted by opposition members purporting to demonstrate a high degree of support for union recognition offshore,[15] the government's stance looked to be more dictated by political preference than genuine interest in the views of the workforce - for all that it characterised the opposition stance as political rather than appropriate to the offshore situation. It was nevertheless significant that both the government and the opposition were now both in favour of, at the very least, some form of workforce involvement in the new approach to safety. This issue simply did not appear on the cognitive map of politics at the time of the passing of the 1971 Act, when the onus of responsibility was taken to be on the government to prescribe a safe working environment and carry out inspections to ensure that it was provided.

There was also extended debate, as there had been after the Burgoyne Report, about the issue of which body should have responsibility for regulation. The opposition wanted to know why the government in the wake of the Cullen Report was content for regulatory responsibility to be transferred to the HSE while following the same minority recommendation in the Burgoyne Committee's Report it did nothing. The government's repeated and simple response was that the situation had changed between

1980 and 1990 and in each case it was following the 'majority' recommendation.[16] Despite extended discussion of this issue, it was effectively one of political point scoring rather than of substance because now all were agreed on the transfer of responsibility to the HSE.

Of greater interest, perhaps, was the political attitude to the industry. While front bench spokesmen for the government presented a fairly upbeat appraisal of the industry's response to the Piper Alpha disaster, government backbenchers felt no hesitation in raising questions in this regard. One criticised UKOOA and its members for its presentation of figures suggesting that two-thirds of the 900 Safety Representatives in the North Sea had by now received training. The question was asked why 100% had not received training in the two and a half years that had elapsed since the disaster. There was also wonderment at UKOOA's apparent self-satisfaction at having made recommendations to the Cullen Inquiry regarding the systematic use of the safety case and formal safety assessment as well as the move away from prescription towards goal-setting which had then been taken up by Lord Cullen. The question was asked why they had to wait for 167 men to die before they could make those recommendations and it was contended that UKOOA ought to have made them five years earlier. The conclusion drawn was that UKOOA's response was 'not something to be proud of'.[17]

A Liberal Democrat member offered some comfort to the industry when he admitted that before the Piper Alpha disaster 'nobody believed that [it] could happen' and he made a very telling observation when he added that now that it had happened, all were aware that 'no matter what the regime, it could conceivably happen again'.[18] The same point was echoed by a Labour member who gave credit to companies who in the aftermath of the disaster admitted that, while they thought that they had done everything they could to make installations safe, now realised how far they still had to go.[19] Another Labour member conceded that he could detect a change in the industry in that it was now taking health and safety issues much more seriously and responding promptly and effectively when such issues were raised.[20]

Lastly, there was clear recognition of the role which other regulatory interventions played in the entire health and safety equation. The need for continuing adaptability on the question of taxation, as had been demonstrated since 1986 in particular, was noted.[21] And, as will be seen later,[22] the ongoing approach to taxation by first the Conservative and then the Labour government has largely been viewed by the industry as appropriate despite periods of concern.

In summary, then, there had been by this time some very significant changes to the political cognitive map. Attitudes to the industry no longer split easily along party lines. Government members did not think that the industry was doing enough in regard to health and safety and were in favour of workforce involvement. Opposition members conceded that improvements had been made and pointed to a different attitude on the part of the industry. Albeit that the sheer cost of the Piper Alpha disaster mentioned at the end of the last chapter undoubtedly helped to focus political attention on offshore health and safety, the political construction of the nature of the problem and of available solutions was markedly different than before. The recognition that no one had actually believed such a disaster could happen pointed up starkly the shortcomings of the previous regulatory approach. Thus, while complacency about the industry had all but disappeared, there was not a simple knee-jerk reaction to the opposite extreme. Instead, the issue of the orientation of law and the appropriate focus for regulation appeared clearly on the political map and the way was clear for sweeping change. It had taken the fact of the disaster, however, as much as the findings of the Cullen Inquiry to shake politics out of its complacent belief in a programme of prescriptive regulation - the orientation of the law had, after all, been an issue nearly ten years earlier at the Burgoyne Committee.

3 The New Regime

3.1 The Legal Changes

In this political context of the total acceptance of Lord Cullen's recommendations, especially with regard to the need for a focus on auditable Safety Management Systems and the use of Quantitative Risk Assessment all demonstrated in a Safety Case,[23] new legislation was brought swiftly and uncontentiously into force. The only problem related to the question of the protection from victimisation of Safety Representatives and members of Safety Committees created under the 1989 regulations.[24] Lord Cullen had recommended that similar protection as was afforded to their onshore counterparts[25] should extend offshore. While the government had accepted this (as well as every other) recommendation, it refused to include this provision along with others in the Offshore Safety Bill on the basis that this was an employment and not a safety issue.[26] Whatever the motivations behind this decision, the government at least did not stand in the way of a private member's bill introduced into the House of Lords by Baroness Turner of Camden on this issue - a bill which passed the Second Reading, Committee, Report and Third Reading Stages in the Commons without debate to become the Offshore Safety (Protection Against Victimisation) Act 1992. This supplemented the 1989 regulations which were also amended to give Safety Representatives the right to be consulted about development of the Safety Case and to have access to the completed document. The political recognition of a need for workforce involvement thus found legal expression.

The main legislation giving effect to Lord Cullen's recommendations, however, was the Offshore Safety Act 1992. Section 1 of this Act effectively completed the transfer of responsibility for the offshore area to the HSE. Each remaining piece of offshore legislation including the MWA 1971 was made an 'existing statutory provision' for the purposes of the HSWA 1974, meaning that their provisions and regulations made under them could be enforced by the HSE until such time as they were repealed and replaced by new provisions. Likewise, the remaining vestiges of the licensing approach relating to health and safety at work offshore under the Continental Shelf Act 1964 were repealed by section 3 of the 1992 Act. Thus, the legal framework was in place for the new approach envisaged by Lord Cullen and by politics.

The 1992 Safety Case Regulations,[27] made under the 1992 Act, set out the requirements for the fundamental part of the new regime. The Safety Case, which in practice can be a very extensive document running to hundreds of pages, typically comprises an executive summary, details of the Safety Management System, a description of the installation, identification and assessment of risks to the installation together with the means for their management and programmes for improvement of identified problems and finally a justification for continued operation.

The regulations require that such a document be submitted at different stages in an installation's life-cycle (design, pre-operational and abandonment, and before moving into relevant waters in the case of mobile units) and that further documents or revisions be submitted in the event of combined operations, major modifications and periodic updating (see regs. 4, 5, 6 & 7). In addition, any procedures or arrangements specified by the operator in a Safety Case must be followed and it will be an offence to breach this requirement (reg. 10). Thus, although the operator is responsible for defining its own procedures, the HSE can ensure that it then follows them. Further, a breach of these procedures would be a breach of a statutory duty and actionable under civil law in the event that damage or loss resulted (see J. Salter 1994, 3). Lastly, well operations and certain construction activities must be notified to the HSE (regs. 11 and 12).

The Safety Case is regarded as a living document which is to be updated to take account of changing activities and technology relative to an individual installation. The principal matters to be demonstrated in a Safety Case are that:

> (i) the management system is adequate to ensure compliance with statutory health and safety requirements;
> (ii) adequate arrangements have been made for audit, and the preparation of audit reports; and
> (iii) all hazards with the potential to cause a major accident have been identified, their risks evaluated, and measures taken to reduce risks to persons to as low as reasonably practicable (ALARP). (HSE 1992a, viii)

There are, therefore, points of similarity with the then current Control of Industrial Major Accident Hazard Regulations 1984 (CIMAH) which implemented the EC Seveso Directive[28] relating to larger onshore industrial installations, but there are also important differences including:

> (i) for offshore installations the operator's standards for the management of health and safety and the control of major hazards are subject to formal acceptance by the HSE and since November 1995 it has been illegal to operate such an installation without an accepted Safety Case;[29]
> (ii) for offshore installations suitable use must be made of quantitative risk assessment (QRA) as part of the demonstration of the adequacy of preventive and protective measures; and
> (iii) for offshore installations there are formal requirements relating to safety management and audit.[30]

In line with Cullen's criticism of prescriptive regulation, the existing regulations are being phased out and replaced with goal-setting regulations which specify general objectives but leave the manner of achieving them to individual operators.[31] Even where guidance from the regulators exists, operators are able to depart from this provided that they demonstrate the safety of their alternative in the Safety Case. This reveals the extent to which the prescription of the former approach has been transcended - in theory at least. But simply leaving the industry free to depart from regulations or from guidance would amount to some form of deregulation and the Safety Management System and risk assessment requirements of the new regime take it far beyond any such approach.

3.2 Safety Management Systems and Risk Assessment

The Safety Case required by the 1992 regulations must demonstrate, *inter alia*, the adequacy of the operator's management system to ensure compliance with statutory requirements which, as mentioned above, are now goal-setting. The management system is defined as the organisation and arrangements established by the operator for managing the undertaking. Equally, the Safety Case must demonstrate the adequacy of arrangements for audit of the management system and for making reports. Audit is defined as the systematic assessment of the adequacy of the management system to achieve its purpose by persons who are sufficiently independent of the system to ensure that such assessment is objective. While each operator is free to establish its own management system specific to its own operations and installation, the HSE has produced guidance on the fundamental aspects of such a system (HSE 1993b) illustrated by the following diagram (Figure 5.1).

(i) *Policy* - the SMS is required to describe the operator's policies for ensuring the health and safety of persons who may be affected by the activities covered by the Safety Case. These policies must recognise the importance of health and safety standards, of organisational structures and resources required to achieve them, of the need to identify and control risk, of the need to be responsive to internal and external changes and for review. Guidance states that policies must be clear and coherent in order to be understandable by all. Performance standards required by the 1992 regulations relate to the Temporary Refuge, routes to and from the refuge, means of evacuation at these points, facilities within the refuge for monitoring and controlling an incident and organising evacuation. Others relate to the support of the SMS: monitoring and auditing arrangements, workforce involvement procedures, the permit to work system, emergency command organisation, the emergency drills and exercises system, OIM

Figure 5.1 Key Elements of the Safety Management System

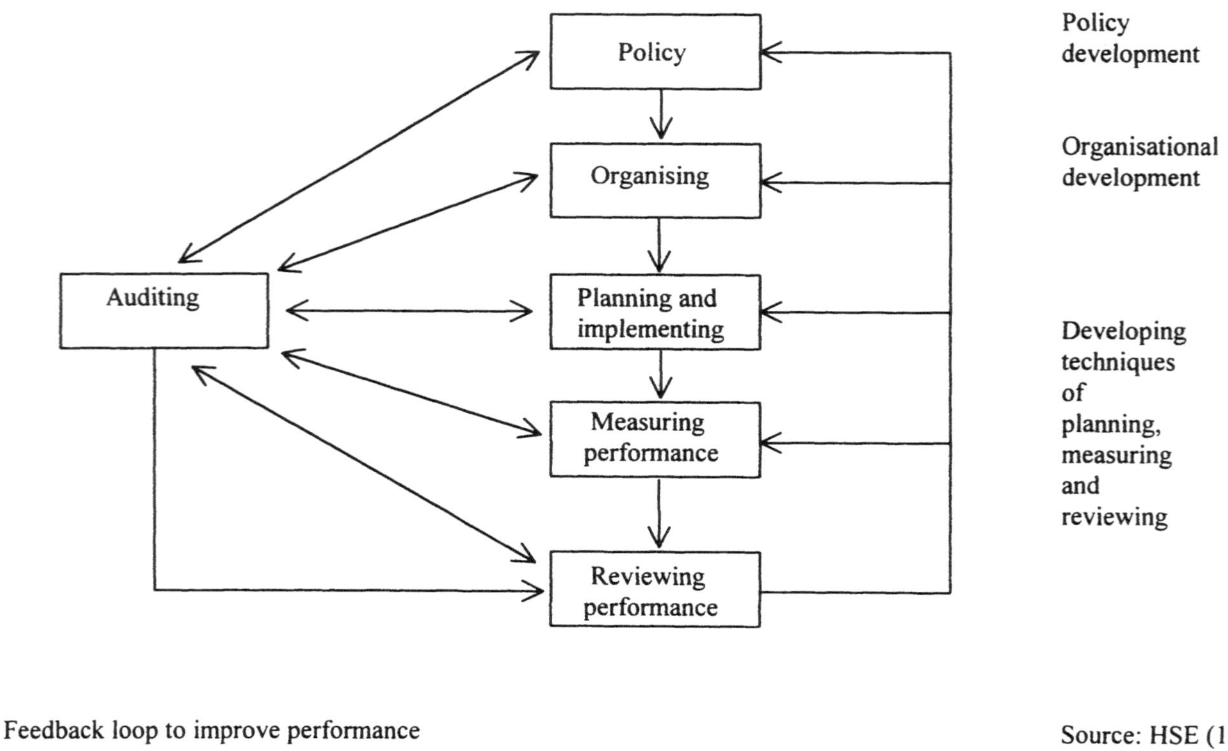

Source: HSE (1993b, 3)

selection criteria and the emergency training system (Barrell 1993, 63-4).

(ii) *Organisation* - what must be demonstrated here is management control of and responsibility for safety systems; the co-operation of all levels of the workforce in all stages of the safety management system from policy formulation to audit and review; the securing of effective communication; and the ensuring of the competence of all levels of the workforce for safe operations.

(iii) *Planning and implementation* - objectives must be set, methods devised for delivering them and monitoring implemented to confirm their achievement.

(iv) *Measuring performance* - this involves both active systems which monitor compliance with performance standards, the control of risks and the achievement of objectives, and passive systems which monitor accidents and other problems. In both cases reporting and response systems are required to ensure that information produced is evaluated and acted upon.

(v) *Auditing and Reviewing performance* - the principal aim here is to ensure that lessons are learned from all relevant experience. Reviewing performance is concerned with making judgements about the adequacy of performance and taking action to remedy deficiencies. This results in a feedback loop to improve performance at all levels of the system. Auditing is the structured process of collecting independent information on the efficiency, effectiveness and reliability of the total system and drawing up plans for corrective action. The key difference between audit and review is that the former employs individuals who are independent from the line management of the area they are studying. A key component of both is the tracking of recommended remedial action, which is achieved by defining responsibilities and setting deadlines.

Beyond the implementation and demonstration of a Safety Management System, an operator is required to demonstrate that this system is based on a rational assessment of the risks relevant to the individual installation. Thus, the operator must:

(i) consider the hazards which have the potential to cause a major accident;

(ii) evaluate the likelihood of these hazards being realised and their consequences; and

(iii) confirm that in the light of such evaluation the risk to persons is as low as reasonably practicable or that measures to achieve this end are in hand together with details of the timescale.

In order to achieve these objectives, an operator must make use of quantitative or probabilistic risk assessment techniques. Probabilistic engineering techniques and risk assessment have been discussed in the preceding two chapters where it was seen that the industry was gradually moving towards their use, albeit largely in respect of isolated technical issues. In the context of the new regime, however, operators must apply such techniques across the board. All risks must be assessed and whereas previously the values produced related, for example, to the probability of structural failure, now they must ultimately be related to the risks to persons. Furthermore, it is not enough simply to calculate the risks. Rather it must also be demonstrated that they are at the lowest reasonably practicable level. If they are not, then the operator must demonstrate what will be done to achieve that level, within which timescale and the options from among which the preferred method has been chosen - all justified on the basis of QRA.

3.3 Reflexivity and Risk

From this brief outline of the new regime, it is possible to make a first assessment of its potential to deal with the issues of communication and of risk raised in the preceding chapters. To what extent does the SMS and QRA approach recognise and deal with the issue of closed communicative systems, both regulatory and regulated? To what extent does this approach recognise the need to consider the issue of risk as the product of decisions within such systems?

On both counts it seems at first sight that the new regime scores well. The fact that performance standards and objectives are to be set by individual operators in relation to individual installations indicates the extent to which the former prescriptive regime has been left behind. But the law does not simply allow operators to set any standard which suits them in terms of being the easiest to achieve. Rather standards must be the product of an assessment of the risks and an appropriate response thereto. The risks which must be assessed are not spelled out in detail by the regulator. Rather the operator must set out to identify the hazards associated with the individual installation and work from there. No risks are excluded by some deterministic formula but rather once a hazard has been identified it must be assessed and may only be disregarded on the basis of a rational process. The system by which safety is managed on the broad basis of assessed risks is not imposed on the operator. The guidance in this respect is but the barest outline of what any management system in any company would comprise. Rather, the guidance sets out to ensure that the bare minimum is in place and thus attempts to ensure that where weaknesses exist in any given organisation these can be identified and remedied - as far as possible by the operator itself. As to the difficulties of communication between different systems, the requirement for an auditable Safety Management System effectively ensures the coupling of engineering, management and workforce so that even if there is not some genuine transfer of information then at the very least these sectors may now construct information on the basis of the same communicative events relative to health and safety at work defined more broadly than ever before.

It can be suggested, then, purely on the evidence of the outline of the new regime, that it does indeed address the issue of risk as a central and underpinning aspect of the management of health and safety and does indeed possess characteristics of reflexive law. In this latter regard, it can be said that in the new approach, law has indeed attempted to influence the 'duration, intensity and quality of structural coupling' by the requirement for a Safety Management System based on risk assessment. And it has indeed shifted its orientation from a 'mis-reading' of socially produced norms for the production of legal norms to the employment of the processes of social norm production for law production - that is, instead of translating engineering or management norms into generalised legal norms, it allows the production of context-specific social norms and holds the operator to compliance with its own standards and procedures.

In theory, then, the new regime looks promising as a mechanism for coping with the issues identified in the preceding chapters. But does it deliver in practice?

4 Engineering in the New Regime

While 'the incident will recede into history, the lesson that a fixed platform to UK standards is vulnerable to complete destruction will remain.' (SREA 1989, 44)

4.1 Positive Developments

Perhaps not surprisingly, the area in which probabilistic techniques saw most development offshore before 1988 is the area where greatest enthusiasm is evident in the wake of the Piper Alpha disaster and the implementation of the new health and safety regime. It would not be overstating the case to say that whatever lingering doubts there were in engineering before about probabilistic risk assessment techniques, these have now all but completely disappeared.[32] The acceptance of such techniques is now practically uniform and the extent to which engineering has moved from a very considerable emphasis on structural integrity to the realisation that many other factors have to be considered is striking. Even before Lord Cullen's report was published, the risk assessment approach was being actively discussed as the most appropriate response precisely on the grounds of its ability to expose the blind spots of determinism:

> Any hazard or accident scenario that can be identified is included for analysis, and the application of probabilities leaves no need for exclusions on the grounds of preconceptions or incredibility. It overcomes the situation where those for and against a particular activity can content themselves with a statement that the activity is safe or not. It forces them to develop their arguments to a greater depth with a view to putting forward a detailed quantitative analysis. (SREA 1989, 42)

Similarly, engineers have begun to view the new approach as allowing for greater freedom to produce the best engineering solution as compared to the constraints of the old prescriptive Construction and Survey Regulations and associated guidance which discouraged the examination of alternatives (Durnin 1994, 7). It is worth noting also that even those who were considered to have been at the forefront of the development of the new programme prior to 1989 admit that they still had a considerable distance to go before meeting the requirements of the new regime (Spence 1994, 1). And it has been admitted that '[n]o full risk analysis was applied to a UK Sector platform prior to the Piper Alpha disaster, although studies were carried out on specific design questions noting risk analysis methods' (Cox 1990, 155). The products of the new approach have been impressive.

A survey carried out by the HSE indicated that, during the assessment of Safety Cases, the largest single group of problems necessitating the sending of Issue Notes[33] related to engineering matters. Often, further risk assessment was required to be carried out which had the effect ultimately of encouraging the replacement or upgrading of equipment without prescribing what should be done. In one instance, the Safety Case was simply withdrawn by the duty holder in relation to a MODU and the rig was removed from the UK sector (see HSE 1995, 12 & 41).

Regarding platform topsides design, this was an issue which was seen in Chapter 4 to be gradually appearing on the cognitive map of engineering. After 1988 it simply could not be ignored. There were frank admissions that previous assessments of blast resistance had been inadequate (Cockbain *et al.* 1990; Walker *et al.* 1991) and that such a lack of awareness had contributed to a relatively minor gas leak escalating into a huge disaster on Piper Alpha (van den Berg & van Wingerden 1991). Previously, topsides had been designed on the basis of lifting abilities and structural weight distribution as well as on deterministic blast calculations. Now more sophisticated calculations were used and a high priority was given to adapting topsides design accordingly (Cockbain *et al.* 1990). Similarly, the location of risers carrying hydrocarbons from the reservoir had been decided by the location of processing or metering equipment or on the basis simply of where space was available and proximity to 'living quarters, fire pumps and other safety equipment does not seem to have been considered' (Coker 1991, 636). This lack of consideration had been compounded by the use of increasingly large diameter risers at higher pressures. Nevertheless, it 'seems that the increased risks of these changes were not recognised' and it 'did not seem that many operators performed safety evaluations of installations which could have identified the risk level' (Coker 1991, 636). All of this has now changed.

Similar findings were made in relation to the design of the systems used for mooring offshore installations. Previously, the resistance capacity of the system was calculated by multiplying the load by a safety factor - a method described in the new risk-aware environment as 'simplistic and deterministic' and implying that load and resistance could be perfectly predicted (Luo & Ahilan 1991, 783). The new reliability based method in contrast 'recognises that perfect safety is unattainable' and that 'uncertainties are inevitable' - it is therefore a question of designing mooring systems so that the probability of failure is acceptable in terms of consequences (Luo & Ahilan 1991, 784).

Risk assessment has revealed further levels of complexity in structural issues, something which engineering has long concentrated on. In addition to the problems which progressively emerged in the North Sea, the new techniques now suggest that loading asymmetry, joint non-linearity, foundation interactions and global deflection criteria have all been inadequately considered (Bolt *et al.* 1996). But it is beyond structural issues that the application of risk assessment techniques have produced some surprises for engineering. The tendency to concentrate on obviously high-risk occupations such as construction and drilling was exposed as misguided by the Piper Alpha disaster when many of those killed were off-duty and included all of the supposedly low-risk catering staff (Brandie 1993, 157). Moreover, it was discovered that in some locations, the risk to an installation from collision by passing shipping was more significant than any other risk including blow-out or structural failure (Massie & Buijs 1991).[34] Similarly, the process revealed that on one installation, the total demand for power from emergency systems was no less than double the supply available (Barrell 1994, 3-4).

Most impressive of all has been the extent to which human factors have come to be considered in engineering with a profound questioning of quite how they had been omitted in the past. Not least among the reasons given are the fact that the concept of human engineering was simply unknown in the offshore industry and the fact that humans were regarded by engineering as adaptable and thus not a major factor in the design of topsides (G. E. Miller 1990). And beyond the simple design and layout of topsides, engineering has become aware of the need to consider human and organisational factors in the calculation of the risks to the entire structure. Indeed, there has even been the admission - extraordinary when one considers the extent to which it was ignored previously - that human and organisational errors are a *greater* source of risk than structural issues (T. M. Miller *et al.* 1991; see also Curole & McKinney 1999; Harrison 1999; Noerager *et al.* 1999; Spigener 1999). There is also greater emphasis in engineering on communication issues at all stages from design to operation (e.g. Velez 1992; Garga 1999; Green 1999). Recognition of this level of complexity has even prompted the questioning of the fault tree/event tree methodology used in risk assessment[35] as in fact too deterministic. Instead, more free-form influence diagrams are being developed which are less limiting in the sequences of events which can be modelled (Moore & Bea 1993). This has particular significance given the reported inability of experts to agree on a common fault tree analysis when asked to attempt to reproduce the same risk assessment results (Cooke 1991, 33) and is perhaps an early example of the influence of the feedback loop encouraged by the review and auditing requirements of the SMS. That said, some operators have encountered difficulties in applying quantitative techniques to human factors and have retained the use of qualitative analysis except in isolated cases where the risk potential seems highest (Spence 1994, 4).

4.2 Tension Points

As regards engineering, then, things look good for the new regime. There is much enthusiasm for the new risk assessment approach, a new awareness of a huge range of issues which were previously completely invisible to engineering while the deterministic programme dominated and constant reference to the impact of the Piper Alpha disaster and the new UK offshore health and safety regime as motivations for the change in approach. But, good as the picture appears, there is no room for complacency on the part of the regulators.

The increased use of probabilistic and other risk assessment techniques in engineering is not simply a result of the new regulatory requirements. The issues which were responsible for their development in engineering in the first place are still present - cost (Rule & Huddleston 1988; CRINE 1994; Cope 1999; Cresswell 1999), life-extension of platforms due to satellite development (Brown & McCann 1989), realisation of the limitations of initial design criteria regarding both structural issues (Shuttleworth & Billington 1989; Lalani & Shuttleworth 1990) and protection from the effects of explosions and fires (Tolloczko 1991), realisation of the extent to which industry practice influenced design regulations without consideration of local conditions (path-dependency) (Arnold & Roobaert 1989) and the maintenance needs of existing platforms (Bea 1990). Equally, new issues are appearing on the cognitive map of engineering, not least the social and political pressure following accidents which result in environmental damage (Owen & Raeburn 1991) and the need to assess and communicate the risks associated with various abandonment options when a platform's working life is over (Dymond 1995) - an issue which came to a head with the debacle over the disposal of the Brent Spar installation by Shell (Reader 1995; Cope 1998). Each of these issues now appears on the cognitive map of engineering and in each case the solution to the problems they raise is the application of probabilistic risk assessment techniques.

There is, then, much else of concern to engineering which provides support for the risk assessment approach. The danger, however, is that some of these issues can from time to time take on such importance that they can focus attention to a great extent on only one dimension of risk and result in health and safety at work becoming the victim of the blind spot thus created. The extent of the international public and political reaction to the decommissioning of the Brent Spar installation - including protests to the UK government from other European governments and public boycotts of Shell products in countries beyond the UK - resulted in the abandonment of the decommissioning plan which had already been approved and consideration of a large range of alternatives.[36] The risk assessments carried out for the initial plan were completely ignored in the media frenzy which ensued and there has been belated recognition that the activities of the environmental group Greenpeace, especially their provision of dramatic video footage of their occupation of the installation to news organisations, forced the issue into the public eye in a way which was not conducive to rational debate.[37] That this is the first of dozens of decommissions, many of which will be vastly more complex and costly (the Brent Spar was not a fixed platform), indicates that regulators will have to be extremely sensitive to the need to balance risks and will have to work hard to ensure that the processes of social norm production do not operate so as to obscure significant dimensions of risk including health and safety at work. Unless care is taken - that is, unless there is mutual observation of difference-minimising programmes - incremental reductions in environmental risk, for example, may mask dramatic increases in occupational risk. One study, for example, suggests that selecting total removal options over partial removal increases risks to worker safety by approximately 50% (Prasthofer 1998, 382). There is evidence of a sensitivity to this issue within engineering where a 'global' or 'total' approach to risk is being advocated. This involves the development of sophisticated and flexible assessment techniques which are sensitive to the limitations of what is possible and to the need to keep options open and under review (see e.g. Owen & Raeburn 1991; Comer & Eades 1991). Again there is perhaps evidence here of the influence of the feedback loop encouraged by the risk assessment programme.

Nor do all the problems lie outwith engineering. It was noted before that when these techniques enjoyed some ascendancy as a result of cost pressures, reservations were voiced as to the extent to which the engineering outlook had to change before they could be effectively employed. And this is a concern which remains. Discussing the new techniques, two professors from the Department of Offshore Engineering at Herriot-Watt University state that '[t]he group which will require perhaps the most extensive revision and updating of their education and training is the engineers who are responsible for the safety and reliability of the design, construction and operation of offshore structures' (Wolfram

& Owen 1991, 17). Proponents of the new techniques continue to warn that their usefulness is dependent on the skills of those who carry them out and those who receive the results. There is a tendency to focus on the final risk figures instead of using the techniques to weigh alternatives on the basis of risk. Thus, the aim must not be to fine tune one set of figures but to make informed decisions on the basis of alternatives (see e.g. Bea 1990; T. M. Miller *et al.* 1991). Engineering must not attempt to use these techniques to remove uncertainty since that would represent a return to determinism. Rather they must be used to allow the expression of degrees of belief in a systematic way, to open up issues otherwise masked and to force a documentation of the thought process (Stahl *et al.* 1992). That there is still some way to go before these points are understood is evident from those who while in favour of the new approach bemoan the fact that different techniques produce different results (e.g. Brekke *et al.* 1990) and from the fact that proponents meet with concerns that risk assessment is a 'black art' and 'academic' and therefore something to be treated with scepticism (Brandie 1993, 158). At the 1996 Offshore Technology Conference, it was stated that despite the introduction of Safety Cases and the requirement for quantitative demonstrations of safety, '[t]he majority of geotechnical engineers distrust statistical techniques, do not believe the answers they provide and hence make little effort to understand the subject' (Horsnell & Toolan 1996, 382). In other words, apparently wholehearted engineering support for the new approach must be viewed more cautiously if there are suspicions that it is not properly understood.

Evidence of this problem can be found in the discussion within the past decade about the update of one American design code which is also used for North Sea structures.[38] The API RP2A-WSD (working stress design) code which imposed deterministic requirements on individual structural components was replaced by the API RP2A-LRFD (load resistance factor design) code which requires probabilistic analysis of components. The advantage of the latter code is that it allows account to be taken of the uncertainty associated with environmental loads (Lloyd & Karsan 1988; Ferguson 1990). Against a background of the considerations mentioned above, the new code has been greeted enthusiastically and the advantages of its use - such as a more consistent level of component reliability and the opportunity for improving design - widely proclaimed (e.g. Turner *et al.* 1992). Its benefits have also been demonstrated by experimentally redesigning existing platforms which were produced on the basis of the WSD code. The results have been impressive with significant weight savings reported in conjunction with better reliability as a result of the ability to take better account of local environmental conditions (e.g. van de Graaf *et al.* 1994). But all is not as well as it might seem.

Alongside these enthusiastic reviews of the new code there are dissenting voices who highlight its shortcomings. Most significant is the point that it still concentrates on individual components. While it may allow each component to be more rationally designed, it says nothing about the interaction of components. Rather there is an assumption that if each component in a structure is rationally designed according to probabilistic criteria and the structure is composed of components possessing a consistent reliability rating then the entire structure must be similarly reliable. Critics point out, therefore, that while the LRFD code is certainly an advance on the WSD version in terms of the rationality of its approach, it may be creating a false sense of security because it still concentrates on individual components and does not address global structural integrity (Arnold *et al.* 1989; Ferguson 1990). This is a significant shortcoming and has the potential to cause a high degree of confusion in the light of studies which find that some conservatively designed platforms have a high degree of reserve and residual strength when reassessed on the basis of global reliability techniques (e.g. Lalani & Shuttleworth 1990), raising questions about the reserve and residual strength of LRFD designed installations which manifest significant reductions in the use of structural steel. Given that Lord Cullen referred specifically to the shortcomings of the prescriptive regime with regard to the interaction of components (1990, para. 21.42), the re-emergence of this problem is particularly troubling.

Thus, while the cognitive map for engineering in the post Piper Alpha era is the very encouraging Figure 5.2 which significantly constructs the new regulatory approach as integral to the new difference-minimising programme, regulators must focus on issues of communication and risk if the potential of this new world construction is to be realised. In particular, they must ensure not only that outside pressures do not act to narrow the focus of risk assessment and thus allow the development of blind spots which the new approach has the ability to expose, but also that within engineering itself, misunderstandings of the new approach based on the remaining vestiges of the deterministic programme do not operate to produce the same effect.

The above debate on the API code also points to another problem confronting the new regulatory approach. It is significant that there is some suggestion that the reluctance to push risk assessment too far in American codes is the perceived inability of those receiving the results to understand what they mean. The example of the American nuclear industry has been

Figure 5.2 Cognitive Map: Engineering (1990s)

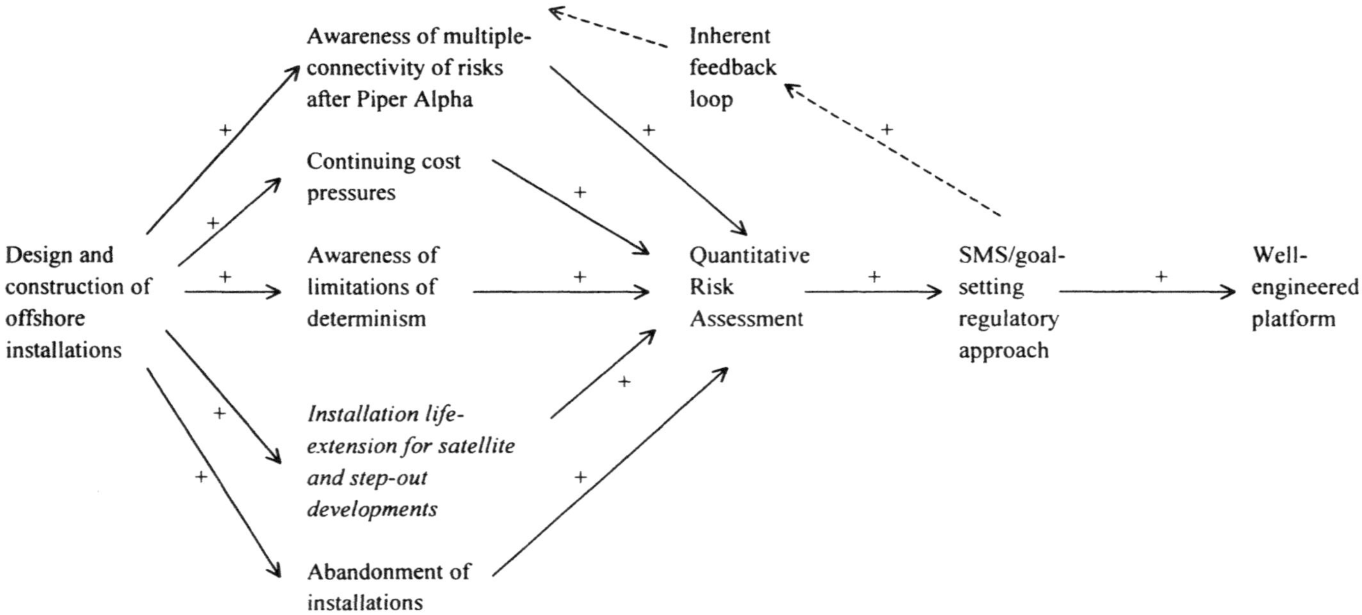

cited in this regard where the release of risk figures designed to indicate the level of safety is seen to have resulted in a public backlash which has brought the development of the industry to a virtual standstill (Visser 1993). Such problems of communication are not restricted to the public, however, but extend also to industry management for whom the risk assessment approach has been altogether new (cf. Faeke *et al.* 1981).

5 Industry Management

5.1 Introduction

If the immediate reaction to the Piper Alpha disaster in industry management was concern that the inevitable political/regulatory response would be 'over the top' in terms of, for example, greater separation between production facilities and personnel,[39] management equally knew that something drastic had to be done. Many of the tenets by which the industry had operated for decades were left severely exposed by the disaster. The UKOOA evidence to the Burgoyne Committee on the industry's own health and safety arrangements[40] bears re-reading in the light of Lord Cullen's findings. Quite simply, nothing of the industry's beliefs from that period remained intact. Its emphasis on its own experience and its own procedures and arrangements was shown by the events of 6 July 1988 to count for nothing. While the industry's previous assumptions about health and safety were comprehensively challenged, it would nevertheless be wrong to suggest that it effectively held its hands up and left itself at the mercy of the Cullen Inquiry. The understanding of the industry and its preference for self-regulation which has been gained in the previous two chapters indicates that it would have been surprising if it had reacted in this way. Its existing rationality was in tatters but that did not mean that it did not try itself to come up with some answers. The preceding chapters have also revealed how an alternative risk-oriented programme had been developing - albeit that its progress was uneven and severely set back by the 1986 price fall. In the aftermath of Piper Alpha, however, it had no competition.

It has been seen that Lord Cullen proposed a radically different approach to health and safety at work offshore. He did not, however, produce this new approach, as it were, from thin air, but rather he offered it as the preferred alternative from among those that had been presented to him in evidence. A substantial proportion of that evidence in Part 2 of the

Inquiry was presented by witnesses representing UKOOA (34 out of 63 expert witnesses). Thus it was UKOOA itself which proposed the goal-setting approach to regulation and the introduction and systematic use of Safety Cases and Formal Safety Assessments. While we saw that politics wanted to know why these recommendations had not been made much earlier,[41] the domination of the deterministic programme - especially after 1986 - can be seen to be the explanation. The extent of that programme's failure helps to account also for the degree to which industry management has embraced the new regime (Taylor *et al.* 1991; Hughes 1994, 1), with frank admissions that it had previously favoured hardware solutions and thought in terms of responding to emergencies rather than preventing them and a recognition that the tendency to blame human error and technical failure often masked management problems (N. Morgan 1992, 15).

Now, this close involvement of the industry in the development of the new approach may appear suspicious to some. Woolfson, Foster and Beck (1996), for example, as has been seen, are less than enthusiastic and Carson's concerns about the growth of a special regulatory framework (1981, 139ff) would appear to reach new levels of justification in such a situation. Whereas it would be naive to suggest that there are no potential dangers, it would equally be wrong to suggest that such a situation fatally contaminates the regulatory process.

A significant lesson of the preceding chapters has been the extent to which both industry management and engineering have been continually 'surprised' by the emergence of unforeseen problems which in large part have arisen as a result of the deterministic communicative systems by which they have operated. Assumptions were made and alternatives were closed off on the basis of tradition-based or path-dependent approaches which were not well-adapted or adaptable to new circumstances. The effect of these systems was to a great extent to prevent or restrict communication about certain possibilities until they occurred - by which time it was often too late in terms of injury or loss of life. A further significant finding has been the extent to which the regulators found themselves in an impossible situation. Always at a disadvantage as regards detailed information about the industry they had to regulate, the findings of the preceding chapters about the difficulties arising within the industry regarding issues of technological safety reveal starkly the insufficiency of the entire regulatory approach.

In these circumstances, it can be seen that viewing the new regime as a reflexive response to the difficulties encountered reveals the involvement of the regulated in its development in a much less problematic light.

Instead, it appears as an attempt to engage the processes of social norm production for law production and to encourage them to confront the issue of dual closure - that is, to allow a mutual observation among systems of how other systems observe. But if it is thus possible to look on the new approach favourably from a theoretical point of view, the question remains as to whether what is delivered in practice measures up.

5.2 The New Regime in Action

The basic principles upon which the new regime is based are not, of course, new to the offshore industry - in theory, at least. The ALARP principle (that risks to the workforce should be reduced to a level as low as reasonably practicable) has applied offshore since the extension in 1977 of the HSWA 1974. However, it was found by the HSE that it was a principle that was not well understood by management (Leiser 1993a, 80), not least perhaps because there was no similar notion in the MWA 1971 which was the dominant concern of all sides of the industry before Piper Alpha. The PED's belated acceptance of the HSWA 1974 as an alternative to the MWA 1971 in appropriate circumstances[42] does not appear, therefore, to have led to any understanding offshore of the main risk-management principle of that Act. The requirement for an auditable Safety Management System incorporating Quantitative Risk Assessment, however, offers a mechanism by which this principle can be rationally implemented. In general, the goals set in the new regulations are to be regarded as an indication of what is as low as reasonably practicable (Leiser 1993a, 81). The great advantage of the SMS approach is that it frees the operator from prescribed solutions which may have served to impede attainment of lowest practicable risk. That said, there is a clear onus on individual *operators* rather than on the *regulator* to ensure that at all times all risks are reduced to a level which is ALARP. Further, ALARP is not in itself the goal but rather the absolute minimum which is permissible (D. Bainbridge 1993, 86). It is worth noting that during the Voluntary Safety Case (VSC) exercise carried out up to 1993, as an aid to both regulator and regulated in discovering how the new approach would work in practice, none of the VSCs prepared demonstrated ALARP to the satisfaction of the regulators (Fox 1993, 16) - and, indeed, none of the VSCs would have been accepted (Powell 1993, 29). While this in itself is not surprising given the novelty of the Safety Case for all concerned, it does give some indication of the relatively limited extent to which risk assessment had been developed in the industry prior to Piper Alpha and serves as a corrective to any overly optimistic reading of UKOOA's claims in this regard. It also gives some impression of the learning curve management has confronted since the new regime has come into force.

ALARP is demonstrated, in accordance with the guidance to the 1992 regulations, by a chain of evidence running from identification of the hazard; through assessment of the likelihood and consequences of the hazard (including by quantitative risk assessment according to the degree of complexity and uncertainty); the provision of evidence that precautions required to achieve ALARP are being followed; the implementation of mechanisms to test performance against this standard; and finally an assessment of whether these measures are in themselves sufficient and if not the identification of other reasonably practicable precautions. The last stage may include further QRA and re-evaluation of existing practices in consultation with both workforce and management.[43]

There is evidence to suggest that this approach is indeed being adopted by industry management - with, indeed, further refinements. The approach in Shell, for example, begins with a hazard identification and assessment procedure. Following this, any problem is notified to the appropriate management group. Short or long term solutions are then identified and evaluated in order to reach a decision. The decision is passed to the management group for approval before being confirmed with workforce Safety Representatives. At this stage, if there are any continuing problems, the issue is returned up the line for the further identification and evaluation of solutions. Upon approval, the solutions are implemented and ongoing review and auditing assesses their performance. The decision making process now takes account of a hierarchy of approaches according to the degree of complexity of a problem and the extent to which it is understood. Thus, the most simple and well understood issues may be assessed on the basis of engineering judgement with progressively greater complexity and uncertainty requiring screening consequence and probability analysis, QRA and finally QRA plus Cost Benefit Analysis. This of course raises the possibility that determinism will be reapplied to problems which appear to be well understood but the review and audit mechanisms lessen the possibility of a long-term failure to recognise problems (Kennedy 1993).[44] It is also interesting to note that the HSE has stressed that the clearer the decision-making process is in the Safety Case the easier (and faster) will be the task of assessment (Pape 1993, 117). In other words, operators can avoid delay now not by cutting corners and reducing all issues to a calculus of time saved but rather by demonstrating that their SMS is adequate. In this regard, at the very least, the new regime in practice has observed the self-steering programme of industry management and employed this observation to encourage the development of an adequate SMS without having to prescribe in detail.

From the point of view of the industry, there are many indications that the new regime is perceived favourably and that it is indeed helping to ensure that a risk-oriented or reflexive programme as opposed to a deterministic one holds sway in management. For example, one confidential survey indicated a substantial number of operators (in excess of 90%) reporting that QRA had been beneficial to their understanding of risk and had helped improve safety on their installations (Kinsella 1994, 7). Further, a survey of senior management carried out for the HSE found that management viewed Safety Cases as having had a positive impact on its approach to health and safety. Benefits mentioned included a focusing of attention on the most important safety issues resulting from the use of risk assessment procedures and a structured approach to decision making which also produced efficiency in safety spending (HSE 1995, 5). But beyond safety spending, management has also reported 'unequivocally' the production of considerable unquantifiable consequential benefits from the new approach due to reduced accident frequencies, reduced plant down-time and reduced loss of production (HSE 1995, 8-9) - and that notwithstanding the outlay of some £2.24 billion to £2.53 billion on safety as a result of all changes due to the Piper Alpha disaster (AUPEC 1999, 31). It is worth noting that while management pointed to the shock of Piper Alpha as the main motivation for immediate changes, it was admitted that these had been largely technical in nature and that changes to management and procedures encouraged by the new regime were of more significance both in relation to safety improvements and rational cost control (HSE 1995, 6). In this regard, management accepted that the risk to personnel fell significantly as a result of remedial work carried out on the basis of risk assessments required by the Safety Case regime, most dramatically on the older installations (HSE 1995, 13). Furthermore, QRA has assisted management in reaching more rational decisions about development options and has encouraged the use of phased, and thus less risky, developments as uncertainties relating to geology and reservoir performance can be better understood before there is a full commitment of capital (Ahmed & Murphy 1996).

Nevertheless, the explicit linking of the new regime to cost issues may be a cause for concern. But this is not necessarily an example of management misunderstanding. Rather, the ALARP principle explicitly allows the consideration of costs by the duty-holder. Indeed following the

Voluntary Safety Case exercise, the HSE pointed out that all options discussed in a Safety Case must be costed so that attainment of ALARP can be judged by the regulators (Pape 1993, 111). The operator is entitled to weigh costs against benefits in deciding how much to spend in averting a particular risk. It is this which allows a decision on what is reasonably practicable. This seems at first sight to raise the sort of problems encountered in Chapter 1 in relation to the economic analysis of law but there are in fact significant differences. In that chapter it was seen that economic analysis fell short of a sufficiently full account of the regulatory process when it made the assumption that a company, for example, would decide whether or not to obey a regulation on the basis of whether the cost of compliance outweighed the cost of non-compliance. One of the questions such an approach did not ask was whether the regulation itself was regarded as rational by the regulated. In the new offshore regime it is not a question of the duty-holder considering cost as regards compliance with an externally imposed regulation but rather a matter, firstly, of the duty-holder assessing risks *itself* as they relate to its own installation and its own operations and then of considering its approach to those risks on the basis of costs and benefits. It could of course be objected that a company could nevertheless manipulate this process so as to save costs on safety issues but there is to the contrary evidence that the requirement to assess risk has revealed blind spots to operators which the previous approach to safety had created and thus also the possible costs of failing to take adequate account of the issue of safety (Perham 1993).[45] Thus, the new regime has the advantage of making use of the main concerns of the regulated so as to achieve the ends desired by the regulators. Similarly, it provides in QRA a means of linking these concerns also to the activities of engineering.

5.3 Problems

The new regime, therefore, appears not only to have theoretical but also practical advantages and the HSE has, in general, been able to report positively on its impact:

> Overall, as a result of the analysis necessary to prepare safety cases, companies have voluntarily made many modifications and changes to their procedures, plant and equipment. This has led to real and substantial risk reduction and is a vindication of the value of the whole Safety Case process. (Barrell 1994, 4)

That does not mean, however, that there are no difficulties - both actual and potential. The HSE itself has noted that of the problems arising during the assessment of Safety Cases some 40% related to hazard identification and risk assessment and 15% to management system issues (HSE 1995, 12). And while the regulators were encouraged to find managers who took the view that the new regime had forced them to go back to first principles and question their assumptions, there were others who were still sceptical. The regulators believe that this scepticism may stem from a lack of proper understanding of what is involved in both QRA and a systematic approach to the management of safety beyond the generation of a great deal of paperwork. Thus, while it found management with a good understanding of QRA insofar as it allowed a ranking of risks, identified previously unknown risks and allowed cost-effective planning, others expressed doubts about the extent of reliance on the technique and about the value of the effort required. As a result, this was often the single area of the Safety Case where there was reliance on external consultants due to lack of in-house expertise and resources. Similarly, concerns were expressed about the bureaucracy of the Safety Case approach.

Thus, while the new approach to the management of safety in the offshore oil and gas industry has the benefit of structurally coupling the different discourses of management, engineering and regulation, such a coupling by no means produces a situation where information is unproblematically transferred from one to another. While the mutual observation of steering programmes that the new approach allows represents a significant advance over the path-dependencies of the past, the temptation to believe that the so-called 'deadly gap' between engineering and management is thereby closed must be avoided (see N. Morgan 1992, 14). The difficulties facing the new regime in this regard can be examined under a number of headings.

(a) *Risk assessment* While probabilistic techniques have, as it were, been given a favourable press in this book, this does not mean that they are problem free. Rather, their importance in this context has been in large part the extent to which their appearance on the cognitive maps of engineering signalled a shift away from determinism towards a greater appreciation of the array of risks which face offshore installations and which determinism had masked - a shift culminating in a long-overdue recognition of the importance of individual occupational safety alongside and as a potential contributor to the more obvious catastrophic possibilities. Probabilistic techniques may offer a means of describing risk in a way which is less

emotive and equally form part of an assessment approach which demands an explicit appraisal of possibilities which cannot otherwise be observed or which can simply be ignored without comment, but they do not solve the problem of reaching a consensus on risk issues as is sometimes assumed (see Luhmann 1993, 48-9).

Risk assessment is relatively new to the offshore industry, certainly in the wide-ranging form required by the new regime, but it has been used more extensively elsewhere for much longer. While it, therefore, appears as a significant improvement offshore, there has been time elsewhere for problems to emerge and for commentators to become sceptical of just what it can achieve. Perhaps the most famous critic is Charles Perrow who cogently points out that the things which he (and many others) perceive to be the greatest risks (such as nuclear power or recombinant DNA) are precisely the things which risk assessments say have done almost no harm and are highly unlikely ever to do so (1984, 305).

The danger, then, as far as Perrow is concerned, is that far from simply assessing the risks of particular decisions, the technique can take on a legitimating function (1984, 307), something which Luhmann describes as the notorious aptness of quantitative analysis to manipulation (1993, 149-150) and which Baron calls the abuse of risk assessment (1992). Perrow has demonstrated in this regard how risk assessment is often blind to the differential imposition of risk on social classes (1984, 310), that QRA is often skewed in favour of industry (1984, 311), and that it is often indifferent to whether risks are imposed or voluntarily undertaken (1984, 312).

It can be said, however, that these criticisms of risk assessment stand only so long as the activity is slotted into what Perrow characterises as 'absolute rationality' or the rationality that believes that it is right, unbounded and free from the disordered thinking of the vast mass of the population (1984, 315-6). While QRA maintains a posture recognising its own limitations and its own need for flexibility, self-criticism and an ongoing process of assessment, it is not tainted by the stain of this presumed absolutism. That is not to say, of course, that the recipients of risk assessment results do not impute that power too it. In this regard, Perrow very definitely points us to a potential problem of risk assessment. As was suggested at the end of the discussion above on engineering,[46] the understanding of engineering QRA by management is precisely a point of tension. Whereas engineering may issue QRA results as a statement of relative uncertainty, they may be constructed by management as absolute values and thus take on the very legitimating function pointed to by

Perrow, by Luhmann and by Baron - something which would mark a dangerous return to determinism.

Nor is this a phenomenon restricted to the offshore industry. The pioneer of the risk assessment approach, NASA, was seen as experiencing precisely this problem in a report prepared for the European Space Agency:

> the problem with quantifying risk assessment is that when managers are given numbers, the numbers are treated as absolute judgments, regardless of warnings against doing so. These numbers are taken as fact, instead of what they really are: subjective evaluations of hazard level and probability.[47]

Similar concerns have been expressed in the nuclear industry, another prime user of probabilistic techniques: '[b]ecause of the complexity and multi-disciplinary nature of PCA [Probabilistic Consequence Assessment] codes, there is a considerable potential for their mis-use by inexperienced users' (OECD 1994, 60).

And there are some worrying indications in this regard in the offshore industry. The extent to which determinism held sway in the industry before Piper Alpha and the possibility of its continued influence can be gauged from the difficulty with which QRA has been applied in accordance with the new regime - whatever management may report to the contrary. The Voluntary Safety Case exercise carried out up to 1993 provided a valuable learning experience for both the industry and the regulators. It revealed that while some companies had a good grasp of the technique and of its application, there were others who struggled with it and those who, even if they could use it, were unable to incorporate it into the decision-making process (Pape 1993, 110). Others simply admitted that it was difficult to adjust to where previously qualitative engineering judgement had prevailed (Watson 1993, 69). Apart from providing a rather sobering insight into the standard of decision-making previously, this finding indicates that the problems experienced in other industries are present also offshore.

Thus, while the risk assessment approach is designed and intended to produce statements about degrees of uncertainty and to aid the process of deciding between alternative approaches to technical and operational problems, there is evidence that the figures it produces are constructed by management as absolute values of reliability. In this way, there can be a tendency either to accept a risk assessment as indicating that an installation is safe on the basis that the figures are within an acceptable range or to manipulate aspects of the risk assessment to bring the overall figure within that range without necessarily considering the knock-on effect of that manipulation. In other words, management applies a sort of ALARP binary code to QRA results - things are either ALARP or they are not (see HSE 1993c, 122ff). This obscures the need to ensure the ongoing assessment of operations and effectively demonstrates the way in which uncertainty is reconstructed as absolute by management. In this way, one manager I spoke to showed me how the probability of fatalities on one installation had been reduced simply by reducing the number of personnel on the installation. The figure before the removal was regarded as too high and the figure after was seen as acceptable. The effect of removing the personnel - for example, on the workload and shift patterns of those remaining and on the ability of that workforce to maintain vital functions - had not been considered in the calculation. Rather the aim was to bring the final result within an acceptable range.[48] It is not surprising, then, that there have been conflicts between industry and regulator as to whether ALARP has been demonstrated (AUPEC 1999, 5).

A number of other similar problems of constructive misunderstanding can be identified:

(i) Sometimes risks to individual groups of workers can be diluted by averaging the risk across all the groups on an installation so that a high risk group is masked. This may in particular affect contractor staff whose high risk status may be offset by low risk operator staff whose well-being has been given greater priority by the operator.

(ii) The so-called 'salami' effect of considering risks in isolation or as individual slices so that they appear negligible but taken all together may be great. This is also a potential shortcoming of the fault tree/event tree approach which, because it effectively specifies one or a number of particular paths, may mask out others. This is an issue, however, which is being addressed by modifying fault/event trees to model events in a more complex way beyond the standard binary possibilities which dominate at the moment (see Cox 1993) and by the use of more free-form influence diagrams (Moore & Bea 1993).

(iii) Averaging risks over time may conceal peaks associated with particular periods, for example, the old age of a platform - a matter of clear significance in a mature province such as the North Sea.

(iv) There have been examples of the rotation of personnel through high-risk jobs as a means of achieving a low individual risk figure rather than tackling the risks themselves and irrespective of the fact that rotation of personnel may actually increase risk as a result of the reduced opportunities for gaining experience.

(v) There have been examples where the off-duty risks to personnel have been omitted from calculations - a particularly problematic omission in the light of the high proportion of off-duty victims on Piper Alpha.

(vi) There has been a tendency to use reliability studies in relation to systems independent of other indicators such as assessments of vulnerability and sensitivity resulting in the production of reliability figures of 99.9% without any real understanding of what is at stake (see generally Pape 1993; Doyle 1993).

(vii) QRA has been used retrospectively to justify the removal of Stand-by Vessels (AUPEC 1999, 15).

In the light of these issues, the tendency for management to point to the opportunities provided by the new approach to increase the awareness of the *workforce* of safety issues (e.g. Chevalier 1993, 154) appears well-intentioned but to direct attention away from a pressing need at the level of management itself in this regard.

The problem of the constructive misunderstanding by management of QRA produced by engineering is a potentially very serious one, not only at the level of the immanent risks which it can mask, but also at the level of the opportunity which the technique offers more generally for transcending many of the problems which have beset the regulation of health and safety at work offshore. The result of the misunderstanding is that a technique which aims to provide an opportunity to communicate uncertainty and to avoid the restrictions which compel the communication of the uncertain as sure, is constructed by management as being a process which produces certainty. The net effect of its misunderstanding may even be more dangerous because management may nevertheless believe that it is behaving more safely because its decisions have the imprimatur of risk assessment. QRA does not eliminate uncertainty, then, but rather forces the issue to be confronted and thus inherently demands that once a decision is taken it cannot be regarded as final but rather must be subject to ongoing review and assessment to check on the inevitably continuing uncertainty.

If any proof were needed that the new approach does not remove uncertainty or lead to an elimination of risk, it came in the form of a series of gas explosions on board the Piper Bravo, the replacement for the Piper Alpha and the first platform in the North Sea to have been designed with safety as an integral feature and to have been subject to Formal Safety Assessments from the conceptual design stage onwards.[49]

Most recently, there is some evidence that the management response to these difficulties with QRA has been to abandon it altogether. The HSE-sponsored evaluation of the offshore safety legislative regime discovered that there 'were major concerns about the methodology and application of QRA [and] a move away from reliance on QRA...to more traditional qualitative concepts such as "sound engineering judgement"' (AUPEC 1999, 6-7). The extent of this reaction is unclear and it needs to be set in the context of the new Risk Decision Support Framework developed by the industry which retains a clear role for QRA (see Tope 1999). Nevertheless, the importance for the regulator of addressing the understanding of QRA by the industry is clear.

(b) Concentration on major events and technical issues The use of QRA can lead to problems manifest in more particular ways than the constructive misunderstanding of the uncertain as certain. One potential problem is the extent to which its use can lead to a renewed concentration only on major events and on technical issues at the expense of lower level occupational matters. While the Safety Management System approach does seem to ensure that occupational matters remain in view, there is a danger that the comparative difficulty of modelling human factors can lead to them being given a lower priority rather than the renewed focus which that uncertainty ought to produce. This has been blamed on a number of factors related to the practices of management, regulators and external consultants alike. On the part of management, for example, some operators involved in the VSC exercise were particularly criticised for the omission of assessments of risk to personnel as opposed to risks to installation components (Fox 1993, 18). Others admitted to a greater facility in demonstrating ALARP in relation to major risks as opposed to minor ones (Redd 1993, 23). Still others have contended that if asset protection was a permitted benefit to be included in Cost Benefit Analysis then everything would automatically be ALARP. This indicates a continuing belief that provided technical integrity is assured, occupational issues will fall into place. The extent to which the fallacy of that belief was exposed by the Piper Alpha disaster renders its continued appearance particularly

worrying. The response of regulators to this issue - that only safety issues should be included in the analysis and that asset protection should be included 'only where further reassurance is required' - does little to reassure insofar as it does not tackle the underlying misunderstanding (see HSE 1993c, 124). It has also been said in this regard that significant problems of ensuring trained and competent staff, especially by contractors, has been ignored by the HSE because of their greater ability to assess technical issues (Spiller 1994, 3). And on the part of external consultants, there is certainly a risk that the increasing use of sophisticated computerised approaches based on the structure of the installation may divert attention away from more 'mundane' issues (see e.g. Cox 1993). The most recent evidence appears at first sight to be more encouraging with management feeling that the industry now focuses more on occupational safety and on minor accidents and incidents (AUPEC 1999, 7). The same report, however, reveals that workers feel 'safest' with regard to 'hazards to the installation' and 'catastrophes' and 'less safe' with regard to 'occupational' and 'work-task' hazards (AUPEC 1999, 47). The blindness to occupational and personnel risk has, therefore, not yet necessarily disappeared because of Piper Alpha and the new regime.

(c) Use of consultants The use of external consultants in risk assessment, while presenting some dangers as hinted at above, also presents some opportunities. Insofar as they possess the highest level of expertise in QRA techniques, they are in a unique position to provide structural coupling regarding the communication of uncertainty to management. Their very status as external to the organisations which employ them, however, introduces constraints in this regard. Nor is the use of external consultants for the carrying out of QRA an isolated practice. While there has been recent evidence of 'less wholesale contracting out of Safety Cases' (AUPEC 1999, 40), this means little when seen in the context of an earlier survey which suggested that only 6% of operators relied solely on in-house staff for risk assessment (Kinsella 1994, 6). If communication between engineering and management within organisations is difficult, then communication between external consultants and management is likely to be doubly so (see Luhmann 1993, 191-2). Nor is this a one-way problem. The issue of the appropriate understanding of industry issues by consultants is just as much a question as the understanding of QRA results by industry management. There is, however, the possibility that things can even go a stage further. It is not unknown for consultants to be used effectively to confirm decisions that have already

been taken or for consultants effectively to 'second guess' what those employing them want to hear.

And yet, despite such problems, there are plenty of examples of consultants operating so as to try to maintain the advantage offered by QRA and the SMS approach. There are those who insist on the need for continual review and the need to avoid the misunderstanding of results as amenable to 'once and for all' decisions (see e.g. Cox 1993; Perham 1993, 17). Similarly, consultants, as the ones who can sometimes contribute to a concentration on major hazards and technical issues, may also hold the key to ensuring that occupational issues are taken more seriously. There is an increasing awareness among human factors specialists of the potential for relatively minor occupational accidents to contribute to the overall risk to the installation. Their demonstrations of the impact of technical issues on human factors and of human factors on technical issues are designed to produce an awareness in a technically predisposed industry of the need to transcend that preoccupation at the risk (at the very least) of increased technical and cost problems if it fails to do so (see e.g. Bellamy 1994; Noerager *et al.* 1999).

(d) Interface with contractors As with the question of consultants, the question of the interface between operators and their contractors provides problems but also possible benefits in the context of the new regime. While, in the abstract, the idea of requiring a Safety Management System appears undoubtedly good and unproblematical, in the context of an industry with such fragmented contracting arrangements the issue is not so straightforward. It was seen in Chapter 1 that Wright (1986) identified contracting as an economically rational approach but one which resulted in greater safety problems. His prescription, therefore, was to reduce the amount of sub-contracting. It was suggested that this was perhaps an unrealistic proposition in the face of an industry belief that the contracting arrangements were a means of dealing with the complex array of tasks which the process of offshore oil and gas extraction involves. Thus, while in the post-Piper Alpha era the amount of contracting and sub-contracting has not decreased and has indeed increased with ever more functions being performed outside the operator's organisation (Durnin 1994, 9), not excluding operational management of installations themselves (AUPEC 1999, 18), there have been significant changes in the relationships between operator and contractor.

Most significant has been a growth in what has become known as 'partnering' where the parties enter into longer-term and more closely coupled arrangements. While exact details of these new arrangements are difficult to come by, the benefits reported give some idea of what is involved: improved communications due to the removal of duplicated project management and documentation, reduced costs and increased certainty for contractors with a secure flow of work.[50] There are reports of vast improvements in the relationships between operators and contractors with the former realising that not only was the previous way of doing business (where contractors could be hired and fired with remarkable rapidity and where time and cost considerations took precedence) not safe, but it was not financially efficient either. The Britannia installation, for example, is put forward as a success story as regards the application of alliance contracting principles which sought, *inter alia*, continuously to 'instigate measures towards alignment of all parties, at all levels and through all phases of the project' (Garga 1999, 461). In particular, the aim was to 'create greater linkage between project and operations phases with rewards to project alliance companies for improved plant reliability, lower opex and safety in order to bring about further improvements in total field life economics' (1999, 461). Quite apart, then, from the requirements of the new health and safety regime, the industry has itself been moving towards a closer coupling of the management systems of operators and contractors. And it is significant that experience to date has suggested that such relationships are most likely to be successful in projects containing 'common characteristics of complexity, uncertainty, technology and duration' (Farrell *et al.* 1996, 589).

That does not mean that this has been an easy process, nor that the industry-inspired moves measure up to what is required to be demonstrated in the respective Safety Cases of operator and contractor. Experience so far suggests that the response by operators to this issue has been varied. While some operators require a joint approach with contractors to SMS development at all times and to a very high degree of detail (Forrest & Reisz 1993; Durnin 1994), others have adopted a slightly more flexible approach depending on the exact circumstances of the work in hand. In such cases, working arrangements range from a combined Safety Case for combined operations, through bridging documents between SMSs for MODU operations, to reliance on bridging documents or even just the contractor's SMS for connected activities and installation support (J. Morgan 1993; see also M. Salter 1993). It might be suggested that the flexible approach is in some respects preferable in that it seems to fit with the non-prescriptive stance of the new regime. But there is a danger that its flexibility is more apparent than real in that it suggests a particular working arrangement for a particular type of circumstance without requiring a consideration of individual particularities as would be the case with the joint approach. It has been pointed out by the HSE in this regard that there is a need for clarity about where independence is possible and where consultation is required and that this is not something that can be decided in the abstract (J. King 1993, 212).[51] The regulator has recently been warned that in this context it needs 'to be more vigilant in monitoring competencies, expertise and management systems of individual parties' (AUPEC 1999, 15).

(e) CRINE Related to the development of new relationships between operators and contractors has been the Cost Reduction Initiative in the New Era which has resonated throughout the offshore industry. Insofar as it focuses on the problems of the previous management approach (what it terms the 'North Sea culture'), it performs an extremely useful function in identifying the problems of prescription. It even reveals that responsibility for these problems rests as much with industry management as with the regulators. The much-discussed need for flexibility and self-regulation on the part of management appears to have found expression in the rigid adherence to in-house standards by individual operators and to have perpetuated obsolete technology and practices. Similarly, the *perception* of the North Sea as a hostile environment is regarded now as having produced an over-reaction rather than a rational response. In short, the reasons for the excessive costs in the North Sea (see Figures 4.1 and 4.2) are found to lie in management specifications rather than in regulatory requirements.

In this regard, CRINE represents a remarkable piece of soul-searching by the industry and a turn-around of astonishing magnitude - an acknowledgement of the masking effect of its deterministic programmes. As a consequence, the worries that can be raised by the emphasis on cost-reduction may be over-stated. In particular, the emphasis on simplifying and clarifying communications between operators and contractors is especially encouraging as is the aim to seek QUASCO administration of an industry-wide concentration on quality and safety in the provision of equipment and services by contractors. Much of this is to be achieved by stripping out the in-house prescriptive preferences of operators which are now seen to have been the most significant barrier to innovation and replacing them with functional specification. This aims to allow operators to specify in simple terms *what* it is that they require to achieve and to allow contractors to answer *how* this will be achieved. So far, then, CRINE looks much less worrying than has sometimes been suggested and does not in itself involve a headlong rush to reduce costs in a way similar to that which followed the price fall of 1986.

But the picture is not all so rosy. In particular, there is one area of fundamental tension evident in the CRINE report. While there is to be a shift to functional specification by operators - in principle allowing greater freedom to contractors to produce appropriate solutions - the expectation is that increasingly contractors will offer standard solutions. And this standardisation is to be encouraged by appropriate modifications to codes and standards. Insofar as these moves towards standardisation are of the goal-setting variety there will be no conflict with the new regulatory regime. This is not something, however, about which there is complete clarity in the CRINE report and taken together with the other problems about constructive misunderstanding by management discussed above, such ambiguity is more than just unfortunate.[52] Beyond that, the period from 1994 when CRINE was launched was one of relative price strength. But with a second price crash in 1998, the initiative risked being the vehicle for another panic reaction as will be discussed below.

5.4 Conclusion

There are, then, reasons to be optimistic about the management response to the new regime but there are equally reasons to be cautious. These reasons, however, do not suggest a need for anything like a return to more detailed regulation and tougher enforcement. Rather they suggest that the aspects of the new approach which allow a closer structural coupling of the different communicative systems and which encourage the communication of what is uncertain as such - as opposed to closing off that possibility - should be supported. Of great importance in this regard is the danger that the closer coupling which the Safety Case encourages and which has coincided with the development of partnering in the industry and the CRINE initiative will contribute to the development of communicative systems which run counter to this aim. The possibility that complacency can creep into communications where everything seems so much better than it was before is very real. The risks associated with such a complacency are especially high at a time when the industry is dealing with ageing platforms in the maturing province of the North Sea, their eventual abandonment and the move into an entirely new set of circumstances West of Shetland.[53] This problem is only compounded when the basis for keeping communications open to risk is often maintained by external consultants and constructively misunderstood by the decision makers who have had no involvement in those processes. The Risk Decision Support Framework to be discussed below may offer some hope for the future but that the task confronted is a complex one is reinforced when the factor of workforce involvement is added to the equation.

6 Workforce Involvement

The issue of workforce involvement in health and safety offshore has tended, as we have seen, to be reduced to a debate about the role of the unions. When the Cullen Report was debated in Parliament, politicians divided down party lines on this issue at least while significantly all coming down in favour of some form of involvement.[54] There is a danger, however, that the issue of unionisation *per se* can serve to obscure much more important matters with regard to health and safety.

There is little doubt that the relative invisibility of the workforce from the cognitive maps of management, engineering and the regulators for a significant period of the history of the North Sea as an oil and gas province can be related in no small measure to the traditional weakness of the unions in this sector. While part of the reason for this weakness was due to the steps taken by operators to prevent unionisation - making it difficult for representatives to speak to the workforce, intimidation of activists, and so forth - the unions themselves must accept part of the blame. It was seen in Chapter 3 that one of the reasons given by management for disliking the thought of unionisation in the early 1970s was the possible effect of inter-union disagreement such as was being witnessed onshore at the time. Whatever the extent to which that statement was a true reflection of management sentiment, the fact remains that the history of union co-operation in the North Sea until comparatively recently is a sorry one. A persistent failure to agree and an ongoing fight for members at the expense of members' interests has undoubtedly weakened the potential of the unions to operate with any force in the offshore industry.[55]

The Offshore Industry Liaison Committee has been an attempt to overcome these problems and in the summer of 1989 it tried to organise industrial action offshore to highlight ongoing safety problems and unacceptable working conditions. Its One Union Discussion Document issued in May 1989 clearly recognised the problems which unions had created for themselves offshore. While the scale of the eventual action, involving the occupation of installations, fell short of what was intended, it nevertheless succeeded in extracting promises from a number of companies that they would allow ballots on union membership. The public face shown by offshore employers concerned with workforce safety during the Cullen Inquiry which was ongoing at this time must be contrasted with the ease with which these promises were forgotten once the men had returned to work (OILC 1991, 48). In these circumstances, it is not surprising that support for further strike action the following summer was strong. Once again the OILC sought a united front.

The Continental Shelf Agreement, drawn up among a number of unions before the industrial action of the summer of 1990 and timed to coincide with the largest ever North Sea maintenance programme - a period of extreme vulnerability to delays - was an example of the level of co-operation that could be achieved. This time, the action was much better co-ordinated and much more effective. Once again, however, the employers revealed a face which was completely at odds with the public face on view at the Cullen Inquiry. By targeting the maintenance period, the operators claimed that the unions were actually having a detrimental effect on safety. Great play was made of the fact that some of the work delayed was the fitting of the Emergency Shut-down Valves required by regulations brought into force as a direct result of the Piper Alpha disaster. Reported in exactly this form in the oil industry press, the claims appeared fair and cogent.[56] But other press sources published company documentation obtained by the OILC which catalogued a safety situation much more serious than that including, significantly, such issues as unfit fire-fighting systems (OILC 1991, 56).

But another management fear of union power which was seen in the cognitive maps of the 1970s was completely justified by this action. Delays in the construction and installation phase of early North Sea projects produced serious knock-on effects which management simply could not countenance. While Shell continually insisted that production was not affected by the strike action in 1990,[57] they were eventually forced to concede in a court action brought to try and end the occupation of the platforms that the dispute was costing them some £4 million per day. Significantly, however, this appears to have contributed to the judge's finding that the cost to Shell of the occupation outweighed any expected benefits to the workers (OILC 1991, 61). From the effects which delays and costs had on operational practices seen in Chapters 3 and 4, this may have been more correct than anyone realised at the time.

The question then arises whether the management attitude to the unions, which has clearly been hostile until very recently, is matched by its attitude to the workforce in general. On the basis of the revelations during the disputes of 1989 and 1990, it would have to be concluded that the issues effectively being covered up were detrimental to the workforce as a whole and, therefore, the public pronouncements of a safer industry with a more open attitude to the workforce would have to be discounted. The standard management view that they knew best and could make the changes necessary in the aftermath of the Piper Alpha disaster was in evidence at this time. Whether this remains the case is a more open question. It has already been seen in the discussion of industry management that the initial response to the Piper Alpha disaster, while it involved a profound reassessment by the industry of how it operated, was largely confined to technical issues. Only later did other issues including the management of safety from a non-technical point of view begin to come to the fore.

Legislation has certainly played a role in this. The guidance to the 1992 Safety Case Regulations includes workforce involvement in the development and implementation of regulations (HSE 1992a, 55-7). Further, the 1989 Safety Representative and Safety Committee Regulations have, as we have seen, been amended by the Offshore Safety (Protection Against Victimisation) Act 1992 to provide for the involvement of Safety Representatives in the development of Safety Cases and for Safety Representatives to have access to the completed Case and to audits. The systematic consultation with Safety Representatives must also be included in the Safety Management System (Leiser 1993b, 132). But while the new regime compels management to engage with the workforce, the attitudes which were evident during the 1989 and 1990 industrial disputes suggest that that engagement may be less than productive. In Chapter 1, reference was made to the work of Tombs (1990; 1991) in which he suggested that management's view of workers and unions was as 'outside groups' meaning that they simply were not taken seriously. He called for the granting to workers of formal legal rights of communication about safety issues and for steps to be taken to redress the power imbalance by increasing the role of unions. Evidence of that management view can certainly be seen in 1989 and 1990. But now that there certainly are legal requirements for communication between management and workforce (especially in the aftermath of the changes to the 1989 regulations effected by the 1992 Act) does Tombs's assessment that none of the Cullen recommendations would result in a shift in the nature and extent of such distorted communication still have relevance?

Tombs was writing before the 1992 changes, for example, and there is certainly evidence to suggest that the management view of consultation with the workforce on safety issues has dramatically changed since the summer of 1990. There are companies who actively seek the involvement of the workforce both through Safety Representatives and Safety Committees and through the line management structure as a direct link to the broader workforce. Such companies have tried to arrange a focal point for safety issues such as a Safety Case co-ordinator and to ensure feedback to the originator of such queries (Forrest & Reisz 1993, 143). There are examples of management ensuring that drafts of Safety Case studies and other relevant documentation are developed and reviewed in consultation with those elements of the workforce who have relevant experience and not just with Safety Representatives as required by the regulations (Forrest & Reisz 1993, 145-6). Similarly, companies have recognised the value of hands-on experience in developing realistic scenarios for risk assessment as opposed to relying simply on the assumptions of onshore, often external, personnel whose expertise in risk assessment techniques is not likely to be matched by expertise in drilling, well control, crane operations, etc. Thus, scenarios are developed by those with direct experience of them which provides data for cross-checking the results produced by experts onshore and equally gives the workforce direct experience of the practice of risk assessment (Forrest & Reisz 1993, 144; Chevalier 1993, 152). The importance of such developments cannot be over-emphasised and one of the pioneers of QRA in the offshore industry has described as 'essential' the 'integration of the experience, insights and judgment of those that have direct and daily responsibilities for field operations' (Bea 1996, 79). The integration of operations personnel from the outset of the design process for the Britannia topsides, for example, has been presented as a key factor in producing both a safe and low-cost facility (Croft-Bednarski & Johnston 1999, 465-6).

Management is, therefore, in many cases not simply consulting with the workforce in the rather formal way that might be expected on the basis of the 1989/90 attitudes as something that had to be gone through to keep the regulators off its back, but rather is actively and creatively developing that consultation to solve some of the problems which were identified above in relation to other aspects of the new regime - especially the requirement for Quantitative Risk Assessment and the consequent need to engage outside expertise. Far from being problems, these issues have led to a closer and potentially productive coupling of the different sectors concerned.

> Structuring and formalising communications between the different participants into a controlled process, with offshore visits and meetings, underlines the value of people's contribution and thus, significantly enhances the quality of the outcome. (Chevalier 1993, 154)

There has also been a recognition that without such integration of the workforce there is no feedback loop to enhance design and construction with the lessons of experience (Skrede 1998, 72-3).

But this apparently rosy picture of improved relations between management, engineering and workforce needs to be more closely examined and a key question answered. How widespread is the change suggested by the above-mentioned examples? Regrettably, the answer to that appears to be at best that improvements are not uniform and at worst that the examples cited may be isolated islands of best practice in a sea of indifference, lip service or simple misunderstanding. The recent HSE-sponsored evaluation of the offshore safety regine (AUPEC 1999) produced some depressing findings about workforce involvement: 'there was evidence that achievements in encouraging workforce participation in safety were more modest' (1999, 9); the data showed little change in workforce understanding of safety cases since the interim evaluation carried out four years earlier (1999, 19); 'there seems to be little evidence to suggest widespread involvement of Safety Representatives or the general workforce in the preparation of Safety Cases' (1999, 40). All of this would be bad enough if there were some indications of future, albeit belated, improvement. But even this modest hope appears dashed by the astonishing findings, firstly, that there is still a lack of clarity about how to achieve workforce involvement and, secondly, *about the fundamental aim* (1999, 9). That this could be the case over ten years after Piper Alpha almost defies belief. And yet there is further evidence of precisely these problems. Despite the extraordinarily clear language of Lord Cullen's criticisms of management in the Piper Alpha inquiry report and his recognition of a role for the workforce and unions in the new offshore safety regime, it was five years before a single solitary member of the workforce was involved in the annual Safety Case conference (Molloy 1993). That only a few Safety Representatives attended the HSE conference on the tenth anniversary of the Piper Alpha disaster – *Changing Health and Safety Offshore: The Agenda for the Next Ten Years* – requires no comment. A safety consultant discussing experience of audits of the offshore industry generally stated that '[o]ne aspect which has scored consistently low from our audits has been worker involvement' (Pomfret 1998, 253). That he also pointed to the fact that 'the lowest scores are for management involvement, leadership and commitment' (1999, 251) raises the question of just who is involved. And while the representatives of management, unions and regulators present at the HSE conference in July 1998 all appeared to be reading from the same script, precisely what that script said indicated more that work needed to be done than that a great deal had already been achieved. UKOOA spokesman, Ian Montgomery, stated that all stakeholders had to be taken into account, including employees and unions. Roger Spiller of the MSF union interpreted this as long-overdue recognition of the role unions could play, largely ignored in reality as they were. The Health and Safety Commission chairman, Frank Davis, called for greater union involvement offshore, while the head of the HSE's OSD, Allan Sefton, pointed to an ongoing failure of communication when he stated that management and unions needed to start talking to each other rather than at each other (see Cresswell 1998). Consequently, the recent very hopeful signs of a more genuine partnership between management and unions offshore – in the form of a union recognition deal between MSF and Total, touted as the first of many,[58] and of a partnership agreement involving seven unions (the Inter Union Offshore Oil Committee) and UKOOA aimed at better co-operation on safety issues[59] – need to be seen in this context. That the TUC General Secretary, John Monks, could only suggest that 'unions and employers in the oil and gas industry have turned their backs on the macho management and union militancy of the past'[60] fully eleven years after Piper Alpha is an indication of the mountain that may still have to be climbed.

The provisions of the Employment Relations Act 1999 relating to union recognition which prompted the Total/MSF agreement will undoubtedly help to promote further positive developments with regard to workforce involvement. But given the history of problems and the continuing evidence of a lack of understanding revealed by the AUPEC (1999) survey, great care will be needed to ensure that these developments are not purely formal without any meaningful contact between the two sides. The basic mechanisms of the new regime possess the potential to assist but they need to be properly understood by all concerned if this potential is to be fulfilled.

In some respects, the offshore industry is just beginning to reach a stage in labour relations that has prevailed for longer onshore under the impetus of the HSWA 1974. Experience there, however, points to the limitations of closer co-operative structures if they are not understood in a sufficiently sophisticated way. Onshore, the simple tripartite approach envisaged by the HSWA 1974 and the 1977 regulations is perceived to have placed too much faith in the ability of procedures on consultation to produce universal consent (e.g. Baldwin 1987, 138-9) - an issue which becomes more serious in the context of more complex health and safety problems where there are particular problems of uncertainty and causation (see Baldwin 1987, 158). In other words, simply getting parties together who previously have not been involved in dialogue is not an automatic recipe for success. The evidence presented in the third and fourth chapters indicates that a key factor in the health and safety situation offshore has been what the communicative systems in play have systematically masked. Thus, the advantage in co-operative structures must be the role they can play in allowing (to the extent possible) an ongoing mutual consideration of the potential fatal blind spots. There is evidence that management and engineering have understood the benefit of the risk assessment approach in revealing previous blind spots. They will ignore the further assistance that the union perspective can provide in this respect at their peril.

To put it in more autopoietic terms, the close structural coupling of management, engineering and workforce around the processes of risk assessment and safety management, significantly in the context of recognition agreements, provides all the benefits of a binding or linkage institution in terms of the 'duration, intensity and quality' of that coupling. The opportunities for one system to observe others' observations can lead to a better understanding of what it is that its own operations may be masking. A very hopeful sign in this regard is evidence of an increasing recognition that the problems confronting management and unions revolve around the issue of communication rather than the traditional issues of power, membership, etc. Workforce Safety Representatives themselves, for example, have identified communication as the key to the success of the Safety Management System and have identified three barriers which stand in the way of success: physical (the fact that much of the work on the Safety Case is carried out onshore away from the workforce); psychological (problems of workforce attitudes, mistrust and fear); and semantic (the problems of the complexity of the new techniques) (see Molloy 1993, 2).

There is already some evidence, as has been seen, that the physical barrier is being overcome by combining and cross-checking onshore and offshore expertise so that the possibility of blind spots occurring in any of the communicative systems is reduced: onshore experts and consultants may model certain processes in overly-simplistic ways which mask risks which are obvious to those who physically work with them; the offshore workforce may lack the theoretical knowledge of certain processes which make other risks obvious to consultants. Semantic barriers are more difficult, especially in the context of the technical language surrounding QRA which risks the development of a closed communicative system with no accessibility - in terms of an ability to observe its observations - to the workforce. There are examples, however, of attempts to overcome such difficulties by applying the principles of hazard identification and risk assessment to everyday experience as well as specifically to the work carried out by particular groups in order that otherwise abstract principles take on practical relevance for the workforce. This is especially important because in much the same way that management may be expected to construct engineering uncertainty as certainty, so may engineering and other experts remote from the physical operational technology construct a risk figure as acceptable which the workforce regard in practice as intolerable (see e.g. Beck 1992, 58). There is equally encouraging evidence of operators reducing the bulk and complexity of Safety Cases to make them understandable to the workforce (AUPEC 1999, 69).

Psychological barriers present another significant problem. Two issues are identified here by Safety Representatives. One is of the remaining vestiges of a management culture which sees it as the job of management to manage and not to consult with the workforce. Such a view demonstrates the concern that if safety is open for discussion today, everything else will be open for discussion tomorrow. The other issue is of the fear and mistrust which the previous experiences of the workforce have engendered (Molloy 1993, 3). Given the evidence discussed above, it would be naive to suggest that there are no remaining examples of this sort of management attitude (see also Spaven *et al.* 1993, 111ff). Even where management is no longer as macho as it used to be, it is clear that the unions will have to convince it that they have a positive contribution to make. In this regard, unions can look to one of the areas of conflict that emerged in the post-Piper Alpha era for an indication of how they might most successfully move forward.

It will be recalled that the political debate on how best to achieve workforce involvement concentrated on whether to adopt the onshore model of *union appointment* of Safety Representatives or to retain the offshore model of *workforce election* of Safety Representatives. Faced with a low level of unionisation and a situation where management could continue to make it difficult for unions to improve that situation by methods well short of the strong-arm tactics of the past meant that there were severe problems in pursuing a stronger role down that avenue. That Lord Cullen was not convinced of the need to apply the onshore model made it very easy for industry management to defend their opposition. Similarly, the fact that the offshore model was more democratic was also a major stumbling block for unions attempting to argue for the extension of the onshore model, since to move to union appointment would be a retrograde step in this regard. It was also the case that in this respect the offshore model was more in line with the EU Framework Directive[61] than the onshore model (see James 1992, 96). Paradoxically, some union spokesmen while complaining about the difference between the onshore and the offshore model in terms of union involvement nevertheless praised the latter's democratic structure (Bibbings 1993, 139).

The approach of the OILC union was, in this regard, more acute. Instead of fighting for the onshore model, it simply put up its members for election as Safety Representatives and if they were not elected then that was an end of it (see McDonald 1993). Predictably, this set the OILC at odds with other unions. But in adopting this approach it demonstrated an understanding of the management construction of the situation. By moving out of a position of confrontation with management and using the means which management approved of for the election of Safety Representatives, they could achieve positions of influence in ways which did not antagonise management. Few would doubt that the support which the backing of a trade union provides can be anything but a benefit in the context of offshore safety and so the likelihood of an OILC (or any union) member being elected over a non-union member was high. This transcendence of the traditional polarisation of management against union fought out over well-defined fields of conflict marked a significant step forward and is one which other unions would do well to follow. The reluctance to trust to the democratic procedure was something which was difficult for those outside the industry to understand and which presented a sitting target for management. For its part, management was always prepared to concede in private that it could clearly see the benefit of training courses which trade unions provide for Safety Representatives, even when its public pronouncements made little or no mention of this. And while the TUC recognised that part of the problem lay in persuading management that it did not have to be perpetually in confrontation with the unions (Bibbings 1993), its approach tended to demonstrate no awareness of the management construction of this issue: despite the changes brought about by the Framework Directive in this regard, it continued to construe the offshore approach negatively (Bibbings 1994).

What this example shows is that communication is the issue that must be focused upon and the question of unions must become one of their role in improving the quality of structural coupling rather than their quest for power - whether in relation to management or, even worse, in relation to each other. For so long as unions conceptualise the situation on the basis of power and position it is highly likely that they will merely confirm the traditional management construction. If they shift to an understanding which stresses their ability to provide the training and resources for Safety Representatives and the workforce at large and which stresses the need for genuine workforce involvement in the management of safety (and consequently the achievement of management objectives), they will have a much greater chance of achieving yet stronger coupling with management and thus their own objectives of a safer working environment.

Such a concentration may help to alleviate some of the confusion that has been evident among the offshore workforce as regards the role of Safety Representatives and of unions. The interim report on the Safety Case regulations (HSE 1995) identified a number of problems which the updated survey (AUPEC 1999) indicates have not significantly improved. While Safety Representatives tend to be dismissive of the role of the unions offshore, despite being predominantly union members, and to look increasingly to the HSE for stronger involvement (possibly due to increased contact between Safety Representatives and the regulator), the workforce as a whole tend to look for stronger union involvement. The fact that the HSE is keen to avoid this stronger involvement and has stressed that it is not the final guarantor of safety offshore (Spaven *et al.* 1993, 78) means that Safety Representatives cannot rely on support from this quarter. Nor should this be particularly surprising given the auditing role of the regulator in the new regime. That there may be some misunderstandings among Safety Representatives about the exact roles of the various parties and about the orientation of the new regulations is shown by their dismay about the shift from prescription to goal-setting in the regulations, which is seen as making their task more difficult (see Spaven *et al.* 1993, 65ff, 116ff). There is a need for support for Safety Representatives and their disillusionment with their own unions is telling. The fact that a report prepared by the Aberdeen University Offshore Study Group (Spaven *et al.* 1993) identifies training as a key issue, both for Safety Representatives and for those who interact with them - notably OIMs - indicates that there is a clear opportunity for unions to deploy their expertise in that role. But they will need to do so on the basis of the merits of training and communication and not on the basis of any other agenda if they are to have any realistic prospect of overcoming the structural obstacles of the management system.

Only by observing how management observes, by taking into account the avenues closed off by management's construction of unions and the opportunities presented by management's new-found recognition of the need for workforce involvement and training, can progress be made. The management system will still construct information internally. Union utterances will not be transferred direct to the heart of management. But unions can, nevertheless, seek to understand the closure of the management system - by observing how it observes - as a means of understanding the limitations and the opportunities. Shortly after the Safety Case regulations appeared, the UK approach to safety representatives offshore was given apparent support by the International Labour Organisation when it explicitly left the question of mandatory union involvement open and concentrated instead on other issues. For example, the new approach was seen to 'require the operator to describe and justify the safety of his operations to an outside authority' in contrast to the prescriptive approach. And in contrast to worries about the technical nature of QRA, the ILO suggested that it offered 'the advantage that the operator cannot hide behind bland, descriptive generalisations'. Lastly, the new approach could 'be made to require that the extent of workforce involvement be documented and subject to the scrutiny of the inspecting authority' (ILO 1993, 76-77). Thus, even after a relatively short experience of the UK regime, the International Labour Organisation took the view that it had 'generally shown the possibility of constructive workforce involvement' (ILO 1993, 77). Six more years down the line and in many more respects the regime still shows the possibility of constructive workforce involvement. But it remains to be seen whether that possibility becomes a reality in more than a few isolated cases.

7 Role of the Regulator

It is perhaps not surprising that in the context of a regulatory approach as innovative as that applying to the offshore industry, many of the problems confronting the regulator relate to the question of the orientation of the law. While the new regime has been shown to possess theoretical potential in terms of both reflexivity and risk and to provide practical benefits with regard to the encouragement of risk-aware programmes in the different communicative systems, much depends on the understanding of the regulator as to whether the theoretical potential is realised and the practical benefits continue to accrue.

It can be said first of all that the regulator has shown a clear understanding of the centrality of communication - particularly in terms of understanding the concerns of the regulated in attempting to ensure a risk-aware approach to the management of safety. This understanding was undoubtedly aided by the early experience provided by the Voluntary Safety Case exercise. During that period, the HSE came in for some criticism from operators regarding its concentration on issues which the latter did not perceive as critical to safety (Fox 1993, 19; Watson 1993, 69). This may have been due to an inappropriate ranking of risks on the part of the regulator but may equally have indicated a failure to understand the nature of the risk on the part of the operator. The HSE itself reported a certain reluctance on the part of industry to open up lines of communication between operators and the regulator and equally a recurrent failure to include options in the VSCs which meant that the regulator was unable to see that choices had been truly risk based - factors which suggest that the latter explanation is more likely than the former (Powell 1993, 30).

The HSE has sought to address this issue by being sensitive to the industry management rationale in its communications relating to the assessment of Safety Cases. Thus, one means of ensuring clearer communication with the industry is by a demonstration that the systematic attention to risks is not just a matter of health and safety but also one of the control of costs and of quality - which in the offshore industry means continuity of production (Bacon 1993, 9). The regulator is, therefore, attempting to tap into the industry's own rationale to achieve a reconstruction there of the health and safety issue - including occupational health and safety - as a factor which does not inevitably increase cost and result in interventions which jar with production but rather as an issue which is integral to the commercial aims of the industry. Insofar as this addresses the concerns noted above with regard to the CRINE initiative,[62] the approach is encouraging. Similarly, in addition to taking the view that the workforce, as those who are in the front-line if something goes wrong, are entitled to be satisfied with the Safety Case and therefore have a right to involvement, the regulator has also attempted to indicate how the experience of the workforce can be used to improve the quality of risk assessments and thus the implementation of measures arising out of the assessment (Bacon 1993, 9-10). Again, the location and style of intervention is encouraging even if as was seen in the last section there is no room for complacency.

On the question of the interface between operators and contractors, the regulator has sought to ensure a comprehensive approach requiring careful case-by-case consideration from the parties concerned rather than the blanket application of predetermined formulae. The HSE view is that this interface must be achieved at the level of the safety management system and has stressed that at all stages, the key is communication. Thus, in line with the diagram at Figure 5.1 above, the following stages are envisaged:

(i) *Policy*: there should be a statement of how consistency and co-ordination will be achieved among the objectives of different groups: operator and contractors.

(ii) *Organising*: there should be detailed communication channels between contractors and operators.

(iii) *Planning and implementing*: details should be provided of selection criteria for contractors on grounds of health and safety (now understood in terms of its link with cost and quality), of review procedures and of co-operation with regard to the setting of standards.

(iv) *Measuring and Reviewing Performance*: the SMS should detail procedures for monitoring performance including that to be carried out by responsible personnel (including contractors and their staff), and procedures for feedback to contractor management.

(v) *Auditing*: operators should check the adequacy of contractor's own controls by audit which involves contractor representatives. (See Caldwell 1993)

While there has been a perception here that the regulator's approach could become too prescriptive, the latter has sought to resolve problems with operators on the grounds of the need for adequate communication rather than on the grounds of technical details. Thus, the regulator has expressed the view that:

> when two management systems are brought together [t]he characteristics of one might be such that minor perturbations from the pure are of no significance but when passed onto the other create havoc.

> Similarly, stress has been put on the possibility for misunderstandings and distortions to arise at the interface between the activities of contractors and operators or other contractors. Good communication across the interfaces are vital for the achievement of effective safety management. (J. King 1993, 216)

Taken in the round, the regulator's approach fares well on the issue of reflexivity and thus bodes well as regards the question of communication problems as between engineering and management in particular as regards the results of QRA. Given that it was the HSE's evidence to Lord Cullen which persuaded him of the value of the technique, it is not surprising to find that the HSE has perhaps the greatest level of expertise in its application and the fullest grasp of both the opportunities and the limitations which it possesses. In contrast to the evidence seen above of the possibility of management misunderstanding of QRA results, the HSE has sought to discourage this by stressing the opportunities in the new regime for 'creative thinking' (Pape 1993, 117). But the use of risk assessment offshore needs to be set in the broader context of its development in the UK.

Risk assessment has been the subject of increasing interest in government since the mid-1980s. First interest arose with regard to nuclear power stations and was quickly followed by a realisation of its potential application to health and safety issues more generally (HSE 1989; 1992b). Thereafter, concern with environmental problems led to a review of the principles and practices used in government for risk assessment with a view to identifying best practice and encouraging common approaches. This review was carried out by the Interdepartmental Liaison Group on Risk Assessment, an informal committee of officials responsible for policy development and the practical application of risk assessment in all major departments. The first report of this Group allowed a timely insight into the thinking of the regulator on this issue (HSE 1996).

An important feature of this report is its rejection of the previous conceptual separation of risk assessment (the evaluation of risks) from risk control (the prioritisation of risks and risk-reduction measures). It is recognised that the science and policy issues cannot be so easily separated - an aspect of which is the way in which there is often a large divergence in the assessment of a particular risk by experts and its perception by the public at large as was noted earlier (HSE 1996, 3; see also Rowe 1992). As a result, the report indicates that while risk assessment provides a rational structure for decision making on risk, account must also be taken of 'values established by political debate and public willingness to tolerate risks in return for benefits' (HSE 1996, 13). Similarly, there was found to be a wariness on the part of regulators of placing too great a reliance on cost-benefit techniques, despite their frequent usefulness, in cases where social preferences and equity-based criteria suggested caution (HSE 1996, 33). There has been identified, then, a need to improve communication about risk in the question of regulation and to this end the report states that there is agreement among regulators on the objectives of sharing power between government and those being regulated, of improving mutual understanding of attitudes to policy in risk areas and of developing effective alternatives to direct regulatory control (HSE 1996, 33-34). In its second report, the Group has been even clearer about these points and linked them specifically to the achievement of trust among the interested parties (HSE 1998, 20-22).

Given this view of the general HSE approach to risk assessment, there is reason to believe that regulators are aware of the need to concentrate on the issue of misunderstanding between engineering and management as well as on the question of the appropriate involvement of the workforce.[63] There is clearly no question of the results of QRA being constructed as absolute by the regulator and the aim is instead to ensure that management is continually kept aware of the need to view the results as a statement of degree of belief and thus inherently calling for continual review - something which is helped by the Safety Management System's review and audit requirements (HSE 1995, 15-16; 42-3). That this will not be a straightforward process can be seen from the raising by management of the question of what will happen should an operator seek to make production changes which will result in the increasing of risk although still within the ALARP range. The regulator's response has been that an operator would have some room for manoeuvre although it hoped that innovative production techniques would be accompanied by innovations with regard to safety (HSE 1993c, 125). Hard cases will not disappear in the new regime but the mechanisms should be there to deal with them in a way which at the very least ensures that the old blind spots are as far as possible absent.

So far so good, but there are indications that not everything is so positive. Despite a lawyer's assessment that '[t]he prescriptive approach, setting out in detail how safety is to be managed, is shelved' (J. Salter 1994, 4), it is significant that during the interim evaluation of the 1992 Safety Case Regulations the most widely expressed fear by management was of a drift back towards prescription and away from the goal-setting approach on the part of the regulators (HSE 1995, 7; see also Perham 1993, 10-11 & 21; Hughes 1994, 3). The updated review revealed continuing concerns in this regard with management suggesting that the HSE had failed to move beyond the prescriptive approach (AUPEC 1999, 9).

For example, despite the apparent flexibility of the new regime, there have been suggestions that the fact that it emerged from an inquiry into a particular incident led it inevitably to prioritise certain aspects which were relevant to that incident and that type of installation and which may, therefore, have less relevance to others. There are echoes here of the old engineering view of regulation, that it is the result of an inevitable political over-reaction to a unique event. Thus, those concerned with MODUs point out that much of the new approach has little relevance to their installations which spend only very little time in contact with hydrocarbon reserves (Forman 1991; Stiff *et al.* 1992; Visser 1993; HSE 1995, 7). This has implications, however, not only from the point of view of the operators of installations who feel that the regime imposes requirements on them which are burdensome, but also from the point of view that there may equally be blind spots in the new regime with regard to risks associated with other types of installation.

The hope must be in this regard that the very fact of the risk assessment approach will deal with both aspects of this problem - on the one hand allowing operators to make a case for avoiding burdensome and unnecessary requirements and on the other helping to identify the potential problems specific to other types of installation. An indication of the degree to which this is happening can be derived from the 'surprises' revealed to management and to engineering detailed in the foregoing sections and in the recent finding that the new regime is seen by managers to have produced an 'installation-based' approach that is 'structured and rigorous' (AUPEC 1999, 10). Similarly encouraging is the fact that the issue of helicopter safety which was alleged to have been missed by the Cullen Inquiry[64] has emerged as significant from the Safety Case exercise (HSE 1993c, 220) and is now more fully understood in relation to the global offshore risk even if concerns remain about the interface between the offshore and civil aviation regulatory regimes (AUPEC 1999, 8).[65]

But beyond problems which may be inherent to the regime, there are also indications that both the regulator and the regulated are on occasion reverting to the old style of safety regulation. For its part, the HSE has been nothing if not keen to get the point across that it is not the ultimate guarantor of safety offshore (Spaven *et al.* 1993, 78) and has criticised a continuing compliance mentality in some operators (Barrell 1994, 4), but in continuing to issue some prescriptive regulations it is implicitly adopting such a role. For its part, management has complained that the risk assessment approach which forms the basis of the new approach has been undermined by this continuing degree of prescription, for example in relation to the requirement for sub-sea isolation valves. It is claimed that risk assessments indicate that in some instances other alternatives are available (McIntyre & McManus 1991). Of course, it is often a question of cost as opposed to an industry belief that it has a better solution. But for so long as the ALARP principle is based on a consideration of cost there will be difficulties for the regulator when prescribed solutions appear to contradict its own guidance on this issue and the industry has sought to remind the HSE of this point (e.g. Kennedy 1993, 92-3).

Part of the difficulty may arise from the fact that the goal-setting regulations were introduced only after the Safety Case system was in place - a situation which the HSE has itself characterised as far from ideal. Nevertheless, the contention on the part of the regulator has been that the regulations have been designed to complement the Safety Case regime (Leiser 1993a, 79). That said, the delay in introducing the new goal-setting regulations led to an awkward transitional phase during which the old prescriptive regulations were in force alongside the Safety Case system with its risk assessment techniques. The difficulty has, therefore, been that the industry became accustomed to applying risk assessment to the parameters of the old prescriptive regulations and the regulator was prepared to allow different approaches where the risk assessment justified it. Now, however, where there are elements of prescription in the new regime the regulator has not been willing to apply the same standard. Beyond that, there has been concern that the regulator, even where there is no prescription, is not always sufficiently open to new alternatives, resulting in *de facto* prescription (see Redd 1993, 23). The reason for this may lie in the suggestion that regulators are beginning to miss the certainty provided by prescriptive standards and that 'the Cullen regime has made offshore safety regulation more difficult' (AUPEC 1999, 14). This is an area which will require to be watched carefully - particularly in the light of Lord Cullen's findings of the problems of a compliance mentality and also in view of the ambiguity noted in the CRINE report about standardisation.[66] Placing so much emphasis on the responsibility of the operator for the organisation of its own installations and safety management systems while continuing to prescribe certain aspects risks setting up contradictions in the new regime which may yet be problematic.

There is a danger that the problems with such an approach could lead to a return to a style of regulation which is at odds with the nature and complexity of the task in hand. Just as such a shift has been called for offshore by Woolfson, Foster and Beck (1996), so the onshore health and safety regime is seen by some as inadequate in its assumptions about the nature of organisational decision-making and consequently in need of more rigorous enforcement and higher penalties (James 1992, 99-101). It has been the finding of this study that the nature of organisational decision-making must indeed not be assumed but rather studied closely to see what the codes and programmes are. If the offshore can for once teach the onshore a lesson it is that applying stricter enforcement and higher penalties is to risk entirely missing the nature of the regulatory problem and indeed masking the build up of significant risks. If higher penalties and stricter enforcement are directed at ensuring that management takes its responsibilities seriously then it is a different matter, but in the absence of an understanding of management concerns such an approach may be highly dangerous.[67]

That this issue may not be solely in the control of the HSE is evident from the tension that has existed between that organisation and the European Commission. It has been said that in the area of safety at work, the lack of a political mandate at a European level 'has lost its explosive quality as the SEA [Single European Act] explicitly established genuine competences for the Community' (Joerges 1993, 323). Nevertheless, other areas of tension between the European and the national level continue to exist which coincide closely with the concerns of this study - namely as regards the orientation of law and regulation. The first ILGRA report on risk assessment (HSE 1996), for example, contains some interesting findings as regards the impact of European regulation. In a number of responses from government departments, it was alleged that movement towards what was described as more rational regulation was impeded by European standard-setting which was in many cases not the result of thorough analysis or assessment. Conversely, in other cases (notably departments affected by the Framework Directive on health and safety at work[68]) there was a more positive attitude to the impact of European regulation. In general the report concluded on this issue that

> [t]he trend for goal-setting as opposed to prescriptive regulation is now firmly established in the UK and slowly gaining ground in directives emanating from the European Union dealing with healthier places of work, safe commercial products and a cleaner environment. (HSE 1996, 38)[69]

And there are other examples of this convergence of approach. The so-called 'new approach' to standard-setting in the internal market produces directives which eschew detailed technical specification, state only essential requirements and leave details to bodies capable of carrying out specific risk analysis. Moreover, those to whom the standards are addressed may either operate in accordance with them or demonstrate by other means that they have complied with the requirements of the directive in question (Baldwin & Cave 1999, 161). The success of this approach will apparently lead to its extension to other areas (see Schepel 1995). The example of health and safety, however, points to the problems. Commentators have pointed to the apparent difference in the standard of the duty imposed on employers on the one hand by the Framework Directive and on the other by the HSWA 1974 (e.g. Baldwin & Cave 1999, 169). Serious as this is, another problem is of more direct concern in the current context. While the Framework Directive is in line with the UK approach in calling for risk assessment and management systems, specific directives issued within that framework impose prescriptive requirements which jar with the more reflexive rationality. With regard to the offshore industry itself, the result of this tension is evident in the 1995 Management and Administration Regulations which give effect to the requirements of the European Directive relating to health and safety in the extractive industries.[70] In the main body of the regulations can be found the goal-setting approach envisaged by Cullen while in the annex to the regulations is a long list of prescriptions as required by the European Directive. The need to address this kind of problem has, however, been recognised within the European Commission. Riccardo Perissich, for example, as Director-General for Industry, conceded that 'risk management and risk assessment are still relatively new concepts in the bureaucratic and legal jargon used in regulatory work in Brussels and the Member States' capitals' (1994, 95) and he went on to call for 'an impact assessment culture...to end the conflict patterns in the dialogue between Community and National authorities' (1994, 110).[71] That his call has not yet been fully heeded is evident from the second ILGRA report which states that 'the absence of information on the cost or benefits of European Directives [is] an impediment to the evaluation of outcomes' (1998, 15). The HSC/E has in its negotiations with the Commission tried to persuade the latter away from the routine use of detailed provisions and to encourage the use of risk assessment techniques to limit rule-making to those areas where the risk justifies it (see Baldwin 1992, 218). It has not always been successful, however. In the field of air pollution, for example, there was initially tension between the uniform emission standards required by directives and the setting of objectives in terms of the putative receiving capacity of the environment favoured by the UK (Weale 1996, 116). Although the UK approach has been described as possessing 'the advantage of being more sensitive to the different environmental circumstances of the member states' (Majone 1996, 267), the European approach eventually prevailed in the Environmental Protection Act 1990. That said, not everyone in the UK regards the prescriptive EU approach as problematic, seeing the UK approach as old-style deregulation (e.g. Szyszczak 1992, 13-15). Part of the difficulty in making progress with this debate lies in providing a conceptualisation which allows such developments to be discussed in terms other than deregulation or prescription.

If there has not so far been any strong conflict between the UK and the European approaches to offshore health and safety regulation - the rather awkward looking Management and Administration regulations notwithstanding - the potential for such conflict in the future clearly exists. One way in which this issue may come to a head arises from the fact that under European law, harmonised standards may not be altered by national law so as to impose a higher standard (see J. Salter 1994, 6). It will be a question how the issue of a higher or lower standard will be resolved in the event of a perceived conflict between UK and EU law offshore when the conflict may lie between different legal orientations - prescriptive and goal-setting - where both may determine the standard by inherently different procedures. Hope that such problems can ultimately be avoided will lie in an acceptance by the European Commission that the completion of the Single Market of necessity requires it to consider seriously the regulation of risk (Dehousse *et al.* 1992).

With these tensions in mind, it is perhaps not surprising to find that other difficulties have emerged in relation to the exact role of the regulator in the new regime. There can be a perception that the regulator's role of auditing is simply too 'hands off' and that it does indeed signal a move to a deregulation of offshore health and safety. The HSE has stated, for example, that the Safety Case regime is first and foremost a question of the operator demonstrating to *itself* that its systems are safe while only secondarily being a question of a demonstration of this to the regulator (Bacon 1993, 9). Of course, it is all very well for the new safety management system to be in place. The real challenge will be in ensuring that it is applied in such a way that it has meaning at all levels of the organisation (Redd 1993, 24). It would be all too easy for such a system to become a self-contained and bureaucratised entity in an organisation, ostensibly carrying out auditing and reviewing functions and producing an auditable output but without actually having a real contact with the workforce and the management of operational safety. If there is a lesson from this study it is that the routinisation of communications, whether at the level of the engineering discourse or that of the permit to work system on an installation, is the setting for potentially and actually catastrophic blind spots. A worrying indication in this respect appears in the industry complaints that the well operations notification procedure contained in the Design and Construction regulations has not improved safety and is little more than a paperwork exercise (AUPEC 1999, 3), a complaint possibly borne out by the leaked internal report into the incident on Cormorant Alpha when gas flowed through an improperly secured flange in April 1999. On that occasion, the platform had been shut down to enable a well from another platform to be tied into the Cormorant and to allow maintenance to be carried out simultaneously. The leaked company report suggested that '[t]here was a general failure to recognise when a series of smaller jobs had become a larger job requiring a more rigorous planning approach'.[72] There must, therefore, be concern when the HSE takes the view that in future offshore visits by regulators may not be necessary since it is the Safety Case that is being assessed and not the installation (Powell 1993, 29). There would seem to be a need, however, for greater emphasis on the auditing and assessment of *systems*, rather than of the *document* and that is something which it would seem cannot be done in isolation from the installation. One of Lord Cullen's main criticisms of the PED was that its inspection regime was not adequate to test the safety on installations. If the HSE limits itself to the verification of bureaucratic procedures it risks finding itself in the same position.

That, however, is not a criticism of the audit function in itself but rather a warning that that function must be properly directed if it is to ensure that mechanisms are in place which achieve a structural coupling not only of communicative systems to each other but also to the technology which is at the heart of the industry. An understanding after the Cullen Inquiry that management systems were as important as technical integrity, if not more, must not result in such a shift in that direction that the regulation becomes abstract and the management systems become uncoupled from the technical.

And beyond the level of the individual installation, there are indications that the HSE's undoubtedly greater vision of the range of issues impacting on health and safety may be beginning to narrow. The audit approach has the potential to be much more revealing than the former inspection approach in that it takes the regulator right into the structures of the company and to issues beyond health and safety as it was narrowly defined in the foregoing prescriptive regime under the PED. This has definite implications in the context of this study where it has been seen that issues well beyond the technical and even operational aspects which have traditionally been the focus of health and safety regulation can have the greatest impact. In this regard it is significant to find in the HSE a clear recognition that commercial and health and safety activities cannot be separated and to this end the regulator has conducted 'top-to-toe' audits of companies (see Sefton 1993; J. King 1993). Equally, they have sought to discover whether company structures can really deliver the stated aims. However, it has been suggested that in future such audits will not be much above platform level (J. King 1993, 193). A step away from the link between the installation and the bureaucratic systems is troubling enough but a step away from the link between the installation and the wider corporate structure risks being considerably worse.

The findings especially of Chapter 4 were that, despite an unwillingness on the part of Lord Cullen to draw concrete causal links between the 1986 price collapse and the Piper Alpha disaster, the blind spots that were reinstated by the new drive, little short of panic, for cost-reductions masked precisely those aspects of risk which came together in that event. Looking only at narrow areas of an organisation's approach to risk may well result in future in a similar false sense of security. Is it significant, for example, that the gas leak and evacuation events in 1999 described at the beginning of this book occurred in the aftermath of yet another dramatic fall in prices? Did the industry yet again enter panic mode and slash costs in areas where short-term reductions in economic risk masked longer term increases in technical and occupational risk? The paradoxical thing is that in the face of these apparent steps away from a more global approach to risk, the HSE seems aware of this issue with a remarkable clarity:

> Health and Safety Management cannot be divorced from the management of business as a whole. Put simply, it is not possible to consider commercial issues without at the same time taking on board the linked health and safety issues. This does not necessarily mean that commercial risks will demand the same safeguards as health and safety risks but that most problems give rise to both and that the solutions should not be considered in isolation. (J. King 1993, 212)

In the following section, after considering the development of management programmes for the minimisation of those broader commercial risks, a potential area of concern will be discussed which may demonstrate a need for a more holistic approach to the auditing of an organisation's risk management programmes.

8 Costs and Prices

8.1 Introduction

In Chapter 4, it was noted that instruments for hedging price risk became progressively available during the 1980s especially in the form of oil futures contracts. Given the extent to which industry thinking and practice revolved around concerns about the future value of money, the ability to absorb some of this risk clearly had great significance for health and safety in terms of reducing the need to rely solely on programmes of intensified operations or cost-reduction. So far in this chapter, it has been seen how far the communicative systems of industry management and engineering manifest a transformation from deterministic programmes to more reflexive programmes of risk-minimisation - a transformation supported and encouraged by the new orientation in regulation. However, since the issue of price risk has had such an important role in the past, it remains to be seen to what extent the potential offered by new price-hedging instruments has been realised over the same period. In addition, the other interventions and cost issues which appeared so prominently on the cognitive maps of management in particular must be examined to see how the originators of those interventions view the new situation and how they in turn are constructed by the industry.

8.2 Taxation

One of the most obvious problems during the 1970s and early 1980s especially was the continuing uncertainty created by political interventions with regard to taxation, participation and depletion policy. The last two have now disappeared from view but taxation, naturally, remains an issue whichever government is in power. In this regard, it can be said in general that the degree of understanding demonstrated by the Conservative government from the early 1980s continued until its demise in 1997 and the industry was largely content with the approach to taxation in the context of lower oil prices after 1986 and a maturing province. Combined with new technologies, a favourable tax regime has meant that lower prices were not seen as a particular problem. A high level of exploration and appraisal drilling in 1988 and 125 applications for licences in the 11th round indicated that confidence was still high (Quinlan 1989, 175) - albeit that initially this was largely sustained by the extraordinary degree of cost-cutting that has been described previously. In this regard, the ability of the Treasury to observe the industry's concerns must be contrasted with the inability of the PED to observe what was happening. This again underlines the need for the HSE to maintain its openness to such issues. Despite such a responsive tax regime, however, there was continuing pressure on the previous government to maintain this stance.[73]

In 1990, the government moved to ease another pressure which had been building up in calculations of field economics, namely the question of abandonment costs. It announced that 100% of such costs would be allowed against Corporation Tax carried back 3 years.[74] While the industry complained that this period was insufficient to cover the costs of the larger platforms, it was none the less encouraged by the government's responsiveness[75] and the general feeling of confidence was again reflected in strong interest in the frontier territory offered in the 12th licensing round (Quinlan 1990, 178). There was more good news in the following budget with CT rate reductions seen as favouring small fields paying only that tax and a widening of the definition of allowable abandonment costs favouring all.[76] And again, industry confidence was evident in the continuing high levels of exploration and appraisal drilling.[77]

Despite a sharp rise in the price of oil at the time of the invasion of Kuwait, this fell back relatively quickly and by 1992 the tax take from the North Sea was significantly down. So much so, in fact, that PRT was by now operating negatively and in FY 1991/92 cost the Exchequer some £200 million. In 1993, therefore, the tax was abolished for new fields and the rate reduced for existing taxable fields from 75% to 50%. Tax relief for exploration and appraisal drilling was removed at this time.[78] The effect of these changes was to impose a penalty on drilling and make further development of existing fields more attractive. Companies able to switch expenditures were unconcerned but those who had made drilling commitments under the 11th and 12th licensing rounds on the assumption that tax relief would be available found themselves in some difficulty (Quinlan 1993b, 18). It was clear, therefore, that even during periods when the political understanding of the industry was seen as good, there could be nasty surprises and the dynamic tool could become the blunt instrument once again. That said, the political reasons for change were regarded beyond the drilling community as sound (Harvie 1995, 344-5) and indicate that management needs just as much to be responsive to politics as to expect things to be handed to it on a platter.

For a period thereafter, however, the Conservative government appeared to keep the industry happy with tax provisions in 1994 aimed at helping companies involved in a pipeline project,[79] and those in 1995 aimed at restricting unrelievable field losses.[80] Similarly, the licensing rounds were responsive to market conditions with the 14th and 16th including frontier areas and the 15th concentrating on natural gas in accordance with an expanding UK market and the generally lower oil price. The 16th also allowed companies to nominate blocks for inclusion in the round.[81] Furthermore, before stepping down as Energy minister, Tim Eggar announced the possible replacement of the discretionary licence system with a competitive bidding system for the round to close in the autumn of 1997 followed by annual licensing thereafter - a move which was well-received by the industry.[82] Indeed, it is a measure of the success of the Conservative government in observing the industry's construction of taxation that, by the end of its term in office, the UK was rated by the international industry as the the most attractive country for the coming year[83] and as possessing the most attractive fiscal regime of the frontier deep-water territories (Kellas & Parish 1997). But as the country as a whole began to consider the possibility of a change of government with relative enthusiasm, the industry watched political developments with greater unease given its previous experiences of Labour administrations. There were, however, early indications that their fears were misplaced. The then Labour Shadow Minister for Energy, John Battle MP, delivering the 1997 Conoco Lecture, stressed the importance of a stable tax regime for the promotion of long-term offshore investment, indicating it seemed a clear observation of industry concerns (Battle 1997). But a few short months later, it looked as if industry fears had been entirely justified. At the very rapidly organised July budget, while the Chancellor offered industry in general some very positive signs in the further reduction of the CT rate,[84] his announcement of a review of offshore taxation looked distinctly negative. No doubt seeking to remind the Energy Minister of his pre-election promises, UKOOA responded by calling for a stable tax regime[85] while the industry looked forward to a long period of uncertainty as it waited for the March 1998 budget.

The prospects began to look bleak as it became apparent that the government was concerned about the unexpectedly high oil price in 1997 and there was talk of a windfall tax similar to that which the government had already imposed on the privatised utilities. In particular, the government was considering a range of options, including the introduction of PRT for post-1993 development consent fields or the introduction of a new oil-specific tax within the existing structure of CT.[86] Once again the industry repeated the position seen in the earliest management cognitive map - high prices over a relatively short period of time had to be set in the context of long-term projects with high front-end loading of costs, frequent negative cash flows in the early years with long lead times to first oil, and the time value of money had to be factored in (Adams 1998). The industry's immediate reaction to the announcement in the March 1998 budget that a decision on any changes would be delayed to allow further consultation was therefore one of relief. But this relief was short-lived as it came to terms with a further extended period of uncertainty. The view was expressed that planning was impossible in the absence of firm information about the future tax regime and UKOOA called for the 18th licensing round to be delayed until there was greater certainty - a call immediately rejected by John Battle.[87]

Events on the global oil market had, however, overtaken the debate between government and industry in the UK as the price fell to levels not seen since 1986. The idea of imposing a windfall tax now appeared absurd and in the late summer of 1998, just before the deadline for 18th round applications, the government announced that there would be no changes to the offshore tax regime.[88] The industry breathed a sigh of relief - albeit a shallow one in the context of the depressed price - but it seemed that a great deal would need to be done to restore the degree of mutual observation of steering programmes that had characterised the situation under the previous government. It is not surprising therefore that, as will be seen in due course, the government has since taken unprecedented steps to establish what might be characterised as a binding institution to improve the 'duration, intensity and quality of structural coupling' (Teubner 1992a, 1458).

8.3 Finance

In the context of government interventions under the Conservatives which sought and largely attained a measure of certainty in the industry, it is paradoxical that one action which was also intended to produce certainty had exactly the reverse effect and undid some of the good work done by other policies. This action related to certain assurances given by the

Secretary of State for Energy to banks financing North Sea operations regarding the revocation or transfer of the licence. The possibility of revocation greatly concerned banks as did the fact that the Secretary of State's consent was required for any transfer of the licence. Such an unknown quantity, well beyond their control, appeared to them to add a substantial risk to what were already regarded as risky loans and the assurances served to allay these fears. During the second Conservative government of the 1980s, however, the previous practice of giving these assurances was stopped on the basis that banks could by now rely on the fact that the government's record in the North Sea was good. The move was explicitly aimed at building confidence but had the opposite effect since the banks remembered 'the manner in which Tony Benn introduced state participation rights' (Vinter 1992, 33). Thus, even at this late stage, banks continued to feel the need 'to control the means of production and not just the production itself' (1992, 34). There was, then, a danger of a return to the situation seen in Chapter 3 of those financing the industry having a very direct say in operational matters - something which it might be difficult to reconcile with the new approach to safety which, for all its openness, does not consider the possibility of direct operational involvement beyond the operator and contractors. The possibility of the HSE stepping back from a position where such issues could come into view again looks problematic. It is to be hoped that the Labour government's CT roll-over relief amendment to the Finance Bill in July 1999 aimed at removing inhibitions to licence transfers will also remove any lingering uncertainty.

Significantly, however, by the early 1990s, banks were also beginning to consider the possibility of taking hedging instruments as security (Vinter 1992, 37) and this possibility was very quickly taken up.[89] The ability of banks to seek the lock-in of prices over a long period greatly reduced the risk that they were taking on in granting loans for development and production.[90] Simultaneously, the risk faced by the producers themselves was reduced both as regards price and as regards their operations, on which there was now a greatly reduced pressure in the context of locked-in prices and less worried lenders.[91] A related benefit for producers was that the reduced risk perceived by banks led to their offering more money. With prices locked-in, banks were prepared to offer up to 90% of proven and deliverable reserves instead of the 70% which had been the previous upper limit.[92] In the context of the use of more accurate 3-dimensional seismic exploration and probabilistic reservoir analysis techniques (which helped to raise estimates as opposed to the previous deterministic techniques while simultaneously reducing costs) this increase in funding was even greater than the percentage figures themselves indicate (see Quinlan 1992, 15; 1993a, 4; 1994, 3).[93]

Thus, banks which had previously contributed to the pressure on oil field developments now used their position to demand risk-reduction strategies. Significantly, their interventions were not now related to technical issues but to economic ones. It is ironic that the only potential problem appearing on the cognitive map of financing at this time was a political move aimed at reducing uncertainty.

It is worth noting here also that the ability of banks to demand that operators enter into to certain risk-reduction strategies has been one way in which the reluctance of the industry to become involved in non-traditional methods has been overcome. The banks as providers of risk-management instruments and as the organisations which have the most experience of their use are in a unique position to provide both the stimulus towards such instruments and the advice on their appropriate use. Whether they always do so is another matter and one that will not be visible if the regulators do not act on their own understanding of the relationship between commercial and health and safety risks and between the different solutions implemented to deal with them.

8.4 Insurance

In much the same way that banks are in a position to encourage risk minimisation programmes in financial matters which rely on economic instruments and not intensified operations or cost-reduction, so insurance companies are in a position to encourage appropriate programmes as regards technical and operational matters. Just as industry management and engineering arrived in the North Sea scaling itself up deterministically on the basis of experience in the Gulf of Mexico, so did the insurance industry. There have been frank admissions, therefore, in the aftermath of the Piper Alpha disaster that the insurance industry did not go into the North Sea with its eyes open, has tended to learn by experience and has not followed a consistent or rational policy with regard to the insurance of offshore structures and operations (Compton-Rickett 1994). A view that 'if it isn't broken, don't fix it' has been modified by the Piper Alpha experience to 'if it isn't broken yet, it nevertheless might be soon' and there has been a greater use of surveyors to assess the safety arrangements of the insured (C. Lee 1995).

Not least for the insurance industry was the realisation that Piper Alpha as a middle ranking platform could result in such a massive claim arising out of consequential losses associated with its satellite developments. While the huge individual values in the North Sea had been well understood by the insurance market, it seems that field interdependencies were not - perhaps yet further evidence that the unprecedented scale of North Sea installations tended to render them the focus of attention to the detriment of other issues. This sudden realisation together with the collapse in 1992 of the London Market Master Energy Lineslip (which had been set up in the 1960s to provide guaranteed support for North Sea development) led to a reduction in the capacity of the market and to premium increases (Gibson 1992).

Another important aspect of Piper Alpha was that the economy's ability to absorb the consequences of failure was pushed to the limit. Simply being able to pay for the occasional catastrophic failure is no longer a possibility. The very fact that this failure could not easily be absorbed but instead had massive knock-on effects throughout the insurance market meant that those with an interest in accepting the risk of failure on payment of a premium became much more concerned about how that risk was being actively managed. Whereas previously insurers might have considered a catastrophic failure as something which might occur, say, every ten years and the loss be restricted to the replacement of the platform, they now became aware of the multiple connectivity of the risk they had underwritten and the difficulty in foreseeing just how far-reaching the effects of high technology failure can be.

The impact on the insurance market was all the greater because of the phenomenon of different levels of reinsurance. Thus, the already sizeable bottom line of approximately $1.5 billion resulted in a knock-on cash-flow cost estimated in 1993 at $7 billion but eventually reaching a figure of $15 billion arising out of some 47,000 reinsurance transactions (C. Lee 1995) which was felt widely in the market. A further complication was that some of the reinsurance ended up, after three or four steps, back in the original market which resulted in the original capacity of the cover being significantly reduced (Redmond 1990). Followed by other large claims from the United States resulting in a total claim well in excess of collected premiums, the attitude of the insurance market to the oil industry has changed beyond recognition and in addition to increased premiums, the market is interested in how a company operates in a way that it never was before. Thus, in addition to the regulatory system and the industry's own awakening to the risks it previously could not observe, another external party with a degree of influence because of its ability to impose costs on the industry is helping to ensure in a very direct way by means of its own quality assurance audits that awareness of risks remains high.

In the aftermath of the Piper Alpha disaster, while the insurance industry has admitted that it is still more concerned about loss of structure as opposed to loss of life - simply on the basis of the size of the likely claims - it now has a much greater awareness of the ways in which human factors can result in loss of structure as opposed to the more obvious causes of blow-out, fatigue failure and severe weather (Compton-Rickett 1994). Realising that structures are basically sound and reassured that engineering seems to have come to terms with the difficulties presented by the North Sea, insurers are now more concerned about how what has been built is actually being operated. The possible costs of paying out on business interruption insurance in such a highly interdependent province has led the newly-enlightened insurance market to suggest not infrequently that premiums may not yet accurately reflect the risk they have taken on (Gibson 1993). The market has, for example, so far resisted industry calls for premium reductions to reflect the improvements brought about in communication between operators and contractors by alliance and partnership arrangements (Sharp 1998). Insurers thus possess the means both of putting pressure on operators and contractors to maintain safety management systems and of facilitating scrutiny of such systems by insurance surveyors.

Once again, a note of caution must be sounded, however, in as much as both insurers and surveyors have indicated that the risk assessment data produced by the latter are not necessarily well understood by the former and so yet again the possibility for constructive misunderstanding arises. Equally, the upheavals in the insurance market eventually led BP to withdraw completely and to self-insure (Gibson 1993). There is, therefore, a limit to the extent to which higher premiums and greater insurance scrutiny of procedures can influence company behaviour. A safety auditor has recently questioned the complacent attitude of the offshore industry: '[c]ontrary to popular belief the safety and risk control standards in the industry are unacceptable, and the industry is paying the price with major increases in insurance coverage' (Pomfret 1998, 249).

8.5 Price Risk

It is possible to see, then, that in the aftermath of Piper Alpha, not only have industry management and engineering become much more risk-aware and not only does the new regime encourage a closer structural coupling of these communicative systems, but also the other communicative systems which have in the past been seen to have a profound influence on operations and thus on health and safety in the offshore industry are also more closely structurally coupled than ever before - significantly in terms of encouraging risk management strategies relating to both economic and technical/operational aspects of the industry. However, just as this closer coupling presents opportunities to the regulator in terms of providing support for its interest in managing risk, ensuring that safety management systems are effectively operated and maintaining communications on the basis of the awareness of risk, so does it raise the possibility of problems. Too much pressure from insurers can be seen to force operators towards self-insurance, thus removing a valuable extra check on safety management. Similarly, there is always the danger that too close a coupling can result in a routinisation of communication which can lead to complacency.

Of potentially even greater importance, however, given the extent to which the cost-cutting panic after 1986 was triggered by unhedged price risk, is the extent to which management has learned from this experience as much as it has from Piper Alpha. While the response in terms of the new safety regime and of the CRINE initiative can be seen as aspects of this learning, the question of the direct management of price risk remains. To what extent have the rapid production and cost-reduction programmes been replaced or at least ameliorated by a programme pitched more at the economic level and away from the technological level - namely the use of financial instruments? This will be considered in the following section.

In considering the development of more advanced price risk management programmes, however, it will be seen that novel questions are raised with regard to the role of the regulator. If such programmes can operate to lessen the pressures on technology and operations and thus on occupational safety, is the regulator in a position to encourage their adoption? If as was suggested earlier, there is evidence that the regulator is withdrawing from a position where it can observe the installation in the broader context of the corporate organisation then is it fatally restricting its ability to observe the operation - or indeed the absence of operation - of steering programmes which aim to reduce ecomomic (specifically price) risks in ways which lessen the blind spots imposed on other dimensions of risk? Is the regulator in any event suitably equipped to deal with such difference minimising programmes? This last question is of particular importance when it is understood that any move by operators towards the use of risk-hedging financial instruments is not in itself risk free but needs to be properly managed if further blind spots are not to be created which may ultimately have an effect on operations and on health and safety.

8.6 Price Risk Management

In the preceding chapters, reference has been made to the increasing use of futures and other derivative financial instruments for price hedging as evidence that the economic risk-minimisation approach of industry management has shifted away from its deterministic programme of rapid production to a much more sophisticated programme which acknowledges the masking effects of the previous programme. It remains to be shown, however, just how these instruments can be used in this way and the extent to which their use does signal a shift in the rationality of industry management. The whole subject of derivatives markets is immensely complicated and the detail is well beyond the scope of this book. What follows, therefore, is aimed at allowing an understanding of why these markets are important to the way the offshore industry conducts its business which in turn has very direct implications, as we have seen, for how much risk the workforce is exposed to.

(a) Futures contracts The basic concern of the offshore producer is that the price of oil will fall and that it will prove impossible to sell future production at a price which guarantees a continuing profit. The producer, therefore, needs to take some form of action by which the losses incurred by such a future fall will be offset by some compensating transaction. In such a situation, the producer could sell an amount of futures contracts equivalent to the production it is concerned about. To take a greatly simplified example, we can assume that a producer is concerned about 100,000 barrels of oil which represents its monthly production and which it needs to sell at the currently available $20 per barrel in order to ensure a profit. Its income from the sale of a month's production at this price is $2 million. The producer is worried that in a few months time the price it will be able to command will have fallen from $20. It, therefore, sells an equivalent amount of futures contracts for the month in question for the market price of, say, $19 and thus receives $1.9 million. When the month in question comes around, the price available for the physical oil has indeed fallen and the producer is only able to achieve $17 per barrel. Accepting this price, it has received some $300,000 less than it needed to stay within budget. However, by this time, the futures price has also fallen

to say $16. Not wishing to actually deliver oil on the basis of the futures contracts it sold, the producer must 'square out' its position and buy equivalent dated futures at this price. Of course, it is able to do so at a price less than it sold them for and thus makes a profit on this futures transaction of $300,000. Thus, the profit from the futures position cancels out the loss from the physicals position and the budgeted profit margin is maintained. The utility of futures contracts in dealing with price risk is abundantly clear from this - albeit simplified - example.

We can consider also what would have happened if the producer's concerns about a falling price proved unfounded. Assume that instead of falling, the price of physical oil rose from $20 to $23 over the same period. When the producer came to square-out its futures position it would then have to buy them at an increased price of, say, $22 meaning that it made a loss of $300,000 on the futures transaction. But this is not necessarily a bad thing. It will, of course, also have made a profit of $300,000 on the sale of physical oil over and above what it had budgeted for. The two transactions therefore cancel each other out and the budgeted profit margin is maintained. This simplified example, therefore, demonstrates also that the 'cost' of 'removing' price risk by means of futures contracts is the loss of the opportunity to take advantage of a favourable price movement over the period in question. In general, however, the offshore producer is more concerned to protect a certain level of profit margin than to enter into speculative guesses about the likely movement of future oil prices.

These are the very basic features of the futures contract and allow one to see how they can be used to hedge price risk. A futures contract is, then, an agreement to buy or sell a standard quantity of oil at a price fixed at the time the contract is made for delivery at a future specified time. For the reasons seen in the above example, only a tiny fraction of these contracts actually ever proceed to delivery - that after all is not their purpose. These contracts are traded on an exchange (principally NYMEX and IPE) according to the rules and procedures of that exchange so that performance of both parties is guaranteed by the exchange. Thus, legally, once the initial deal is done, the exchange becomes the counterparty to what is then effectively two deals. Parties are required to post an initial payment or margin with the exchange and these are followed by further daily payments in both directions according to the difference between the contract price and the market price. There are, then, also considerations of bureaucratic complexity in the use of futures to hedge price risk, but the bottom line is that '[h]edging allows a firm the freedom to pursue its line of business without having to worry about forecasting prices in the future' (Errera & Brown 1999, 86).[94]

(b) Options While the above example demonstrates that futures are very useful for hedging price risk, not all producers are willing to forego so completely the opportunity to take advantage of favourable price movements. In such cases, other derivative instruments are available. In the event that a producer does not wish to give up the possibility to participate in a buoyant market as required by a futures transaction but nevertheless wants to provide insurance for a price level below which it regards its operations as at risk, it can buy a put option. Options are traded on the same exchanges as futures contracts since they are effectively agreements to buy or sell the right to buy or sell futures contracts by a specified date on payment of the specified premium (Sas 1992, 52). Here the producer effectively sets a floor on the price which it will receive for its oil. In this case, the option writer agrees to pay to the producer the difference between the spot price and the strike price (the price level about which the producer is concerned) when the spot price falls below the strike price. Provided that the price does not fall, the producer does not have to worry about the option and can participate in any favourable movements in the market. In the event of the price falling to its nominated crisis level, the producer will receive compensating payments to maintain the price at that level. Of course, for such a service, an up-front premium must be paid. Equally, no option-writer would enter into a contract for an extended period of time since his risk is potentially unlimited and thus such put options tend to be available in the three to six month range (Mansfield 1990, 16).

A variation on the floor is the collar where the producer buys a floor and sells a cap. A cap is the opposite of a floor and is normally used by consumers of a commodity to set a limit on the price they pay. In this case the producer not only sets a lower limit on the price it will receive in the event of a falling market but also an upper limit on the price it will receive in a rising market. In this way, it is protected from a price fall, can participate in a rising market up to a certain point and gains the advantage of a reduced premium as a result of the cap since the option provider will take the benefit of a rise above that level (Robinson 1991b, 22-3).[95]

(c) Swaps The downside of futures and options contracts is the fact that they are relatively complex and labour intensive. Equally, they are relatively limited in the period of price-hedging they can offer. Long-term futures and options contracts are simply not available. Producers

especially, however, are interested in long-term certainty. While long-term sales contracts were a feature of the industry historically, progressive deintegration and the developing spot market meant that they became less of an alternative. Indeed with the development of the spot market, long-term sales contracts were often related to the spot price in any case (Sas 1992, 51). The same degree of certainty, however, is offered by oil swaps. These are contracts negotiated between parties off-exchange relating to the price of a specified amount of oil over a specified period extending to several years. They involve the parties periodically (say quarterly) exchanging payments based on the fixed and variable or floating prices of the fixed quantity of oil for the agreed period of time. The variable or floating price is determined according to an agreed index such as Brent. The swaps market in particular has grown considerably during the 1990s and has developed to include swaptions or the option to enter into an agreed swap at a future date and agreed price. The best way to understand a swap is once again to take an example.

We can assume that a production company aims to fix the price at which it sells crude oil for a period of three years. It produces one million barrels every six months which it sells on the spot market. Field projections indicate that a barrel price of at least $20 would provide a suitable margin. It is impossible to be certain that the spot market will provide such a price over the period of three years in which the company is interested. It, therefore, enters into an oil swap which consists in effect of two parallel contracts: under the first contract, the producer sells one million barrels at $20; under the second, it buys one million at the spot price on the day of delivery. This arrangement by itself is speculative in that if the spot price is above $20 the company profits whereas if the spot price is lower, the company loses money. However, since the producer also has 1 million barrels of production which it sells on the spot market at the same time, the effect of the additional arrangement, the oil swap, is to lock-in the price at $20. If the spot price is higher, its loss on the swap is offset by its gain on the sale of production. Crucially, however, if the spot price is lower, then the reduced amount from the sale of production is offset by the gain from the swap. While the possibility to take extra profits from a buoyant spot market is lost, the risk of losses on a depressed market is extinguished (see Walmsley 1990).

Swaps are provided by banks and other financial institutions and have progressively extended in the periods over which they allow the price to be locked in. Periods up to 10 or even 20 years are possible (Clubley 1998, 93), although in all cases it is a question of the view the parties to the transaction take of the credit risk of the counterparty. Their advantages include the fact that they involve no up-front premium for the insurance effectively bought and have no effect on existing sales, purchase and delivery procedures. The fact that swaps have been the fastest growing hedging instrument (Williams 1990a, 37) indicates the extent to which a desire for certainty of profit dominates the desire for profit *per se* in the oil industry and the extent to which long-term price risk management is now a concern of the industry (Sas 1992, 59). Many producers saw the price hike after the invasion of Kuwait as a good opportunity to buy swaps to lock in the price while it was high (Robinson 1991b, 21). Prices could have gone still higher than they did - there were those who predicted severe shortages associated with the supply interruptions which occurred at that time. But producers seem to have been content to lock in prices higher than anything they could have anticipated a few months earlier and even forego the profits associated with a further rise in exchange for the security offered by swaps at that level.

A variation on the standard swap has, however, developed in response to the producer's interest in participating to some extent in a rising market - the commodity participating swap. A 50% participating swap, for example, possesses the advantage of the standard swap in locking-in a minimum price but also allows the producer to take half the difference between the fixed price and the spot price when the market is rising (Robinson 1991b, 23).

(d) Industry acceptance As was noted earlier, the industry was slow to get involved in these markets but it has been suggested that a 'critical threshold' (see Sas 1992, 54) has been crossed and that the industry now regards even sophisticated and complex tools as an indispensable part of its risk-management strategy.

The contrast which this approach to the management of price risk makes with the headlong rush which characterised the 1970s and the panic cost-reduction after the 1986 price fall is stark and the implications for health and safety at the cutting edge of the offshore production industry are clear. If management no longer has to worry about either intensifying operations or seeking cost reductions in operations as programmes for minimising economic risk but can actually lock-in guaranteed prices related to the margins required to continue operations then the entire outlook of the industry is different. When the funding possibilities of such instruments are added into the equation, the contrast with the situation in the 1970s is even more marked (Bossley 1999). In addition, apart from the possibility of hedging risk, the markets provide different parties in the industry with an opportunity to express their views about the price of oil into the future thus contributing to, if not price stability, then at least some price certainty (Williams 1990a; 1990b; Robinson 1991a; 1991b).

One of the most interesting features of the entire phenomenon of risk-management instruments in the oil industry as was mentioned earlier is the extent to which it has emerged and developed without any political or regulatory intervention. The only presence of law is at the level of contract law and the regulations of the exchanges on which the instruments are traded - all operating within the broad framework of the national financial regulation of the jurisdiction of the exchange or financial institution. Thus, the providers of instruments are able to develop instruments which they think will suit the market and in the event that these fail they can be swiftly withdrawn and replaced by instruments which seem closer to market needs. For example, the growing demand for OTC instruments from producers led to an increasing need from the providers of these instruments for longer futures contracts with which to hedge their own risk (Fusaro 1995, 16; see also Sas 1992, 53; Clubley 1998, 93). In this way, the complex of energy instruments on the New York Mercantile Exchange was made up of no fewer than thirteen instruments by 1995 (Rappaport 1995, 27).

But while many producers have taken advantage of the new opportunities, others have continued to be concerned that the new markets are being driven by 'outsiders' for their own purposes.[96] It should be clear, however, that just as there are producers who are willing to forego further profits to lock-in a price by using risk-management tools, there are speculators (in the form, for example, of large banks and portfolio managers) who are willing to take risks on potentially large profits (and losses) in order to provide the risk-management tools that the producers require (Williams 1990b, 56; Robinson 1991b, 21). When producers become speculators, however, there is indeed cause for concern.

8.7 Crossing the Line Between Hedging and Speculation

Given the extent of upheaval in the industry following the 1986 price collapse and the dramatic cost-cutting which followed, the role of price risk management in the overall health and safety picture is clear. The short-termism of the producers (in terms of their desire to get oil out of the ground as quickly as possible or to slash costs in order to minimise economic risk) is said to have been modified by the presence of banks in the oil market with their much greater experience and expertise in dealing with risk on a longer term basis (see Williams 1990b, 54-55). But while the industry has undoubtedly made great strides forward in dealing with this issue by means of price hedging instruments, it is by no means the case that the picture is now one of an entirely risk-aware and risk-managing industry. There is instead evidence that new blind spots are in place which may be masking significant risks. Thus in the new era of opportunity for oil producers as regards financial markets, there seem to be two distinct programmes in operation. One restricts the use of such markets to clear risk-hedging strategies. The other views them instead as an opportunity to supplement the income of the core business by speculating.[97]

Nor is this only a potential problem. Two oil companies have already suffered dramatic losses on these markets - Kashima Oil of Japan which lost $1.5 billion over several years and Germany's Metallgesellschaft which ran up losses of $1 billion - and other companies, such as Total and Elf, have been known to take on 'significant exposures' in the name of risk management which may cross the line between hedging and speculation.[98] Part of the problem is that while a company's treasury is supposed to limit its financial risks, when the core business finds itself in difficulty (as when the oil price is depressed, for example) there is a temptation to move beyond hedging to speculation. In other words, at precisely the time when risk-hedging mechanisms ought to have cushioned the blow of the falling price, concerns about trying to boost profits can lead the treasury to take risks on losses on futures markets which may push the company to the brink of disaster. Given what we know about the response of industry management when such pressures arose after the 1986 fall, the implications for health and safety are clear.

The case of Metallgesellschaft (MG), therefore, merits closer attention and in the following discussion I draw very heavily upon the excellent accounts provided in Edwards (1994) and Edwards & Canter (1995). The initial reaction to the company's substantial losses was that it had indeed over-stepped the mark. It was assumed that it must have been operating in the market to a much greater extent that its physical contracts justified: '[t]hat would indicate that prudent hedging had turned into imprudent speculation'.[99] But closer inspection revealed a less clear-cut situation.

Very basically, MG appeared to be doing exactly what has been suggested in this and the foregoing chapter is a prudent and rational way to manage the price risks inherent in the markets for crude oil and crude oil products. To be clear, MG was not a producer but a refiner and trader and therefore had to consider the risks involved in the price it paid for crude oil and the price it received for products supplied. Nevertheless, the basic principles remain the same. Having entered into a substantial number of fixed-price long-term supply contracts for petrol and heating oil with a range of customers at a time when prices were low, MG sought to hedge the risk of future losses caused by rising prices by entering into short-dated futures and swap contracts. Its position on the derivatives markets matched its position for the supply of physicals almost exactly (around 160 million barrels in each case). Because its derivatives position was in the form of short-term contracts, these had to be rolled forward when they matured in order for the hedge to be maintained against the long-term physicals contracts. The derivatives position was reduced in accordance with the amount of physicals which had been supplied in the intervening period.

When prices actually fell rather than rising as MG had feared, the company found itself experiencing unrealised losses on these derivatives contracts. The problem was exacerbated by a number of factors, especially cash-flow difficulties arising from margin and supermargin calls by NYMEX. When this situation was revealed, it caused substantial concern to the company's investors and creditors on its supervisory board. The full extent of the unrealised loss stood at a sum in excess of $1 billion when the derivatives position was liquidated by new management and a rescue operation costing $1.9 billion was required to save the company from disaster.

However, with the initial panic over, it was possible to see that other factors were at work. First of all, MG was certainly involved in a risky strategy of rolling contracts which required dynamic positioning and raised the possibility of cash-flow problems. That is not to say, however, that MG was speculating rather than hedging. Note, however, that its actions clearly show that it assumed greater funding risk and greater rollover risk in exchange for better protection against rising prices. Secondly, the requirements of German accounting practice meant that MG was compelled to reveal the unrealised losses without being able to link them to the favourable position the company now found itself in with regard to its fixed-price supply contracts which of course produced more profit the further the price fell.

It is possible to suggest, therefore, that the debacle surrounding MG arose as much from confusion about the nature of the position it was in both within and outside the company. The inability to see the unrealised losses on the derivatives contracts in the context of the increased profits from the fixed-price contracts indicates the extent to which derivatives are still not properly understood. This is clear from the actions of the new board in liquidating the derivatives position at a time when prices were at their lowest in years and then getting rid of the remaining risk on forward supply contracts by liquidating them too. That said, there is also evidence that MG did not itself initially understand its hedging needs.

Funding problems arose for the company because the value of unrealised losses on short-dated derivatives depended on spot prices and the value of unrealised gains on forward supply contracts depended on forward prices. There is not a one-to-one relationship between these prices since long-term volatility is much less than short-term volatility and thus the one-to-one relationship between MG's derivative and supply contracts was only apparent. Similarly, the NPV of expected cash flows from the supply of oil in the future would be less than the value of cash outflows due to losses on short-term derivatives. Taking this factor into account demonstrates that MG needed a hedging position of less than half of its forward supply position. The impact on its unrealised losses and margin calls would have been significant.

In short, as soon as the risk is hedged by means of contracts which differ in term and type from the underlying physical contracts there is a danger that this mismatch will create cash-flow risks. The possibility of using further derivatives (such as puts, as might have been possible for MG) merely serves to demonstrate that both prudence and sophistication are required when derivatives are used for hedging.

It can be seen that the simple fact that a company is making use of derivative instruments to hedge price risk does not mean that it has moved from a deterministic to a more risk-oriented programme. Rather it is clear that further blind spots are always created, and unless the company is clear about the risks it is masking by adopting one strategy over another the magnitude of that risk may have devastating effects if it is realised. Hedging price risk is not necessarily a risk-minimising strategy if it increases other risks. In short, use of derivatives itself requires a risk management strategy (Pilipovic 1997, 197ff).

It has been noted elsewhere that banks have been responsible for encouraging oil producers to become involved in risk-management strategies based on financial instruments. Not only has this occurred through the straightforward sale of, for example, swaps, but also as part of the risk reduction strategy required by banks when organising finance for producers. Thus, it would seem that the onus is also on these banks (beyond refusing to sell overly exotic instruments to those who do not understand them) to ensure that client companies are not over-stepping the line from hedging to speculation unless they are well aware of the risks they are running. There is already evidence that some banks are actively pursuing such a line with client companies - even to the extent of discontinuing business in the event that treasuries are unco-operative.[100] Beyond this, of course, the Metallgesellschaft case may indicate that while some treasuries may know what they are doing, that will count for nothing unless the risk-management strategy is known and understood throughout the management structure of the company. Whether banks can become involved in that degree of education is perhaps more doubtful but by no means out of the question. The bottom line would seem to be, however, that for all the advantages brought by futures markets and derivative instruments in terms of risk-management, unless they are properly understood there is a danger of catastrophic problems for companies. In short, the risk-management tools used have to fit with the needs of the producer in question, its 'cash-flow and culture' (Mansfield 1990, 17).

If the regulators thus ignore the total risk-management approach of operators, all their good work at the level of the installation could be undone by activities elsewhere in the corporate structure. Even if it is felt to be too much to expect the regulator actively to seek statements of company policies on such issues, at the very least the maintenance of installation visits would provide a means of seeing whether risks realised elsewhere in the corporate structure were impacting on health and safety at work. The simple audit of the bureaucratic output from the Safety Management System will not provide that assurance. And while catastrophic losses on the scale of those suffered by Kashima and MG inevitably become public, it does not seem unreasonable to suspect that smaller losses arising from derivative speculation or mis-handled hedging which nevertheless affect cash-flow will remain hidden from public view.

8.8 The 1998 Price Crash

So much for the theory, but the 1998 price crash, in many respects more serious than the fall of 1986, provided an opportunity to observe whether or not the industry had indeed learned the lessons of the past and had shifted to the more sophisticated risk reduction steering programme with sufficient conviction to be able to meet the new crisis with comparative equanimity.

The graph of the oil price in the Appendix indicates the extent to which the industry had to come to terms with price volatility after the 1986 crash and we have already noted how it used the opportunity provided by the rise after the Kuwait invasion to lock-in prices using derivative instruments. But there is evidence to suggest that, as prices rose steadily from 1994 through 1997 in the context of a strong global economy, there were those in the industry who began to think that the period of depressed levels/volatility was over and that oil was once again a commodity whose value only rose. One indication of this can be seen in the reducing volume of trading on the IPE from 1995 to 1997 following previous steady growth (see Errera and Brown 1999, 161). But further evidence emerges from the period after the fall.

While the average price of Brent crude over 1997 was $19, by March 1998 the price had fallen by over 30% in just four months. Over the course of the year the average price was $13 with periods below $10. The Asian economic crisis signalled early on that this would be no temporary blip but rather a long period of depression as demand for oil was unlikely to be increased by the falling price. While some companies did seem to have foreseen the fall and were relatively unmoved, others manifested all the signs of panic that were seen post-1986. The UK sector was particularly badly hit because of the strength of the pound against the dollar.[101] Cost-reduction was once again the priority[102] and UKOOA's Assistant Director of Policy suggested that in 1998, as in 1986, the industry in the North Sea had entered a 'survival phase' as profits fell by an average of 30% (see Cope 1999) with some companies experiencing 50% drops.[103]

It has been concluded that 'recent history shows that exploration and production companies are ill-equipped to deal with oil price risk' (Bossley 1999), but it remains a question whether we should only be concerned because the industry seems not to have moved as decisively towards sophisticated economic risk reduction programmes as might have previously appeared, or also because once again it reverted to drastic cost-cutting in ways which impacted on occupational health and safety. It is more difficult to reach a conclusion on this last point. Post-Piper Alpha, the industry is more careful about making the sorts of admissions that were made between 1986 and 1988, now admitting only 'drastic short-term measures' including 'significant cost-cutting' (see Russell 1999). It is therefore necessary to turn to more controversial evidence in the form of the leaked company documentation relating to the serious gas escapes which occurred during 1999 mentioned at the beginning of this book.

On 6 April, in an event reminiscent of the supposed cause of the Piper Alpha disaster, gas flowed through a flange which had not been properly secured on Shell's Cormorant Alpha platform. On 10 May, in a particularly worrying occurence, gas flowed into the main control room and the Temporary Refuge on Marathon's Brae Alpha platform. Internal reports into these events leaked to the *Scotsman* newspaper seem to reveal a reaction to the 1998 price fall that is disturbingly similar to that occurring in 1986. There are suggestions that key maintenance programmes are being reduced in an attempt to cut costs. Safety checks on safety critical systems such as deluge systems, gas detectors and lifeboat launching systems are similarly being reduced. The Shell report admits that at the time of the Cormorant leak '[t]here was a general failure to recognise when a series of smaller jobs had become a larger job requiring a more rigorous planning approach'.[104] Reading these reports, it is almost as if Piper Alpha had never happened and the industry had not been subjected to a regulatory approach aimed specifically at encouraging it to avoid such short-sighted behaviour. Nor are concerns limited to the major operators. The price-slashing in 1998 has had a dramatic effect on contractors who have once again been called on to offer better value for money. Is it therefore possible to see similar corner-cutting in the failure of two companies to test lifting equipment - one of them offering a false certificate - which led to an accident in January 1999 which could have had catastrophic effects?[105]

Industry observers have been quick to point to the economic risks to companies of their apparent failure to make use of derivative instruments to ease the pressures on operations and to proof them against price falls. There has been renewed encouragement to use derivatives in the financing of projects (Bossley 1999) and to move to so-called 'life-cycle costing' to escape the problems associated with the previous approach of heavy front-end capital expenditure and a fast-track to production (Russell 1999). This is sound advice but it will miss the point if it is not linked to an overall risk strategy which aims to produce a stance where operators remain vigilant for the negative effects of the blind spots that inevitably arise from their operational codes and programmes. An extremely detailed examination of risk assessment techniques in the oil industry has recently been produced by two economists and it is highly significant that they stress that their focus on financial risk should not be construed as a statement that other dimensions of risk are unimportant. 'Quite the contrary can be true - they are often the most important factors' (Lerche & MacKay 1999, 352). But for all the potential of the Cullen regime with regard to raising and maintaining awareness of the multi-dimensional and inter-related nature of the risks to health and safety offshore, it seems that work remains to be done to ensure that it is realised.

8.9 Positive Developments and Points of Concern

Despite this rather depressing conclusion, there are more positive recent developments to report - although once again it needs to be made clear that they possess a positive potential with regard to safety offshore but require to be understood and operated appropriately if this potential is to be realised.

(a) Step Change[106] The first development occurred in September 1997 with the launch of the Step Change in Safety initiative launched by UKOOA and two contractors organisations. Since the launch, other industry bodies including trade unions have expressed support for the initiative. Looking at the issues which the initiative aimed to address, it is clear that the industry was in advance of the recently published HSE-sponsored survey (AUPEC 1999) in identifying the areas where problems required urgent attention. Thus the initiative seeks to:

- (i) establish model performance contracts for senior management which compel them to demonstrate visibly their personal concern for safety as an equal to business performance;
- (ii) develop guidelines for safety case workforce communication as a continuous process;
- (iii) improve the induction process for people new to an installation.

The initiative has moved forward to work on collecting data about incidents which had the potential to lead to more serious accidents, demonstrating a heartening attempt to deal with potential blind spots. There is also remarkable candour about the failure to engage the workforce and about the tension between safety and production, with an admission that there has been an 'innate bias towards action' which may have been at odds with the need to take time to consider actions from the perspective of safety. There is also a recognition that the progress that has been made under CRINE towards better co-operation to improve business performance needs to be repeated with regard to safety. The ultimate aim of the Step Change initiative is an ambitious 50% improvement in the whole industry's safety performance over three years.

While all of this is highly creditable, the events of 1998 and 1999 in terms of the price fall, the apparent lack of readiness on the part of the industry, the drastic cost-cutting and the worrying and apparently not unrelated accidents demonstrate the difficulty faced in translating all the good intentions of Step Change into meaningful action. That the CRINE initiative in 1998 launched a drive effectively to reduce production costs by a dollar per barrel per year over four years (that is, from $12/b to $8/b by 2002) (Potter 1998, 12) and that the CRINE president has spoken of his preference for an ultimate production cost of $6/b (Cresswell 1999, 34) indicates the continuing difficulty Step Change will have in ensuring that the tension between production and safety is not once again resolved in favour of the industry's 'innate bias towards action'.

(b) Oil and Gas Industry Task Force In the same way that Step Change has sought to improve the structural coupling between operators and contractors and between management and workforce with regard to safety, the Oil and Gas Industry Task Force is an attempt to improve the structural coupling between government and industry where problems were revealed by the uneasy period between the announcement of a review of offshore taxation in the summer of 1997 and the ultimate decision to leave the regime untouched a year later. The Task Force is concerned very much with business performance (dealing with such issues as taxation, regulation and licensing, innovation and technology, skills and training, competitiveness and sustainable development) and aims ultimately 'to produce a shared vision for the industry for 2010 and beyond'.

Insofar as it allows government to observe how industry observes then it can only contribute to a reduction in the risk that unforeseen side-effects will arise for occupational health and safety from regulatory or taxation interventions which are at first sight remote from such concerns. But again a note of caution must be sounded. To the extent that the government appears wholeheartedly to be embracing the industry's drive for cost reductions there is always the danger that it may inadvertently favour the industry's innate bias towards action in the eternal struggle between safety and production.

In such circumstances, the pressure on the regulator to maintain an adequate view of the way the industry is operating risks becoming overwhelming. It has been abundantly clear since Piper Alpha that the regulator cannot prescribe in detail and the withdrawal of the law from such pretensions can only be welcomed. The paradox is that as regulation has become more reflexive and has sought to encourage operators to assess and manage risks on an installation-specific basis, it has become increasingly clear just how complex the factors are that can impact on occupational health and safety. The regulator therefore no longer needs to run the unwinnable race to keep track of every individual component and to keep pace with every minute advance in technology, but it does now need to broaden its perspective to keep in view not only the technological aspects of the industry but also the economic, political and management dimensions which can transform an installation from a model of safe operations to a hotbed of masked risk more or less overnight. As the review of the offshore safety legislative regime concluded,

> HSE has a major role to play both in promoting good practice in safety management but also in ensuring, through inspection and monitoring, that safety management systems remain robust in difficult economic circumstances. (AUPEC 1999, 51)

This is a significant challenge and one, it is submitted, that can only be met if, once and for all, the debate on the possible range of regulatory responses to risk offshore broadens its scope beyond the binary pair of prescription and deregulation and encompasses more adequately complex concepts that can accommodate the distinctive nature of risks problems. Understanding the limitations of traditional regulatory options and the potential of a reflexive orientation, the regulator needs to take full advantage of the opportunities offered by the Cullen regime in order to take full advantage in turn of the developments within the industry itself which can ensure a posture of ongoing risk awareness, assessment and management. In this regard, whereas developments mentioned so far may be seen to represent in certain respects mixed blessings insofar as they may very rapidly produce problematic masking effects when, say, political or economic pressures mount, a further very recent development may represent the regulators best chance to harness an industry structure to reach the desired goal of improved safety.

(c) Risk Decision Support Framework Developed by UKOOA and other industry organisations, this framework aims to provide transparency on the range of issues considered when taking decisions relating to safety offshore and to facilitate the deployment of different approaches required for different situations. Compelling decision makers to identify the nature of the decision context it then directs them to the tools necessary to achieve a resolution. Significantly, this framework explicitly recognises the need for stakeholder participation, a posture of continuous improvement, the need to integrate different assessments and to allow for different individual and organisational values (see Tope 1999). The framework is still very new

and there is always a danger that the best intentions at the development stage will be thwarted in practice by, for example, a mechanistic application or its use as window-dressing. There must also be concerns that it appears, at least at this early stage, to focus principally on technological risk. And there is also the danger that it will be seen by operators as just one other piece of jargon to emerge in the post-Piper Alpha era which they have to repeat mantra-like in public while trying to minimise its impact in private. This is where the regulator has a chance to act decisively and positively by encouraging this development but ensuring that it acts as a 'binding institution' which brings together the different dimensions of risk, the different discourses in play in the industry, and encourages a mutual observation of how each observes as a means of encouraging an awareness of what cannot be seen, what lies behind the mask of operational assumptions, of constructivist codes and – paradoxically but crucially – risk-minimising programmes themselves.

9 A New Map of Management?

On the basis of the foregoing discussion of the more recent history of offshore industry management, it would be possible to propose tentatively Figure 5.3 as its cognitive map of the current situation within which it operates and of how it has been arrived at.

Put very simply, there is recognition of the two responses to the 1986 price collapse: the deterministic cost-cutting programme and the longer-term shift to more active price risk management. We saw the evidence in Chapter 4 of just what was regarded as acceptable within the cost-cutting context. While this deterministic response offered short-term relief from cost pressures, there is now recognition that this produced, at the very least, long-term technical problems which ultimately increased costs. The result of this recognition has been the development of a rational approach to cost reduction (CRINE) and an awareness of the need to link this to a more actively managed approach to safety manifest especially in the Step Change initiative.

And yet despite the undoubted progress, the 1998 price crash exposed the fragility of this system. It may have gained increasing acceptance after Piper Alpha but it appears that as prices recovered from 1995 to 1997 the old cognitive map re-exerted its influence and left the industry exposed when prices fell again. No doubt in different parts of the industry the two competing maps could have been discerned to differing

Figure 5.3 Cognitive Map: Industry Management (1986-1999)

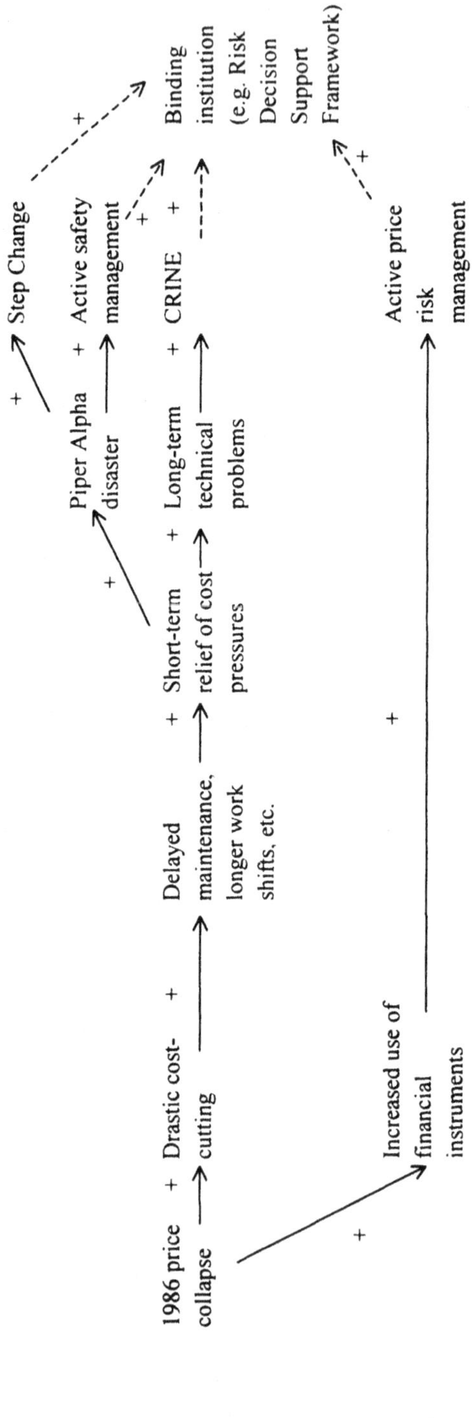

extents; no doubt some will have abandoned the old map for good in the early 1990s in the face of the manifest evidence of its inadequacies. But the fact remains that 1998 revealed once again the disturbing inability of some to learn the lessons of the past. Thankfully this time the ultimate price did not have to be paid. But those events reinforce the need for a concentration of effort on the development of a risk-aware orientation – an obvious possibility being to encourage the Risk Decision Support Framework as a mechanism that both binds and opens up the disparate strands of risk-responsive reactions to the events of the period from 1986 to 1988.

Insofar as these different approaches to the management of different dimensions of risk are coupled there is indeed hope that matters have significantly improved. Insofar as they are not coupled, however, and begin to operate as independent systems then each risks masking other dimensions of risk once again. This may even be more problematic because now in each case there is increased confidence due to the very fact that it appears that risk is being actively managed. It is, however, a short step form confidence to complacency.

10 Conclusions

> The possibilities of self-control that are held up by all possessors of monopolies must be supplemented by opportunities for self criticism. (Beck 1992, 234)

Beginning with the recognition that the regulation of health and safety at work in Britain's offshore oil and gas industry has proved both difficult and contentious, the first chapter of this book reviewed the history of the subject from the point of view of the law and from the point of view of a number of academic commentators who have been critical of the law's record. Over the roughly 35-year history of the North Sea as an oil province, British governments have adopted three successive approaches to the regulation of health and safety offshore. Initially, government adopted a *formal* approach in which the industry was left to decide on its own safety measures without any detailed regulation or inspection from outside. In the wake of the first serious accident in 1965, however, an inquiry found that this approach was inadequate and recommended the introduction of detailed prescriptive regulation backed up by inspection and penalties. This *substantive* regulatory approach was gradually introduced but was beset by difficulties associated with the rapidity of change and frequently criticised

- not least because the body entrusted with the development and implementation of the detailed regulations was part of the same department responsible for maximising the country's energy production. Following the Piper Alpha disaster in 1988, this approach to regulation was severely criticised by a further inquiry both because of the 'compliance mentality' which prescription could produce and because the inspection regime was found to be inadequate to determine whether safety was being appropriately managed.

As a consequence, a new regulatory approach was recommended in which regulations would set general goals but individual operators in the industry would be left to determine themselves how they would achieve them. This would require formal safety assessment and quantitative risk assessment in the preparation of a Safety Case for each offshore installation which would demonstrate *inter alia* that an appropriate Safety Management System was in place. The role of the regulators would, as a consequence, shift from one of detailed prescription and implementation to one of accepting or rejecting Safety Cases and auditing their context-specific implementation. Now fully introduced, this new approach bears some hallmarks of a style of regulation that might be described as *reflexive* following the theoretical literature which has attempted to recommend appropriate new strategies for law as conventional regulation reaches it limits. Be that as it may, critics of the new approach describe it as *deregulation* (in other words, a return to formal law) and insist that only the reimposition of prescription can ensure an adequate level of health and safety in the offshore industry.

Examining these different approaches and the evaluations of the various critics, it was suggested in the first chapter that a vicious circle of debate between prescription and deregulation would continue for so long as conventional models of law and regulation were adhered to and for so long as conventional legal sociological methods (such as economic analysis and capture theory) were deployed. Evidence was presented from the realms of science and economics as well as of law which suggested a growing concern with the limits of each of these disciplines which was in contrast to the explanatory powers traditionally claimed for them. In each case, the contingency of the models constructed by law, economics or science has been recognised, exposing the fact that such models may mask as much as they reveal - a recognition that has profound implications for both prescriptive regulatory approaches to offshore health and safety and deregulatory alternatives.

The implications of this recognition were considered further in the second chapter where the need to find an approach to law and legal sociology which could accommodate these constructivist insights was considered. The theory of *autopoiesis* was selected as meeting this criterion and its understanding of law and society examined. Proposing that society is composed of self-referential communicative systems which exhibit a high degree of closure and often of path-dependency, the theory offers the possibility to legal sociology of reconstructing the study area in a more adequately complex manner than is permitted by approaches which effectively assume the primacy of economic or political relations. Thus, any number of different rationalities in the study area could be considered on the basis of an identification of the stable *codes* by which they constructed their own realities and the variable *programmes* by which they steered themselves. Understanding systems such as law, science and economics in this way was shown to have serious implications for regulation - not least in a technologically complex and economically important industry such as offshore oil. Operating according to different codes and programmes, the different systems observe different realities. They can only observe that to which their particular code and programmes gives them access and cannot observe that which lies in the *blind spot* created by the very operation of their unique code - the basic assumption upon which they proceed. Similarly, steering in such a context must be understood as *self*-steering with systems seeking to minimise or reduce internally-constructed differences.

Regulatory pronouncements must thus overcome the limits of law's own construction of reality and the fact that the systems it seeks to regulate operate on the basis of different constructions and steer according to individual difference-minimising programmes. In such a situation, the outlook for traditional approaches to regulation is bleak. Instead, law must adopt a *reflexive* orientation in which it takes account of this dual closure - seeking to observe how other systems observe and trying to encourage them to adopt a similarly reflexive outlook. In order to make this operational, the technique of *cognitive mapping* was proposed by which the world constructions of different systems could be reconstructed. In this way, what each system could observe and what it could not observe would become evident.

This technique was employed especially in the third and fourth chapters to examine the different world constructions of legislators, industry management, engineering and regulators from the beginnings of operations in the North Sea up until the Piper Alpha disaster which marked the end of the prescriptive regulation of health and safety. The codes and programmes by which each system operated were revealed - what each system could and could not observe. It was found in this way that industry management constructed the world according to an economic code and steered itself initially by a programme of rapid production aimed at the minimisation of economic risk. Many events, including political interventions, labour disputes and engineering problems, were thus constructed as increasing *economic* risk and in each case the response was an intensification of operations aimed at reducing that risk. The difficulty with this way of operating, however, was shown to be its inability to observe the *occupational* and *technical* risks which could be built up as operations were intensified. During the same period, when uncertainties about the North Sea were at their greatest, engineering occupied a particularly uneasy position between science and economics. Constructing the world on the basis of deterministic assumptions derived from experience in other provinces, it attempted to accommodate the uncertainties of the new province with a risk-reduction programme of conservatism. The emergent limitations of that approach - both with regard to technical issues and to questions of cost - led engineering to take tentative steps towards a probabilistic programme of risk minimisation.

For both systems the realisation that the 1979 price hike had saved most North Sea projects rather than the inherent ability and adequacy of their programmes was a watershed. The masking effects of their path-dependent constructions of reality were laid bare. Nevertheless, the days of plenty which followed meant that newer and more sophisticated risk-minimisation programmes which sought to transcend the path-dependencies had to compete with the vestiges of the old. And when the price crash came in 1986, any sophistication gave way to a programme of drastic cost-reduction which was as restricted in its vision of risk as the programmes of rapid production and conservative determinism had been in the 1970s.

In the midst of this understanding of the systems of the regulated area, the world constructions of politics and regulation with regard to offshore health and safety appeared in a different light. Politics was seen to be envisaging a prescriptive approach long after its shortcomings had become evident in other systems. And the regulators, for all that they may have been flexible enough to prevent the worst problems of prescription by operating with detailed guidance notes instead of detailed regulations, essentially never abandoned the prescriptive approach. Believing that ultimately everything could be defined in detail and subjected to law's code (legal/illegal) they were unable to observe the risks to health and safety building up behind the masks of the industry's basic assumptions - certainly during the 1970s and the early 1980s but most notably after the price collapse in 1986.

It can be said at this stage that the commentators reviewed in the first chapter and the approaches adopted by them are not in some sense revealed to be 'wrong' by autopoiesis and the cognitive mapping approach. Rather, autopoiesis contextualises those approaches and harnesses them to the production of information about the fields they belong to. The risks in failing to recognise the limitations of context, however, are great. An ongoing debate between academic commentators and the industry has been, as was noted at the beginning of Chapter 1, about the interpretation of statistics. While there is undoubtedly a place for statistics in the regulation of health and safety at work, they may be of considerably less utility than the sort of approach advocated in this book. If further proof were required, we need only note that between 1986 and 1987 the numbers of fatalities and serious injuries reported in the North Sea fell dramatically, indicating a rapidly improving situation.[107] The findings of this study, however, were that in both industry management and in engineering at that time there was a level of systemic blindness to occupational and technological risk which had never before been experienced. That period, of course, was the context for the Piper Alpha disaster.

With this in mind, the new regulatory regime was found in the fifth and final chapter to possess significant advantages in terms of addressing the closure of different communicative systems (reflexivity) and the central issue of risk. In this regard, however, while there were many encouraging signs, the possibility of dangerous blind spots re-emerging was noted. Difficulties associated with the constructive misunderstanding of the figures produced by quantitative risk assessment were noted, for example. In addition, the example of the way in which economic (price) risk is now being managed by means of financial instruments in contrast to the previous programmes of intensified operations and cost-reduction was examined. It was demonstrated that unless there is a global appreciation of the interconnectivity of risk, then the sort of systemic blindness that allowed the dramatic build-up of risks in the aftermath of the price collapse which was the setting for the Piper Alpha disaster may reoccur with similarly serious consequences for health and safety in the industry.

The fact that the industry did not prepare for such events until they actually happened - despite the availability of more appropriate risk management programmes - demonstrates the systemic blindness that can occur when systems evolve on a path-dependent basis without questioning their basic assumptions. The challenge for the regulators accordingly lies in ensuring that the channels by which uncertainty is communicated are kept open and as clear as possible. That there is some recognition within the industry of this ability to learn from major events but an inability to learn from near misses (for example, the recent developments in this direction in the Step Change initiative discussed in the foregoing section; see also Spence 1994, 2) indicates the sort of level at which the regulators can intervene to foster improved reflexivity and learning. The lessons of the past and of recent events in financial markets suggest that even the current arrangements for the communication of uncertainty between management and engineering - significant advance though they undoubtedly are - may not be sufficient to prevent the spillover effects of financial risk on technical and especially operational risk of a magnitude similar to that experienced after 1986 and perhaps again after 1998, albeit that it may be restricted to individual operators. Similarly, the ease with which the totality of risk might be transferred to economics in the industry management system by means of financial instruments and the comparative novelty of this approach to risk management counsel a cautious approach from all parties (see Luhmann 1993, 186). Nor is this intended to identify the most likely location of unacknowledged risk. Rather it is but one example of how the sort of interconnectivity of risk clearly identified by the regulator may currently be being ignored. The lesson is that unless there is reflexivity, unless blind spots - basic assumptions - are continually challenged, risk is not being appropriately managed.

The HSE, as was seen in the final chapter, is certainly aware of this interconnectivity - the fact that, for example, commercial risks and solutions cannot be viewed in isolation from health and safety risks and solutions more narrowly defined. Whether it is able to address that degree of complexity in its current configuration and within the terms of its current regulatory mandate is another question. But it is a question which history, as revealed by the cognitive maps of the autopoietic approach, suggests will have to be addressed. That there is also some awareness of this issue within the industry is encouraging (see e.g. Bentley & Stockley 1992; Alderman & Lewis 1994). Just as the new regulatory regime has been able to take advantage of developing risk-aware programmes within management and engineering, it must not then allow these to become new path dependencies but must ensure ongoing reflexivity, must seek to foster this new *global* risk awareness. The aim must not be to put ever more responsibility and informational demands on the regulator but rather to ensure that its range of audit and possible interventions is not unduly restricted and that it encourages ongoing questioning and communication (reflexivity) rather than routinising it. By adopting such a stance, law can help to ensure that it is not in the future found once again to be part of the problem rather than the solution. The Risk Decision Support Framework represents an opportunity to harness the disparate strands of risk-awareness, assessment and management which have developed throughout the industry.

The Piper Alpha disaster and the subsequent inquiry have been described as 'a unique learning opportunity for the industry' (Hall 1991, 653) but unless care is taken the implementation of the lessons may be as dangerous as the problems they are supposed to be addressing. It is perhaps significant that one industry insider who is close to the whole question of offshore safety has suggested recently that 'we are only now beginning to understand properly' the potential of the Cullen regime (O'Ferrall 1999). Contemporary critics are surely taking too restrictive a view when they associate the new regulatory regime offshore with deregulation, but care must be taken to ensure that it does not by default or inattention *become* deregulation. Ongoing problems of health and safety resulting from a failure to fulfil the reflexive potential of the new regime may prompt a return to prescription which would surely carry greater risks. If the new regime is understood as a *reflexive* approach to health and safety, however, the outlook is more optimistic. But that must be a full understanding of reflexivity. Insofar as the opportunities for self-criticism are limited and the possibilities of self-control are over-estimated, the risks to health and safety offshore are once more behind the mask.

Notes

1. See Chapter 4, Section 5.
2. Hansard HC (Debs) 12 Nov. 1990 cols. 329-345; 7 March 1991 cols. 472-567.
3. For example, Frank Dobson MP at col. 332.
4. Secretary of State for Energy, John Wakeham MP, at cols. 473-4.
5. Secretary of State for Energy at col. 329.
6. Robert Hughes MP at col. 519.
7. Secretary of State for Energy at col. 474.
8. Secretary of State for Energy at col. 479.
9. 'I am prepared to accept that the appointment of offshore safety representatives by trade unions could be of some benefit in making the work of safety representatives and safety committees effective, mainly through the credibility and resistance to pressure which trade union backing would provide' (Cullen 1990, para 21.84)

quoted, for example, by Frank Doran MP at col. 343 and by Alex Salmond MP at col. 541.

10 Quoted, for example, by the Secretary of State for Energy at col. 344 and by the Parliamentary Under-Secretary of State for Energy, Colin Moynihan MP at col. 564.

11 Stanley Orme MP at col. 335.

12 Secretary of State for Energy at col. 335.

13 See, for example, the cases cited by Alex Salmond MP at cols. 540-2 and by Frank Doran MP at cols. 547-8.

14 For example, the Parliamentary Under-Secretary of State for Energy at col. 563.

15 Ernie Ross MP at col. 529 cited the example of seven ballots on the question of union recognition organised by the Manufacturing, Science and Finance union on offshore installations, all of which had shown a large majority of workers in favour of recognition. Despite these findings, it seems that other companies, including the likes of Conoco who were often cited as a good example of a company with a 'safety culture', were not interested in holding similar ballots.

16 For example, the Secretary of State for Energy at col. 333.

17 Dr. Michael Clark MP at cols. 504-5.

18 Malcolm Bruce MP at col. 506.

19 Robert Hughes MP at col. 516.

20 Frank Doran MP at col. 551.

21 For example, John Greenway MP at col. 536.

22 See Section 8 below in this Chapter.

23 See Chapter 1, Section 1.4.

24 Offshore Installations (Safety Representatives and Safety Committees) Regulations 1989 (SI 971) introduced by the DEn during the Cullen Inquiry.

25 By s58(1)(b) of the Employment Protection (Consolidation) Act 1978.

26 Hansard HC (Debs) Vol. 213 col. 682, Secretary of State for Employment.

27 Offshore Installations (Safety Case) Regulations 1992 (SI 2885).

28 Respectively (SI 1984/1902) and Directive 82/501/EEC.

29 The HSE procedure for assessment of Safety Cases and review procedures in the event of rejection is described in HSE (1993a).

30 It is worth noting that while there is a recurrent criticism of the speed with which change has been implemented offshore as opposed to onshore as regards health and safety, similar if not greater time lags have occurred onshore. For example, the HSE set up the Advisory Committee on Major Hazards following the Flixborough disaster in 1974. The CIMAH regulations were finally brought into force in 1984 and the deadline for the first round of safety cases under those regulations was 1989 (Barrell 1994, 1-2).

31 See Chapter 1, Section 1.4 for details.

32 That offshore engineering was not alone in its failure fully to adopt risk assessment techniques is evident from the publication in 1992 of a Code of Professional Conduct by the Engineering Council entitled *Engineers and Risk Issues*. This called for a balance between reliance on codes of practice and project specific risk assessment and also called on engineers to be open-minded and not 'hide behind regulations'. Among a series of disasters mentioned as leading to this conclusion was the Piper Alpha. See Engineering Council (1993).

33 Issue Notes are notes drawing attention to issues which would (level 1) or could (level 2) prevent acceptance of the Safety Case.

34 This is a finding which vindicates the concerns expressed some years previously by legal researchers (see Barrett & Howells 1984).

35 See Chapter 4, Section 6.2 (Figure 4.5).

36 For details of the 30 schemes under consideration see *PR* October 1996, 472-3.

37 Compare the announcement of the removal ashore for decommissioning of the Leman BK compression platform which passed entirely unnoticed by the non-specialist media. *PE* March 1996, 48.

38 For example, the Tern platform designed in 1986 (see van de Graaf *et al.* 1994).

39 See *PE* 1988, 271.

40 See Chapter 4, Section 3 above.

41 Section 2 above in this Chapter.

42 See Chapter 4, Section 9.2.

43 See especially paras. 9 to 11 of Schd. 2 to the 1992 regulations; see also D. Bainbridge (1993, 87) and Pape (1993, 118).

44 For other examples of the new regime in practice in other companies see Koenig (1993) and, with special reference to the review and audit procedures, Cracknell (1993) and S. Jones (1993).

45 For example, Conoco suspended production from its Viking A complex of platforms for 'factors including safety considerations, age and current production levels...the proximity of gas production risers is considered to be unsatisfactory by today's standards'. *PE* December 1991, 40.

46 Section 4.2 above in this Chapter.

47 Wiggins (1985) quoted in Cooke (1991, 23).

48 See in this regard Spiller (1994, 4) who argues that reducing numbers on an installation increases individual risk.

49 *PE* March 1993, 47. See also *The Press & Journal* 28 March 1997 for evidence of continuing problems.

50 *PE* June 1994, 93.

51 That the new approach of open management structures is not a cure-all is evident from the case of the Foinaven field being developed West of Shetland. At one time this leading-edge development was being presented as an example of the remarkable advances that could be achieved by 'rethought relationships' between operators and contractors with the expectation that the project would be brought to first oil in one third of the time required for an equivalent North Sea development; *PE* June 1995, 85. More recently, the project has been beset by both technical difficulties with installed equipment and labour problems in a Spanish fabrication yard; *PR* September 1996, 408. There is no room, therefore, for complacency.

52 See CRINE (1994) in general and especially Annex 1A, 65-77. See also Woolfson *et al.* (1996, 310ff).

53 So far, the developments to the West of Shetland (the so-called Atlantic Frontier) do not appear to have captured public attention in the way that those in the North Sea did. But the magnitude of the challenge facing the industry there - and hence the magnitude of the risks - is considerable. While the deepest North Sea field (Magnus) lies in 186m of water, Schiehallion lies in 375m and Foinaven in 500m. Moreover, the ocean currents occurring in this area are among the most complex in the world because of the interaction of the Gulf Stream and the Atlantic Stream, which produces opposing strong and variable currents running almost to the seabed. Beyond the ocean conditions, the reservoirs tend to be shallow and of wide extent,

requiring multiple drilling sites. The fact that these conditions render the use of fixed platforms impossible and have led instead to the use of Floating Production Storage and Offloading vessels (FPSOs) which look like little more than modified ships, may account for the lack of public attention. Nevertheless, the difficulties and risks associated with, for example, the flexible risers and dynamic positioning which are features of this approach are considerable (see Ball & Brookes 1996).

54 Section 2 above in this Chapter.

55 See OILC (1991, 26-28) for a list of the unions vying for members offshore and a list of inter-union organisations. The image is one of anything but coherence. What follows is a relatively brief account of the union position in the aftermath of Piper Alpha and the implications for workforce involvement in the new regulatory regime. For an extremely detailed account of this period see Woolfson *et al.* (1996, Part 4).

56 See, for example, *PE* September 1990, 38.

57 *ibid.*

58 BBC Online Network 23 July 1999.

59 BBC Online Network 11 August 1999.

60 *ibid.*

61 Framework Directive for the Introduction of Measures to Encourage Improvements in Safety and Health of Workers (89/391/EEC) enacted in the UK by the Management of Health and Safety at Work Regulations 1992 (SI 1992/2051).

62 Section 5.3(v) above in this Chapter.

63 The joint HSE/UKOOA conference on health risks to offshore workers in Aberdeen in March 1996 is an example of the advances in this regard. See HSE Press Release E39:96. Similarly, HSE sponsored research into workforce risk perception has recently been published (Flin *et al.* 1996).

64 See Chapter 1, note 46.

65 See the HSE leaflet *How Offshore Helicopter Travel is Regulated* (HS(G)142) 1996.

66 Section 5.3(v) above in this Chapter.

67 Note that penalties under the Offshore Safety Act 1992 s.4 are much higher than those previously available. Breach of any health and safety regulation carries a maximum of 2 years imprisonment or an unlimited fine or both. Failure to comply with a prohibition or improvement notice or a remedy order carries a maximum of 6 months or a £20,000 fine or both in a lower court and, on indictment, 2 years or an unlimited fine or both.

68 Framework Directive on the Introduction of Measures to Encourage Improvements in the Safety and Health of Workers (89/91/EEC, OJL 183/89).

69 See also Perham (1993, 10) for evidence that the European Commission and continental European companies are looking to the UK approach for future direction.

70 Extractive Industries (Boreholes) Directive (92/91/EEC).

71 The European Commission has also been encouraged to use more risk assessment in recent reports from business organisations. See AGDG (1995) and UNICE (1995).

72 BBC Online Network 8 September 1999.

73 The chairman of Shell UK, Bob Reid, for example called for an 'imaginative review of tax' in order to encourage investment in older fields where expenditure was needed to extend the life of platforms beyond what had been originally planned because of the development of satellite fields. *PE* 1989, 389.

74 FA 1990 ss60-61.

75 *PE* 1990, 131.
76 FA 1991 ss62 & 103; *PE* April 1991, 20.
77 *PE* June 1991, 19.
78 FA 1993 ss185, 186 & 188.
79 FA 1994 ss231ff.
80 FA 1995 ss 146ff.
81 *PE* June 1994, 93.
82 *PE* August 1996, 53.
83 Robertson's International Ventures Survey 1997 quoted in *PE* April 1997, 19-20.
84 FA (No.2) 1997 s18. The 31% rate was retained for FY1998 and has been further reduced to 30% for FY1999; see FA 1998 ss28-29.
85 *PE* December 1997, 39.
86 *PE* April 1998, 54.
87 *PE* May 1998, 2.
88 PE October 1998, 37.
89 *PE* November 1993, 15-23.
90 For further examples of financing arrangements taking advantage of risk-management instruments, see Williams (1990a, 45-46).
91 *PE* November 1993, 15-23, 16.
92 *PE* November 1993, 15-23, 19.
93 Although locked-in prices would appear to conflict with the earlier industry management concern with NPV, the current acceptance must be seen in the context of a vastly different inflation situation.
94 For fuller details of futures contracts in the context of oil production see Battley (1989, 7-8); Clubley 1990, (90-92). The above example draws on these sources.
95 For fuller details, see Battley (1989, 90ff).
96 *PE* 1990, 11; see also Roeber (1993, 45).
97 *ibid.*
98 See *PE* February 1994, 16 and *The Economist* 4 June 1994, 107-8.
99 *PE* February 1994, 16.
100 *The Economist* 4 June 1994, 108.
101 *PE* June 1998, 11.
102 *PE* March 1998, 2.
103 *PE* November 1998, 2.
104 BBC Online Network 8 September 1999.
105 BBC Online Network 9 August 1999.
106 See www.ukooa.co.uk for details.
107 See *Offshore Accident and Incident Statistics Report 1996 [Provisional Data]* Offshore Technology Report – OTO 96 955, Figure 7.

Appendix Crude Oil Prices 1960-1998

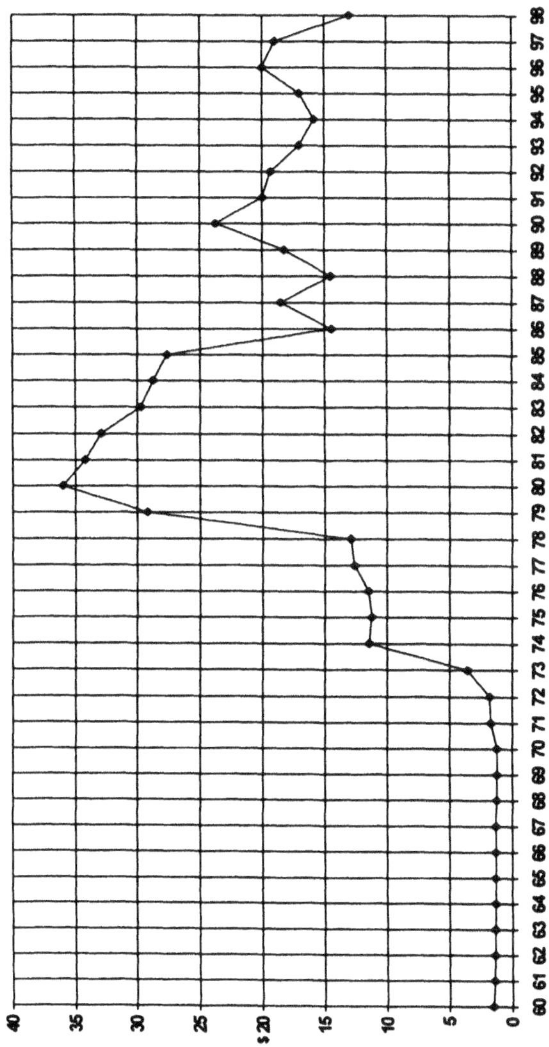

Sources: Jenkins (1989); International Energy Authority (1994); US Department of Energy (1996); *Petroleum Economist* 1997-8

Bibliography

Abbot, P. A., L. E. Farmer, G. J. Blight and D. Osborne-Moss (1980), 'A New Integrated Deck Concept', *OTC*, IV, 231-44; no. 3879.

Abdel-Aal, H. K. and R. Schmelzee (1976), *Petroleum Economics and Engineering*, New York and Basel: Marcel Dekker Inc.

Adams, R. (1998), 'A Vibrant Oil and Gas Industry Relies on Fiscal Stability', *Petroleum Economist*, March, 38-9.

Ahmed, S. and S. J. Murphy (1996), 'Use of Decision Risk Analysis in Selecting Field Development Options: A Case Study: Alba Field Phase II', *OTC*, II, 93-8; no. 8038.

AGDG (1995), *Deregulation Now*, London and Bonn: Anglo-German Deregulation Group.

Alderman, J. A. and S. J. Lewis (1994), 'Essential Elements of a Formal Risk Management Program', *OTC*, I, 119-25; no.7383.

Allott, A. (1980), *The Limits of Law*, London: Butterworths.

Almar-Naess, A., P. J. Haagensen, B. Lian, T. Moan and T. Simonsen (1982), 'Investigation of the Alexander L. Kielland Failure - Metallurgical and Fracture Analysis', *OTC*, II, 79-94; no. 4236.

Andersen, S. S. (1987), *British and Norwegian Offshore Industrial Relations: Pluralism and Neo-Corporatism as Contexts of Strategic Adaptation*, Aldershot: Avebury.

Ansquer, P. F. and R. S. Carton (1980), 'Field Measurements of Correlation Between Waves and Platform Responses versus Significant Wave Height and Wave Direction', *OTC*, III, 25-35; no. 3797.

Arnold, G. (1978), *Britain's Oil*, London: Hamilton.

Arnold, K. E., P. J. Koszela and J. C. Viles (1989), 'Improving Safety of Production Operations in the US OCS', *OTC*, III, 349-58; no. 6079.

Arnold, K. E. and D. B. McCafferty (1997), 'Safety and Environmental Programs as a Mechanism for Establishing ALARP', *OTC*, II, 89-104; no. 8364.

Arnold, K. E. and N. C. Roobaert (1989), 'Comparison of North Sea and Gulf of Mexico Design Philosophies', *OTC*, III, 623-30; no. 6117.

Ashford, N. A. (1976), *Crisis in the Workplace: Occupational Disease and Injury*, Cambridge, Mass: MIT Press.

AUPEC (1999), *Evaluation of the Offshore Safety Legislative Regime: A Study Undertaken for the Safety Policy Division, Health and Safety Executive* (Report Overview), Aberdeen: Aberdeen University Petroleum Economic Consultants.

Axelrod, R. (1976a), 'The Cognitive Mapping Approach to Decision Making', in Axelrod (ed.), 3-17.

Axelrod, R. (1976b), 'The Analysis of Cognitive Maps', in Axelrod (ed.), 55-73.

Axelrod, R. (1976c), 'Limitations', in Axelrod (ed.), 251-65.

Axelrod, R. (ed.), (1976), *Structure of Decision: The Cognitive Maps of Political Elites,* Princeton, New Jersey: Princeton University Press.

Bacon, J. (1993), 'Keynote Address', in HSE (1993c), 8-11.

Bainbridge, C. A. (1975), 'Certification of Fixed Steel Platforms in the North Sea', *OTC,* III, 737-56; no. 2410.

Bainbridge, D. (1993), 'ALARP in Practice', in HSE (1993c), 86-9 .

Baird, R. W. (1976), 'Explanation of Shallow Blowouts and Lost Time Incidents with some Recommendations', *OTC,* II, 925-41; no. 2610.

Baldwin, R. (1987), 'Health and Safety at Work: Consensus and Self-Regulation', in Baldwin and McCrudden (eds), 132-58.

Baldwin, R. (1992), 'The United Kingdom' in Baldwin and Daintith (eds), 203-22.

Baldwin, R. and M. Cave (1999), *Understanding Regulation: Theory, Strategy and Practice*, Oxford: Oxford University Press.

Baldwin, R. and C. McCrudden (eds), (1987), *Regulation and Public Law,* London: Weidenfield and Nicholson.

Balekjian, W. H. (1979), 'Legal Reasoning and Economic Reasoning: Interactions', *Rechtstheorie,* 10, 371-7.

Ball, I. G. and D. A. Brookes (1996), 'Technical Challenges of Opening the Atlantic Frontier', *OTC,* II, 21-9.

Bankowski, Z. (1994), 'How does it Feel to be on your own? The Person in the Sight of Autopoiesis', *Ratio Juris,* Vol. 7, No. 2, 254-66; also in Nelken (ed.), 63-80.

Banks, F. E. (1980), *The Political Economy of Oil,* Lexington, Mass. and Toronto: Lexington Books, D. C. Heath and Co.

Baram, Michael (1985), 'Implementation and evaluation of regulations', in Otway and Peltu (eds), 57-75.

Baron, D. S. (1992), 'The Abuses of Risk Assessment', in Waterstone (ed.), 173-8.

Barrell, A. C. (1993), 'Objective Setting and Performance Standards', in HSE (1993c), 62-4.

Barrell, T. (1994), 'The HSE Position and the Safety Case Regime', in Waterfront (1994), Paper 2.

Barrett, B., B. Hindley and R. Howells (1987), *Safety In the Offshore Petroleum Industry: The Law and Practice for Management,* London: Kogan Page.

Barrett, B. and R. Howells (1984), 'Safe Systems for Exploiting the Petroleum Resources of the North Sea', *International and Comparative Law Quarterly* 811-24.

Battle, J. (1997), 'From Waste to Potential', 1997 Conoco Lecture, *Petroleum Review,* April, 160-4.

Battley, N. (1989), *An Introduction to Commodity Futures and Options,* London: McGraw-Hill.

Bauman, Z. (1992), *Intimations of Postmodernity,* London and New York: Routledge.

Bea, R. G. (1990), 'Reliability Criteria for New and Existing Platforms', *OTC,* II, 393-408; no.6312.

Bea, R. G. (1996), 'Quantitative and Qualitative Risk Analyses - The Safety of Offshore Platforms', *OTC,* II, 79-91; no. 8037.

Bea, R. G., R. W. Litton and A. K. Vaish (1985), 'Requalification of Existing Platforms', *OTC,* I, 163-76; no. 4858.

Bea, R. G., F. J. Pusker, C. Smith and J. S. Spencer (1988), 'Development of AIM (Assessment, Inspection, Maintenance), Programs for Fixed and Mobile Platforms', in *OTC,* II, 193-206; no. 5703.

Bea, R. J. (1973), 'Selection of Environmental Criteria for Offshore Platform Design', *OTC,* II, 185-96; no. 1839.

Beck, U. (1992), *Risk Society,* London: Sage.

Bell, D. and Irving Kristol (1981), *The Crisis in Economic Theory,* New York: Basic Books.

Bellamy, L. J. (1994), 'The Human Element', in Waterfront (1994), Paper 10.

Benedict, C. P., N. I. Allanach and A. C. H. Hammer (1982), 'Offshore Evacuation - Past and Future', *OTC,* IV,, 25-32; no. 4373.

Bengtsson, B. and S. Thulin (1985), 'An Offshore Evacuation System: A Safe Haven and an Emergency Control Centre', *OTC,* IV, 523-38; no. 5077.

Benn, T. (1989), *Against the Tide: Diaries 1973-76,* London, etc.: Hutchinson.

Benn, T. (1990), *Conflicts of Interest: Diaries 1977-80,* London, etc.: Hutchinson.

Bennion, F. A. R. (1984), *Statutory Interpretation: Codified with a Critical Commentary,* London: Butterworths.

Bentham, R. W. (1984), 'Offshore Accidents: The Relationships Involved', in IBA (1984), 591-8.

Bentham, R. W. (1991), 'The United Kingdom Offshore Safety Regime: Before and After Piper Alpha', *Journal of Energy and Natural Resources Law,* 273-80.

Bentley, P. D. and J. D. Stockley (1992), 'Hazard Management and Safety Management Systems', *OTC,* II, 471-6; no. 6925.

Bernard, B. (1999), *Century: One hundred years of human progress, regression, suffering and hope,* London: Phaidon.

Bibbings, R. (1993), 'Workforce Involvement in Safety Case Production and Development: A Trade Unions View', in HSE (1993c), 136-40.

Bibbings, R. (1994), 'TUC: Working for Health and Safety', [Typescript], January 1994.

Biewer, F. N. and H. N. Wallin Jr. (1970), 'Minimising Offshore Risk', *OTC,* II, 607-11; no. 1284.

Black, J. (1996), 'Constitutionalising Self-Regulation', *Modern Law Review,* 24-55.

Bland, D. (1988), *UK Oil Taxation* (2nd edition), Longman.
Blankenberg, E. (1984), 'The Poverty of Evolutionism: A Critique of Teubner's Case for "Reflexive Law"', 18 *Law and Society Review*, 274-89.
Bolt, H. M., C. J. Billington *et al.* (1996), *A Review of the Ultimate Strength of Tubular Framed Structures*, London: HSE Books.
Bond, C. R. and P. G. H. Shaw (1986), 'The Lessons from 8 Years' Operation of a First-Generation North Sea Platform and Planning to its End-of-Field Life', *OTC*, I, 73-85; no. 5091.
Bond, S., M. Devereux and M. Saunders (1988), *North Sea Taxation for the 1990s*, London: Institute of Fiscal Studies.
Bossley, L. (1999), 'Use of the forward price curve for project financing', *Petroleum Economist*, August, 6-8.
Boyd, N. G. (1986), 'Topsides Weight Reduction Techniques for Offshore Platforms', *OTC*, III, 309-11; no. 5257.
Brader, J. (1970), 'Ocean Platform - State of the Art', *OTC*, II, 557-592; no. 1282.
Bradshaw, H., E. G. Stokes and M. J. Leece (1985), 'Hutton TLP Installation', *OTC*, II, 159-68; no. 4913.
Brandie, E. F. (1993), 'Risk Reduction in Offshore Production', in *OTC*, I, 153-63; no. 7097.
Brannon, H. R. (1977), 'Platform Verification - A View from a Member of the Industry', *OTC*, II, 21-32; no. 2809.
Bråten, S. (1992), 'Paradigms of Autonomy: Dialogical or Monological?', in Teubner and Febbrajo (eds), 35-65.
Brekke, J. N., R. B. Campbell, W. C. Lamb and J. D. Murff (1990), 'Calibration of a Jackup Structural Analysis Procedure Using Field Measurements from a North Sea Jackup', *OTC*, IV, 357-68; no. 6465.
Brown, E. (1975), 'Finance for the North Sea', in Saeter and Smart (eds.), 111-30.
Brown, G. M. and D. C. McCann (1989), 'Improving Structural Integrity by Injection of Grout into Fatigue-Critical Nodes in Offshore Structures', *OTC*, II, 253-8; no 5984.
Bunce, J. W. and T. A. Wyatt (1982), 'Development of Unified Design Criteria for Heavy Lift Operations Offshore', *OTC*, I, 307-20; no. 4192.
Burgoyne (1980), *Offshore Safety - Report of the Committee*, Chairman Dr J. H. Burgoyne (Cmnd. 7866), London: HMSO.
Buslov, V. M., J. B. Valdivieso and R. D. Holdworth (1987), 'Inspection, Maintenance, and Repair of Offshore Platforms: A System Approach', *OTC*, I, 269-76; no. 5386.
Cairncross, Sir Alec (1992), 'Devaluing the Pound - the Lessons of 1967', *The Economist*, 14 November, 25-8.
Caldwell, S. (1993), 'The Interface between Contractors and Operators: An Introduction', in HSE (1993c), 162-6.
Cameron, P. D. (1983), *Property Rights and Sovereign Rights: The Case of North Sea Oil*, London, etc: Academic Press.

Cannell, C. and N. Stasmore (1980), 'A Retrospective Assessment of Fatigue Damage Suffered by West Sole Platform WE', *OTC*, IV, 491-500; no. 3904.

Carlisle, B. A. (1978), 'Corporate Financing: International Integrated Companies', in White (ed.), 40-55.

Carson, W. G. (1970), 'Some Sociological Aspects of Strict Liability and the Enforcement of Factory Legislation', *Modern Law Review*, 396-412.

Carson, W. G. (1981), *The Other Price of Britain's Oil: Safety and Control in the North Sea*, Oxford: Martin Robertson.

Carter, R. M., P. W. Marshall, P. D. Thomas and T. M. Swanton (1969), 'Materials Problems in Offshore Platforms', *OTC*, I, 443-70; no. 1043.

Carter, J. H. T., Albert Muster and Bruce Skinner (1992), 'Gannet Cluster: Development After the 1986 Oil Price Collapse', *OTC*, III, 163-78; no. 7002.

Castle, G. R. (1985), 'Assessment of North Sea Field Performance', *Petroleum Economist*, 358-9.

Chapman, A. B. (1983), 'Future Requirements for Safety Training', in Commission of the EC (1983), 393-401.

Chelius, J. R. (1974), 'The Control of Industrial Accidents: Economic Theory and Empirical Evidence', *Law and Contemporary Problems*, Vol. 38, No. 4, 700-29.

Chen, H. T. (1980), 'Long Term Prediction of Offshore Vessel Responses for Design and Operability Evaluation', *OTC*, III, 61-8; no. 3800.

Chevalier, J (1993), 'Workforce Involvement: An Industry View', in HSE (1993c), 152-4.

Clark, J. and Lord Wedderburn (1987), 'Juridification - A universal trend? The British experience in labour law', in Teubner (ed.), (1987a), 163-90.

Clubley, S. (1998), *Trading in Oil Futures and Options*, Cambridge/Boca Raton: Woodhead/CRC.

Clune, W. H. (1992), 'Implementation as Autopoietic Interaction of Autopoietic Organizations', in Teubner and Febbrajo (eds), 485-513.

Cockbain, G., A. Jermstad and D. Stenhouse (1990), 'Design of the Draugen Topsides for the Effects of Gas Explosions', *OTC*, IV, 489-96; no. 6477.

Cockburn, D. (1985), 'Financing', in *UK Oil and Gas Guide*, 1985/86 Edition, London: Arthur Anderson and Co., 123-31.

Coker, J. W. A. (1991), 'Design of Gas and Oil Riser Installations for Offshore Platforms', *OTC*, II, 635-40; no. 6628.

Collingridge, D. and C. Reeve (1986), *Science Speaks to Power - The Role of Experts in Policymaking*, London: Frances Pinter.

Comer, P. J. and M. Eades (1991), 'The Application of Risk Assessment in Offshore Projects', *OTC*, II, 743-56; no. 6642.

Commission of the European Communities (1983), *Safety and Health in the Oil and Gas Extractive Industries - Proceedings of an International Symposium*, Luxembourg, 19-20 April 1983, London: Graham and Trotman Ltd.

Compton-Rickett, C. (1994), 'The Insurance Risks', in Waterfront (1994), Paper 8.

Connolly, P. F. (1978), 'Project Financing: Petroleum Production', in White (ed.), 74-90.

Cooke, R. M. (1991), *Experts in Uncertainty: Opinion and Subjective Probability in Science,* New York and Oxford: Oxford University Press.

Cope, G. (1998), 'When NGOs target individual oil companies', *Petroleum Review,* November, 27-9.

Cope, G. (1999), 'The third oil crisis', *Petroleum Review,* March, 33-9.

Corti, G. (1983), 'North Sea Oil', in Tempest (ed.), 59-72.

Cotterrell, R. (1992), *The Sociology of Law: An Introduction* (second edition), London, Dublin, Edinburgh: Butterworths.

Cotterrell, R. (1993), 'Sociological Perspectives on Legal Closure', in Alan Norrie (ed.), (1993), *Closure or Critique: New Directions in Legal Theory,* Edinburgh: Edinburgh University Press, 175-93.

Cox, R. F. and M. H. Walter (eds.), (1991), *Offshore Safety and Reliability,* London and New York: Elsevier Applied Science.

Cox, R. A. (1990), 'The Application of Risk Assessment to Existing Installations', in Institution of Chemical Engineers (1990), 153-66.

Cox, T. (1993), 'Maintenance of a "Living" QRA' in IBC (1993), Day 2, Paper 6.

Cracknell, D. (1993), 'Audit and the Living Safety Cases', in IBC (1993), Day 1, Paper 4.

Cranston, R. (1979), *Regulating Business: Law and Consumer Agencies,* London: Macmillan.

Craven, J. P. (1973), 'Industry/Government Relations in Offshore Resource Development' *OTC,* II, 939-68; no. 1919.

Cresswell, J. (1998), 'Improving North Sea Safety', *Petroleum Review,* September, 25.

Cresswell, J. (1999), 'Crine Drives Down Development Costs', *Petroleum Review,* April, 34-5.

CRINE (1994), *CRINE - Cost Reduction Initiative in the New Era,* London: Institute of Petroleum on behalf of UKOOA.

Croft-Bednarski, S. and K. Johnston (1999), 'Britannia Topsides: A Low Cost, Safe and Productive North Sea Facility', in *OTC,* II, Part 2, 465-77; no. 11018.

Cullen, Lord (1990), *The Public Inquiry into the Piper Alpha Disaster*, Chairman The Hon. Lord Cullen (Cm. 1310), London: HMSO.

Curole, M. A. (1997), 'Mars Risk Management Program', in *OTC,* II, 69-80; no. 8362.

Curole, M. A. and A. McKinney (1999), 'Human and Organisational Factors in Deepwater Applications', in *OTC,* I, 503-12; no. 10878.

Dahle, L. A. (1985), 'Mobile Platform Stability: Project Synthesis with Recommendations for New Philosophies for Stability Regulations', *OTC,* III, 269-78; no. 4988.

Daintith, T. and R. Baldwin (eds.), (1992), *Harmonization and Hazard: Regulating Health and Safety in the European Workplace,* London: Graham and Trotman.

Daintith, T. C. and I. W. Gault (1979), 'Oil and Gas: National Regimes', in Mason (ed.), (1979), 53-70.

Daintith, T. and G. Teubner (eds), (1986), *Contract and Organisation: legal analysis in the light of economic and social theory,* Berlin: de Gruyter.

Daintith, T. and G. Willoughby (1984), *Manual of United Kingdom Oil and Gas Law,* London: Sweet and Maxwell.

Dam, K. W. (1976), *Oil Resources: Who Gets What How?,* Chicago and London: University of Chicago Press.

Daniel, J. J. S. (1982), 'Stand-by Rescue Ships - Their Role and the Factors Involved in Performing Them', *OTC,* IV, 53-9; no. 4374.

Darity, W. Jr. (ed.), (1993), *Labor Economics: Problems in Analyzing Labor Markets,* Boston, Dordrecht, London: Kluwer Academic Publishers.

Dawson, S., P. Willman, A. Clinton and M. Bamford (1988), *Safety at Work: The Limits of Self-regulation,* Cambridge: Cambridge University Press.

Dehousse, R., C. Joerges, G. Majone and F. Snyder with M. Everson (1992), 'Europe after 1992: New Regulatory Strategies', European University Institute: Florence, EUI, Working Paper LAW No. 92/31.

de Smith, S. and R. Brazier (1994), *Constitutional and Administrative Law* (seventh edition by R. Brazier), Harmondsworth: Penguin.

Dodd, N. (1995), 'Whither Mammon? Postmodern Economics and Passive Enrichment', *Theory, Culture and Society,* Vol. 12, No. 2, 1-24.

Doyle, E. (1993), 'Identification and Assessment of Safety Systems in Safety Cases', in IBC (1993), Day 1, Paper 6.

Dupuy, J.-P. (1987), 'On the Supposed Closure of Normative Systems', in Teubner (ed.), (1987b), 51-69.

Durnin, D. (1994), 'The Contractor's Experience', in Waterfront (1994), Paper 5.

Durning, P. J. (1971), 'Prediction of Maximum Wave Height from Historical Data', *OTC,* I, 165ff; no. 1343.

Dymond, P. F. (1995), 'The Operators' Perspective on the Decommissioning of UKCS Offshore Installations', *Petroleum Review,* 176-8.

Edelman, G. M. (1989), *Neural Darwinism,* Oxford: OUP.

Edwards, A. R. (1991), 'Communication and steering: what the science of public administration could learn from Habermas and Luhmann', in in 't Veld *et al.* (eds), 183-91.

Edwards, F. R. (1994), 'Derivatives Can Be Hazardous to Your Health: The Case of Metallgesellschaft', *LSE Financial Markets Group Special Paper Series,* Special Paper No. 64, December 1994.

Edwards, F. R. and M. S. Canter (1995), 'The Collapse of Metallgesellschaft: Unhedgeable Risks, Poor Hedging Strategy or Just Bad Luck?' *LSE Financial Markets Group Special Paper Series,* Special Paper No. 71, April 1995.

Edwards, G. (1984), 'Some Recent Applications of Reliability Theory in Offshore Structural Engineering', *OTC,* III, 427-36; no. 4827.

Ehrlich, E. (1936), *Fundamental Principles of the Sociology of Law*, Cambridge, Mass.: Harvard University Press.

Ellickson, R. C. (1987), 'A Critique of Economic and Sociological Theories of Social Control', *Journal of Legal Studies*, 67-99.

Ellis Jones, P. (1988), *Oil: A Practical Guide to the Economics of World Petroleum*, Cambridge: Woodhead-Faulkner.

Elwes, P. J. G. (1978), 'Corporate Financing: Independent Oil Companies', in White (ed.), 55-71.

Engineering Council (1993), *Guidelines on Risk Issues*, Lloyd's Register.

Eri, J. (1975), 'Development and Implementation of Regulations for Permanent Offshore Structures', *OTC*, III, 757-8; no. 2413.

Errera, S. and S. L. Brown (1999), *Fundamentals of Trading Energy Futures and Options*, Tulsa OK: PennWell.

Evan, W. M. (1990), *Social Structure and Law: Theoretical and Empirical Perspectives*, London, etc.: Sage Publications.

Ewald, F. (1987), 'The Law of Law', in Teubner (ed.), (1987b), 36-50.

Faeke, D. C., W. G. Lesso and R. M. Knapp (1981), 'An Offshore Planning Model Incorporating Risk Analysis', *OTC*, IV, 211-21; no. 4138.

Fairclough, N. (1992), 'Discourse and text: linguistic and intertextual analysis within discourse analysis', *Discourse and Society*, 193-217.

Farrell, S., J. R. McDermott, A. Ramsay and J. Watzke (1996), 'Best Intentions: Lessons Learned on International Partnering and Alliance Contracts' *OTC*, II, 589-99; no. 8091.

Faulds, E. C. (1982), 'Structural Inspection and Maintenance in a North Sea Environment', *OTC*, III, 713-24; no. 4360.

Febbrajo, A. (1992), 'The Autopoietic Approach and its Form', in Teubner and Febbrajo (eds), (1992), 19-33.

Feenberg, A. (1991), *Critical Theory of Technology*, New York and Oxford: Oxford University Press.

Ferguson, M. C. (1990), 'A Comparative Study Using API, RP2A-LRFD', *OTC*, II, 341-51.

Fjeld, S. (1977), 'Reliability of Offshore Structures', *OTC*, IV, 459-72; no. 3027.

Flin, R., K. Mearns *et al.* (1996), *Risk Perception and Safety in the Offshore Oil and Gas Industry*, London: HSE Books.

Foerster, H. von (1984), 'On Constructing a Reality', in *Observing Systems*, Seaside, California: Intersystems Publications.

Foerster, M. C. (1985), 'Leg Strengthening of a North Sea Jacket', *OTC*, I, 347-56; no. 4880.

Forman, B. J. (1991), 'The Application of Regulations for Certificate of Fitness of Jackup Structures in the British Sector of the North Sea', *OTC*, II, 469-82; no. 6610.

Forrest, J. E. and J. D. Reisz (1993), 'Involvement in the Beryl "Alpha" Safety Case', in HSE (1993c), 142-9.

Fox, C. (1993), 'UKOOA Overview of the Voluntary Safety Case Experience', in HSE (1993c), 14-20.

Frankel, P. H. ([1946], 1968), *Essentials of Petroleum: A Key to Oil Economics* and *Essentials Revisited 1968,* London: Frank Cass.

Freudenthal, A. M. and W. S. Gaither (1969), 'Design Criteria for Fixed Offshore Structures' *OTC,* I, 623-46; no. 1058.

Frihagen, A. (1983a), 'Offshore Contracting: Some Legal Issues', in Page (ed.), 1-29.

Frihagen, A. (1983b), *Offshore Tender Bidding: Contracting for Oil and Gas Development in the North Sea - The Offshore Tender Bidding System,* Bergen: Universitetsforlag.

Frug, G. E. (1989), 'Law and Uncertainty: A Comment on Karl-Heinz Ladeur', in Joerges and Trubek (eds), 591-6.

Fusaro, P. (1995), 'Markets Look for New Options after Financial Fiascos', *Petroleum Economist,* November, 16-18.

Garga, P. K. (1999), 'Britannia Topsides: A Safe and Productive North Sea Facility at Lowest Cost', in *OTC,* II, Part 2, 455-64; no. 11015.

Garnaut, R. and A. Clunies Ross (1975), 'Uncertainty, Risk Aversion and the Taxing of Natural Resource Projects', *Economic Journal,* 272-87.

Gentile, Cazzola, Schenato and Torricelli (1983), 'An overview of safety training for onshore and offshore working', in Commission of the EC, 73-93.

Gerwick, B. (1977), 'Verification of Offshore Platform Design and Installation: The Marine Board Panel View', *OTC,* II, 7-14; no. 2807.

Gibson, F. (1992), 'Realism Returns to Loss-hit Markets', *Petroleum Economist,* North Sea Special Report, August/September, 38-9.

Gibson, F. (1993), 'Rates Climb Higher as Capacity Shrinks', *Petroleum Economist,* Special Report, July 16.

Goodrich, P. (1986), *Reading the Law: A Critical Introduction to Legal Method and Techniques,* Oxford: Basil Blackwell.

Gordon, R. M. (1983), 'Operators, contractors and governments: towards peaceful co-existence', in Commission of the EC, 214-26.

Graver, H. P. (1979), 'Normative and Purposive-rational Reasoning: A Case Study of the Norwegain Petroleum Directorate', *Rechtstheorie,* 10, 47-56.

Grecco, M. G. (1987), 'Deepwater Development Economics', *OTC,* III, 519-29.

Green, J. M. (1999), 'Lessons Learned from the Schiehallion FPSO's Design and Construction', in *OTC,* II, Part 2, 59-66, no. 10901.

Green, M. B. (1983), 'Experience with Fatigue Analysis and Inspection Results in the North Sea', *OTC,* II, 103-12; no. 4524.

Gudeman, S. (1986), *Economics as Culture: Models and Metaphors of Livelihood,* London: Routledge and Kegan Paul.

Habermas, J. (1970), 'Towards a Theory of Communicative Competence', in H. Dreitzel (ed.), *Recent Sociology,* New York: Macmillan.

Hall, J. N. (1988), 'Competition in project development planning', in ICE, 13-22.

Hall, J. N. (1991), 'Safety Survey Using Piper Alpha Disaster Evidence', *OTC,* II, 651-61; no. 6630.

Hallam, M. G. and N. J. Heaf (1978), 'Dynamic and Fatigue Analysis of Murchison Tower Structure', *OTC,* II, 1001-1010; no. 3163.

Hamilton, A. (1978), *North Sea Impact: Offshore Oil and the British Economy,* London: International Institute for Economic Research.

Harland, R. (1993), *Beyond Superstructuralism,* London and New York: Routledge.

Harré, R. (1986), *Varieties of Realism: A Rationale for the Natural Sciences,* Oxford: Basil Blackwell.

Harris, D. R. and C. G. Veljanovski (1986), 'The Use of Economics to Elucidate Legal Concepts: The Law of Contract', in Daintith and Teubner (eds), 109-20.

Harrison, P. I. (1999), 'Achieving Performance Enhancement Where it Counts; Management Strategies for Exploiting Best Human Factors Practices in Design and Operations Offshore', in *OTC,* II, Part 1, 665-71; no. 10879.

Harvie, C. (1995), *Fool's Gold: The Story of North Sea Oil,* Harmondsworth: Penguin.

Haun, O., H. R. Hansen, J. Nylund and O. A. Hafnor (1979), 'Safety Aspects Related to Hydrocarbon Production and Processing Offshore Plants' *OTC,* IV, 2535-46; no. 3650.

Hausman, D. M. (1984), 'Introduction' in Hausman (ed.), *The Philosophy of Economics: An Anthology,* Cambridge: Cambridge University Press 1-50.

Hawkins, K. (1983), *Environment and Enforcement: Regulation and the Social Definition of Pollution,* Oxford: Clarendon Press.

Hay, J. T. C., H. D. Hay and G. F. Debnam (1982), 'Environmental Protection in the Beatrice Field Development', *OTC,* IV, 481-92; no. 4419.

Hayllar, R. F. and R. T. Pleasance (1977), *UK Taxation of Offshore Oil and Gas,* London: Butterworths.

Heaf, N. J. (1988), 'Cost effective structures for the North Sea', in ICE, 41-52.

Heller, T. (1987), 'Accounting for Law', in Teubner (ed.), (1987b), 283-311.

Henderson, G., P. D. Wyatt and N. G. Bradshaw (1986), 'The Tern Platform: A New Generation Steel Jacket for the Northern North Sea', *OTC,* III, 313-20; no. 5259.

Henning, J. A. and H. M. Mann (1981), 'An Appraisal of Model Building in Industrial Organisation', *Research in Law and Economics,* Vol. 3, 1-14.

Heyne, P. (1988), 'The Foundations of Law and Economics: Can the Blind Lead the Blind?', *Research in Law and Economics,* Vol. 11, 53-71.

Holloway, E. C. (1983), 'Operators Contracting Selection Procedures and Commercial Prequalification of Contracts', in Page (ed.), 47-59.

Holmes, R. (1980), 'The Fatigue Behaviour of Welded Joints Under North Sea Environmental and Random Loading Conditions', *OTC,* I, 219-30; no. 3700.

Holter, E. and K. Hagen (1976), 'Integrated and Semi-integrated Deck Concepts for Production Platforms with Emphasis on Capital Cost Optimization', *OTC*, III, 789-806; no. 2686.

Horgan, J. (1995), 'From Complexity to Perplexity', *Scientific American*, June 74-79.

Horsnell, M. R. and F. E. Toolan (1996), 'Risk of Foundation Failure of Offshore Jacket Piles', *OTC*, I, 381-92; no. 7997.

Horsnell, P. and R. Mabro (1993), *Oil Markets and Prices: The Brent Market and the Formation of World Oil Prices*, Oxford: Oxford University Press for the Oxford Institute for Energy Studies.

Houseman, C. T. (1970), 'Role of the Commercial Bank in Financing Offshore Mineral Exploitation', *OTC*, 273-7; no. 1255.

Howe, R. J. (1986), 'Evolution of Offshore Drilling and Production Technology', *OTC*, IV, 593-603; no. 5354.

HSE (1989), *Quantified Risk Assessment: Its input to decision making*, London: HMSO.

HSE (1992a), *A Guide to the Offshore Installations (Safety Case), Regulations 1992* London: HMSO.

HSE (1992b), *The Tolerability of Risk From Nuclear Power Stations* (revised edition: first published 1988), London: HMSO.

HSE (1993a), *Offshore Safety Case Assessment*, London: HSE.

HSE (1993b), *Successful Health and Safety Management* (fourth impression with revisions), London: HMSO.

HSE (1993c), *Offshore Safety Cases Conference: Conference Proceedings*, Aberdeen Conference Centre, 1-2 April, 1993, organised by the Health and Safety Executive.

HSE (1995), *An Interim Evaluation of the Offshore Installations (Safety Case), Regulations 1992*, London: HMSO.

HSE (1996), *Use of Risk Assessment Within Government Departments*, London: HMSO.

HSE (1998), *Risk Assessment and Risk Management: Improving policy and practice within government departments*, Sudbury: HSE Books.

Huang, P. and H.-M. Wu (1994), 'More Order Without More Law: A Theory of Social Norms and Organizational Cultures', *Journal of Law, Economics and Organization*, 390-406.

Hughes, H. (1994), 'The Operator's Response', in Waterfront (1994), Paper 3.

Hutter, B. M. (1988), *The Reasonable Arm of the Law? The Law Enforcement Procedures of Environmental Health Officers*, Oxford: OUP.

Hutter, M. and G. Teubner (1994), 'The Fat Plunder of Society: Homo Iuridicus and homo oeconomicus as communicative fictions', [Typescript].

IBA (1984), *International Energy Law*, Proceedings of the Sixth Energy Law Seminar organised by the International Bar Association's Section on Energy and Natural Resources Law - Houston, Texas - February 1984, London: IBA.

IBC (1993), *Offshore Safety Cases: The Living Documents - Where next?*, Conference Documentation; 1 and 2 December 1993, London: IBC Technical Services Ltd.

ICE (1988), *Cost Reduction in Offshore Engineering* - Proceedings of the conference organised by the Offshore Engineering Society of the Institution of Civil Engineers and held in London on 10-11 February 1988, London: Thomas Telford.

ILO (1993), *Safety and related issues pertaining to work on offshore petroleum installations*, Report of Tripartite Meeting, Geneva 1993, Geneva: International Labour Office.

Ingram, G. E. and P. A. Dee (1973), 'Reliability Engineering Applied to Offshore Petroleum Production Systems', *OTC*, I, 303-12; no. 1756.

Institution of Chemical Engineers (1990), *Piper Alpha - Lessons for Life-cycle Safety Management: A two-day symposium organised by the Institution of Chemical Engineers*, London: Hemisphere Publishing Corporation.

International Energy Authority (1994), *Energy Prices and Taxes 1994* (4th Quarter), Paris: OECD.

in 't Veld, R. J. *et al.* (eds.), (1991), *Autopoiesis and Configuration Theory: New Approaches to Societal Steering*, Dordrecht: Kluwer.

Jahnke, U. H. and P. G. Webb (1983), 'A Bankers' View of Project Funding', *Petroleum Economist*, 383-6.

James, P. (1992), 'Reforming British Health and Safety Law: a framework for discussion', *Industrial Law Journal*, 83-105.

Jasanoff, S. (1990), *The Fifth Branch: Science Advisers as Policymakers*, Cambridge, Mass. and London: Harvard University Press.

Jenkins, G. (1989), *Oil Economists' Handbook* (2 Vols.), (5th ed.), London: Elsevier Applied Science.

Jessop, B. (1992), 'The Economy, the State and the Law: Theories of Relative Autonomy and Autopoietic Closure', in Teubner and Febbrajo (eds), (1992), 187-263.

Joerges, C. (1993), 'Product Safety in the European Community: Market Regulation, Social Regulation and Legal Structures', in Snyder (ed.), 321-38.

Joerges, C. and D. M. Trubek (eds.), (1989), *Critical Legal Thought: An American-German Debate*, Nomos Verlagsgesellschaft, Baden-Baden.

Johnson, C. (1979), *North Sea Energy Wealth 1965-85: Oil and Gas in the British and Norwegian Sectors* (2 Volumes), London: The Financial Times Limited.

Jones, A. (1981), *Oil: The Missed Opportunity*, London: André Deutsch.

Jones, D. (1989), 'Energy Policy: The New Uncertainties', in Pearson (ed.), (1989), 1-10.

Jones, M. and L. Brooks (1994), 'Addressing Organisational Context in Requirements Analysis Using Cognitive Mapping', *University of Cambridge, Research Papers in Management Studies*, 1993-1994 No. 17.

Jones, S. (1993), 'Continuous Improvement through Effective Management Systems', in IBC (1993), Day 2, Paper 1.

Jones, W. (1977), 'Is there a conflict of interest?', *Petroleum Economist,* 183-186.

Joosten, M. W. and G. C. Robinson (1983), 'Development of a Specification for Christmas Tree and Wellhead Components', *OTC,* I, 39-44; no. 4447.

Kasperson, R. E. (1977), 'Societal Management of Technological Hazards', in Kates (ed.), (1977), 49-80.

Kates, R. W. (1977), 'Summary Report', in Kates (ed.), (1977), 1-48.

Kates, R. W. (ed.), (1977), *Managing Technological Hazard: Research Needs and Opportunities*, Program on Technology, Environment and Man, Monograph #25, Institute of Behavioral Science: University of Colorado.

Kaufman, B. E. (1994), *The Economics of Labor Markets* (4th ed.), Fort Worth, etc.: Dryden Press.

Kellas, G. and S. Parish (1997), 'Examining Fiscal Terms for the New Frontiers', *Petroleum Economist,* April, 21-3.

Kelly, G. A. (1955), *The Psychology of Personal Constructs: A Theory of Personality,* New York: Norton.

Kemp, A. G. (1986), 'Scope for Tax Changes', *Petroleum Economist,* 289-290.

Kemp, A. G. and D. R. Cohen (1981), 'Impact of Oil Production Tax', *Petroleum Economist,* 16-19.

Kemp, A. G. and D. R. Cohen (1982), 'North Sea Economics Revised', *Petroleum Economist,* 133-7.

Kemp, A. G. and G. Kellas (1988), 'Impact of Budget Tax Changes', *Petroleum Economist,* 156-7.

Kemp, A. G. and D. Rose (1981), 'Budget Changes in Oil Taxation', *Petroleum Economist,* 147-8.

Kemp, A. G. and D. Rose (1983a), 'Dangers of Relying on Oil Revenues', *Petroleum Economist,* 81-3.

Kemp, A. G. and D. Rose (1983b), 'Tax Changes Give New Incentives', *Petroleum Economist,* 163-5.

Kemp, A. G. and D. Rose (1984), 'Tax Changes in 1984 Budget', *Petroleum Economist,* 148-50.

Kenley, R. M. (1982), 'Measurement of Fatigue Performance on Forties Bravo', *OTC,* IV, 289-302; no. 4402.

Kennedy, B. (1993), 'ALARP in Practice - An Industry View', in HSE (1993c), 92-106.

Kickert, W. J. M. (1991), 'Applicability of Autopoiesis to Administration Science', in in 't Veld *et al.* (eds), 193-205.

Kidder, R. L. (1983), *Connecting Law and Society: An Introduction to Research and Theory,* New Jersey: Prentice-Hall Inc.

King, J. (1993), 'SMS Interfaces', in HSE (1993c), 212-6.

King, M. (1993), 'The 'Truth' About Autopoiesis', *Journal of Law and Society,* Volume 20, Number 2, 218-36.

King, M. and C. Piper (1990), *How the Law Thinks about Children,* Aldershot: Gower.

King, M. and A. Schütz (1994), 'The Ambitious Modesty of Niklas Luhmann', *Journal of Law and Society,* Volume 21, Number 3, 261-87.

Kinnersley, R. (1973), *The Hazards of Work: How to Fight Them,* London: Pluto Press.

Kinsella, K. (1994), 'The Application of QRA for Fixed Offshore Installations in the UK', A position paper prepared for the European Safety and Reliablity Association QRA Work Group.

Kitchen, J. (1977), *Labour Law and Off-shore Oil,* London: Croom Helm.

Kloss, D. M. (1998), *Occupational Health Law* (third edition), Oxford: Blackwell Science.

Koenig, D. W. (1993), 'The Corporate Safety Culture: Its Workings and Its Importance', in *OTC,* I, 145-52; no. 7096.

Koppen, I. J. (1991), 'Environmental mediation: an example of applied autopoiesis?', in in 't Veld *et al.* (eds), 143-50.

Koppenjan, J. F. M. and J. A. M. Hufen (1991), 'Autopoiesis, learning and governmental steering', in in 't Veld *et al.* (eds), 171-81.

Krapels, E. N. (1983), 'Growing Influence of Oil Stocks', *Petroleum Economist,* 211-15.

Kriger, G., E. Piermattei, J. D. White and R. W. King (1983), 'Risk Analysis Applied to Offshore Platforms During the Unpiled Installation Phase', *OTC,* I, 9-18; no. 4442.

Kumar, R. and G. L. Michael (1985), 'Instrument Control Systems on Brae "A" Platform', *OTC,* IV, 177-85; no. 5040.

Ladeur, K.-H. (1987), 'Perspectives on a Post-Modern Theory of Law: A Critique of Niklas Luhmann, "The Unity of the Legal System"', in Teubner (ed.), (1987b), 242-82.

Ladeur, K.-H. (1989), 'From Universalistic Law to the Law of Uncertainty: On the Decay of the Legal Order's "Totalizing Teleology" as Treated in the Methodological Discussion and its Critique from the Left', in Joerges and Trubek (eds), 567-90.

Lalani, M. and E. P. Shuttleworth (1990), 'The Ultimate Limit State of Offshore Platforms using Reserve and Residual Strength Principles', *OTC,* II, 353-64; no. 6309.

Latour B. (1988), 'The Politics of Explanation: an Alternative', in Woolgar (ed.), (1988), 155-74.

Lawson, T. (1997), *Economics and Reality,* London and New York: Routledge.

Lee, C. (1995), 'Engineers Have Their Say in Risk Assessment', *Petroleum Economist,* August 8-9.

Lee, G. C. (1977), 'Verification of Platform Design and Installation - A Contractor's View', *OTC,* II, 15-19; no. 2808.

Leiser, H. (1993a), 'ALARP Philosophy and the Safety Case Regulations', in HSE (1993c), 78-83.

Leiser, H. (1993b), 'Involving the Workforce', in HSE (1993c), 130-3.

Lempert, R. (1987), 'The Autonomy of Law: Two Visions Compared', in Teubner (ed.), (1987b), 152-90.

Lerche, I. and J. A. MacKay (1999), *Economic Risk in Hydrocarbon Exploration*, San Diego, etc.: Academic Press.

Nesje, J. D., R. Aggarwal, C. Petrauskas, J. E. Vinnem, G. L. Keolanui, J. Hoffman and R. McDonnell (1999), 'Risk Assessment Technology and its Application to Tanker Based Floating Production Storage and Offloading (FPSO), Systems', in *OTC*, II, Part 2, 347-57; no. 10998.

Levy, G.-P. (1984), 'The Relationship between Oil Companies and Consumer State Governments in Europe, 1973-1982', 19, *Journal of Energy and Natural Resources Law*, 9-29.

Lévy-Bruhl, H. (1964), *La preuve judiciaire: Étude de sociologie juridique*, Paris: Rivière.

Lloyd, J. R. and D. I. Karsan (1988), 'Development of a Reliability-Based Alternative to API, RP2A', *OTC*, IV, 593-600; no. 5882.

Lovegrove, M. (1983), *Lovegrove's Guide to Britain's North Sea Oil and Gas* (2nd Ed.), Cambridge: Energy Publications.

Lowe, E. A. and A. J. Odone (1980), 'The History of the Piper-Claymore-Flotta Pipeline System', *OTC*, II, 415-30; no. 3785.

Lucas, H. Jr. (1976), 'The State v Oil Industry Expansion', *Petroleum Economist*, 346-348.

Luhmann, N. (1985), *A Sociological Theory of Law*, London, etc.: Routledge and Kegan Paul.

Luhmann, N. (1986a), 'The Individuality of the Individual', in T. C. Heller, M. Sosna and D. E Wellbery (eds.), *Reconstructing Individualism: Autonomy, Individuality, and the Self in Western Thought*, Stanford, Cal.: Stanford University Press, 313-25.

Luhmann, N. (1986b), 'The Autopoiesis of Social Systems', in F. Geyer and J. van der Zouwen (eds.), *Sociocybernetic paradoxes: observation, control and evolution of self-steering systems*, London-Beverly Hills: Sage 172-92.

Luhmann, N. (1993), *Risk: A Sociological Theory*, Berlin, New York: Walter de Gruyter.

Luhmann, N. (1995), *Social Systems*, Stanford, Cal.: Stanford University Press.

Luhmann, N. (1997), 'Limits of Steering', *Theory, Culture and Society*, Vol. 14(1), 41-57.

Lumsden, A. (1978), 'North Sea tests new technology', *Petroleum Economist*, 142-4.

Luo, Y. and R. V. Ahilan (1991), 'Mooring Safety Assessment Using Reliability Techniques', in *OTC*, II, 783-92; no. 6783.

Mabro, R. (ed.), (1988), *The 1986 Oil Price Crisis: Economic Effects and Policy Responses*, Oxford: OUP.

MacKay, D. I. and G. A. Mackay (1975), *The Political Economy of North Sea Oil*, London: Martin Robertson.

Mackay, W. B. (1974), 'North Sea Offshore Cathodic Protection', *OTC*, I, 245-51; no. 1957.

Majone, G. (1989), *Evidence, Argument and Persuasion in the Policy Process*, New Haven and London: Yale University Press.

Majone, G. (1996), 'The future of regulation in Europe', in Majone (ed.), 265-83.

Majone, G. (ed.), (1996), *Regulating Europe*, London and New York: Routledge.

Mansfield, S. (1990), 'Hedging Energy Risk', *Petroleum Economist*, August 15-17.

Marin, B. (1992), 'Contracting Without Contracts: Economic Policy Concertation by Autopoietic Regimes Beyond Law?', in Teubner and Febbrajo (eds.), 295-349.

Mason, C. M. (ed.), (1979), *The Effective Management of Resources: The International Politics of the North Sea*, London: Frances Pinter - New York; Nichols Publishing Co.

Massie, W. V. and A. H. E. Buijs (1991), 'Analysis of Platform Collision Chances', *OTC*, II, 757-63; no. 6646.

McCloskey, D. (1985), *The Rhetoric of Economics*, Madison, Wisconsin: Harvester Press.

McDonald, R. (1993), 'New Regulations and Workforce Involvement', Paper presented on behalf of OILC at the Human Factors in Emergency Response Offshore Conference, Aberdeen 29-30 September 1993.

McDonnell, T. E. and J. W. Hasz (1985), 'Hutton TLP Integrated Deck', *OTC*, II, 145-58; no. 4912.

McIntyre, H. and H. McManus (1991), 'Installation of Subsea Isolation Valves: A Review of Recent Operations in the North Sea', *OTC*, II, 551-7; no. 6617.

McIntyre, J. E. (1973), 'The Development of Rational Standards for the Offshore Drilling Industry', *OTC*, II, 529-37; no. 1880.

McKay, R. R. (1970), 'Offshore Property Insurance', *OTC*, I, 663-6; no. 1213.

McKenzie, R. B. (1983), *The Limits of Economic Science: Essays on Methodology*, Boston, etc.; Kluwer-Nijhoff Publishing.

Merkey, R. K. (1978), 'The Development of Petroleum Financing', in White (ed.), 29-38.

Miller, G. E. (1990), 'The Omission of Human Engineering in the Design of Offshore Equipment and Facilities: How Come?', *OTC*, IV, 521-6; no. 6481.

Miller, K. (1991), 'Piper Alpha and the Cullen Report', *Industrial Law Journal*, 176-87.

Miller, R. S. (1974), 'The Occupational Safety and Health Act of 1970 and the Law of Torts', *Law and Contemporary Problems*, Vol. 38, No. 4, 612-40.

Miller, T. M. and D. K. Dolan, M. L. Eskijian and M. J. K. Craig (1991), 'Requalification of an Older California Platform: API, and Risk-Based Approaches', *OTC*, III, 19-32; no. 6648.

Ministry of Power (1967), *Report of the Inquiry into the Causes of the Accident to the Drilling Rig Sea Gem* (Cmnd. 3409), London: HMSO.

Molloy, J. (1993), 'Workforce Involvement in Safety Case Development', in IBC (1993), Day 1, Paper 5.

Moore, W. H. and R. G. Bea (1993), 'Human and Organisational Error in Operations of Marine Systems: Occidental Piper Alpha and High-Pressure Gas Systems on Offshore Platforms', *OTC*, I, 383-96; no. 7121.

Morey, R. S. (1974), 'Mandatory Occupational Safety and Health Standards - Some Legal Problems', *Law and Contemporary Problems*, Vol. 38, No. 4, 584-611.

Morgan, J. (1993), 'SMS Interfaces - An Operator's View', in HSE (1993c), 168-86.

Morgan, N. (1992), 'Managing to Avoid Risk', *Petroleum Economist*, March 14-15.

Moses, F. and B. Stahl (1978), 'Reliability Analysis Format for Offshore Structures', *OTC*, I, 29-38; no. 3046.

Murphy, W. T. (1994), 'Systems of Systems: Some Issues in the Relationship between Law and Autopoiesis', *Law and Critique*, Vol. V, no. 2, 241-64.

Nagel, S. and M. Neef (1978), 'Causal Analysis and the Legal Process', *Research in Law and Sociology*, Vol. 1, 201-27.

Nahamowitz, P. (1992), 'Difficulties with Economic Law: Definitional and Material Problems of an Emerging Legal Discipline', in Teubner and Febbrajo, (eds), 515-77.

Nehring, R. D. (1985), 'Prospects for Offshore Petroleum Resources', *OTC*, I, 507-8, no. 4875.

Nelken, D. (1987), 'Changing Paradigms in the Sociology of Law', in Teubner (ed.), (1987b), 191-216.

Nelken, D. (1990), *The Truth about Law's Truth*, EUI, Florence Working Paper LAW No. 90/1.

Nelken, D. (ed.), (1996), *Law as Communication*, Aldershot, Brookfield USA, Singapore, Sydney: Dartmouth.

Niering, F. E. Jr. (1983), 'Oil Futures Trading', *Petroleum Economist*, 223-227.

Nisbet, R. (1975), *Twilight of Authority*, New York: OUP.

Noerager, J. A., M. E. Danz-Reece and W. A. Pennycook (1999), 'HFAST - A Tool to Assess Human Error Potential in Operations', in *OTC*, I, 521-7; no. 10881.

Nolte, K. G. (1978), 'The Effect of Uncertainty in Wave Force Coefficients for Offshore Structures', *OTC*, I, 177-85; no. 3066.

Nonet, P. and P. Selznick (1978), *Law and Society in Transition: Towards Responsive Law*, New York, etc.: Harper and Row.

Noreng, Ø. (1980), *The Oil Industry and Government Strategy in the North Sea*, London: Croom Helm for the International Research Center for Energy and Economic Development, Boulder, Colorado.

Odell, P. R. (1975), 'The Economic Background to North Sea Oil and Gas Development', in Saeter and Smart (eds.), 51-80.

Odell, P. R. (1983), 'An Alternative View of the Outlook for the International Oil Market', *Petroleum Economist*, 392-4.

Odell, P. and K. E. Rosing (assisted by Hester Vogelaar), (1976), *Optimal Development of the North Sea's Oilfields: A Study in Divergent Government and Company Interests and their Reconciliation*, London: Kogan Page.

Odell, P. and K. E. Rosing (1977), 'Conflict of interest in the UK North Sea?', *Petroleum Economist*, 226-8.

OECD (1994), *Probabilistic Accident Consequence Assessment Codes: Second International Comparison: Overview Report*, Paris: OECD.

O'Ferrall, P. (1999), 'The Business of Safety', *Petroleum Review*, January, 11-12.

Ogus, A. I. (1994), *Regulation: Legal Form and Economic Theory*, Oxford: Clarendon Press.

Oi, W. Y. (1974), 'On the Economics of Industrial Safety', *Law and Contemporary Problems*, Vol. 38, No. 4, 669-99.

OILC (1991), *Striking Out: New directions for offshore workers and their unions*, Aberdeen: Offshore Information Centre.

O'Riordan, T. (1985), 'Approaches to Regulation', in Otway and Peltu (eds), 20-39.

Orts, E. W. (1995), 'Reflexive Environmental Law', *Northwestern University Law Review*, 901-1010.

Ost, F. (1987), 'Between Order and Disorder: The Game of Law', in Teubner, G. (ed.), (1987b), 70-96.

Otway, H. and M. Peltu (eds.), (1985), *Regulating Industrial Risks*, London: Butterworths.

Owen, D. and G. Raeburn (1991), 'Developing a Safety, Occupational Health, and Environmental (SOHE) Program as Part of a Total Quality Program' *OTC*, I, 33-7; no. 6502.

Page, A. (ed.), (1983), *Offshore Contracting in the North Sea*, Dundee: University of Dundee, Centre for Petroleum and Mineral Law Studies.

Page, J. A. and P. N. Munsing (1974), 'Occupational Health and the Federal Government: The Wages are Still Bitter', *Law and Contemporary Problems*, Vol. 38, No. 4, 651-68.

Pape, R. P. (1993), 'ALARP, QRA and Temporary Refuges', in HSE (1993c), 108-20.

Park, J. D. (1979), 'Oil and Gas: Governments and Companies', in Mason (ed.), (1979), 71-99.

Pascoe, K. J., A. G. Lusted, P. G. F. Sliggers and W. Vissers (1987), 'Self-Elevating Mobile Offshore Drilling Units: An Operator's Viewpoint', *OTC*, I, 47-53; no. 5359.

Passemard, P. R. (1988), 'Cost effective quality appraisal', in ICE, 107-14.

Paterson, J. (1995), 'Who is Zenon Bankowski talking to? The Person in the Sight of Autopoiesis', *Ratio Juris*, Volume 8, Number 2, 212-29; also in Nelken (ed.), (1996), 81-104.

Paterson, J. and G. Teubner (1998), 'Changing Maps: Empirical Legal Autopoiesis', *Social and Legal Studies*, 7(4), 451-86.

Patterson, G. R. (1983), 'Safety and Health Offshore: A Survey of North Sea Legislation', in Commission of the EC, 28-55.

Pavia, A. P., P. K. Yin and P. R. Corder (1977), 'Effect of Design, Fabrication and Installation on the Structural Reliability of Offshore Platforms', *OTC*, IV, 451-8.

Pearce, D. (1976), 'The Limits of Cost-Benefit Analysis as a Guide to Environmental Policy', *KYKLOS*, vol. 29, 97-112.

Pearson, P. (ed.), (1989), *Energy Policies in an Uncertain World*, London: Macmillan.

Perham, A. J. (1993), 'Implementing Cost-effective Safety: With Goal Setting Regulation Helping (or Hindering?) the Offshore Workforce', in IBC (1993), Day 1, Paper 3.

Perissich, R. (1994), 'Risk Assessment and Community Legislation', [Typescript].

Perrow, C. (1984), *Normal Accidents: Living with High-Risk Technologies*, New York: Basic Books, Inc.

Peters, E. J. (1985), 'Trends in Passive Fire Protection Favor the Use of Ceramic Fibre Systems', *OTC*, IV, 557-60; no. 5080.

Peterson, W. T., J. T. Sinnot, L. R. Whalen and R. F. Sammis (1981), 'Availability and Pricing of Insurance for Offshore Operations' *OTC*, IV, 263-71; no. 4142.

Pilipovic, D. (1997), *Energy Risk: Valuing and Managing Energy Derivatives*, New York, etc.: McGraw-Hill.

Planeix, J-M, J. Ciolina, J. Deleuil and J. Y. Heas (1979), 'Are Offshore Structures Over-designed? Relative Influence of Environmental Data', *OTC*, I, 269-80; no. 3387.

Pokol, B. (1990), 'Law as a System of Professional Institutions', *Rechtstheorie*, 21, 335-51.

Pomfret, B. (1998), 'Offshore Facilities Audit Results', in *OTC*, I, 249-57; no. 8705.

Popper, K. (1972), *The Logic of Scientific Discovery* (6th Impression - Revised), London: Hutchison.

Posner, R. (1986), *Economic Analysis of Law*, Boston and Toronto: Little Brown and Co.

Potter, N. (1998), 'Driving Well Costs Down', *Petroleum Review*, December, 11-13.

Pound, R. (1953), *An Introduction to the Philosophy of Law* (Revised Edition), New Haven and London: Yale University Press.

Pound, R. (1960), *Law Finding through Experience and Reason,* Athens, Georgia: University of Georgia Press.

Powell, T. (1993), 'HSE Experience of Voluntary Safety Cases', in HSE (1993c), 26-50.

Prasthofer, P. H. (1998), 'Decommissioning Technology Challenges', in *OTC,* III, 379-86.

Praught, D. W. (1983), 'Safety Features of Offshore Structures, a Designer's Viewpoint', in Commission of the EC, 197-213.

Praught, M. W., D. S. Hammett, J. E. Hampton and C. N. Springett (1985), 'Industry Action on Stability of Mobile Offshore Drilling Units', *OTC,* III, 251-62; no. 4986.

Priest, W. C. (1988), *Risks, Concerns and Social Legislation*, Boulder, Colorado: Westview Press.

Prosser, T. (1999), 'Theorising Utility Regulation', *Modern Law Review,* 62:2, 196-217.

Quinlan, M. (1978), 'One Million Barrels Daily', *Petroleum Economist,* 337-9.

Quinlan, M. (1980), 'The Danger of Complacency', *Petroleum Economist,* 16-18.

Quinlan, M. (1981), 'The Need for New Oil', *Petroleum Economist,* 247-50.

Quinlan, M. (1982a), 'New Tax for Old?', *Petroleum Economist.* 103-4.

Quinlan, M. (1982b), 'Development slowing down', *Petroleum Economist,* 232-4.

Quinlan, M. (1982c), 'Britoil Sale to Go Ahead', *Petroleum Economist,* 449-50.

Quinlan, M. (1986), 'Companies Press for Urgent Action', *Petroleum Economist,* 205.

Quinlan, M. (1989), 'Major Loss of Production Capacity', *Petroleum Economist,* 175-6.

Quinlan, M. (1990), 'Raising the Drilling Stakes', *Petroleum Economist,* 178-9.

Quinlan, M. (1992), 'Oil and Gas Reserves Up', *Petroleum Economist,* June, 15-20.

Quinlan, M. (1993a), 'All's Well - Apart from the Oil Price', *Petroleum Economist,* April, 4.

Quinlan, M. (1993b), 'Less Exploration but More Development', *Petroleum Economist,* July, 18-19.

Quinlan, M. (1994), 'Oil Price Stability, 1990s Style', *Petroleum Economist,* May, 3.

Radford, T. S. (1988), 'Hidden benefits of cost reduction', in ICE, 23-8.

Ramberg, S. E. and J. M. Niedzwecki (1979), 'Some Uncertainties and Errors in Wave Force Computations', *OTC,* III, 2091-2101 no. 3597.

Rappaport, D. (1995), 'The Present and the Futures', *Petroleum Economist,* April, 27.

Ravetz, J. R. (1990), *The Merger of Knowledge with Power: Essays in Critical Science,* London and New York: Mansell Publishing Company.

Reader, C. (1995), 'New Look at the Fate of Brent Spar', *Petroleum Review*, 500-1.

Redd, E. (1993), 'Voluntary Safety Case Experience', in HSE (1993c), 22-4.

Redmond, T. C. (1990), 'Piper Alpha - Cost of the Lessons', in Institution of Chemical Engineers (1990), 113-9.

Regg, James B. (1999), 'Floating Production, Storage, and Offloading Systems in the Gulf of Mexico OCS: A Regulatory Perspective', in *OTC*, I, 11-15; no. 10701.

Regg, J., A. Verret, M. A. Stair and W. Hauser (1996), 'The Future of Regulations for the Deepwater Gulf of Mexico', *OTC*, IV, 829-34; no. 8243.

Rehbinder, E. (1992), 'Reflexive Law and Practice: The Corporate Officer for Environmental Protection as an Example', in Teubner and Febbrajo (eds), 579-608.

Renn, O. (1992), 'Concepts of Risk: A Classification', in Sheldon Krimsky and Dominic Golding (eds), *Social Theories of Risk*, Westport, Connecticut and London: Praeger, 53-79.

Rhodes, G. (1981), *Inspectorates in British Government: Law Enforcement and Standards of Efficiency*, London: George Allen and Unwin.

Richardson, G., A. Ogus and P. Burrows (1982), *Policing Pollution: A Study of Regulation and Enforcement*, Oxford: Clarendon.

Rimell, J. (1975), *Oil and Gas in Offshore Areas of NW Europe*, Paris: Eurofinance.

Robens, Lord (1972), *Safety and Health at Work; Report of the Robens Committee*, (Cmnd. 5034), London: HMSO.

Robinson, C. and J. Morgan (1976), 'Comparison of Tax Systems', *Petroleum Economist*, 1976, 170.

Robinson, C. and C. Rowland (1978), 'Marginal Effect of PRT Changes', *Petroleum Economist*, 501.

Robinson, D. (1991a), 'Futures and Options: Ups and Downs of the Exchanges', *Petroleum Economist*, November, 18-21.

Robinson, D. (1991b), 'Futures and Options: Energy Derivatives Catch On', *Petroleum Economist*, November, 21-3.

Robinson, G. H. (1986), *Offshore Oil Production: Reducing the Costs*, London: Financial Times Business Information Ltd.

Robinson, R. J. (1975), 'Regulations and their Impact on Permanent Offshore Structures', *OTC*, III, 761; no. 2415.

Rodrigues, P. E. L. B., W. K. Wong and J. H. Rogerson (1980), 'Weld Defect Distributions in Offshore Platforms and the Relevance to Reliability', *OTC*, I, 151-6; no. 3693.

Roe, M. J. (1996), 'Chaos and Evolution in Law and Economics', *Harvard Law Review*, 641-68.

Roeber, J. (1993), *The Evolution of Oil Markets: Trading Instruments and their Role in Price Formation*, London: The Royal Institute of International Affairs.

Rose-Ackerman, S. (1992), *Rethinking the Progressive Agenda: The Reform of the American Regulatory State*, New York: Free Press.

Rosenfield, I. (1992), *The Strange, Familiar and Forgotten: An Anatomy of Consciousness*, London: Picador.

Rossbach, S. (1993), *The Author's Care of Himself: On Friedrich Neitzsche, Michel Foucault and Niklas Luhmann*, EUI, Florence, Working Paper, SPS No. 93/10.

Rottleuthner, H. (1989), 'The Limits of Law - The Myth of a Regulatory Crisis', *International Journal of the Sociology of Law*, 17, 273-85.

Rowe, W. D. (1992), 'Risk Analysis: A Tool for Policy Decisions', in Waterstone (ed.), 17-31.

Roxburgh, J. (1983), 'Basic Safety Training for Personnel', in Commission of the EC, 97-109.

Rule, D. D. and R. R. Huddleston (1988), 'Facilities Design in the UKCS: Setting Weight Objectives by Multi-Variant Analysis of Past Design', *OTC*, III, 549-54; no. 5806.

Rundt, R. J. and J. C. Luppens (1981), 'Simultaneous Activities Offshore Norway: A Review of Practices and Results', *OTC*, I, 475-84; no. 4006.

Rye, H., R. C. Byrd and A. Tørum (1974), 'Sharply Peaked Wave Energy Spectrum in the North Sea', *OTC*, II, 739-48; no. 2017.

Saeter, M. and I. Smart (eds.), (1975), *The Political Implications of North Sea Oil and Gas*, Oslo: Universitetsforlaget - Guildford: IPC Science and Technology Press Ltd.

Salama, M. M., P. C. Warwick and S. T. McClaury (1985), 'Fabrication of Hutton TLP', *OTC*, I, 221-8; no. 4865.

Salter, J. (1994), 'The Legal Position of the New Regime', in Waterfront (1994), Paper 7.

Salter, M. (1993), 'Safety Management Systems; Interface between Contractors and Operators: The Contractor's View (2),' in HSE (1993c), 208-10.

Sanderson, T. J. O. (1988), 'Cost-cutting in the oil industry', in ICE 1-12.

Santos, B. de S. (1987), 'Law: A Map of Misreading. Toward a Postmodern Conception of Law', *Journal of Law and Society*, 279-302.

Sas, B. (1989a), 'Legal Aspects of Risk Management and Forward Oil Trading: The "Forward" Oil Markets and their Contracts', *Journal of Energy and Natural Resources Law*, 1-33.

Sas, B. (1989b), 'Legal Aspects of Risk Management and Forward Oil Trading: The US and UK Regulatory Regimes', *Journal of Energy and Natural Resources Law*, 142-60.

Sas, B. (1992), 'Legal Aspects of Risk Management in Energy Markets', *Petroleum Economist, Energy Law Supplement*, July, 50-9.

Saunders, G. C. (1983), 'Problems Associated with the Specification of Castings for Offshore Application', *OTC*, I, 45-56; no. 4448.

Savelsberg, J. J. (1987), 'The Making of Criminal Law Norms in Welfare States: Economic Crime in West Germany', *Law and Society Review,* Volume 21, No. 4, 529-61.

Schepel, H. (1995), 'Standard-Setting in the Internal Market - A Brief Overview', [Typescript].

Schüeller, G. I, and H. S. Choi (1977), 'Offshore Platform Risk Based on a Reliability Function Model', *OTC,* IV, 473-82; no. 3028.

Sefton, A. (1993), 'Inspection Programmes and the Safety Case', in HSE (1993c), 188-97.

Shapiro, M. J. (1981), *Language and Political Understanding: The Politics of Discursive Practices,* New Haven and London: Yale University Press.

Sharp, D. (1998), 'Risks in New Relationships', *Petroleum Economist,* August, 23-24.

Shuttleworth, F. P. and C. J. Billington (1989), 'A New Approach to Designing Repair Clamps for Offshore Structures', *OTC,* III, 317-30; no. 6076.

Simitis, S. (1987), 'Juridification of Labor Relations', in Teubner (ed.), (1987a), 113-61.

Simon, D. (1988), 'Coping With Low Oil Prices', in Mabro (ed.), (1988), 49-60.

Simon, H. A. (1976), 'From Substantive to Procedural Rationality', in S. J. Latsis (ed.), *Method and Appraisal in Economics,* Cambridge: Cambridge University Press, 129-48.

Simon, H. A. (1978), 'Rationality as Process and as Product of Thought', *American Economic Review,* vol. 68, 1-16.

Skeet, I. (ed.), (1989), *Paul Frankel: Common Carrier of Common Sense - A Selection of his Writings, 1946-1988,* Oxford: Oxford University Press for the Oxford Institute of Energy Studies.

Skrede, R. O. (1998), 'Ekofisk II, - Planning for Low Operating Costs Through Lifetime', *OTC,* 69-76; no. 8655.

Slovic, P., B. Fischhoff and S. Lichtenstein (1977), 'Risk Assessment: Basic Issues', in Kates (ed.), (1977), 81-107.

Slovic, P., B. Fischhoff and S. Lichtenstein (1985), 'Regulation of Risk: A Psychological Perspective', in R. G. Noll (ed.), *Regulatory Policy and the Social Sciences,* Berkeley, Los Angeles and London: University of California Press, 241-78.

Smith, R. S. (1974), 'The Feasibility of an "Injury Tax" Approach to Occupational Safety', *Law and Contemporary Problems,* Vol. 38, No. 4, 730-44.

Smith, S. C. (1991), 'Beyond 'Mega-theory' and 'Multiple Sociology': A Reply to Rottleuthner', *International Journal of the Sociology of Law,* 19, 321-40.

Smulders, B. H. N., J. C. Franklin and B. N. Logan (1987), 'The Eider Production Platform Concept: A Platform in Deep Water with Small Reserves', *OTC,* III, 541-8; no. 5547.

Snellen, I. Th. M. (1991), 'Autopoiesis and steering: the role of identity', in in 't Veld *et al.* (eds), 151-60.

Snyder, F. (ed.), *European Community Law*, Vol. II, Aldershot, etc.: Dartmouth.

Søreide, T. H., J. Amdahl, T. Granli and O. C. Astrud (1986), 'Collapse Analysis of Framed Offshore Structures', *OTC*, IV, 95-102; no. 5302.

Spaven, M., H. Ras, A. Morrison and C. Wright (1993), *The Effectiveness of Offshore Safety Representatives and Safety Committees: A Report to the Health and Safety Executive* (2 vols.), Aberdeen: University of Aberdeen Offshore Study Group.

Spence, E. (1994), 'Safety Case Implementation - A Case Study', in Waterfront (1994), Paper 4.

Spidsoe, N., H. P. Brathaug and O. Skjåstad (1986), 'Nonlinear Random Wave Loading in Fixed Offshore Platforms', *OTC*, I, 183-91; no. 5101.

Spigener, J. (1999), 'Behavior-Based and Human Factors - There is Synergy', *OTC*, I, 513-8; no. 10880.

Spiller, R. (1994), 'The Employee Response', in Waterfront (1994), Paper 6.

Sporn, P. (1969), *Technology, Engineering and Economics*, Cambridge, Mass.: MIT Press.

SREA (1989), *Offshore Business No. 28: Offshore Safety - The Economic Implications*, Canterbury: Smith Rea Energy Analysts.

Stahl, B. and J. F. Geyer (1985), 'Ultimate Strength Reliability of Tension Leg Platform Tendon Systems', *OTC*, I, 151-62; no. 4857.

Stahl, B., G. J. Shoup, J. F. Geyer, J. E. Vinnem, C. A. Cornell and R. G. Bea 'Methodology for Comparison for Alternative Production Systems (MCAPS)', *OTC*, II, 389-98; no. 6915.

Stender, J. H. (1974), 'Enforcing the Occupational Safety and Health Act of 1970: The Federal Government as Catalyst', *Law and Contemporary Problems*, Vol. 38, No. 4, 641-50.

Stewart, R. (1981), 'Regulation, Innovation and Administrative Law: A Conceptual Framework', *California Law Review*, Vol. 69, No. 5, 1259-1377.

Stewart, R. (1990), 'Madison's Nightmare', *University of Chicago Law Review*, Vol. 57, 335-56.

Stewart, R. (1995), 'Markets versus Environment', *Jean Monnet Chair Papers*, No. 19, R. Schuman Centre, EUI, Florence.

Stiff, J. S., M. Kucharski, J. C. Trickey and R. L. Jack (1992), 'Risk Analysis of MODUs Following Lord Cullen's Report', *OTC*, II, 491-502; no. 6928.

Street, W. R. (1975), 'United Kingdom Regulations for Permanent Offshore Structures', *OTC*, III, 731-6; no. 2409.

Summers, R. S. (1979), 'Economics and the Autonomy of Law, Legal Analysis and Legal Theory', *Rechtstheorie*, 10, 395-408.

Svehla, K. M. and P. Elliot (1988), 'Platform monitoring as a tool for cost reduction' in ICE 53-66.

Symonds, E. (1978), 'The problems of financing future oil investment - 2', *Petroleum Economist*, 101.

Szyszczak, E. (1992), '1992 and the Working Environment', *Journal of Social Welfare and Family Law*, 3-16.

Taber, C. (1992), 'POLI: An Expert System Model of US Foreign Policy Belief Systems' *American Political Science Review*, 55, 888-904.

Tannahill, C. A. (1971), 'Methods of Strengthening Existing Offshore Structures', *OTC*, II, 699-704; no. 1488.

Taylor, B. G. S. (1993), 'A Goal-Setting Approach to Offshore Regulations', Paper presented at Offshore Europe Conference, Aberdeen, 7-10 September, 1993 (also Society of Petroleum Engineers, paper no. PE 26745).

Taylor, B. G. S., I. G. Wallace and A. Ward (1991), 'The Response to Piper Alpha: Recent Offshore Safety Developments in the UK', *OTC*, II, 641-9; no. 6629.

Tebbett, I. E. (1987), 'The Last Five Years' Experience in Steel Platform Repairs', *OTC*, I, 261-8; no. 5385.

Tebbett, I. E. and M. Lalani (1986), 'Recent Developments in the Reassessment, Maintenance, and Repair of Stell Offshore Structures', *OTC*, I, 305-14; no. 5113.

Tempest, L. P. (1979), 'The Financing of North Sea Oil 1975-1980', *Bank of England Quarterly Bulletin*, Vol. 19, No. 1, 31-4.

Tempest, P. (ed.), (1983), *Energy Economics in Britain*, London: Graham and Trotman.

Teubner, G. (1983), 'Substantive and reflexive elements in modern law', 17 *Law and Society Review*, 239-85.

Teubner, G. (1984), 'Autopoiesis in Law and Society: A Rejoinder to Blankenburg', 18 *Law and Society Review*, 291-301.

Teubner, G. (1985), 'After legal instrumentalism? strategic models of post-regulatory law', in Teubner (ed.), 299-325.

Teubner, G. (1987), 'Juridification - concepts, aspects, limits, solutions', in Teubner (ed.), (1987a), 3-48.

Teubner, G. (1989), 'How the law thinks: toward a constructivist epistemology of law', *Law and Society Review*, Volume 23, Number 5, 727-57.

Teubner, G. (1992a), 'The Two Faces of Janus: Rethinking Legal Pluralism', *Cardozo Law Review*, Volume 13, No. 5, 1443-62.

Teubner, G. (1992b), 'Regulatory Law: Chronicle of a Death Foretold', in *Social and Legal Studies*, Vol. 1, 451-475.

Teubner, G. (1993a), *Law as an Autopoietic System*, Oxford: Basil Blackwell.

Teubner, G. (1993b), 'The "State" of Private Networks: The Emerging Legal Regime of Polycorporatism in Germany', *Brigham Young University Law Review*, Volume 1993, Number 2, 553-75.

Teubner, G. (ed.), (1985), *Dilemmas of Law in the Welfare State*, Berlin: de Gruyter.

Teubner, G. (ed.), (1987a), *Juridification of Social Spheres: A Comparative Analysis in the areas of Labour, Corporate, Antitrust and Social Welfare Law*, Berlin: de Gruyter.

Teubner, G. (ed.), (1987b), *Autopoietic Law: A New Approach to Law and Society*, Berlin: de Gruyter.

Teubner, G. and Alberto Febbrajo (eds.), (1992), *State, Law and Economy as Autopoietic Systems: Regulation and Autonomy in a New Perspective*, European Yearbook in the Sociology of Law 1991-92 (Double Issue), Milan: Dott. A. Giuffrè Editore.

Thaler, J. and R. Geminder (1972), 'Offshore Insurance - Is Anyone the Winner?', *OTC*, II, 387-92; no. 1657.

Tolloczko, J. J. (1991), 'Blast and Fire: The Engineering Background', *OTC*, II, 685-94; no. 6633.

Tombs, S. (1990), 'Piper Alpha - A Case Study in Distorted Communication', in Institution of Chemical Engineers, 99-111.

Tombs, S. (1991), 'Piper Alpha and the Cullen Inquiry - Beyond "Distorted Communication"?', in Cox and Walters (eds), 28-41.

Tope, I. (1999), 'Offshore industry risk decision support framework', *Petroleum Review*, August, 44-45.

Tucker, E. S. (1987), 'Demand for Oil: How Responsive to Price Change?', *Petroleum Economist*, 402-403.

Tugendhat, C. (1976), 'A Politicians View of Oil', *Petroleum Economist*, 253-5.

Tuohy, C. J. (1985), 'Procedural Rationality and Regulatory Decision-Making: A Decision Framework Approach', *Law and Policy*, Vol. 7, No. 3, 345-73.

Turner, B. (1978), *Man-Made Disasters*, London: Wykeham.

Turner, L. (1975), 'State and Commercial Interests in North Sea Oil and Gas: Conflict and Correspondence', in Saeter and Smart (eds), 93-110.

Turner, L. (1983), *Oil Companies in the International System* (3rd edition), London: The Royal Institute for International Affairs, George Allen and Unwin.

Turner, R. C., C. P. Ellinas and G. A. N. Thomas (1992), 'Towards the Worldwide Calibration of API, RP2A-LRFD', *OTC*, II, 513-20; no. 6930.

Tveit, O. J., B. Myklatun, T. Bohler and O. Vesterhaug (1980), 'Risk Analysis of a Typical North Sea Petroleum Production Platform', *OTC*, IV, 501-8; no. 3905.

UNICE (1995), *Releasing Europe's Potential through Targeted Regulatory Reform: The Unice Regulatory Report 1995*, Brussels: Union of Industrial and Employers' Confederations of Europe.

US Department of Energy (1996), *International Energy Outlook: Fourth Quarter*, Washington: Energy Information Administration, US Department of Energy.

van de Graaf, J. W., P. S. Tromans and M. Efthmiou (1994), 'The Reliability of Offshore Structures and its Dependence on Design Code and Environment', *OTC*, I, 105-18; no. 7382.

van den Berg, A. C. and C. J. M. van Wingerden (1991), 'Numerical Simulation of Offshore Gas Explosions', *OTC*, II, 705-11; no.6635.

Velez, P. K. (1992), 'A Major Oil Company's Safety Program', *OTC*, I, 157-68; no. 6842.

Veljanovski, C. G. (1984), 'The Economics of Regulatory Enforcement', in K. Hawkins and J. M. Thomas (eds), *Enforcing Regulation* Boston, etc.: Kluwer-Nijhoff Publishing 171-188.

Verleger, P. K. Jr. (1984), 'Promises and Problems', *Petroleum Economist*, 293-6.

Vinter, G. (1992), 'Square Pegs into Round Holes', *Petroleum Economist, Energy Law Supplement*, July, 32-7.

Visser, R. C. (1993), 'Offshore Platform Accidents, Regulations, and Industry Standards', *OTC*, I, 345-53; no. 7118.

Walker, S., Chunsheung Hu and J. R. Williams (1991), 'Assessment of the Blast Resistance of Offshore Topsides Structures', *OTC*, II, 713-22; no. 6636.

Wallis, W. A. (1977), 'Law and Economy', in Bernard H. Siegan (ed.), *The Interaction of Economics and the Law*, Lexington, Mass.: Lexington Books 1-11.

Walmsley, J. (1990), 'Price Hedging through Swaps', *Petroleum Economist*, 94-5.

Waterfront (1994), *Offshore Safety Case Management: A Conference on safety case work and safety management systems after the Cullen Report*, 19 April 1994, Conference Papers, London: The Waterfront Partnership.

Waterstone, M. (ed.), (1992), *Risk and Society: The Interaction of Science, Technology and Public Policy*, Dordrecht, Boston, London: Kluwer Academic Publishers.

Watson, K. (1993), 'Objective Setting and Performance Standards', in HSE (1993c), 66-70.

Weinberg, A. M. (1972), 'Science and Trans-Science', *Minerva* 10, 209-22.

Weale, A. (1996), 'Environmental regulation and administrative reform in Britain', in Majone (ed.), 106-30.

White, N. A. (ed.), (1978), *Financing the International Petroleum Industry*, London: Graham and Trotman.

Wiggins, J. (1985), *ESA Safety Optimization Study*, HEI, 685 Houston, Texas: Hernandez Engineering.

Wildavsky, A. (1995), *But is it True? A Citizen's Guide to Environmental Health and Safety Issues*, Cambridge, Mass. and London: Harvard University Press.

Williams, L. (1990a), 'Boom in Energy Derivatives', *Petroleum Economist*, November, 35-46.

Williams, L. (1990b), 'Energy Exchanges: Golden Opportunity', *Petroleum Economist*, November, 46-56.

Willke, H. (1990), 'Political Intervention - Operational Preconditions for Generalized Political Exchange', in Bernd Marin (ed.), *Governance and Generalized Exchange - Self-Organising Policy Networks in Action*, Frankfurt/Boulder, Col.: Campus/Westview.

Willke, H. (1992), 'Societal Guidance Through Law?', in Teubner and Febbrajo (eds), 353-87.

Wilson, G. J. (1973), 'Integrated Approach to Deep Water North Sea Drilling', *OTC*, II, 351-68; no. 1860.

Wingate, P. M. and F. R. Taylor (1980), 'Simulation: A New Tool in Offshore Process Control', *OTC,* IV, 537-46; no. 3908.

Wolfram, J. and D. G. Owen (1991), 'Education and Training for Safety and Reliability in the Offshore Industry', in Cox and Walter (eds), 12-27.

Wood, D. (1993), *The Power of Maps,* London: Routledge.

Woolfson, C., J. Foster and M. Beck (1996), *Paying for the Piper: Capital and Labour in Britain's Offshore Oil Industry,* London: Mansell.

Woolgar, S. and M. Ashmore (1988), 'The Next Step: An Introduction to the Reflexive Project', in Woolgar (ed.), 1-11.

Woolgar, S. (ed.), (1988), *Knowledge and Reflexivity: New Frontiers in the Sociology of Knowledge,* London, Newbury Park, Beverly Hills, New Delhi: Sage Publications.

Wright, C. (1986), 'Routine Deaths: fatal accidents in the oil industry', *Sociological Review,* Vol. 34 (1), 265-89.

Yellin, J. (1983), 'Science, Technology, and Administrative Government: Institutional Designs for Environmental Decisionmaking', *Yale Law Journal,* Vol. 92, no. 5, 1300-33.

Young, J. Z. (1988), *Philosophy and the Brain,* Oxford: Oxford University Press .

Ziegert, K. A. (1983), 'The Theory and the Measurement of the Effectiveness of Legislation', *Rechtstheorie,* 14, 204-45.

Ziman, J. (1978), *Reliable Knowledge: An Exploration of the Grounds for Belief in Science,* Cambridge: Cambridge University Press.

Zolo, D. (1992), 'The Epistemological Status of the Theory of Autopoiesis and its Applications to the Social Sciences', in Teubner and Febbrajo (eds), 67-124.

Index

For Product Safety Concerns and Information please contact our EU representative GPSR@taylorandfrancis.com Taylor & Francis Verlag GmbH, Kaufingerstraße 24, 80331 München, Germany

Batch number: 10726013

Printed by Printforce, the Netherlands